RADICAL INTERPRETATION AND INDETERMINACY

RADICAL INTERPRETATION
AND INDETERMINACY

Timothy McCarthy

OXFORD
UNIVERSITY PRESS
2002

OXFORD
UNIVERSITY PRESS

Oxford   New York
Auckland   Bangkok   Buenos Aires   Cape Town   Chennai
Dar es Salaam   Delhi   Hong Kong   Istanbul   Karachi   Kolkata
Kuala Lumpur   Madrid   Melbourne   Mexico City   Mumbai   Nairobi
São Paulo   Shanghai   Singapore   Taipei   Tokyo   Toronto

Copyright © 2002 by Timothy McCarthy

Published by Oxford University Press, Inc.
198 Madison Avenue, New York, New York 10016

www.oup.com

Oxford is a registered trademark of Oxford University Press

Library of Congress Cataloging-in-Publication Data
McCarthy, Timothy, 1951–
Radical interpretation and indeterminacy / Timothy McCarthy.
p. cm.
Includes bibliographical references and index.
ISBN 0-19-514506-2
1. Language and languages—philosophy. I. Title.
P107 .M37 2002
401—dc21   2002009848

1 3 5 7 9 8 6 4 2

Printed in the United States of America
on acid-free paper

For Noreen and Johanna

ACKNOWLEDGMENTS

I have learned much from discussions with many people about the problems treated in this book, from the prehistory of the project through relatively recent times. Given the chance, I should like to thank Kathleen Akins, Hiroshi Aoyama, Akeel Bilgrami, Hugh Chandler, Marian David, Michael Detlefsen, Michael Devitt, Joshua Finkler, Arthur Fine, Kit Fine, Marjorie Hass, Patrick Hayes, Jaegwon Kim, Philip Kitcher, Michael Kremer, Saul Kripke, William Lycan, Joe Malpeli, David McCarty, Hilary Putnam, Peter Railton, Stewart Shapiro, Gila Sher, Larry Sklar, Sean Stidd, William Taschek, Steven Wagner, and Stephen White for helpful discussions over many years. The late Peter Winch was a source of kind encouragement until his untimely death in 1997, as different as the philosophical orientation of the present work is from his own. Philip Kitcher, North American delegate for Oxford University Press, expressed interest in the manuscript several years ago, and has ever since patiently urged me to finish it. Joshua Finkler provided invaluable and unflagging help in the preparation of the manuscript, as well as more or less constant philosophical companionship over the past seven years. The University of Illinois afforded me an extended sabbatical leave of absence during which some of the crucial work was done, and while writing an early draft of chapter 2 of the project the University of Notre Dame gaciously hosted me for a term in which my formal responsibilties were largely confined to teaching a seminar on the topics of this book. Finally, I want to acknowledge with love the support and encouragement of my wife Noreen and my daughter Johanna, whose kindly but persistent entreaties to finish this book were a not inconsiderable stimulus to my doing so.

PREFACE

This book has been a long time in the making. This is due in part to the nature of its subject, which brings together various strands of thought, each requiring separate, and extended, treatment. The origins of the present study lie in the early 1980s, when I was occupied with some problems that in the end receive but scant attention. In this original phase, I was much concerned with the problem posed in Paul Benacerraf's seminal article "Mathematical Truth." The question was originally framed as a problem about knowledge, but it is equally and even more fundamentally a problem about reference: how do causal theories of reference and knowledge allow for the possibility of semantic and cognitive relations to numbers and sets? The idea I had was to somehow derive the central aspects of the causal theory of reference for the core cases of ordinary proper names and natural kind words from a more basic semantical framework that would allow for the possibility of reference to numbers, sets, and other abstract objects. But since at the time I could not at all see my way clear to defining the nature of such a framework, the problem was set aside.

A second motivation for this book was the desire to find a convincing response to the problem of the indeterminacy of reference. While still a graduate student I began thinking about Quine's arguments for the indeterminacy of reference and translation, the argument about translation having been described at about that time as "the most fascinating and the most discussed philosophical argument since Kant's transcendental deduction of the categories."[1] I have been thinking about them ever since. The original setting of Quine's discussion—radical translation—was subsequently generalized by Donald Davidson and David Lewis to the broader context of *radical interpretation*: the project of characterizing, from scratch, the language and attitudes of an unknown agent or population. In the mid-80s, Hilary Putnam described a significant generalization of a construction used by Quine in "Ontological Relativity" to exhibit the extent of the indetermi-

---

[1] Hilary Putnam, "The Refutation of Conventionalism," in *Mind, Language and Reality: Philosophical Papers*, vol. 2 (Cambridge: Cambridge University Press, 1975), p. 159.

nacy of reference. That construction was part of a certain sort of invariance argument, purporting to show that the class of acceptable schemes of reference for a language is closed under a very wide range of reference-disturbing transformations. The related frameworks for radical interpretation developed by Davidson and Lewis did not enable a resolution of these putative cases of indeterminacy, and so part of the problem became to devise and, more importantly, to motivate additional constraints on ascriptions of reference that would block the Quine-Putnam construction. Working out a solution to this problem has been a major theme of the present study. The solution I have to offer is based upon a theory of the interpretive role of the concept of reference developed in chapter 2 of this book. And when that was fully worked out, I found that the ingredients of a solution to my first problem were at hand.

A third source was in play. I argue in chapter 3 below that the interpretive framework developed in chapter 2 enables natural characterizations of the reference of expressions in various extra-logical categories (proper names, qualitative predicates, natural kind words), and that the conditions imposed by these accounts are not preserved by transformations of the Quine-Putnam sort. But a characterization of reference for an entire language requires a semantical characterization of the logical forms of the language, since the semantic properties of an arbitrary sentence are determined from those of the lexical primitives only in conjunction with the interpretations of the logical constants. The approach taken in this study to the interpretation problem for logic emerged from situating some earlier work of mine on the nature of the logical constants within the framework for radical interpretation developed in chapter 2. The odd result is that a generalization of the very sort of interpretive invariance that is argued to be defeated for the indicated lexical categories by that framework can be used to *characterize* the logical constants; and that thus constrained the specific interpretations of the logical expressions in a language are determined by the intentional data afforded by an interpretation of its speakers. In a nutshell, that is the story of chapter 4.

The concern with invariance arguments constitutes one over-arching theme of the present study. But the interpretive conditions that a class of transformations must be argued to preserve or not to preserve in order to support or defeat a type of indeterminacy concern in each case the stability of a certain type of explanation under transformations of that sort. Explanation thus constitutes another over-arching theme. Chapter 2 is largely occupied with defining an explanatory role for ascriptions of semantic properties; and, as it turns out, the role thus defined has to do with the ability of a semantical characterization of a subject's language and attitudes to underwrite explanations of a broadly causal sort within that language, explanations that the subject himself might frame. Chapter 3 consists of an extended derivation of mechanisms of reference for several lexical sorts precisely on the basis of their contribution to interpretive explanations of the type described in chapter 2b. The postscript to chapter 2 explores asymmetries in the explanatory role of rule-following ascriptions, asymmetries that can be used, or so I argue, to ground such ascriptions. Finally, in chapter 4, a characterization of the logical constants is justified on the basis of its role in explaining why model-theoretic implications are entailments of a certain sort. In each case, then, a type of semantic property is characterized by the structural role of ascriptions of such properties in a type of interpretive explanation, and in each case ascriptions of particular such properties are grounded in these explanatory roles.

A cautionary note is in order about the nature of the text below. The reader who is put off by formal techniques and models will find these pages discouraging. I have endeavored to find formal representations of various familiar problems about reference, intentionality, and indeterminacy not because formalization seemed a worthwhile end for its own sake, but because framing the problems in these particular ways has helped me to sharpen and to clarify them, and in a number of cases to separate what is really essential in a philosophical argument about these matters from more or less dispensable erudition. One of the publisher's readers was led to comment sympathetically that these problems are often treated in ways that are unsatisfactory precisely because the detailed issues requiring formal presentation are ignored, and that is something I have believed for some time. Beyond that, I am tempted to fall back on a motto extracted from Galileo's *Dialogue* by J. M. Jauch in his book on the foundations of quantum mechanics. Simplicio says at one point: "Concerning natural things we need not always seek the necessity of mathematical demonstrations." Sagredo replies: "Of course, when you cannot reach it. But if you can, why not?" A similar spirit animates much of the discussion below, even though such demonstrations as there are to be found here are confined to the notes and appendices. The point is that framing a conceptual landscape in such a way that questions arising within it could be answered with Sagredo's exactitude can be philosophically fruitful as well as technically satisfying.

CONTENTS

RADICAL INTERPRETATION AND INDETERMINACY

ONE

INTRODUCTION

1.1 Prospect

This book develops a theory of radical interpretation, with applications. The following chapter lays out a general framework for radical interpretation; the ensuing chapters apply that framework respectively to the theory of reference and to the philosophy of logic. The broad theme is that a relatively modest set of constitutive principles of interpretation, properly applied, can serve to constrain the semantic description of the language and attitudes of an idealized agent or population in such a way as to resolve the indeterminacies of interpretation that naturally present themselves. The book thus constitutes an extended, but still partial, response to Quine's indeterminacy arguments.

A word is in order about the structure of this discussion. The body of the book is divided into three substantial studies, each consisting of a chapter and a postscript: an appendix connected to central themes in the associated chapter. These are in some cases technical addenda and in others illustrative studies but in several instances represent substantive extensions of the discussion in the main text. The postscript to chapter 2 develops a response to the skeptical argument about rule-following advanced by Kripke's Wittgenstein, here regarded as a kind of indeterminacy argument. The response centers on the problem of what we mean when we say that an actual finite system 'approximately' instantiates a computational architecture such as a Turing machine. My treatment of this problem is separable from the body of the chapter, which develops a framework for radical interpretation within which interpretations are targeted on a class of idealized intentional systems for which the problem of approximate realization does not arise. Chapter 3 applies this framework to the problems of the classical theory of reference. Natural kind terms are a central theme. I distinguish two classes of such expressions. One sort I call 'homogeneous'. These are roughly general terms associated with definite real essences in the Lockean sense; inhomogeneous terms are characterized only by a more or less loosely connected set of such properties. Inhomogeneous terms, I argue, are vague, and the postscript to chapter 3 pursues the discussion of inhomogeneous terms in the context of two theories of vagueness. Finally, chapter 4 addresses the problem of the determinacy of logic within the interpretive framework of the present study. The postscript presents two technical results that are used in the body of the chapter.

The remainder of this introduction will serve three purposes. The first is to lay out the methodological point of view of the study; the second is to situate the book in the context of the recent history of its subject; and the third is to sketch some of the substantive conclusions reached. I have felt this last purpose to be particularly important for chapter 4, which deals with the foundations of logical theory. Some readers who will readily follow the earlier chapters may find it difficult to follow this one (or may not care to follow it, in full detail), and so it is appropriate to provide an informal brief of how the problem of radical interpretation arises for *logic*, and at least a hint of the nature of the solution I have to propose.

1.2   Some Recent History

One can distinguish several lines of development in philosophical discussions of the foundations of semantics since 1970. These positions embody alternative conceptions of what a semantic theory is *about* that evolved in the aftermath of the Quinean arguments alluded to. Quine argues for the indeterminacy of several semantic notions in several different ways, but in the form primarily relevant here, the argument concerns the notion of reference. The familiar strategy is to take a preferred scheme of reference for a canonical language, use a more or less arbitrarily chosen correspondence between the preferred ontology and some other set to define an alternative reference relation, and then to argue that the alternative scheme of reference thus generated fits the facts as well as the initial one.[1] Someone who takes this argument to be successful will take it to show that reference is substantially indeterminate: 'inscrutable', not in the sense that we lack the empirical means of discerning the reference relation for a given language, but that, within the limits of plasticity established by the argument, there

---

[1] See W.V. Quine, *Ontological Relativity* (New York: Columbia University Press, 1969), the title essay. Variants of the same argument abound; see, for example, John Wallace, "Only in the Context of a Sentence Do Words Have Any Meaning," in *Contemporary Perspectives in the Philosophy of Language*, edited by Peter French et al. (Minneapolis: University of Minnesota Press, 1979), pp. 305–25; and Donald Davidson, "The Inscrutability of Reference," in *Inquiries into Truth and Interpretation* (New York: Oxford University Press, 1984), essay 16. The construction is rehearsed in some detail in 2.4.

is nothing to be right or wrong about. The popular term 'inscrutable' is unfortunate.

1.2.1   The Theory of Reference

Someone who does *not* accept the conclusion of the indeterminacy argument is faced with a fairly standard skeptical situation. The 'straight' response would be to produce a candidate for the reference relation, and then to explain why reference consists in just that relation and not something else. This is the approach represented in what I shall call the 'theory of reference' tradition. The tradition and its representatives are various, but it is not inappropriate to date it back to three lectures given at Princeton University by Saul Kripke in 1970, subsequently published under the title "Naming and Necessity." Kripke gave a direct answer, or a sketch of one, to the question of how the reference of proper names (and, with somewhat less specificity, natural kind words) is fixed. The now familiar picture of the reference of a name in terms of a chain of referential transmissions grounded in a 'baptism' by agents who may introduce the denotation of the name by description, but who more characteristically have direct ostensive contact with it, became a paradigm for the theory of reference. That theory was not, however, at least in Kripke's hands, viewed as a response to Quine's argument; in fact, Kripke doesn't talk about that argument at all. Indeed, some of the central notions in Kripke's story are overtly intentional, and would clearly beg the question if deployed without further explanation against Quine.

Kripke's lectures were first published in 1972.[2] At about the same time, Hartry Field published an important article, "Tarski's Theory of Truth," which forcefully presented a methodological brief for a naturalistic theory of reference and truth.[3] The vehicle for it is a critique of the semantical conception of truth inherited from Tarski's *Wahrheitsbegriff*. Field argued that a theory of truth of Tarski's sort (directed, say, on a regimented fragment L of English) fails to provide an explanatory account of the notion of truth for L, but at most a reduction of the concepts of truth and reference for L to the reference relation for the lexical primitives (what Field called 'primitive denotation'). An explanatory account would result, Field suggests, by *combining* Tarski's recursive analysis of satisfaction with a reductive account of primitive denotation. The problem is that Tarski's description of the semantic contributions of the primitives is nothing more than a list of pairings of each primitive with a representation of its reference; it does

---

[2]In *Semantics of Natural Language*, edited by Donald Davidson and Gilbert Harman (Dordrecht: Reidel, 1972); republished with an introduction as *Naming and Necessity* (Cambridge, Mass.: Harvard University Press, 1980).

[3]*Journal of Philosophy* 69 (1972): 347–75.

nothing to explain why such an item has, or what it is for it to have, the reference that it does. Field's well-known 'valence' analogy is intended to illustrate what is supposed to be missing here: it is as if an account of the chemical notion of valence terminated in a list of clauses that paired each chemical element with its numerical valence (i.e., 'for any x and n, x has valence n if $x =$ hydrogen and $n = +1$ or $x =$ oxygen and $n = -2$ ...', etc.), whereas what is clearly wanted in this context is an account of what valence is that would facilitate explanations of the chemical facts codified by means of the notion of valence. Field's claim is that the clauses in Tarski's theory covering the lexical primitives have a theoretical status similar to that of the bogus valence theory.[4]

Field cites Kripke's work as providing a possible framework for a properly explanatory account of reference in the case of proper names and natural kind words. To play the required role in the context of Field's naturalistic methodology, however, the intentional notions in Kripke's story must be given appropriate interpretations in naturalistic terms. Thus the 'baptism' (in the nondescriptive case) will be identified with a particular sort of causal interaction between the bearer of the name and its introducers, and referential transmission with a causal, or causal-cum-functional, relation within the population of the language in question. The problem of carrying out such interpretations constitutes a major theme of the causal theories of reference developed in the 1970s and 1980s.[5]

What is the status of Quine's argument in the light of these develop-

---

[4]Field's article raises many interesting questions that I will not discuss at this point. One that links up with some themes taken up later in this chapter concerns a claim that Field makes *for* Tarski's theory, might be mentioned in passing. The claim is that a theory of Tarski's sort *does* provide a reduction of the notions of truth and satisfaction, via the Tarskian recursion clauses for the logical constants, to the concept of primitive denotation. That is puzzling, for the description given of the semantic role of the logical constants by the theory is in rather obvious ways similar to that given of predicates and function symbols. *All of* these expressions (and not, as is sometimes supposed, only the logical ones) are characterized by recursive clauses that describe how they affect the extensions of the expressions on which they operate: in the case of the logical constants, the relevant arguments are formulas (or variable-formula combinations); in the case of predicates and function symbols, they are terms (which are infinitely numerous if the language contains any function symbols). The question, then, is why, if a reductive analysis is needed of the semantic properties of predicates and function symbols, one is not needed also for the connectives and quantifiers. In the approach taken in chapter 4 the logical and nonlogical expressions are all initially, so to speak, on the same 'level'. There is *just as much of a problem* about interpreting the one as the other, though I would argue that the problems are solved in very different ways.

[5]A sustained systematic attempt to develop such interpretations may be found in Michael Devitt's book *Designation* (New York: Columbia University Press, 1981). The conclusions of causal theories are played off against the approach of this study in chapter 3.

ments? The consensus seems to be that, unfortunately, it has not gone away. The problem is quite general and has little to do with the details of particular causal theories. Any such theory will characterize a relation, call it R, holding between certain expressions of the language in question and the items to which the theory takes them to refer. Quine's skeptical question, in a now standard formulation, then becomes the following. Consider any permutation of the set that the given theory identifies as the ontology of the language in question. Use this permutation to define an alternative scheme of reference; call it R^* in the obvious way. What fact can be adduced to defeat the claim that R^* and not R is the actual reference relation for the language?

There are many properties of the relation R that need not be shared by R^*, of course; in particular, the relation R may be a *causal* relation, at least in the weak sense that its characterization for the lexical primitives involves reference to certain causal connections between uses of those expressions and their referents.[6] But the mapping of preferred to alternative contents induced by the permutation that generates R^* from R need not preserve the relevant causal relations. This, then, is a difference between R and R^*; what is not clear is why the difference should *make* a difference. More is required to answer the skeptical question than to point to an asymmetry between a preferred reference relation and a skeptical alternative to it. What is required is an asymmetry that distinguishes the two relations in terms of their explanatory roles, a function that we wish the notion of reference to perform that R can perform but R^* cannot. It is this question which has proved to be so difficult to answer, in large part because of pervasive unclarity about what the explanatory role of reference is.

1.2.2 Reference, Conceptual Role, and Success

An alternative approach emerged somewhat earlier. Frege had notoriously identified the sense of a sentence with its truth-condition, on the one hand, and with what a speaker grasps in understanding it on the other. Against the background of a reference-based conception of truth, this duality has seemed to many philosophers to pose insuperable difficulties. What a com-

---

[6]It has been often enough pointed out that the unvarnished claim of causal connection must be restricted to the non-logical primitives (and a subset of them at that) if it is to be at all plausible. It is clearly false that there is a causal relation of any sort between the uses of a descriptive expression such as Kaplan's 'the shortest spy' and *its* referent. For some elaboration of this point, see Hilary Putnam, "A Theory of Reference," in *Renewing Philosophy* (Cambridge, Mass.: Harvard University Press, 1993), which is a discussion of Jerry Fodor's proposal in *A Theory of Content* (Cambridge, Mass.: MIT Press, 1990).

petent speaker grasps in understanding a sentence cannot, so the story goes, outrun what the speaker acquires in learning how to use the sentence in normal linguistic interactions, and it is unclear how what is so acquired can fix a truth-condition that outruns the speaker's ability to know that it obtains when in fact it does obtain. As early as 1959 Dummett was arguing the case that what is understood in learning a language settles, for declarative sentences of the language, at most conditions of warranted or justified assertability, and that these fail to determine 'realist' truth-conditions.[7] The most direct approach to making conditions of warranted assertion the basic ingredients in a semantic description of an elementary language leads to a quasi-intuitionistic account that purports to explain how the conditions of justification of a compound statement are determined by those of less complex statements.[8] More generally, on such an approach, the fundamental semantic notions are epistemic in character, and a semantic description of a language will associate each sentence of the language with a representation its relevant epistemic properties (assertability condition, proof condition, confirmation-to-a degree condition, etc.).[9]

The question, then, as it was usually posed, was whether the semantics of a given fragment of a natural language, or of natural languages generally, is 'realist', or truth-conditional, taking a reference-based and recognition-transcendent notion of truth as fundamental; or 'antirealist', verificationist, quasi-intuitionistic or whatnot, taking some epistemic notion(s) as fundamental. These two sorts of account were thought to conflict, because they were interpreted as providing answers to the *same question*: that of explaining the nature of a speaker's understanding of a natural language. In the late 1970s, however, a different point of view emerged. The idea that the two sorts of account answer *different* questions, and so should not properly be regarded as conflicting, surfaced in some transitional writings of Hilary Putnam.[10] Putnam argued that a broadly verificationist account is plausi-

[7]Michael Dummett, "Truth," *Proceedings of the Aristotelian Society* 54 (1959): 141–62; reprinted in *Truth and Other Enigmas* (Cambridge, Mass.: Harvard University Press, 1978). The argument is pressed further in, among other places, "What Is a Theory of Meaning" (II), in *Truth and Meaning: Essays in Semantics*, edited by G. Evans and J. McDowell (Oxford: Clarendon Press, 1976), pp. 61–137.

[8]Dummett himself favors an account that directly reflects the approach of intuitionistic logic; see "Truth," concluding section, and "The Philosophical Basis of Intuitionistic Logic," in *Truth and Other Enigmas*, pp. 215–47.

[9]Other representatives of this approach include Hartry Field in "Logic, Meaning and Conceptual Role," *Journal of Philosophy* (1977): 379–408; and Ned Block, "Advertisement for a Semantics for Psychology," in *Midwest Studies in Philosophy*, v. 10, edited by P. French, T. Uehling, and H. Wettstein (Minneapolis: University of Minnesota Press, 1986), pp. 615–78.

[10]See "Reference and Understanding," in *Meaning and the Moral Sciences* (London:

bly the right approach to a theory of understanding for a natural language, but that a theory of reference for the language may play an entirely different theoretical role, in explaining the 'contribution of linguistic behavior [of users of the language] to the success of their total behavior.'[11]

Although Putnam's suggestion is quite close in spirit to the stance I shall defend in this book, it faces several difficulties. One question concerns the notion of 'success' itself. Success is, at least apparently, a semantically contaminated notion: to say that an agent's behavior is successful is to say that the truth-conditions associated with a certain range of the agent's desires come to be satisfied. Since 'explanation of success' is supposed to be a criterion of adequacy for ascriptions of content, the criterion seems circular. To apply the criterion, it would seem, we must already have at hand a truth-conditional characterization of at least a subset of the agent's attitudes. Putnam's proposal would seem to beg the question against semantic skepticism, the standpoint that questions the need for an explanatory deployment of the notions of reference and truth in the first place. From that standpoint, it is circular to rationalize the introduction of semantic properties as explanatory devices by appealing to a set of explananda specified in terms of those same semantic properties.

However, the reference to success in Putnam's account seems somewhat incidental. The real problem, it might argued, is to explain the *products* or *outcomes* of actions or of patterns of activity. Such actions may be correctly described, relative to an assumed semantical characterization of the agent's language and attitudes, as successful, but their products *can* generally be specified in nonsemantic terms. Thus, for example, we should wish to explain, not an agent's success in building bridges, but the fact that bridges are built. The real problem bequeathed by this suggestion is twofold: first, to specify precisely how the notion of reference is relevant to explaining such products or outcomes; second, to explain how the explanatory role thus specified can justify a choice *between* semantic descriptions of the agent's language and attitudes.

1.2.3 The Theory of Interpretation

Here is a noncircular implementation of the success idea. Treat success maximization as a constraint on a project that might be called an *interpretation* of the agent or population in question. An interpretation of an agent is given, at a minimum, by the following data:

Routledge and Kegan Paul, 1978), pp. 97–119. This point of view is also advocated by Field in "Logic, Meaning and Conceptual Role."

[11]Field, "Logic, Meaning, and Conceptual Role," p. 101.

(a) A description of the agent's attitudes in the agent's language;
(b) An assignment of truth-conditions to the sentences of that language in our language;

these in turn generate

(c) A specification of the agent's attitudes in our language.

We view the belief-component of (a) as being derived, in part, from a representation of the agent's *inductive method*, that is, roughly, a set of cognitive strategies instantiated by the agent; and we view (b) as being derived from a recursive theory of truth for the agent's language, phrased in our language. The requirement is then in part that such a theory lead to an assignment of truth-conditions that *optimizes potential success*, in the rough sense that it by and large validates beliefs that conditionalize desired outcomes on actions of the agent; that of two otherwise acceptable interpretations, one is to be preferred if it does a better job of rendering sentences that express such connections true. In the best interpretive circumstances, against the background of a further constraint, which says that an acceptable interpretation should enable intentional explanations of the agent's basic actions, we would hope to explicate the fact that the agent by and large gets what she wants.[12]

The theory of interpretation is a natural stance for someone who takes semantic skepticism seriously but who wishes to stake out a theoretical role for the notions of reference and truth that is explanatory and not merely logical or instrumental in character.[13] Most basically, the idea is to compile a list of constraints that express the things we wish a successful interpretation of an agent or population to do, and then to solve for an interpretation that satisfies those constraints. There may be no solution, a

---

[12] The theory-of-interpretation tradition was inaugurated by Donald Davidson and David Lewis in two seminal articles, both entitled "Radical Interpretation," which figure prominently hereafter. The articles are reprinted in Davidson, *Inquiries into Truth and Interpretation* and Lewis, *Philosophical Papers*, vol. 1 (New York: Oxford University Press, 1983). Page references will be to these sources.

[13] Skepticism about reference and truth as explanatory concepts leaves room for other accounts of their status. A 'deflationist' account of truth has been suggested by a number of philosophers, for example, by Stephen Leeds, "Theories of Reference and Truth," *Erkentnis* 13 (1978): 111–29, and Paul Horwich, *Truth* (Oxford: Blackwell, 1990). Leeds in particular argued that a 'homophonic' truth theory has utility independently of any explanatory role for it in enlarging the expressive capacity of the object language. For a useful overview of the relations between explanatory and deflationist conceptions of truth, see Hartry Field, "The Deflationary Conception of Truth," in *Fact, Science and Value, Essays on A. J. Ayer's Language, Truth and Logic*, edited by G. MacDonald and C. Wright (Oxford: Basil Blackwell, 1986). For a recent presentation of the deflationist perspective taking account of a number of difficulties, see Scott Soames, *Understanding Truth* (New York: Oxford University Press, 1999), ch. 10.

unique solution, or many solutions. From the present point of view, success-maximization may be treated as one among various structural constraints on radical interpretation, constraining the *relation* between (a) and (b), the cognitive and semantic components of the interpretation.

Thus construed, however, the success-optimization constraint does little to limit the indeterminacies of reference arising on the Quinean schema considered earlier. The difficulty is that such a requirement is too easy to satisfy. A given interpretation explicates the success of an agent's behavior by appealing to the fact that the agent 'acts on beliefs which are true.' A bit more explicitly, in a typical case, the agent holds a conditional belief in a goal-specifying sentence **g** relative to a set of action-specifying sentences that, in conjunction with a subset S of her standing beliefs, expressed in her language, entails **g**; we can then infer that her goal will be realized if she acts in the specified ways and the sentences in S are *true*. The difficulty is that *any* truth-preserving reinterpretation of the agent's language will serve this purpose if it respects the interpretation of the relevant action-specifying sentences. Of course, such a reinterpretation may change the goal expressed by the sentence **g**, but the agent's *goals* are not given prior to interpretation. In particular, reinterpretations of the Quinean sort generally preserve truth. Thus (assuming the initial interpretation to construe the agent's language in purely elementary terms), any such reinterpretation will fit equally well into the predictive schema described earlier, assuming only that it preserves the conditions under which sentences of the agent's language specify her basic actions. They will differ only in the content assigned to sentences that specify the agent's beliefs and desires.

If the success-optimization requirement is to play a role in constraining the ascription of content, then, it can do so only in combination with further substantive constraints. The seminal papers of Davidson and Lewis cited earlier offer a number of candidates that will be considered in the following chapter. Unfortunately, none of these help with what I am calling 'examples of the Quinean sort', with or without the success-optimization requirement.[14] Consider, for example, the *Principle of Charity* in the form advocated by Lewis. This constraint requires the subject of interpretation and the interpreter to instantiate a common inductive method, a set of cognitive strategies that would lead approximately to their respective belief systems in their respective evidential situations.[15] Suppose, then,

---

[14] Both Davidson and Lewis accept the thesis of the inscrutability of reference, and the intractability of Quine's examples in particular. See Davidson, "The Inscrutability of Reference," in *Inquiries*, and Lewis, "Radical Interpretation," p. 118.

[15] See Lewis, "Radical Interpretation," pp. 112–13. While I think the present suggestion the most plausible of the several versions of the principle of charity that have been suggested, I criticize this version of the principle in 2.3.2. The principle is unduly

an interpretation of an agent to be given that assigns first-order semantic structures to sentences of her language and that satisfies the Principle of Charity. In a large class of cases, an alternative interpretation generated in the Quinean fashion will also satisfy that constraint. Assume the transformation, call it f, that generates such an alternative is a *permutation* of the given domain, that is, a one-to-one correspondence mapping that domain onto itself. The equivalence of the alternative contents assigned to any sentence by the respective interpretations is a logical consequence of the claim *that f* is a permutation. So suppose that, according to the given interpretation, the agent *recognizes* that f is a permutation (relative to a chosen specification of f in her language). If the agent can reason a little, then the given interpretation will represent her as accepting the initial content if and only if she accepts the alternative content; and so will the deviant interpretation. Thus, although the rival interpretations systematically clash in the accounts they give of the referential basis of the agent's language and attitudes, they will *globally* ascribe to her *the same beliefs*. They will thus equally satisfy the Principle of Charity.

1.3   Conformal Interpretation

Quine's examples have proved to be remarkably resilient in the face of a variety of remedial strategies. The way I wish to suggest out of this impasse begins by rethinking the explanatory role of the notion of reference, and of reference-based notions of truth. I begin, in subsection 2.4.1, with a primitive illustration of the explanatory relevance of semantic notions. In the imagined case, we encounter a robotic device that, when suitably prompted, traverses a path of minimal length out of a maze from any starting-point. Skepticism about the relevance of the concept of reference to explaining instances of this regularity is likely to begin with the observation that the motion of the device at any time is causally determined by its internal physical state at that time (in conjunction with relevant boundary conditions). It would then seem that if we were in a suitably idealized epistemic situation, we could explain the fact that the device's motions over a given interval bring about an optimal egress in purely causal, non-semantic terms. First, we compile causal explanations of the successive internal physical states of the device and of how these bring about its successive motions. We may thus explain the particular path taken by the device. Next, we assemble a complete catalog of the possible paths of the device that consti-

---

hegemonistic: the agent's inductive method, or the structure of the agent's understanding, is part of what an acceptable interpretation must uncover. A general framework for radical interpretation should take account of the possibility that fully interpretable agents instantiate divergent inductive methods.

tute egresses, and order them by length. We then observe that the actual path of the device, explicated in terms of its successive basic motions, falls into the collection of paths minimal with respect to this ordering, and thus conclude that the device exits the maze via a minimal path.

The difficulty is this. We can indeed obtain, via the indicated procedure, a complete causal explanation of the *trajectory* of the device; but the trajectory of the device is not exactly what we want to explain. The trajectory of the machine is constituted by its successive motions over the relevant interval. But what we want to explain is not the successive motions of the device, but the fact that these generate a minimal path out of the maze from the initial position. The indicated explanation proceeds by deriving the trajectory of the device and then *observing* that it constitutes a minimal egress. Beyond that, the explanation does not purport to provide an informative answer to the question of why it should *have* this property.

Some 'why'-questions lack informative answers. Perhaps the present question is one of them. There are indeed circumstances in which an analogue of the indicated explanation provides the best possible answer to such a question. (Consider, for example, a particle of dust that traverses, by random walk, a minimal path out of the maze from the initial position.) In some cases, however, a more informative answer to the question may be given, and it is the aim of section 2.4 to describe the relevance of broadly semantic properties to such an answer. I will suggest that the optimality property of the device's path may be explained in terms of (a) an effective strategy that, in an appropriate sense, is *instantiated* by the device and (b) a correspondence mapping certain data for the strategy onto states of affairs in its environment. Under that correspondence relation, these inputs afford the strategy information about the causal structure of a set of outcomes in which the possible basic actions of the device are embedded, in particular, about the ways in which actions of the device affect its position in space. In the present case, the idea for answering our question might be that the basic motions of the device are controlled in an appropriate way by a process that, under the correspondence relation in question, can be interpreted as *selecting optimal paths*. I shall argue that this idea is the basis of an explanation of why in this case the device's actions in fact generate an optimal path.

The story of the robotic device in the maze will serve as a simple prototype for explanations in which, I wish to argue, the concept of representation plays an ineliminable role, explanations of a sort I call *conformal*. In the case of a subject of radical interpretation, the relevant explanatory vehicle is a semantical characterization of the subject's language and attitudes. The analogue of the data in (b) above is a collection of formal sentences that, within the interpretation in question, constitute semantic representations of beliefs ascribed to the subject. Under that interpretation, these sentences constitute an approximately correct description of the causal structure of one of the agent's contexts of interest, in particular of the ways in which her prospective behaviors can effect outcomes that, according to the interpretation, she desires. The idea is that the subject be able to frame a conditional causal explanation that links her prospective basic actions to the realization of such an outcome. A central theme of section 2.4 is that the availability of such an explanation to the agent can sometimes help to explain the fact that her actions bring about the outcome in question when she does act in the relevant ways. I shall study in some detail the consequences of grafting onto a minimal framework for radical interpretation adapted, with some modification, from Davidson and Lewis, a constraint reflecting the idea that one aim of interpretation is to provide conformal explanations of *generative properties* of the subject's behavior, that is, of the subject's bringing about various states of affairs in the world. The constraint says roughly that of two otherwise equally acceptable interpretations, one is to be preferred if it better facilitates such explanations. I call this constraint the Principle of Conformality.[16]

A constitutive principle of radical interpretation constrains one or more interpretational invariants, and in the case of the Principle of Conformality the invariant thus constrained concerns the class of explanations which are generated by the belief-contents ascribed to the subject by the interpretation in question. The Principle of Conformality tells us roughly that part of the point of interpretation is to explicate the subject's activity in conformal terms, an aim that favors an interpretation that as far as possible represents the subject as believing stories which correctly describe causal-explanatory connections between her prospective basic actions and outcomes she desires. These stories are the basis of conditional explanations of the relevant outcomes that the agent can frame herself. The interpretation must then incorporate resources that allow us to discern the structures in the agent's language and states of thinking that constitute *explanations*. What these are taken to be will of course depend on our substantive views about the

---

[16]The Principle of Conformality can be formulated in several ways. One alternative formulation I consider is based on an analysis of the connection between conformal explanation and intentional action (2.4.6). I argue that if there is a conformal explanation of an agent Ag's bringing about an outcome *o*, then by the relevant basic action(s) Ag brings about *o* intentionally; and that, for a large class of causative verbs *V*, a necessary and sufficient condition for the intentionality of the action reported by a sentence of the form 'Ag *V*-ed *a*' is that there exist a conformal explanation of Ag's performing an action that brings about the relevant outcome. Against the background of that equivalence, the Principle of Conformality may be seen as the requirement that the interpretation in question make possible a certain sort of narrative of the agent's activity in intentional terms; see 2.5.1.

nature of explanation. I shall not, however, present a theory of explanation to accompany the Principle of Conformality, and so the status of that principle may seem, to that extent, to be up in the air. That is intentional: I mean the framework for radical interpretation developed here to apply against the backdrop of varying accounts of the nature of explanation. As it happens, I favor a broadly realist conception of causal explanation, on which an adequate explanation of this type describes objective mechanisms in the world; but scant use will be made here of assumptions specific to such a conception. The present deployment of explanation as an interpretational invariant is compatible with epistemic or pragmatic conceptions of explanation. What is required is only what is required of any account of the notion, that it respect our judgments about explanatory adequacy in particular cases. Different models of explanation suggest contrasting interpretations of the Principle of Conformality. I think a realist interpretation is the most natural; but to a considerable extent that judgment can be set aside.

To return to the problem of indeterminacy: if a given interpretation and a Quinean alternative to it are to equally satisfy the Principle of Conformality, they must enable conformal explanations of the same data or, at least, of comparable ranges of data. A bit more precisely, the two interpretations should generate, for the same range of sentences of the agent's language, conformal explanations of the agent's bringing about the realization of the truth-conditions they associate with those sentences. An argument that a deviant interpretation of the Quinean sort satisfies the Principle of Conformality will naturally proceed by showing that if we substitute the alternative semantic characterization of the subject's language and attitudes it provides for that of the initial one, patterns of conformal explanation will be *preserved*. A conformal explanation of an agent's bringing about an outcome, I said, refers to a causal explanation available to the agent, linking her performance of certain basic actions to the realization of that outcome. Thus the conformal-explanatory symmetry of the two interpretations requires an underlying symmetry in a class of causal explanations they make available to the agent: if, according to the initial interpretation, the agent can assemble a causal-explanatory story linking her performance of an action to an outcome described by a sentence of her language, this should also be true in the deviant interpretation, with respect to the outcome answering to the alternative content it associates with that sentence.

This requirement is argued to significantly constrain the semantic characterization of the agent's language and attitudes. Consider, for example, Quine's discussion of 'blanket pythagoreanism', the thesis that for any given interpretation of a first-order language, there is an equally acceptable isomorphic interpretation generated by a transformation that maps each object in the given ontology onto an abstract object such as a number or pure set that serves as its proxy or code.[17] Such an alternative interpretation will generally preserve the truth-values of sentences, but not their causal-explanatory roles, and it is the latter sort of invariance that is required to ensure the conformal-explanatory parity of the alternative interpretations. If sets are the sort of entities they are normally taken to be, an agent's actions cannot *bring about* a purely set-theoretic outcome. However, Quine also motivated the inscrutability thesis by reference to examples such as the following: consider a transformation that maps each physical object onto the mereological sum of its momentary stages or time-slices. It is not implausible that any causal-explanatory story involving reference to ordinary physical objects can be reconfigured in such a way as to involve reference to only to their stages (which may involve, of course, appropriately reconstruing the explanandum), and in this case the time-slice-sum transformation may indeed give rise to an alternative interpretation that satisfies the Principle of Conformality as well as the initial interpretation does. For these cases, then, a different remedy will have to be sought, and is developed in an argument that is woven through chapter 2.[18] The argument attempts to motivate a constraint on indeterminacy-generating transformations: that an object in the initial ontology and its correlate under the transformation coexist in each of a certain range of possible worlds. I argue that the present requirement further and significantly constrains the indeterminacies arising on Quine's schema. The putative indeterminacy generated by a transformation mapping each physical object onto the sum of its time-slices affords a case in point: a physical object and its actual stages do not generally coexist in each of the relevant possible worlds.

In chapter 3, the present framework is applied to the problem of reference for proper names, observation terms, and natural kind terms. In each case, a mechanism of reference is proposed that is argued to optimize the availability of conformal explanations. These proposals are not, like the Principle of Conformality, constitutive principles of radical interpretation. They are rather what I shall call *enabling proposals* with respect to the satisfaction of such principles, in this case the Principle of Conformality itself. My arguments that these proposals are conformally optimal are guarded. Strategies will emerge for constructing an open-ended class of conformal explanations on the basis of the suggested accounts of reference for the indicated categories, but it would seem that more is required than that.

---

[17]See *Ontological Relativity*, pp. 55–61. A set is called 'pure', roughly, if its construction involves only sets; in more exact technical terms, a pure set is one whose transitive closure contains only sets.

[18]See especially sections 2.3.3 and 2.5.3.

We require some evidence to the effect that the suggested mechanisms of reference do the *best possible* job of securing such explanations. It is unclear what form a fully general argument to this conclusion would take; in any case, no such argument will be attempted here. I will, however, assemble some piecemeal evidence, obtained by comparing the consequences of these proposals to those of a number of alternative accounts of reference suggested in the literature. In each case I shall argue that the points of divergence favor the present proposals in terms of our judgments about what the extensions of the terms in the test cases should be, an outcome that I wish to urge is connected to the fact that the suggested mechanisms of reference better underwrite conformal explanations than the alternative accounts with which they are compared.

In certain respects, the models of reference I will suggest for proper names and natural kind words cut across the accounts given by description theories and by causal theories. The present approach is in one way radically 'externalist', depending primarily on our ability to coordinate beliefs within a population with aspects of the causal structure of its environment relevant to explicating its activity in conformal terms. But such a coordination problem is solved, in general, ahistorically, without special attention to the *origin* of the correspondence relation that underlies a putative solution; and a successful solution trades on the accuracy, under he correspondence relation it specifies, of the agents' conception of the causal structure of their situation, in particular of the generative relations between their prospective basic actions and outcomes relevant to their desires and interests. Both aspects of this account contrast sharply with the picture presented by Kripke in *Naming and Necessity*, and it will be a matter of some delicacy to get straight the relationship between these two views.[19]

The discussion of reference in this book is restricted to proper names, natural kind words and observation terms (which are here construed, in effect, as a sort of limiting case of natural kind terms), and is motivated primarily in terms of the Principle of Conformality. But a word is in order about some cases which have not been considered here. Missing in partic-

---

[19]Having said this, it may be noted that the account of the reference of names given in chapter 3 agrees with the conclusions suggested by Kripke's picture, and disagrees with descriptive accounts, in a number of familiar test cases. It is argued, for example, that in the Gödel-Schmitt case (*Naming and Necessity* [Cambridge, Mass.: Harvard University Press, 1980], pp. 83–92), holding the reference of other expressions fixed, the denotation for the name 'Kurt Gödel' that best contributes to conformal explanations involving the reference of that name is the reference suggested by both Kripke's account and by intuition. Where the accounts begin to come apart is in cases where the object that best satisfies what might be called the 'causal profile' of the reference of a name diverges from the object standing at the end of the Kripkean chain of referential transmissions. For a discussion of these cases, see 3.1.2–3.1.4.

ular is an account of reference for the languages of classical mathematics. The cases here divide. There are parts of classical mathematics—roughly those thought of as associated with multiple set-theoretic reductions—for which I believe that an account of reference of the usual sort is inappropriate. The grounds for my belief are broadly 'structuralist' in character, and are alluded to at the conclusion of chapter 4. These grounds do not, I would argue, extend to classical set theory: but missing from these pages is a story about reference to *sets*.[20] This is not because I think the problem of reference for set theory is insoluble, or impermeable to the methods of the present framework. Rather, I believe that the resources for solving the problem are again at least partly contained in the Principle of Conformality. What is at issue in this case is how seeing a part of the object language as being about the standard interpretation of set theory contributes to conformal explanations, and that is ultimately a matter of the contribution of such an interpretation to causal explanations in the object language itself. It has sometimes been supposed that the properties of a fragment of classical mathematics relevant to any explanatory purpose are preserved by isomorphisms of interpretations of the fragment (a thesis that is a consequence, and may even be considered to be a formulation, of the structuralist conception of truth for the fragment). It is this thesis that I believe to be false for classical set theory: the explanatory role of, for example, Zermelo-Frankel set theory is not, I should argue, preserved by isomorphisms of interpretations of that theory. To fully justify this conclusion requires a study of the theoretical role of set theory beyond the scope I have set myself here; and to get from that claim to anything like the thesis of the determinacy of reference for classical set theory is a further, and difficult, stretch.

1.4   Logic and Radical Interpretation

Field argued that Tarski's theory of truth constitutes a reduction of the concepts of truth and satisfaction to that of primitive denotation (the reference relation for the nonlogical primitives), but fails to give an explanatory account of the latter. I suggested (see n. 4 above) that even this claim seems too strong, for at face value the semantic properties of the logical constants stand as much in need of explanation as those of lexical items such as proper names or natural kind words. In the context of radical interpretation, there is no prior division of the semantically primitive expressions of the object

---

[20]Some reasons for the negative claim are contained in my review of Geoffrey Hellman' *Mathematics without Numbers* (New York: Oxford University Press, 1990); and in *Notre Dame Journal of Formal Logic* 38 (1997): 136–61.

language into logical and non-logical sorts. The problem of identifying and interpreting the logical devices of a language on the basis of the sort of information provided by an interpretation of its speakers is what I shall call the *interpretation problem for logic*.

An approach to the problem emerges by revisiting what seems an entirely different issue, the putative indeterminacies of the Quinean sort described earlier. Consider a permutation of a domain D for a simple quantificational language. We observed that such a correspondence induces a reconstrual of the extensions assigned to the primitives of the language over D by an initially given interpretation. The question concerned the grounds for saying that the given interpretation is correct and the induced alternative interpretation incorrect. But one could imagine a predicate, call it P, that resists this skeptical construction in the following way. Suppose that a permutation of D always maps the extension of P over D onto *itself*. More generally, suppose that any correlation of the domain D with an alternative domain D' maps the extension of P over D onto its actual extension over D' according to the given interpretation.[21]

This is clearly an unusual property. It certainly fails, for example, for descriptive terms such as color-predicates, the extension of which over any domain is the set of items therein having the relevant color, for the obvious reason that arbitrary correlations fail to preserve color. But for a small minority the condition obtains. Thus, for example, consider the identity predicate, whose extension over any domain is the identity relation over that domain. Any correlation of a given domain with any other maps the identity relation over the former precisely onto the identity relation over the latter. Let us say that such a predicate is *extensionally invariant*.

It is easy to see that a unary predicate is extensionally invariant if and only if its extension over any domain is either universal or empty. For a two-place predicate, the relevant condition is that over each domain its extension is the universal binary relation, the empty binary relation, the identity relation, or its complement, the distinctness relation. Analogous conditions characterize predicates of higher degree. In the general situation, one has an operator Q applying to strings of expressions of types $\sigma_1, ..., \sigma_n$

---

[21] For this we require the assumption that the given interpretation fix an extension for the predicate over each domain. If P is an n-place predicate, the interpretation will associate P with a class E of n-tuples and the extension of P over a domain D will be the restriction of E to D, that is, the set $\{(a_1, ..., a_n) \in E \mid a_1, ..., a_n \in D\}$. For the general case, considered hereafter, where we have an operator applying to expressions of types $\sigma_1, ..., \sigma_n$ to yield an expression of type τ, the assumption would be that for any domain D the interpretation determines a function mapping sequences of extensions of the sort had by expressions of types $\sigma_1, ..., \sigma_n$ over D to extensions of the sort had by expressions of type τ over D.

to give an expression of type τ. The invariance condition for an operator Q may be expressed as follows: let D be any nonempty domain, and consider any expressions $e_1, ..., e_n$ of types $\sigma_1, ..., \sigma_n$ assigned extensions over D. Now suppose that we are given a one-to-one correspondence of D with an alternative domain D' that maps the extension of each e_i over D onto the extension of an expression e_i' of type σ_i over D'. The requirement is then that such a transformation *also* map the extension of the expression $Q(e_1, ..., e_n)$ over D isomorphically onto the extension of $Q(e_1', ..., e_n')$ over D'.[22]

Mostowski used something like this condition in characterizing the expressions now called 'generalized quantifiers'.[23] In a lecture given in 1966, Tarski suggested a rather similar condition as a criterion of an expression's being a logical constant.[24] The invariance condition for Q says roughly that the structure of the extension of an expression formed by applying Q should be determined by the structure of the extensions of the expressions to which it is applied. Such a requirement may be employed to confer a clear content on one very traditional thesis about logical words, namely, that they are 'topic-neutral' expressions.[25] In this context, the interesting thing about the expressions meeting Mostowski's requirement is that their semantic properties are, in one salient respect, better determined than those of expressions that do not. Invariant expressions systematically defeat indeterminacies of the Quinean sort: for the transformation deployed by such an example will automatically map the extension of any expression over the initial domain onto its actual extension over the relevant alternative domain. This suggests that invariance properties may bear on the interpretation problem for logic, although I shall argue that Mostowski's property is not, by itself, quite what we want.

In modern logic, a demarcation of the logical constants of a language L is preparatory to a semantical definition of a relation of *logical consequence*

---

[22] See 4.3 for a fuller discussion of this condition.

[23] A. Mostowski, "On a Generalization of Quantifiers," *Fundamenta Mathematicae* 44 (1957): 12–36.

[24] A. Tarski, "What Are Logical Notions?" (1966), posthumously published under this title with an introduction by John Corchoran, *History and Philosophy of Logic* 7:143–54. In an article published in 1981, I argued Mostowski's condition to constitute a *necessary* condition for logical constanthood, on grounds not dissimilar from Tarski's (whose lecture on the topic was at the time unpublished, and unknown to me; see "The Idea of a Logical Constant," *Journal of Philosophy* LXXVII, 9 (1981): 499–523). This article is in part a response to a criterion suggested by Christopher Peacocke, "What Is a Logical Constant?" *Journal of Philosophy* 73 (1976): 221–40. My reasons for thinking Mostowski's condition not to constitute a sufficient condition for logical status will emerge below, and are related to the considerations developed in Peacocke's paper.

[25] See "The Idea of a Logical Constant," sec. 3, for a discussion of this concept.

for L. The familiar idea is roughly that a sentence φ is a logical consequence of a set S of sentences in L if φ is true on any semantical valuation of L realizing each member of S that assigns to any logical expression its actual or intended interpretation over the domain of the valuation.[26] One difficulty for this picture is that to be properly called a notion of logical consequence for L, the converse of such a relation should constitute a type of implication or entailment, and for this it seems obligatory, for any set S and sentence φ, that φ be a logical consequence of S only if, *necessarily*, if each member of S is true in L, then φ is true in L. Call this constraint the *Necessitation Condition*. The content of the Necessitation Condition depends, of course, on the concept of necessity used in formulating it. But however it is interpreted, on the semantical conception of logical consequence articulated by Tarski, the claim that a model-theoretically characterized entailment relation for L satisfies the Necessitation Condition is problematic.[27] In fact, in the absence of *any* restrictions on which expressions are to count as 'logical', the condition may easily be seen to fail in some cases. Consider, for example, two predicates, $A(x)$ and $P(x)$, whose extensions contingently coincide. Let us suppose that *both* of these predicates are treated as constants in a semantical characterization of the concept of logical consequence for L. Then the schema

[i] $A(c)/P(c)$

will count as valid; but it is not necessarily truth-preserving. The Tarski-Mostowski condition helps here, but only so far. (Thus, for example, if A is '— is red' and B is '— is round', and all and only the round things are red, then the present example fails because neither predicate is extensionally invariant.) But suppose that $P(x)$ in [i] is a primitive predicate of L translated into regimented English by the phrase

$$(x = x \ \& \ \varphi) \ \vee \ (\neg x = x \ \& \ \neg \varphi),$$

where φ is a contingently true sentence of English. Let $A(x)$ be $x = x$. If $P(x)$ is treated as a logical constant, then, its interpretation is universal over

---

[26]This idea goes back to Löwenheim, and received an important formulation in Tarski's article "Uber den Begriff der logischen Folgerung" (1936; reprint, "On the Concept of Logical Consequence," in *Logic, Semantics, Metamathematics*, translated and edited by J. H. Woodger (Oxford: Clarendon Press, 1956). See also my exposition in 4.2.

[27]This problem has been discussed at length by John Etchemendy in *The Concept of Logical Consequence* (Cambridge, Mass.: Harvard University Press, 1990). A version of the same problem is discussed in my "Modality, Invariance, and Logical Truth," *Journal of Philosophical Logic* 16 (1987): 423–43.

any domain, so that [i] is again counted as valid. But it is not necessarily truth-preserving, as we see by considering possible situations in which φ is false. In this case, however, both $A(x)$ and $P(x)$ satisfy the extensional invariance condition.

The difficulty illustrated by such examples is that there can be accidental invariance; and the natural remedy that suggests itself is to strengthen Mostowski's condition to require the invariance of a logical expression over *all possible situations*. To apply this idea, we require the assumption that the semantic description of the agent's language fix an extension of the appropriate type for each expression *at any possible world*. Thus, in the preceding example, the requirement would be that any correlation of the domains of two worlds would map the extension of $P(x)$ in the first onto its extension in the second, a condition that will fail if the sentence φ holds in one world but not in the other. In the case of a quantifier symbol Q applying to a variable-formula pair $x, A(x)$ to yield a formula $(Qx)A(x)$, the modalized invariance requirement would say that any correlation of the domains of two worlds that maps the extension of a formula $A(x)$ in the first world isomorphically onto the extension of a formula $B(x)$ in the second *also* maps the extension of $(Qx)A(x)$ in the first world onto the extension of $(Qx)B(x)$ in the second. An expression satisfying this condition will be said to be *rigidly invariant* over the relevant class of possible worlds. In our present context, the most important fact about rigid invariance is that, under quite general conditions, if the expressions which are treated as constants in a semantical characterization of validity are rigidly invariant over a chosen class of possible worlds, then the resulting consequence relation satisfies a necessitation requirement with respect to that class: that is, a sentence φ is a consequence of a set of sentences only if φ is true in every world of this sort in which each member of the set is true.[28]

The relevance of these considerations to the theory of radical interpretation emerges when we ask what form the necessitation requirement should take when applied to a model-theoretic characterization of logical relations in a chosen interpretive target language. The question here is whether (and, if so, in what way) a natural entailment relation for such a language is determined by a complete interpretation of its speakers. If such a relation can be discerned, then a form of the necessitation condition may be viewed as a constitutive principle of radical interpretation. It would say that a demarcation of the logical expressions of the agent's language is acceptable only if it gives rise to a notion of logical consequence that is a species of

---

[28] See my "Modality, Invariance, and Logical Truth," for a proof and discussion of this result. A version of the proof is also given in the postscript to chapter 4. For a general discussion of these issues at an introductory level, see my entry "Logical Constants" in the *Routledge Encyclopedia of Philosophy* (London: Routledge, 1997).

the entailment relation for that language. I call this condition the *Completeness Principle*. I shall argue that such an entailment relation is in fact fixed by a suitable representation of the inductive method of the agent in question. Thus the methodological role of the Completeness Principle in radical interpretation will be to control the relation between the inductive method ascribed to an agent and the logic ascribed to the agent's language.

The question then becomes how to solve the demarcation problem for the logical expressions of the agent's language in such a way as to ensure that the Completeness Principle is satisfied. The solution developed in chapter 4 exploits the connection between rigid invariance and entailment alluded to earlier. Suppose that a total interpretation of an agent determined the complete descriptions of the world that are *epistemically possible* for the agent. Call these descriptions the agent's *epistemic alternatives*. The problem of characterizing the entailment relation for the agent's language then has a very natural solution: a set S of sentences entails a sentence φ if φ holds in each epistemic alternative for the agent realizing each member of S. Logical constanthood for that language will then be identified with the rigid invariance property *defined with reference to the entire class of the agent's epistemic alternatives*. The indicated link between rigid invariance and the necessitation condition then explains why model-theoretic implication in the agent's language is a species of entailment therein, and thus underwrites satisfaction of the Completeness Principle.

There is one loose end: *how* does a complete interpretation of the agent fix a description of the configurations of the world which are epistemically possible for the agent? I shall suggest a quasi-syntactic specification of the agent's alternatives, identifying them with sets of semantic representations of the sort accorded to sentences of her language.[29] Such a set will be taken to describe an alternative for the agent roughly if the beliefs it specifies are in an idealized type of reflective equilibrium with respect to the agent's inductive method, and that set is maximal among all sets with this property.[30] The inductive method of the agent will in turn be identified with an effective strategy for the manipulation of semantic representations of this sort.[31] The upshot, then, is that the basic scheme of epistemic rules ascribed to the agent by an interpretation fixes the agent's epistemic alternatives, the class of configurations of the world that are epistemically

---

[29]Although for the present purpose the required semantic representations may go *beyond* those accorded to sentences of her language.

[30]This is a gloss on a construction developed in 4.3.2 and 4.5, and further extended in 4.9. The notion of 'reflective equilibrium' for such a set is characterized in terms of the closure of the set under a notion of implication generated directly by the agent's inductive method.

[31]See 2.2.2.

possible for the agent; and these in turn determine the expressions which count as logical in the agent's language.

We have thus arrived at a broad determinacy property, of a relative sort, for logic: the *demarcation* of the logical constants of an agent's language is settled once a suitable description of the structure of the agent's understanding is given. That leaves open the more specific question of how the interpretations of particular logical expressions are determined by such a description. The logical expressions, I suggested, are just those that behave invariantly over the entire collection of the agent's epistemic alternatives; and in fact it is not difficult to see, under quite general conditions, that the semantic interpretation of such an expression is determined uniquely (4.4.2). An example will serve to illustrate the general idea. Consider again a quantifier symbol Q applying to a variable-formula pair $x, A(x)$ to yield the sentence

[ii] $(Qx)A(x)$.

Given a possible assignment of extension for $A(x)$ over some nonempty domain, then, we need to determine the truth-value of [ii]. To this end, locate a copy of the given extension for $A(x)$ in some alternative. That is to say, we shall find a predicate $B(x)$ whose extension in that alternative is isomorphic to the given interpretation of $A(x)$. We then ascribe to [ii] the truth-value assigned to the sentence $(Qx)B(x)$ in that alternative. By the rigid invariance property of Q, this procedure must yield *the same* truth-value for [ii] no matter which alternative is considered; and for the same reason this value must coincide with whatever may be taken to be the correct truth-value for [ii] on the given assignment.[32]

To sum up: an overall interpretation of an agent sees that person as exemplifying an *inductive method*, roughly, a rule-based conception of epistemic rationality, which in turn makes possible a representation of the agent's epistemic alternatives, the configurations of the world that are epistemically possible for the agent. Alternatives are identified roughly with maximal sets of semantic representations of the sort accorded to the agent's language that are coherent with respect to the agent's inductive method. These structures then determine both the demarcation of the logical expressions of the agent's language and the semantic interpretation of the expressions counted as 'logical'. The ground of the demarcation lies in the ability of the property that characterizes the logical constants (invariance

---

[32]This argument requires the assumption that the relevant semantic values are, in a suitable structural sense, realized in some alternative for the agent. The required assumption is more precisely stated, and its justification discussed, in 4.4.1.

over all alternatives) to ensure satisfaction of a constitutive requirement of interpretation (the Completeness Principle).

In the concluding sections of the book, the foregoing observations, developed initially with reference to extensional languages, are generalized to intensional ones. In the intensional case, the relation of reference or satisfaction is relativized to indexical elements of various sorts (speakers, places, times, possible worlds, and so forth), and so the natural way of extending the suggested account of the logical constants to the intensional case would appeal to a relativized notion of invariance, characterized in terms of a class of alternatives that peg propositional contents to indices of the relevant sort.[33] An expression falling under such a relativized invariance property may be said to be logical *relative to* the indexical features in terms of which it is interpreted; but this, by itself, is not quite enough to ensure that the expression is logical. Thus, for example, temporal modalities such as 'always' and 'never' satisfy this requirement (see 4.8.2), but they are not logical expressions. They are rather analogous to relativized quantifiers, whose nonlogical status stems not from their quantificational aspect, but from the sort to which they are relativized. Similarly, the nonlogical status of 'always' stems not from its modal character per se, but from the nonlogical character of time.

This last sentence should seem a bit odd; it suggests something like a category mistake. The terms 'logical' and 'nonlogical' apply to quantificational devices, connectives, and so on, or perhaps to their semantical correlates (whatever these may be), not to kinds or sorts of things, unless, of course, *such a sort can itself be regarded as the semantical correlate of a logical constant.* But what is the semantical correlate of a logical constant? One answer is that it is a class of valuations or *structures*, in the model-theoretic sense; for example, a unary quantifier Q introduces the class of all structures of the form $\langle D, E \rangle$, where D is a nonempty set and E a subset of D, such that the sentence $(Qx)A(x)$ is true when the quantifier is taken to range over the domain D and $A(x)$ is assigned extension E over D. My suggestion will be that such a class of structures may be said to be *logical* if it is definable in terms of some (possibly complex) logical constant. The concept of logical constanthood for the intensional case is then a product of the relativized invariance requirement and the assumption that the relevant indexical features are logical in the present sense. Thus, the indices will themselves be relational structures picked out by some logical term. As in

---

[33]To make this rough suggestion precise is a rather delicate matter. See 4.8.2 for a treatment of the relativized invariance concept, and 4.9 for a construction of intensional alternatives.

the extensional case, a form of the Completeness Principle is validated, and
a relative determinacy property for the logical constants is secured.

1.5   The Limits of Determinacy

I have not claimed, nor need I claim, that the present framework provides
a *complete* set of constraints on radical interpretation; it is left open here
whether all the constraints are in, or whether in fact they are ever all
in. Neither is an attempt made here to draw a sharp line between intentional and nonintentional systems: indeed, the status of the Principle of
Conformality as a maximizing constraint without a definite threshold of
satisfaction suggests that such an attempt would be misguided. The broad
design of this project is rather to try to motivate as clearly as possible
a quite austere system of interpretational constraints and then to explore
how much can be done with so little. I argue that the system of constraints
adopted here allows us to address a number of the most salient claims of indeterminacy. In conclusion it is thus natural and appropriate to ask which
indeterminacies may survive. The question proves to be entangled with
some difficult metaphysical issues.

Consider the circumstances under which an example of the Quinean
sort might be *successful*. Assume given an *admissible* interpretation of an
agent, that is, one that satisfies each of the suggested constraints, which,
for simplicity, we suppose to assign semantic representations of a first-order
kind to sentences of the agent's language. Any one-to-one correspondence
defined on the ontology ascribed to the agent by the given admissible interpretation induces an alternative interpretation of that agent. The question
is under what conditions the resulting interpretation will also be admissible.
I argue in subsection 2.3.1 below that a reinterpretation of this sort may be
defined in such a way as to meet the requirements of the present framework,
exclusive of the Principle of Conformality. The question, then, is when the
alternative interpretation will satisfy the Principle of Conformality.

The conformal explanations generated by the given interpretation refer
back to causal explanations accessible to the agent; and any such object-
language explanation is potentially available for such a role. Thus a complete conformal-explanatory symmetry between the two interpretations
would require that the same constructions in the language of the agent
constitute causal explanations under those interpretations. Such a requirement is certainly a strong constraint on the admissible reconstruals of that
language, but what have been called 'equivalent' or interreducible theories
may afford a significant illustration of how it may be satisfied.[34] Typical

---

[34]Related explications of the notion of equivalence are suggested by Putnam in his

cases of equivalence include alternative formulations of classical mechanics in terms of fields on the one hand and forces acting at a distance on the other, and the alternative formulations of quantum mechanics due to Heisenberg and Born on the one hand and to Schrödinger on the other.[35] Somewhat easier to digest is Putnam's example of alternative spacetime geometries, one of which takes spacetime points as primitive and identifies regions with sets of points; the other takes regions as primitive and identifies any point p with the sequence $\langle N_k(p) \rangle$, where for each natural number k, $N_k(p)$ is the piece of spacetime corresponding to the open ball around p of radius $1/2^k$. There are then translations mapping each of these geometries into the other. Thus, for example, the term 'point' in the first description will be rendered in the second by something like 'contracting sequence of spheres'; in the other direction, the term 'region' in the second version is interpreted in the first by something like 'connected open set of points'.

In the clearest cases of equivalence, then, there are given (normally first-order) theories T_1 and T_2 and a pair of translations s_1 and s_2 between them that constitute *relative interpretations* of the one theory in the other. That is to say, in the T_1 to T_2 direction, that s_1 is a translation of the language of T_1 into the language of T_2 that preserves logical form and maps consequences of T_1 onto consequences of T_2.[36] This means only that T_1 and T_2 stand to one another in a relation of formal intertranslatability: what is required to ensure their *equivalence*? What invariants are relevant to such a requirement? One plausible constraint is that, under the translations in question, there should be a symmetry between the *explanations* available in the two theories. Putnam has suggested the following formulation of this requirement: first, T_1 and T_2 share a common observational language, in terms of which they can frame a description of the phenomena to be explained; second, the translations in question coincide on this invariant

---

article, "Equivalence," in *Realism and Reason: Philosophical Papers*, vol. 3 (Cambridge, Mass.: Cambridge University Press, 1983), and by Quine, "On Empirically Equivalent Systems of the World," *Erkentnis* 9 (1978): 313–28. Putnam's discussion is in part a critical reaction to Hans Reichenbach's doctrine of coordinating definitions in *Experience and Prediction* (Chicago: University of Chicago Press, 1938). Reichenbach seems to have been the first philosopher to discuss the phenomenon of equivalent theories.

[35]This example was studied by Reichenbach, *Philosophic Foundations of Quantum Mechanics* (Berkeley: University of California Press, 1944), who uses the case as a prototype of the concept of equivalence.

[36]The translation normally involves an appropriate relativization of quantifiers in T_2, to counterparts of the items in the domain of T_1. The notion of relative interpretability of theories was introduced by Tarski, who first described the essential formal properties of the concept. See A. Tarski, A. Mostowski and R. Robinson, *Undecidable Theories* (Amsterdam: North-Holland, 1953), section 1.

sublanguage; and finally, the translations *preserve explanations* of phenomena described in that observational sublanguage. Thus, in one direction,
applying s_1 to an explanation of a given event in T_1, we obtain an explanation of that same event in T_2; and symmetrically for the other direction.[37]
I shall adopt this picture as providing at least a necessary condition for the
equivalence relation in question.

Consider now the situation in which we have two interpretations of an
agent related by a pair of Quinean transformations, in the specified way,
that ascribe *equivalent* belief-systems to the agent. In this situation, there
will be a complete symmetry between the two interpretations with respect
to the causal explanations they make available to the agent of connections
between her prospective basic actions and outcomes that according to the
interpretations, she desires.[38] There will thus exist an induced symmetry
between the conformal explanations that may be given on the basis of
the alternative interpretations, and thus those interpretations will equally
satisfy the Principle of Conformality. I shall show in subsection 2.3.1 that
they also satisfy to just the same degree the other constraints on radical
interpretation to be introduced hereafter. The two interpretations are thus
on a par with respect to the constitutive principles I shall entertain and,
perhaps, with respect to any it would be reasonable to entertain.

Consider, for example, the alternative formulations of spacetime geometry discussed above. If, according to a given admissible interpretation,
an agent's geometrical beliefs are described by one of these formulations,
there exists an equally admissible interpretation of the agent that recon-
strues them in terms of the other. The alternative interpretations can be
considered as arising from a pair of Quinean transformations that embed
the alternative geometric ontologies in each other; the transformations in
question are generated by the dual constructions of points and regions indi-

---

[37]See Putnam, "Equivalence," pp. 38–40. It may seem tendentious to assume that
the items in the equivalence relation come equipped with a set of phenomena to be
explained and a determinate notion of explanation. These assumptions lend a dimension of relativity to Putnam's condition of equivalence for theories, according to which
parameters are chosen for explanation by the theories and which constructions within
the theories are taken to explain them. However, in the usual examples of the relation
this relativity can be suppressed, since there is agreement in these cases about what is
to be explained and about what constitutes, modulo truth, an explanation. Thus, for
example, rewriting a physical theory that takes spacetime points as primitive in terms of
a construction that identifies points with nested sequences of regions plausibly yields an
equivalent theory; any explanation in one theory can, by a straightforward transcription,
be converted to one in the other, assuming certain set-theoretic resources to be common
property. It is of interest that from a nominalistic standpoint, this symmetry fails; see
Hartry Field, *Realism, Mathematics and Modality* (Oxford: Blackwell, 1989), pp. 45–48.

[38]Assuming the outcomes in question to be observational in the relevant sense.

cated above. The term 'point' in the language of the agent will then receive divergent readings within the two interpretations. On the first it will refer to mereologically atomic parts of spacetime; on the second, to certain functions mapping the natural numbers to mereologically composite parts of spacetime. The two interpretations thus conflict. If, as seems plausible, they equally satisfy all relevant constraints, then it would seem that we have a genuine case of indeterminacy.

The following conjectures naturally suggest themselves:

(1) In the context of a complete set of constraints (those suggested here, or an appropriate extension thereof), the present sort of indeterminacy is the only sort possible. That is to say, any pair of interpretations of an agent satisfying such a set ascribe equivalent belief-systems to the agent.

(2) If two interpretations of an agent satisfy a complete set of constraints, then they are equivalent as theories.[39]

Conjectures (1) and (2) are not, in our present situation, susceptible of demonstration. To establish (1) and (2)—or even to invest them with a precise content—we would require on the one hand a specification of all of the relevant constraints, and on the other a satisfactory criterion (necessary *and sufficient* conditions) for equivalence.[40] Neither is quite at hand. In the end, I think that (1) and (2) should properly function as constraints on our *calling* a framework for radical interpretation 'complete'. But I will defer that point for a moment.

What is the significance of the concept of equivalence for theories? One answer to this question, sometimes broadly termed 'irrealist', has been developed, in somewhat different ways, by Reichenbach, Putnam, and Quine in the sources cited earlier. This stance rests on the idea that, if we are given two formally incompatible but equivalent theories, then appearances

---

[39]Note that this assertion is not trivial: to say that theories of any sort are equivalent is to say more than that they equally satisfy all relevant theoretical constraints; it is also to say that they are *intertranslatable* in such a way as to preserve relevant properties and relations.

[40]Putnam argued that the explanatory symmetry requirement is in fact a sufficient condition for cognitive equivalence; unfortunately, however, I believe it is not. The reason is that Putnam's criterion does not distinguish between genuine equivalence and certain cases of global causal-explanatory redundancy. In these cases, the phenomena are overdetermined by two isomorphic systems of causes. Thus the complete theory of the situation, call it 'T' is of the form $T_1 \cup T_2$, where T_1 and T_2 constitute complete descriptions of the causal systems in question. Then T_1 and T_2 are mutually relatively interpretable in such a way as to satisfy the explanatory symmetry requirement, but they do not seem to be equivalent in the informal sense described above; they do not constitute, so to speak, 'alternative complete descriptions of the same state of affairs', however that is to be properly understood.

to the contrary it makes no sense to ask which one is right; that a pair of equivalent theories should be taken to have the same objective content, and to constitute alternative descriptions of what is in some not very clearly understood sense the same state of affairs. Thus, for example, in virtue of their equivalence the alternative versions of spacetime geometry considered earlier should on this view be taken to have the same objective content, notwithstanding the fact that their ontological commitments differ. From this point of view, the question of *what there is* makes sense only relative to such a theory; the relativity is a consequence of a sort of indexicality, an artifact of what might be called 'ontological perspective'.

The picture I have just sketched is as problematic as it is seductive, and cannot be disentangled here. Nor shall I try here to adjudicate between it and a rival metaphysical standpoint which might reasonably be called 'realist' that would affirm, for example, that there *is* a fact of the matter which of the alternative spacetime geometries is correct. No need, for as far as I can see the present framework can be deployed against the background of both of these metaphysical views. I will allow myself just one comment of a defensive nature. If the irrealist view is to seem anything other than a version of Protagorean relativism crafted with the tools of modern logic, then there has to be a notion of 'rightness' or 'goodness of fit' for descriptions of the world in virtue of which some fit the world and others to not. One's immediate inclination is to ask how this property is to be characterized; but perhaps, as Arthur Fine has suggested, it is a mistake to look for a general characterization of it at all.[41] In any case, would an answer to this question that does not take the notion of reference as fundamental render superfluous any characterization of truth in terms of reference? Not at all. On the 'irrealist' view, the suggested rationale of the notion of reference in terms of conformal explanation is fully available, save that the question of the correctness of the underlying object language explanations must be referred to a 'description' (Reichenbach), 'theory' (Putnam), or 'theory formulation' (Quine).

1.6   Credo

In the concluding paragraphs of his seminal paper, Lewis canvasses the possibilities of indeterminacy:

> It seems hopeless to deny, in the face of such examples as have been offered by Quine, that the truth conditions of full sentences in M [the

---

[41] See Arthur Fine, *The Shaky Game: Einstein, Realism, and the Quantum Theory* (Chicago: University of Chicago Press, 1986), p. 9; and see chapter 8, "And Not Anti-Realism Either."

semantic component of the interpretation] do not suffice to determine
the rest of M: the parsings and the meanings of the constituents of
sentences.[42]

That, for Lewis, is one source of indeterminacy, acknowledged as arising
because of the absence of any but some rather weak structural constraints
on M. Here is another:

> It also seems hard to deny that a more general sort of indeterminacy
> can arise because no solution fits all the constraints perfectly, and many
> different ways to strike a balance give many different compromise solu-
> tions. The 'unsharp analyticity' of some so-called definitions in physics,
> or the confused desires of a compulsive thief, might exemplify this inde-
> terminacy of compromise.[43]

Indeterminacies of compromise, one suspects, will arise on any
constraint-based approach to radical interpretation. They do within the
present framework, in view of the sorts of cases Lewis mentioned, but also
because of features distinctive to that framework, in particular, the operation of the Principle of Conformality. I shall largely assume that subjects of
interpretation are in one respect ideal in applying that principle: conformal
explanations proceed on the assumption that the particular beliefs they ascribe to the agent are *true*. This assumption would block the deployment
of conformal explanations in a great many actual situations to which they
might apply if the concept of conformal explanation were extended in one
slightly loaded way. In many cases agents act successfully on information
that is only approximately true, and it would seem a relatively minor matter to adapt the schema for conformal explanation developed in chapter 2
to accomodate these cases. Thus, for example, the laws of classical mechanics should be available as belief-contents in a conformal explanation
if those laws *very nearly* describe the physical situation to which the explanation is applied. Such a stance, however, risks another indeterminacy
of compromise, owing to the fact that, while there is no acceptable physical interpretation of the beliefs in question under which they are true, any
number of divergent interpretations may be tied at optimum in making
them approximately true. Hartry Field observed that classical mechanics
exhibits such an indeterminacy: no physical magnitude exactly satisfies the
constraints placed on mass in Newtonian mechanics, but both inertial mass
and relativistic mass do so approximately under suitable circumstances. We
might call these cases 'indeterminacies of approximation'.[44]

---

[42] "Radical Interpretation," p. 118. My interpolation.

[43] Ibid.

[44] See Field, "Theory Change and the Indeterminacy of Reference," *Journal of Philosophy* (1974): 462–81, for an illuminating discussion of the issue of approximative

Setting aside Quinean indeterminacies and indeterminacies of compromise, Lewis asks:

> Could indeterminacies also arise because two different solutions both fit all the constraints perfectly? Here is the place to hold the line. This sort of indeterminacy has not been shown by convincing examples, and neither could it be shown—to me—by proof. Credo: if ever you prove to me that the constraints we have yet found could permit two perfect solutions, differing otherwise than in the auxiliary apparatus of M, then you will have proved that we have not yet found all the constraints.[45]

Lewis's rather sanguine acceptance of Quine's examples has always puzzled me, because it has always seemed to me that the indeterminacies of interpretation putatively exhibited by some of these are as shocking to common sense as almost any that might arise by tampering with the truth-conditions of whole sentences. Much of this study is a sustained attempt to address examples of the sort offered by Quine, precisely by locating additional constraints on Lewis's M, the theory of the semantic structure of the agent's language. In the aftermath of this enterprise, however, it is tempting to look for an appropriate modification of Lewis's 'credo'. We should properly draw the line well in front of his: the familiar sorts of tinkering with the auxiliary devices of M, I shall argue, are largely excluded within the framework developed hereafter. We have seen, however, that referential divergence is possible across *equivalent* interpretations. The appropriate question here is then the following: could two interpretations perfectly satisfy all of the relevant constraints and yet differ otherwise than in terms reconcilable by the relation of equivalence illustrated above? *There*, I suggest, is the place to hold the line.

---

interpretation and of this example in particular. Another type of indeterminacy of approximation has already been mentioned. It arises when we say, as I shall wish to say, that an actual agent 'approximately instantiates' a computational scheme describing her inductive method. Here I would argue that the situation is complicated by the fact that we have no very clear idea of what we mean when we do say this (see the postscript to chapter 2 for a discussion of this issue). Even when this matter is cleared up, however, the possibility exists that a given agent approximately instantiates, in the relevant sense, and to the same degree, many incompatible inductive methods.

[45] "Radical Interpretation," p. 118.

TWO

RADICAL INTERPRETATION

In this chapter, I set out elements of a framework for radical interpretation. I begin by examining, adapting, and then adopting some constraints on interpretation that have been suggested by Donald Davidson and David Lewis. I shall then introduce the problem of the indeterminacy of semantic description by showing that the constraints in question admit many incompatible semantic descriptions of a simple extensional language if any at all. This result amplifies similar conclusions already reached by these philosophers, and largely anticipated by Quine. I shall then investigate some obstructions to extending this argument to languages involving certain modalities. This will lead us to a limited remedy for indeterminacies of the relevant sort based on broadly logical considerations. In the remainder of the chapter, I shall develop and motivate a further constraint on radical interpretation that is argued to resolve a wide range of referential indeterminacies.

2.1 The Problem

I begin with some basic concepts. Let L be the language of an agent whom, following tradition, we call 'Karl'. We shall assume given a syntactic description of L. We may view a **scheme of reference for** L as being defined by a triple

$$\mathbf{R} = \langle H, L^{\#}, S \rangle,$$

where $L^{\#}$ is an (uninterpreted) formal language, H is a relation holding between sentences of L and sentences of $L^{\#}$, and S is a theory of truth for $L^{\#}$. By the **language** of $\mathbf{R}$ we will mean that of S. The theory S is assumed to be finite and to recursively associate each sentence of $L^{\#}$ with a representation of its truth-condition. The phrase 'scheme of reference' is an artifact of an implicit conception of how this is to be accomplished: the methodology is to associate each lexical primitive of $L^{\#}$ with a reference of some sort, then to explain how the truth-value of any sentence of $L^{\#}$ is determined by its structure from the referential interpretations of the lexical primitives. A scheme of reference may relativize the reference relation for Karl's language to contextual factors, or **indices**, of various sorts. This feature will allow the truth-condition assigned to a sentence of Karl's language to vary with the context in which he tokens it.

The correlates of a sentence of L under the relation H will be called the **semantic representations** or **readings** of the sentence in **R**. The fact that H is a relation, rather than a function, arises from the possibility of ambiguity in L: if each sentence of L has just one reading, then each will possess a unique semantic representation under H. For the sake of simplicity, I shall for the most part suppose that H is the identity function, so that sentences of Karl's language are identified with their semantic representations. In this case, we can simplify matters considerably by identifying the scheme of reference **R** with the underlying semantic theory S.

Our problem is that of saying when a given scheme of reference for L is a *correct* description of L, or whether any scheme of reference at all is a correct description of L. The problem is not, at least primarily, an epistemological one. The question is not how we can *know* how the facts stated by a semantic description of L obtain, but what sort of facts these are. The question of course requires the assumption that the 'trivial' answer—that an expression refers to an item just because it refers to it—is not to the point; that semantic notions stand in need of explanation in some important sense.

But the constraints on an acceptable answer are unclear. The problem, as I shall frame it, concerns the relationship between two sorts of fact. On the one side, there are the nonsemantical, nonintentional facts. These include, but are not necessarily limited to, the physical facts: facts statable in the language of physics about Karl and his natural and social environment. However, if Karl's mental states cannot be identified with physical states, the first realm may also contain facts about Karl's mental states, insofar as these can be specified in nonsemantic and nonintentional terms. On the other side, we have facts about the content of Karl's states of thinking and the semantic properties of his language. What unifies this second domain is the phenomenon of intentionality, or 'aboutness'. Some at least of the sentences of Karl's language and some at least of his states of thinking have content: they are *about* things (objects, events, states of affairs) in the world. An answer to our question will explain how facts of the first sort underly, constitute, or determine facts of the second sort. It is the supposition that some such determinative connection exists that generates our problem; without it, the problem doesn't make much sense. In more recent terminology, it is the assumption that the semantic/intentional facts supervene upon the nonsemantic, nonintentional facts. Intentionality is not intrinsic.[1]

I shall work within a general framework for answering this question first developed by Donald Davidson and later modified by David Lewis and others.[2] In a number of articles subsequent to "Truth and Meaning," Davidson described a role for a theory of truth for Karl's language in an overall theory of Karl as a person, a theory that seeks, among other things, to render Karl's behavior intelligible on the basis of ascriptions of beliefs and desires. The rightness of a theory of truth for Karl's language is to be judged, in part, in terms of its suitability for such an explanatory role. It will be seen that that both Davidson's and Lewis's implementation of this idea leave us with pervasive semantic indeterminacies at least at the lexical level, and perhaps at higher levels as well. Our task will then be to define an explanatory role for semantic notions that further and significantly constrains the semantic description of Karl's language and attitudes.

2.2   The Minimal Framework

The explanatory scheme I will describe in section 2.4 is a way of understanding Karl in relation to his social and natural context, and goes along with a familiar decision-theoretic scheme of explanation which in turn is a refinement of our commonsense strategem for explaining behavior in terms of beliefs and desires. Both are properly part of an overall scheme of radical interpretation for Karl. To explain Karl's behavior in intentional terms, we will want an interpretation of Karl to incorporate, in some way, a specification of his beliefs and desires; to deploy the sort of explanatory framework I have in mind, we will want it also to incorporate a scheme of reference for Karl's language L. I begin with some structural constraints on theories of reference.

---

[1] This inquiry may still be of interest for someone who believes that intentionality *is* primitive; for there is still the question of *where* the fixation of content by Karl's physical circumstances and nonintentional mental states *breaks off*.

[2] See Davidson, "Radical Interpretation," in *Inquiries into Truth and Interpretation* (New York: Oxford University Press, 1984), and Lewis's article of the same title reprinted in his *Philosophical Papers*, vol. 1 (New York: Oxford University Press, 1983). I further extended Lewis's framework in ways relevant to what follows in "Representation, Intentionality and Quantifiers," *Synthese* 60 (1984): 369–411. As will be apparent later, I no longer believe that the form of the Principle of Charity advocated in that article is acceptable.

2.2.1   Structural Constraints on **R**

Following Lewis, we might represent an interpretation of Karl by a triple

$$\langle \mathbf{A}o, \mathbf{A}k, \mathbf{R} \rangle,$$

where $\mathbf{A}o$ and $\mathbf{A}k$ give Karl's attitudes in our language and in L, respectively, and $\mathbf{R}$ is a scheme of reference for L. As earlier, $\mathbf{R}$ will be construed to be a compositional account of truth for a formal language $L^{\#}$ together with a relation that reads L into $L^{\#}$. $L^{\#}$ may incorporate various syntactic categories, but at least these three: variables, formulas, and terms; variables are a special sort of term. Names (individual constants) may also be taken to be a special sort of primitive term. In the simplest cases, formulas and terms of $L^{\#}$ are built up by applying operators that apply to finite sequences of expressions from these three categories to generate formulas or terms. Thus, for example, 1-place function symbols are operators taking terms to terms; unary predicates map terms to formulas; and (unary) quantifiers map variable-formula couples to formulas.

Consider now the form of a scheme of reference for $L^{\#}$. We distinguish extensional from intensional schemes. In the extensional case, there is a specified domain D associated with $L^{\#}$ by the scheme. We say that D is the **ontology** of L for the given scheme and that D is **Karl's ontology** for any interpretation of Karl incorporating that scheme. Any scheme of reference for $L^{\#}$ in the extensional case associates each lexical item in $L^{\#}$ with a **reference** or **extension** as follows. The extension of a variable over D is a *projection function* mapping sequences of items in D to D; if ζ is the n'th variable (in a standard enumeration), the reference of ζ over D is the function mapping any sequence over D onto its n'th component. If ζ is a name, the extension of ζ over D is a constant function mapping any sequence to a fixed element of D, the same for each sequence. The extension of a formula ϕ over D is a set of such sequences: the idea is that a sequence specifies an assignment of denotations to the variables free in ϕ, relative to which those variables behave like constants; the extension of ϕ contains a sequence if ϕ is *true relative to* the assignment of parameters to free variables in ϕ given by that sequence. Finally, if α is an operator mapping expressions of type σ to expressions of type τ, the extension of α over D is a function that returns extensions over D of the sort had by expressions of type τ when applied to extensions over D of the sort had by expressions of the type σ. It is thus implied that the extension of each semantically valuable expression of $L^{\#}$ is determined compositionally from the extensions of its lexical constituents, and it is assumed that for any theory of the sort being considered there is an explicit set-theoretic representation of the extension of each such expression derivable in the theory.[3] This is, of course, a familiar generalization of the model-theoretic semantics for first-order languages inherited from Tarski.

In the intensional case, we proceed in an essentially similar way except that we must take account of the relativity of reference to indexical factors: persons, places, times, possible worlds, and so forth. It is customary to package these data as finite sequences consisting of all of the relevant indexical items. The reference of a compound expression at a given index may depend on the references of its constituent expressions at that *and other* indices; thus the indicated compositionality assumption for extensions must be relaxed. In its place, however, we have a quite natural parallel assumption. By the **intension** of an expression relative to a theory of the present sort we mean the function mapping each relevant index onto the extension of the expression at that index. Our compositionality assumption is then that the *intension* of an expression is determined by its structure from the intensions of its constituents.[4] The assumption is secured by coordinating each operator with a function mapping intensions of the sort appropriate for its arguments to intensions of the sort appropriate for the expressions it returns (and similarly for operators defined on a product of syntactic types). In this context, it is assumed that an explicit representation of the *intension* of each formula or term of $L^\#$ is derivable in a theory of the present sort.[5]

A scheme of reference of either of these two sorts will be called **standard**, and the first structural constraint I shall impose on an interpretation of Karl is that it incorporate a scheme of reference that either is or can be put into a form that is standard in the present sense. However, even reading this much detail into a constitutive constraint on the semantic description of Karl's language may seem suspicious. Is it not tantamount to an a priori stipulation that every natural language must *admit* a semantic description of the sort we have called 'standard'? No: that a given natural

---

[3]In particular, then, an explicit representation of the truth-condition of each sentence is derivable in the theory, a sentence being counted as true if its extension consists of all sequences over D. It should be noted that the present compositionality assumption for $L^\#$ does not require that such a condition apply directly to the given syntactic decomposition of L.

[4]For classical statements of the present idea for describing indexicality, see for example, Richard Montague, "Pragmatics," and "Pragmatics and Intensional Logic," both reprinted in *Formal Philosophy*, edited by R. Thomason (New Haven: Yale University Press, 1975), and Lewis, "General Semantics," reprinted in *Philosophical Papers*, vol. 1.

[5]The previous two paragraphs give a capsule description of my semantical framework that is adequate for the purposes of this chapter. The technical details are largely irrelevant here, but will loom larger when I take up the problem of characterizing logical relations in Karl's language in chapter 4.

language admits a description that satisfies the present constraints is indeed an empirical matter. The requirement intended here is that a theory that *purports* to describe a reference relation for Karl's language recursively associate each semantically valuable expression of the language with an appropriate representation of its reference. The question, of course, is why an interpretation of Karl *should* purport to do this. My answer to this question will emerge from the account of the explanatory role of theories of reference developed hereafter.

2.2.2 Attitude Ascription

$\mathbf{A}o$ and $\mathbf{A}k$, I said, comprise Karl's attitudes as given 'in our language' and 'in Karl's language' L. However, within the present framework, both $\mathbf{A}o$ and $\mathbf{A}k$ will be related to a more fundamental representation $\mathbf{A}$. $\mathbf{A}$ is a pair $\langle \mathbf{B}, \mathbf{D} \rangle$, the components $\mathbf{B}, \mathbf{D}$ being sets containing specifications of Karl's beliefs and desires, respectively. But $\mathbf{B}$ and $\mathbf{D}$ are populated neither by sentences of our language nor by sentences of Karl's, but by semantic representations of the sort accorded to sentences of Karl's language. These may be identified with sentences in the formal language $L^{\#}$, in the extensional case, and with pairs of such sentences together with a selection of relevant indices in the intensional one.[6] Where $\mathbf{R} = \langle H, L^{\#}, S \rangle$ is a given scheme of reference for L, recall that H is a relation that reads L into $L^{\#}$: if s is a sentence of L, the sentences r in $L^{\#}$ such that $\langle s, r \rangle \in H$ are the possible semantic representations, or 'readings', of s. $\mathbf{A}k$ will then be comprised of those sentences in L that are related by H to some sentence in $\mathbf{A}$. Thus, for example, if $\mathbf{B}k$ gives Karl's beliefs in L, we may put

$$\mathbf{B}k \;=\; \{s|\ (\exists r)(\langle s, r \rangle \in H \ \& \ r \in \mathbf{B})\}.$$

$\mathbf{A}o$, on the other hand, will be obtained by applying the assignment of truth- conditions in our language generated by $\mathbf{R}$ to the formal sentences comprising $\mathbf{A}$. The relation between $\mathbf{A}k$ and $\mathbf{A}o$ ensures that our interpretation of Karl will automatically fulfill a constraint that Lewis called the '**Triangle Principle**': Karl's attitudes should, modulo the translation induced by $\mathbf{R}$, be the same as expressed either in his language or in our own.

---

[6] A refinement of the present framework, occasionally touched on in what follows, relativizes ascriptions of belief and desire to degrees, represented by real numbers in the unit interval $[0, 1]$. In the nonintensional case, then, attitudes would be represented by couples $\langle r, \phi \rangle$ where $r \in [0, 1]$ and ϕ is a sentence of $L^{\#}$. Such a refinement will allow intentional explanations of Karl's behavior to be framed in decision-theoretic terms; see the discussion of Lewis's Rationalization Principle in 2.2.3.

Three supplements to the present framework for describing attitudes will play a role in what follows. First, it may be suggested that a quite natural set of objects for Karl's propositional attitudes are, plausibly enough, *propositions*, and (what may be less plausible) that propositions are properly construed as sets of possible worlds. In order to answer the familiar objection that, for certain purposes, such a representation describes Karl's attitudes too coarsely, we shall want to take a fairly liberal point of view about what to count as *possible*. Karl's attitudes will be described by sets of syntactic structures that represent configurations of the world that are *epistemically possible for Karl*, so that attitudes given by coincident sets of worlds will stand to one another in a fairly strong relation of cognitive equivalence.[7] Indeed, it seems to me that providing a demarcation of what is *epistemically possible* or *thinkable for Karl* is an independently defensible goal of radical interpretation. It is pursued in chapter 4 for a quite special purpose: the demarcation is required to ground a satisfactory characterization of logical relations in Karl's language.

The second way in which we might wish to extend the present framework concerns the case in which we seek to describe Karl's attitudes not only in the actual situation but also in various counterfactual situations in which the interpretation of Karl's language L is in some sense held fixed. The obvious suggestion for implementing this idea is to treat the relevant possible worlds as indexical elements, and require that **R** fix the reference of each expression of L at each world. If Ω is the set of worlds in question, we shall wish to specify an assignment of attitudes to Karl at each world of Ω. Call such an assignment, together with the required intensional version of **R**, an interpretation of Karl **over** Ω. In order to specify the required map of Karl's beliefs through Ω, Karl will be exhibited as a realization of an inductive method that, when applied to Karl's life-history of evidence in any world belonging to Ω, returns a representation of his beliefs at that world. We should wish to do much the same sort of thing for desires.

The provision of an effective description of Karl's inductive method is also an independently defensible goal of radical interpretation. We want to know not simply what Karl believes, but how he has formed those beliefs; not merely Karl's cognitive output, but *what Karl is doing* in arriving at that output. In brief, we desire a description of *the structure of Karl's understanding*. Such a description, however, can be given in a variety of ways. My goal is not an explanation of how Karl arrives at his beliefs in neurophysiological terms, nor even an explanation in terms of the func-

---

[7]For a vigorous defence of possible worlds representations of attitudes, see R. Stalnaker, *Inquiry* (Cambridge, Mass: MIT Press, 1984), ch. 1. For a detailed implementation of the present idea, see 4.5 and 4.9.

tional organization of Karl's nervous system, but an explanation in terms of Karl's instantiation of cognitive rules. For this purpose, I shall factor Karl's inductive method, call it 'M' into two components, β and Φ. The component β, the **basis** of M, is a function mapping each relevant evidential situation e onto a set of sentences in $L^{\#}$ that specify Karl's properly basic or underived beliefs in e.[8] Φ, the **method of evaluation** of M, is just that: a set of rules for the epistemic evaluation of information coded in $L^{\#}$. Suppose, then, that σ is a finite set of sentences in $L^{\#}$ that describes Karl's underived beliefs in the situation e, and let π do the same for Karl's prior beliefs. Φ will be identified with a function that applies to any such pair $\langle \sigma, \pi \rangle$ to return the collection of sentences in $L^{\#}$ specifying Karl's beliefs in e.

We wish to regard Φ as being constructed in some way from a basic scheme of epistemic rules. As applied to any input $\langle \sigma, \pi \rangle$, Karl's method of evaluation will proceed in stages, represented by positive integers. At any stage n, let $\Phi^{(n)}(\sigma, \pi)$ be the set of sentences of $L^{\#}$ that describes Karl's epistemic situation after n steps in the inductive evaluation of $\langle \sigma, \pi \rangle$. The function which, for fixed σ and π, maps each integer n to $\Phi^{(n)}(\sigma, \pi)$ is assumed to be effectively computable, and will be called the **rule of revision** for $\langle \sigma, \pi \rangle$. This rule of revision is a representation of the basic cognitive strategies that Karl brings to the epistemic situation described by $\langle \sigma, \pi \rangle$. Such a rule is, in general, nonmonotonic, in the sense that it is *not* generally true that

[i] $$n \leq m \;\Rightarrow\; \Phi^{(n)}(\sigma, \pi) \subseteq \Phi^{(m)}(\sigma, \pi);$$

this is owing to the fact that Karl's rule of revision will generally incorporate nondeductive inferences.

At this point, I shall make a somewhat loaded idealizing assumption about Karl: Karl's beliefs are those which would result by applying his method of evaluation ideally, that is, correctly and exhaustively, to his initial epistemic situation. This assumption would have a clear content if the rule of revision for $\langle \sigma, \pi \rangle$ were monotonic in the sense described by [i]: Karl's beliefs would then be represented as resulting by accumulation from application of that rule. In that case, we would put

[ii] $$\Phi(\sigma, \pi) = \bigcup_n \Phi^{(n)}(\sigma, \pi).$$

---

[8] An underived belief is simply one that, within the interpretation in question, Karl is not represented as having inferred from other beliefs. Observational beliefs may be of this kind, but so might, for example, the axiom of choice.

Without monotonicity, however, this would not make sense: so construed, Karl's beliefs in the given situation may and typically will contain explicitly contradictory semantic representations.

We want to say that Karl's beliefs in this situation are given by those sentences of $L^{\#}$ which he is, in some suitable sense, constrained to accept by his inductive method, that is, by the rule of revision for $\langle \sigma, \pi \rangle$. But there is a quite natural interpretation of the concept of constraint in the non-monotonic situation. The interpretation appeals to a notion of stability: place a sentence in $\Phi(\sigma, \pi)$ if it appears at some stage $\Phi^{(n)}(\sigma, \pi)$ and is stable under further evaluation. If $\{X_n\}$ is a sequence of sets of sentences in $L^{\#}$, we denote by '$\lim_n X_n$' the collection of all sentences that appear in X_m for each sufficiently large integer m. Formally, then, in place of [ii], I suggest that we put

[iii] $$\Phi(\sigma, \pi) = \lim_n \Phi^{(n)}(\sigma, \pi).^9$$

In this representation, Karl's beliefs are regarded as being in an idealized sort of reflective equilibrium with respect to his inductive method. In this, we follow a familiar tradition wherein the subject of radical interpretation is more often than not treated as an idealized hyperrational cognizer. We ought to be wary of claiming any direct relevance of such a conception of an idealized intentional system to the understanding of actual agents. It might be thought that a model of an idealized cognizer can apply *approximately* to an actual system such as a human being in much the same way as explanations of the behavior of an ideal (frictionless) pendulum can apply approximately to actual pendulums. But this analogy is premature. The difficulty is that, while at least in certain contexts in classical physics, we have a fairly clear conception of what it is for an actual system to approximate an ideal one, such a conception is so far lacking in this context. Crucially missing is an explanation of what it is for an actual agent to *approximately instantiate* Karl's inductive method. I take up these issues in the postscript to this chapter. Meanwhile, I shall confine my attention to intentional systems which are idealized in the sense described above. We shall find the problems of the determinacy of reference and intentionality sufficiently difficult in the case of the ideal systems; when we turn to actual systems, the possibility of a different sort of indeterminacy arises. This

---

[9]Peirce similarly used a social notion of epistemic stability to characterize *truth*. In our use, the present notion of stability characterizes not truth but an idealized sort of warranted assertability. The limit notation '$\lim_n X_n$' is from Hilary Putnam, who investigated recursion-theoretic properties of the notion of stability; see "Trial and Error Predicates, and the Solution to a Problem of Mostowski," *Journal of Symbolic Logic* (1965): 49-57.

is owing to the fact that, even if we can successfully explain what it is for an actual system to approximately instantiate an idealized inductive method, as I believe we can, it may still happen that a given actual system approximately instantiates, in the relevant sense, many divergent inductive methods.

Finally, consider the question of how we are to situate an interpretation of Karl in relation to interpretations of other members of his kind. This question would be uninteresting if its answer could be obtained by simply amalgamating independently framed interpretations of the members of Karl's population (call it 'P'). The question is whether an interpretation *of Karl* can be fixed in the absence of interpretations of others in P. Ultimately, I believe, this question must be answered negatively: specifying the semantic properties of Karl's language and attitudes may (and typically does) require reference to the attitudes of others in his population.[10] In this case, then, we must solve simultaneously for the attitudes of members of P, both in our language and in their shared language, and for a semantic interpretation of that language. A possible solution will be called an **interpretation of P**.

2.2.3 Other Constraints

I now turn to some further constraints on radical interpretation. We wish an adequate interpretation of Karl to explain Karl's behavior in terms of his beliefs and desires. Thus, Lewis's **Rationalization Principle**:

> Take a suitable set of mutually exclusive and jointly exhaustive propositions about Karl's behavior at any given time; of these, the one that comes true according to **P** [the physical data base] should be the one (or: one of the ones) with maximum expected utility according to the total system of beliefs and desires ascribed to Karl that time by **A**o.[11]

The behaviors thus explicated are Karl's basic actions: those things, roughly speaking, that Karl can bring about 'by himself', without the cooperation of external circumstances. It is far from clear, however, what these things are. It might be supposed, for example, that while Karl's extraction of a frozen cork from a bottle of Chateau Lafite-Rothschild is a nonbasic action, the pulling movement by which Karl brings this about is basic.[12]

---

[10]The point is by now familiar, and surfaces repeatedly in the discussion of reference in the following chapter. For classical antecedents, see especially Hilary Putnam, "The Meaning of 'Meaning'," reprinted in his *Mind, Language and Reality, Philosophical Papers*, vol. 2 (Cambridge: Cambridge University Press, 1975), and Tyler Burge, "Individualism and Psychology," *Philosophical Review* 95 (1979): 3–45.

[11]Lewis, "Radical Interpretation," p. 113. My interpolation.

[12]Following Davidson, it might be held that we should not regard these as distinct

Clearly, however, such an action is not wholly independent of Karl's physical context; there are many internal and external circumstances that might prevent it. This suggests that either we must recognize the specification of certain boundary conditions to be generally relevant to explanations of basic actions, or we shall have to take an even more restrictive view of what a basic action is.[13] In the end, these two responses may come to the same thing: for, on the second response, we will take as the explanandum in our example something like an *attempt* to bring about a certain motion; but this event is presumably to be characterized in terms of a counterfactual that says that it would give rise to the motion if the relevant boundary conditions were satisfied.

The way out of this impasse is to recognize a suppressed component in our interpretation of Karl. Part of what an acceptable interpretation must tell us is *what Karl's basic actions are*, and specifying these involves saying what, if any, boundary conditions are relevant to their explanation in intentional or decision-theoretic terms. It will then be a constraint on the interpretation that the attitudes it ascribes to Karl can be mapped onto states of Karl as a physical system in such a way that, assuming satisfaction of the relevant boundary conditions, any intentional explanation of a basic action in terms of a given set of attitude-ascriptions corresponds, under the mapping, to a causal explanation of that event. Thus understood, intentional explanations of Karl's behavior acquire an obvious causal-explanatory content: the inference structure that links attitude-ascriptions to an action-specifying sentence in an intentional explanation of a basic action reflects a causal connection that links corresponding states of Karl as a physical system to that action. Thus supplemented, I shall adopt the Rationalization Principle; it codifies part of what we are about in an idealized process of radical interpretation.

Thus far we have acquired the indicated structural constraints on a scheme of reference for Karl's Language and two additional constraints on the intentional structure of the interpretation: the Rationalization and Triangle principles. Lewis offers three other constraints: the **Principle of Charity**, the **Principle of Truthfulness**, and the **Manifestation Principle**. The Principle of Charity is taken up in subsection 2.3.2. Here I shall comment briefly on the Manifestation and Truthfulness principles.

The Manifestation Principle says that Karl's beliefs should normally be

---

events but as the same event under different descriptions. But of course the object of explanation here is not an event, but a sentence or proposition describing it; to speak of 'explaining actions' is apt only if each action has a *privileged description*. Otherwise, we must speak not of explaining actions, but action-describing sentences.

[13]The second avenue is taken by Jennifer Hornsby, *Actions* (London: Routledge, 1980), ch. 3.

manifested in his dispositions to speech behavior. The qualifier 'normally' here is important, for we do not expect Karl's beliefs to be *in all cases* manifested in his dispositions to speech behavior; those very beliefs might, after all, afford Karl good reasons for insincerity. The Principle of Truthfulness says that some of the attitudes ascribed to Karl by the interpretation should fit into a Gricean convention of truthfulness in L: that is, that Karl should normally desire to utter a sentence of L only if he holds it to be true (that is, only if it is part of the belief-fragment of $\mathbf{A}k$); that he intend to utter it under appropriate circumstances if he holds it true; that he believe that others of his kind are endowed with similar attitudes; and so on.[14] Notice that a form of the Manifestation Principle is explicable in terms of the Rationalization and Truthfulness principles: the Truthfulness Principle requires that Karl will normally desire to utter a sentence only if he holds it to be true, the Rationalization Principle that Karl normally utters a sentence only if he desires to utter it.[15] So the two together imply that Karl will normally utter a sentence only if he holds it true.

Lewis motivated the Principle of Truthfulness in terms of the conditions Karl's attitudes must satisfy in order for his language to play a certain role in communication. Still, one might ask why it *must* play such a role merely for Karl to qualify as a subject of interpretation. For my purposes here, it is not necessary to stake out a position on this issue.[16] However, whether or not it is derived from the Truthfulness Principle, the Manifestation Principle has an obvious heuristic rationale: it allows Karl's utterances to afford a route of access to his beliefs. The Manifestation Principle provides that Karl's utterances are normally a guide to the belief-fragment of $\mathbf{A}k$, from which we may recover our representations of Karl's beliefs by applying the semantic description of L associated with the interpretation in question.

The Rationalization, Triangle and Truthfulness principles, together with the indicated structural constraints on the semantic description of L, constitute what I shall call the **Minimal Framework** for radical interpretation. As noted, a version of the manifestation requirement is a byproduct of this framework. To what extent does the Minimal Framework constrain the semantic interpretation of Karl's language and attitudes? I shall describe

---

[14]This is a slight recasting of Lewis's requirement ("Radical Interpretation," p. 114), which as originally formulated constrained the relation between $\mathbf{A}o$ and $\mathbf{M}$ (our $\mathbf{R}$). But the two formulations are equivalent, given my version of the Triangle Principle.

[15]Assuming speech-episodes to constitute basic actions.

[16]My immediate concern in what follows will be to exhibit indeterminacies of interpretation, and any framework for radical interpretation that admits a type of indeterminacy with the Principle of Truthfulness will admit such indeterminacies without it. On the other hand, that principle will not play a role in the further constraints that I shall offer.

a type of referential indeterminacy affecting this framework and many of its extensions. I then present an assessment of how various principles of charity affect these indeterminacies. To look ahead a bit, I will argue that such principles are in general to be rejected, and that the ones that help the most with the indeterminacy problem are especially implausible. This will set the stage for the introduction of the main additional constraint I have to offer in this chapter, which I go on to argue does significantly reduce referential indeterminacy.

2.3 Isomorphism and Indeterminacy

2.3.1 Quinean Alternatives

Here is a familiar recipe for exhibiting indeterminacies.[17] Let **R** be a scheme of reference for Karl's language L; we think of **R** as being associated with an interpretation of Karl meeting the requirements of the Minimal Framework. To begin with, we will suppose, rather unrealistically, that **R** assigns semantic representations to sentences of L in an elementary (first-order) language. Let f be a one-to-one correspondence, definable in our language, mapping the ontology that **R** ascribes to L onto a set D. We may use this correspondence to define an alternative scheme of reference $\mathbf{R}(f)$ for L as follows. $\mathbf{R}(f)$ assigns to any sentence of L just the formal semantic representation assigned to it by **R**, but the interpretation that $\mathbf{R}(f)$ assigns L is, so to speak, the *image under the function* f of the interpretation assigned it by **R**. Thus, according to $\mathbf{R}(f)$, D is the ontology of L. If, according to **R**, a predicate ϕ applies to just the couples belonging to a relation A defined over the given ontology, then according to $\mathbf{R}(f)$, ϕ applies to just the couples $\langle f(x), f(y) \rangle$ such that $\langle x, y \rangle \in A$. Singular terms refer in $\mathbf{R}(f)$ to the objects returned by the function f when applied to the items they refer to in **R**. And so on. Since f is a one-to-one correspondence, the interpretation ascribed to L by $\mathbf{R}(f)$ is *isomorphic* to the interpretation ascribed to L by **R**; and it is a consequence of this fact that a sentence of L is true on **R** if and only if it is true on $\mathbf{R}(f)$. It is clear that $\mathbf{R}(f)$ may be arranged to satisfy the structural constraints subsection 2.2.1 if **R** does.

Two examples of this construction will appear hereafter. Both involve a one-to-one correspondence that is a *permutation* of the ontology initially

---

[17]The present stratagem originated with Quine in *Ontological Relativity* (New York: Columbia University Press, 1969), title essay; variants of it close to the one considered hereafter were described by John Wallace in "Only in the Context of a Sentence do Words Have Any Meaning," in *Contemporary Perspectives in the Philosophy of Language*, edited by P. French et al. (Minneapolis: University of Minnesota Press, 1978) and by Davidson, "The Inscrutabiilty of Reference," in *Inquiries into Truth and Interpretation*.

ascribed to L, that is to say, a correspondence mapping that set onto itself. For the first example, we imagine that the physical objects in Karl's ontology are coded in a one-to-one fashion by positive integers in some way, and we define a permutation σ on that ontology that exchanges each object with its numerical code. If $\mathbf{R}$ is the given scheme of reference for L, then, under the deviant scheme $\mathbf{R}(\sigma)$, those parts of Karl's discourse that $\mathbf{R}$ construes as being about objects in his environment will be interpreted instead as being about positive integers. The ontology of Karl's arithmetic, on the other hand, will harbor some curious impersonators: just as each ordinary object is replaced by its numerical code, so too does the object replace the number. But the objects play the same structural or model-theoretic role in Karl's arithmetic as the numbers they replace.

For the second example, suppose that somewhere in our galaxy there is a planet exactly similar to the Earth. We might call it 'Twin Earth.'[18] Consider a permutation π defined on the domain of a scheme of reference $\mathbf{R}$ for L that exchanges each terrestrial object with its counterpart on Twin Earth. Thus, where $\mathbf{R}$ construes Karl's discourse as referring to objects in his environment, $\mathbf{R}(\pi)$ will construe it as referring to their counterparts on Twin Earth. Thus if, under $\mathbf{R}$, Karl expresses the desire that Hans acquire a bottle of Chateau Lafite-Rothschild, under $\mathbf{R}(\pi)$ he expresses the desire that Hans's counterpart on Twin Earth acquire the counterpart of such a bottle, and so on. Again, the initial interpretation and the deviant one will be structurally convergent.

If, as we have supposed, $\mathbf{R}$ is part of an interpretation of Karl satisfying the constraints of the Minimal Framework, we may use any permutation of the ontology ascribed to Karl by $\mathbf{R}$ to construct an alternative interpretation of Karl that will equally satisfy those constraints. We may do this, in any case, if we are granted one rather weak assumption about the permutation. The assumption is that the permutation preserve the resources of Karl's language relevant to specifying his basic actions, in the sense that the devices in L that specify Karl's possible basic actions on the given interpretation do so again under the deviant one. Call the present assumption

---

[18]Not to be confused with Hilary Putnam's planet of the same name, whereon kinds are exemplified which are superficially similar to but microstructurally distinguishable from the corresponding terrestrial kinds. In my example, the corresponding kinds are indistinguishable all the way down.

the **Action-Invariance Condition**.[19] If ρ is the permutation in question, then the deviant interpretation arises from the given one by substituting $\mathbf{R}(\rho)$ for $\mathbf{R}$: Karl's attitudes in the new interpretation will be given by just the same formal semantic representations, and by just the same sentences of L, as in the initial interpretation, but in the revised interpretation these will be interpreted in terms of $\mathbf{R}(\rho)$.[20]

In order to show that the alternative interpretation of Karl generated by the permutation ρ falls under the Minimal Framework, we must show that it fulfills the Triangle Principle, the Rationalization Principle, and the Truthfulness Principle; as I noted above, it must then also satisfy a form of the Manifestation Principle. The Triangle Principle is an immediate byproduct of our construction of $\mathbf{A}o$ and $\mathbf{A}k$; it is valid in the revised interpretation for just the same reason it is in the initial one. Consider next the Rationalization Principle as interpreted by Lewis. Suppose the given interpretation generates an intentional explanation of a basic action α. The explanation

---

[19]For most purposes, we can operate with this loose formulation of the Action-Invariance Condition. It can, however, be made more precise in the following way. Suppose that Karl's basic actions are specified canonically via sentences of the form

$$(*) \qquad\qquad (\exists e)(\mathrm{By}(e, Karl) \,\&\, A(e))$$

(Here it is assumed that in the initial interpretation $A(e)$ describes a class of basic actions and $\mathrm{By}(e, a)$ the relation 'e is a basic action performed by agent a'.) Let α be a basic action performed by Karl. Say that the sentence $(*)$ *specifies* α within the given interpretation if relative to the semantics it provides $A(e)$ is true of α and of no other action performed by Karl. The action-invariance requirement is then, if π is the permutation in question, that π map Karl onto himself and also fix the extensions of predicates designating basic act types and the by-relation. Suppose now that π satisfies the present formulation of the action-invariance condition and that $(*)$ specifies α in the given interpretation. Then $(*)$ specifies $\pi(\alpha)$ on the alternative to it generated by π. However, if E is the set of basic actions performed by Karl and F the extension of $A(e)$, we have:

$$\begin{aligned}\{\pi(\alpha)\} &= \pi(E \cap F)\\ &= \pi(E) \,\cap\, \pi(F)\\ &= E \cap F\\ &= \{\alpha\},\end{aligned}$$

where the intermediate identity follows by the action-invariance condition. Thus $\pi(\alpha) = \alpha$, whence $(*)$ specifes α also in the alternative interpretation. The same considerations show that if each of Karl's basic actions is specifiable in the foregoing sense in the initial interpretation, then $\pi(\alpha) = \alpha$ for each basic action α.

[20]Of course, the Action-Invariance Condition will occasion some adjustments in the examples σ and π preceding. In particular, σ will not assign numerical codes to Karl's basic actions or to objects constitutive of such actions, and π will not exchange them for their Twin counterparts; as restricted to these items, both σ and π will be construed to be the identity function.

will say that α belongs to a maximal set A of prospective actions such that some set Σ of sentences specifying A in L has maximum expected utility according to the overall configuration of attitudes ascribed to Karl by the given interpretation, relative to any specification of an alternative such set. However, in the presence of the Action-Invariance Condition, just the same explanation will be available in the alternative interpretation of Karl generated by ρ: under that deviant interpretation, Σ still specifies A, and the probabilities and utilities Karl assigns to all prospective behavioral stories and outcomes as expressed in L are the same. The point is that, modulo the Action-Invariance constraint, it makes no difference what revision of *content* is applied to Karl's attitudes, as long as the decision-theoretic relations linking Karl's attitudes to his prospective basic actions are preserved under the reconstrual.

The given interpretation, then, will satisfy the Rationalization Principle if and only if the deviant interpretation does. The two interpretations will also equally satisfy the Truthfulness principle, assuming Karl's speech-episodes to constitute basic actions; for in this case, since Karl's attitudes are given in L by just the same sentences in the two interpretations, again by the Action-Invariance Condition, Karl's attitudes toward his prospective utterances will be the same in both. Thus any regularity characterizing the given interpretation that links the conditions under which Karl desires to utter sentences of L to the conditions under which he holds them true will be duplicated in the deviant one. I shall call an alternative interpretation arising in this way from a given interpretation $\mathcal{I}$ of Karl a **Quinean alternative** to $\mathcal{I}$. Any interpretation and its Quinean alternatives, then, equally satisfy each of the constraints of the Minimal Framework, and indeed are also on a par in terms of other standards. For example, I have noted that the distribution of truth-values over the sentences of L fixed by any interpretation of Karl must coincide with those generated by its Quinean alternatives.[21] It follows that no requirement constraining the distribution of truth-values generated by an acceptable interpretation of Karl can give us a reason to prefer a given interpretation to its Quinean alternatives.

2.3.2 Principles of Charity

The phenomenon of Quinean alternatives shows that the Minimal Framework leaves us with pervasive indeterminacies at the lexical level. I will now investigate various constraints on radical interpretation that might be

---

[21]The general result appealed to here being that truth is preserved by isomorphisms of model-theoretic interpretations of an elementary language. This sort of invariance lapses if L contains intensional devices. However, this observation has analogues in the intensional case which will be considered in section 2.3.3.

deployed to address them. One candidate is the **Principle of Charity**, of which there are several versions. In the form originally suggested by Quine, it tells us, other things being equal, to *maximize truth*; in a form described by Davidson, it tells us to maximize *agreement*, in the sense that we should ascribe to an agent beliefs that so far as possible are correct by our own lights.[22] In Quine's form, the principle is quite powerless to resolve the sort of indeterminacy described earlier (as Quine recognizes); for, as just noted, the sentences of Karl's language which are counted true by a given interpretation are precisely those that will be counted as true by any of its Quinean alternatives. They will thus equally satisfy any truth-maximizing constraint.

What of Davidson's version? In earlier articles, Davidson formulated the Principle of Charity to require that Karl's beliefs be given largely by sentences of our language that we, the interpreters, hold true. But that is not much better. Suppose that we have an interpretation of Karl that 'maximizes agreement' in the sense required and that assigns semantic representations to Karl's beliefs in an elementary language. Indeed, suppose that under the given interpretation Karl holds *only* true beliefs by our lights. We can then use any function that *we can recognize* to be a permutation of Karl's ontology to define a Quinean alternative to the given interpretation under which Karl also holds only true beliefs by our lights. In general, an instance of the original construction survives the imposition of the 'agreement' constraint if we can specify the relevant generating transformation in such a way that we can recognize it to be a one-to-one correspondence.

However, Davidson has described a refinement of his constraint that may help. This third version of the Charity Principle constrains interpretation by requiring that the beliefs assigned to Karl be approximately those that *we would have formed in his evidential situation.* Davidson writes:

> Understanding can only be secured by interpreting in a way that makes for the right sort of agreement. The 'right sort,' however, is not easier to specify than to say what constitutes a good reason for holding a particular belief.[23]

This might be taken to suggest that Karl and the interpreter must instantiate a *common inductive method* that would lead, at least approximately, to their respective systems of belief in their respective evidential situations; this is essentially Lewis's formulation of the Charity Principle.

---

[22]Quine, *Word and Object* (Cambridge, Mass.: MIT Press, 1960), p. 59; Davidson, "Radical Interpretation"; see also "Belief and the Basis of Meaning" and "Thought and Talk," all reprinted in *Inquiries into Truth and Interpretation*, especially pp. 136–37, 152–53, 159, 168–69.

[23]*Inquiries into Truth and Interpretation*, p. xvii.

Can that principle, thus understood, help us to divorce a preferred interpretation of Karl from its Quinean alternatives?[24]

Here we need to distinguish two cases. We have thus far supposed Karl's attitudes to be specified in any interpretation by closed formulae of the sort that give the semantic representations of sentences in L. That is to say that Karl's beliefs are accorded only *de dicto* or 'notional' representations, not *de re* or 'relational' representations. Now let π be a permutation of the ontology ascribed to Karl by the initially given interpretation. Then for the alternative generated by π, the answer to the question concluding the preceding paragraph is 'no' if the description of Karl's beliefs in our language provided by the interpretation includes a sentence that says, by means of a suitable specification of π, that π *is a permutation*. Thus, let A and A^π respectively be the alternative translations assigned to a sentence of Karl's language by the initial interpretation and the Quinean alternative to it generated by π. Since the equivalence of A to A^π is a rather trivial first-order consequence of the claim that π is a permutation, Karl should hold A true if and only if he holds A^π true on *either* interpretation. That is to say if, according to the initial interpretation, Karl *recognizes* that π is a permutation, and Karl can reason a little, then that interpretation should ascribe to Karl *just the same* notional or *de dicto* beliefs as the Quinean alternative to it generated by π. They must therefore equally satisfy Davidson's charity constraint as restricted to notional beliefs.[25]

However, the situation changes in an interesting way if we allow the

---

[24]See Lewis, "Radical Interpretation," p. 112. It is well to pause here to clear up a question raised by the notion of 'evidential situation' itself. As Lewis seems to conceive it, Karl's life-history of evidence occurs at his sensory surfaces, and would be the same for duplicate (physically or functionally indiscernible) Karls (p. 121). Thus duplicate Karls should be accorded the same beliefs by an acceptable interpretation. However, for now familiar reasons, the two Karls are generally not doxastically indiscernible. They will hold beliefs about individuals and kinds populating their environments, but these will not be the same unless the environments are relevantly similar. Lewis deals with this problem by imposing a restriction on the sentences that count as specifications of attitudes: a sentence is a candidate for ascribing an attitude only if the attitude is *autonomous* ('in the head', in Putnam's phrase), invariant as between Karl and his replicas. However, for the purposes of the type of explanation to be described below, we shall require a specification of Karl's attitudes toward arbitrary propositions, and in particular his beliefs about individuals and kinds; and these attitudes are typically non-autonomous. In imposing the indicated restriction, Lewis has somewhat altered my original question. The question concerned Karl's attitudes generally, not simply his autonomous ones; an interpretation that stops at a description of Karl's autonomous attitudes is seriously incomplete. This Charity Principle will be understood to refer to a broader conception of Karl's evidential situation, including not only the happenings at his sensory surfaces, but facts about his physical context as well.

[25]This is of course rather similar to the indeterminacy affecting the second version of the charity principle, save that in this case the indeterminacy is created by the fact

given interpretation to incorporate a description of Karl's genuinely singular (relational, or *de re*) attitudes. In this case, Karl's attitudes might be given in our language by couples $\langle \alpha, F \rangle$ where α is an object (more generally, an n'tuple of objects) and F a predicate of our language, expressing our ascription to Karl of a belief or desire that α fall under F.[26] The Principle of Charity would then be understood to require not only that Karl's *de dicto* beliefs be approximately those that we would form in his place, but also that his *de re* beliefs be invariant in this sense as well. Thus construed, the alternative to the given interpretation induced by π need *not* satisfy the Principle of Charity. Suppose, for example, that π is the permutation that differs from the identity function only by mapping objects in Karl's environment onto their counterparts on Twin Earth in the second example above; and suppose that Karl is causally isolated from Twin Earth. Given Karl's life-history of evidence, we would form no attitudes at all toward the counterpart objects. The deviant interpretation would not then satisfy the relational Principle of Charity if, according to the given interpretation, Karl holds any relational beliefs at all about the objects in his environment. In order to ensure the charitability of the deviant interpretation, we must require that the permutation π preserve *de re* attitudes toward objects in each evidential situation. This is a strong constraint on the construction of Quinean alternatives; it requires, in effect, that given knowledge of an object in the domain of the relevant permutation, Karl can know a priori what the corresponding value is.[27]

However, either version of the Principle of Charity faces the question of whether it is reasonable to require of Karl, merely to qualify as a subject of interpretation, that he form, even approximately, the beliefs that we would form in his evidential situation. The obvious difficulty is that agents might instantiate very different inductive methods. For example, Einstein's life-

---

that *Karl* recognizes the relevant generating function to be a permutation. This type of indeterminacy could be mitigated somewhat by applying the notional charity constraint across counterfactual evidential situations in which he does not hold this belief. But we could still generate substantive indeterminacies using functions that Karl believes to be permutations in each such situation. For example, let R specify an arbitrary relation defined on Karl's ontology. Define a function f on Karl's ontology by setting $f(x)$ equal to the unique y such that $R(x, y)$ on the condition that R is a permutation, and $f(x) = x$ otherwise. Specified in this way, then, Karl can know a priori that f is a permutation. If R does specify a permutation of Karl's ontology, the extensions of expressions in Karl's language will be reconstrued in the corresponding way.

[26] This familiar representation of *de re* attitudes originates with David Kaplan in "Quantifying In," in *Words and Objections*, edited by D. Davidson and J. Hintikka (Dordrecht: Reidel, 1975), 206–42.

[27] See my "Representation, Intentionality, and Quantifiers," sec. 5, for a more detailed discussion of the relational Principle of Charity.

history of evidence led him to the field equations for General Relativity, a model of spacetime that he believed to be at least approximately correct. A more conservative Einstein might have followed van Fraassen's advice and have formed only the belief that the model is empirically adequate.[28] Others, less talented, would be led to neither belief. The various belief-systems that arise from a given life-history of evidence on the basis of divergent inductive methods cannot simultaneously satisfy any very strong form of the Principle of Charity. If such a constraint were a constitutive principle of radical interpretation, we could not, for example, solve simultaneously for the beliefs of both these Einsteins. At least one, then, would be precluded from instantiating beliefs. This seems to me very implausible, as it has to others.[29]

However, it might be maintained that the Principle of Charity has here been interpreted too strongly. Davidson writes:

> The method is not designed to eliminate disagreement, nor can it; its purpose is to make meaningful disagreement possible, and this depends entirely on a foundation—*some* foundation—in agreement.[30]

Perhaps the most natural suggestion for implementing this idea is to restrict the application of the Principle of Charity to a certain core class of beliefs. For example, the two Einsteins differ in their beliefs about theory, but might be presumed to agree about observation. It might then be suggested that the application of the Charity Principle be restricted to the beliefs registered by *observation sentences*.[31] Such a restriction would preserve a significant methodological role of the Principle of Charity, which is to enable Karl's beliefs to be fixed, in part, by his observable circumstances. The idea is that, in any fixed situation, the observations would by and large be common property to Karl and his interpreter.

But this will not do. The obvious problem concerns the demarcation of the observation sentences of Karl's language. Even if the notion of 'observation sentence' is well defined for the home language, we lack a transcendent notion of the observational. What is observably true and what not *for Karl* is a problem to be solved in radical interpretation; its solution is not a resource that can be *assumed* in radical interpretation. Suppose, for example, that Karl is an agent with perceptual deficits (or perceptual surpluses). I

---

[28]See Bas C. van Fraassen, *The Scientific Image* (New York: Oxford University Press, 1981).

[29]For a discussion of the Principle of Charity in a similar spirit, see Michael Devitt, *Realism and Truth* (New York: Oxford University Press, 1991), pp. 191–99.

[30]"Thought and Talk," p. 169.

[31]Perhaps among other privileged classes of sentences, for example, uncontentious logical truths.

said that one methodological role of charity is to enable Karl's beliefs to be constrained by his observable circumstances. But there is an ambiguity here, as between what we can observe and what *Karl* can observe. At the outset, we don't know what Karl can observe. Karl may have perceptual deficits that prevent him from observing what we can observe, and so it is inappropriate to project into the belief-fragment of **A**o the sentences that we would perceive to be true in his situation. On the other hand, Karl may have perceptual capacities that we lack, and so it is not generally to be expected that we will assent to the translations of his perceptual reports.

These observations are especially damaging to the relational form of the Principle of Charity, the version of the principle requiring the invariance of genuinely singular or *de re* beliefs; and it is this version, I argued, that was needed to help with the problem of Quinean alternatives. It is widely held that the *de re* character of Karl's beliefs is determined, in part, by their grounding in perception (not necessarily Karl's perceptions, but those at least of members of his kind with whom he is in the appropriate sort of contact). If, as I have urged, the limits of what is observable for Karl (or Karl's kind) are not given in advance, but are fixed by interpretation, then the notion of *aboutness* for Karl's beliefs is as well. It is consequently inappropriate to require in advance that Karl be represented as holding beliefs about just the objects toward which our beliefs would be directed in his situation.

2.3.3 Generalizing the Basic Construction: Rigid Invariance

The argument of subsection 2.3.1 assumes that the initially given interpretation construes Karl's language L to be an elementary first-order language, for Quinean alternatives have been defined only for such languages. In this section, I shall consider the problem of generalizing the basic construction of 2.3.1 to languages involving certain modalities. The discussion will bear directly on a quite general issue concerning indeterminacy. It might be supposed that if a type of indeterminacy is exhibited by a given interpretation, it must also arise for any interpretation that differs from the given one in reading additional expressive resources into Karl's language (the additional expressive devices, one might suppose, should if anything make the situation *worse*). But I want to argue that this need not be so: that adding expressive capacity can, in certain circumstances, help to *reduce* indeterminacy.

Suppose that L arises from an elementary language L_0 by the addition of a modality '$\Box$'. We suppose given an interpretation that accords to L a simple intensional interpretation in terms of possible worlds, wherein each world is regarded as accessible from any other. Thus, on the given interpretation, '$\Box$' signifies metaphysical or 'broadly logical' necessity. Hilary Putnam has described an analogue of the basic construction that would ensure the stability of truth-values of sentences in the elementary language L_0 between the alternative interpretations *in each possible world.*[32] Putnam's idea is roughly to simultaneously apply the procedure of 2.3.1 to a family of structures describing the interpretation of L_0 at each world. We coordinate to each world α a permutation π_α of the domain of α. We then use these permutations to simultaneously define isomorphic copies of the structures for L_0 corresponding to each possible world, and thereby an alternative intensional interpretation of L_0. Thus, for example, for a fixed world α, the extension of a two-place predicate P at α on the alternative interpretation will consist of just the couples

$$\langle \pi_\alpha(\mathbf{a}), \pi_\alpha(\mathbf{b}) \rangle$$

such that $\langle \mathbf{a}, \mathbf{b} \rangle$ belongs to the extension of P at α on the initial interpretation. If the logical constants are interpreted standardly, it follows that the truth-value of any sentence of L_0 on this alternative interpretation coincides with its truth-value on the initial one at each world.

Let us try to extend Putnam's construction to the modal language L, which supplements L_0 with the modality '$\Box$'. To this end, we must show that the two interpretations fix the same truth-value for modal sentences at each world, where a sentence of the form $\Box\phi$ is valued as true at a world if and only if ϕ is valued as true at each world. But there is a problem here: suppose that, according to the initial interpretation, there is a predicate $P(x)$ of L such that the sentence

[i] $(\exists y)\Box(\forall x)(P(x) \leftrightarrow y = x)$

is true in the actual world. In this case, we say that the predicate $P(x)$ **distinguishes** or is a **distinguishing predicate for** the unique object **a** answering to '$(\exists y)$' in [i], and that an object is **distinguishable** in L if there exists a predicate that distinguishes it in L.[33] In this case there is trouble if the permutations π_α and π_β associated with two worlds α and β map **a** onto distinct objects, for the sentence [i] would then be false in the actual world on the deviant interpretation. In order to avoid changing the truth-value of [i] in this way, we must suppose that the permutations $\{\pi_\alpha\}$

---

[32]See *Reason, Truth and History* (Cambridge: Cambridge University Press, 1981), pp. 32–48, 217–18.

[33]Notice that, if names behave rigidly, a sufficient condition of **a**'s being distinguishable in L is that there exist a name η of **a** in L, for in this case **a** will be distinguishable via the condition $x = \eta$.

agree on **a**: that is, that for any worlds α and β, if **a** belongs to the domain of both α and β, we have $\pi_\alpha(\mathbf{a}) = \pi_\beta(\mathbf{a})$. Now, however, a new difficulty emerges: suppose that the common image $\pi_\alpha(\mathbf{a})$ of **a** for each world α fails to inhabit a possible world β in which **a** exists. In this case, the sentence $(\exists x)P(x)$ is true in β according to the given interpretation but false in the deviant one. In order to ensure the stability of this sentence, we must suppose that **a** *coexists* with its image at each possible world (that is, exists in any world if and only if its image does); to solve the problem generally, we must require this to be true for each distinguishable object. Let us call this requirement the **Rigidity Condition**. The Rigidity Condition, then, is a constraint on the permutations that generate an alternative to a given interpretation of L, a constraint that must be satisfied if each sentence of L is to receive the same truth-value in the two interpretations at each possible world.

The Rigidity Condition somewhat mitigates the indeterminacies of reference arising from Putnam's construction. In particular, it is interesting to note that neither of the stock examples given in subsection 2.3.1 survives. Since a distinguishable object on Earth need not exist in each possible world in which its counterpart on Twin Earth exists, the permutation that exchanges each terrestrial object with its counterpart in the second example violates the Rigidity Condition; and since distinguishable objects in the first example do not rigidly coexist with their code-numbers, the permutation in the first example does as well. As a third example, consider the permutation that maps each physical object onto the mereological sum of its time-slices, or momentary stages. Since, for example, the clock on this table could have existed without its current actual stage existing, there are possible situations in which the clock exists but the sum of its (actual) timeslices does not.[34] If the clock is distinguishable in L, then, the indicated permutation similarly fails to satisfy the Rigidity Condition.

I began by claiming that under certain circumstances adding expressive capacity to a language can help to reduce the indeterminacies of interpretation affecting that language. We are now in a position to see why. Putnam's construction shows that any family of permutations of domains of worlds leads to a reinterpretation of an elementary language that assigns the same truth-value to each sentence as does a given interpretation *at each possible world*. Not so, I have shown, if the language in question is expanded to incorporate the broadly logical modality '$\Box$' and distinguishing predicates for a set Σ of actual objects: in this case, for the permutations in ques-

---

[34]I am relying on the plausible mereological assumption that a sum of parts $\zeta_1, ..., \zeta_n$ exists in any world just in case each of the objects $\zeta_1, ..., \zeta_n$ exist therein. The *stage* of an object at a time consists roughly of its material content at that time.

tion to preserve truth-values of sentences at each world, they must agree on Σ and map each member of Σ onto an object with which it coexists at each world. Of course, this conclusion can be reached explicitly only for objects that can be distinguished by some predicate within the initial interpretation. However, by increasing the distinguishing capacity of Karl's language,[35] we inflate the category of distinguishable objects, and correspondingly diminish the number of alternative interpretations arising from Putnam's construction which agree with the initial interpretation rigidly on truth-values in L. In the limiting case, in which we suppose each actual object to be distinguishable, the permutations that generate an alternative interpretation must agree on all actual objects and map each onto a rigid worldmate. Indeterminacies that can be eliminated simply by considering situations in which Karl acquires additional descriptive resources seem both artificial and inessential; and if we impose the requirement that a putative example of indeterminacy survive when additional predicates are introduced into Karl's language, then we obtain the conclusion adverted to for the limiting case in which all actual objects are distinguishable therein.

However, it is necessary to be careful here. Putnam's argument sought to establish a strong sort of indeterminacy: that the interpretations of the lexical primitives of an elementary language are substantially indeterminate even if the truth-values of sentences are fixed *over all possible worlds*. The preceding considerations mitigate the indeterminacies of reference arising from Putnam's construction only if it is assumed that each sentence of L *receives* the same truth-value at each world in each of the interpretations considered, but we have seen no reason, as yet, to suppose that this sort of stability is exhibited by any pair of acceptable interpretations. I shall find some support for a limited form of this assumption at the conclusion of this chapter. Second, however, Putnam's construction assumes that in the alternative interpretations considered the *logical* expressions (identity, the connectives, and the quantifiers) are construed standardly. This is not an assumption that Putnam needs to justify, for his argument sought to establish only that the invariance-of-truth-value requirement is compatible with many interpretations of the *nonlogical* primitives: if the interpretations of the logical devices are also variable, Putnam might argue, so much the worse! But the assumption is not innocuous in the context of an argument that seeks to *reduce* indeterminacies of interpretation. Indeed, not only have I assumed that the deviant interpretations treat the elementary logical constants standardly; in our extension of Putnam's construction to the modal case, I also assumed that the interpretation of the necessity operator

---

[35] For example, by considering situations in which Karl acquires names to which the given interpretation can be extended; see n. 33.

is held fixed. But the conclusions reached earlier would be of little interest if they could be undermined simply by gerrymandering the interpretations of identity, necessity and the quantifiers. To forestall such a tactic, one would need reasons to suppose that the interpretations of these expressions are substantially determinate. I think there are such reasons; but I must defer that matter until chapter 4. In the meantime, I have largely exhausted, I believe, the responses to indeterminacies of the Quinean sort which are available within the Minimal Framework on the basis of broadly logical considerations. I shall now begin to lay a foundation for a substantive extension of that framework.

2.4 Conformal Explanation and Semantic Content

2.4.1 Conformal Explanation

Part of the intractability of the indeterminacy problem stems from the fact that we lack a clear conception of the explanatory role of the notion of reference and of reference-based notions of truth. In this section, I shall describe a type of explanation in which reference plays a central role, and in the following section a model of this sort of explanation in the interpretive context will be sketched. I will then introduce a constraint on interpretation that says, in effect, that the admissible schemes of reference for a language are those which best play this explanatory role.

We begin with a simple example that is already familiar from the introductory discussion earlier. Suppose that we wish to explain Karl's ability to efficiently find his way out of a large building (when suitably prompted, for example, by a fire-alarm). One way in which this might come about is that Karl can normally identify his location in the building and can somehow pair each location with a finite sequence of basic actions that when performed in the relevant order take him through a path of minimum length out of the building. Let us suppose that Karl's procedure is entirely clerical, so that we may as well have considered a robotic device (also called 'Karl') whose behavior in the indicated circumstances may be described in this way. The device instantiates an effective procedure, or 'program' (call it P), that generates its basic actions; when performed in sequence these actions propel Karl through various paths in the building. Given an input of the appropriate type, P determines a finite sequence of basic actions that describe an optimal path out of the building from Karl's initial position.

I now wish to ask what role the semantic notion of *representation* (or reference, broadly construed) has to play in explaining the behavior of such a device. I will distinguish the following objects of explanation:

(1) That in a particular case, Karl leaves the building via an optimal route;

(2) that when suitably prompted in any initial position, Karl will leave the building via an optimal route.

Object (2) describes a capacity that Karl has in the indicated situation; object (1) reports a particular instance in which that capacity is exercised.

It might be claimed that there is a satisfactory explanation of (1) in entirely nonsemantic terms. Let q be the path followed by the device from the given initial position. There is, in the first place, a purely causal explanation of the following:

(1*) Suitably prompted at the initial position, Karl traverses q.

The motion of the device at any time is causally explained by its current internal physical state (in conjunction with relevant boundary conditions). By sequentially compiling these explanations, we can explain any trajectory of the device in purely causal terms that, apparently, do not presuppose semantical notions such as 'reference', 'correspondence,', and so on. Since (1*) specifies such a trajectory, we may thus explain (1*) in nonsemantic terms. To get from (1*) to (1), we may simply observe, in light of the building layout, that q constitutes a minimal path out of the building from the initial position, and that the relevant boundary conditions are satisfied. (Of course, this strategy for explicating Karl's egress is available only if we have rather extensive knowledge of his internal physical states and the causal relations between them. And as we do not generally possess such knowledge, it may be argued that reference to semantic properties is pragmatically indispensable for the prediction of items like (1).[36] But still it might be claimed that semantic notions play no proper part in a fundamental explanation of the fact reported by that sentence.)

In the same way, it might be thought that a purely causal explanation may be given of (2). For any initial position of the device, we may obtain a causal explanation of its capacity to emerge from that position via a minimal egress of the sort indicated above: we explain the successive basic actions of the device on the condition that it is in the relevant initial state and position, and then observe, in light of the building design, that the path generated by these actions is a minimal egress from the initial position. It may then be suggested that (2) be explained by assembling these various causal explanations.

The suggestion, then, is that semantical notions play no ineliminable role in explaining items like (1) and (2); the explanations just adverted to are, it may be claimed, the fundamental ones, and in these semantical

---

[36] As I did argue, in "Representation, Intentionality, and Quantifiers," pp. 379–80.

notions play no part at all. Nevertheless, I want to argue that these explanations are unsatisfactory. Consider first (2). The suggested explanation of this sentence assembles explanations of instances of the regularity it describes, but it is a familiar fact that *compiling* explanations of instances of a regularity does not always yield a good explanation of the regularity. What is missing is a structure that *unifies* the divergent explanations. Let us note this problem, and set it aside. (Perhaps there *is* no significant explanatory unification possible here.) There is, I believe, a more fundamental problem with the suggested explanation of (1) itself, which was briefly exposed in section 1.3. The problem is that explaining (1*) does not, by itself, suffice to explain (1). To explain (1*), we explain why, under the relevant circumstances, Karl executes a certain sequence of motions: a trajectory. The indicated explanation does indeed account for Karl's *trajectory* in purely causal terms. But (1) doesn't report Karl's following that trajectory. (1) says that Karl follows a trajectory that describes a path out of the building and, moreover, a minimal one. The suggested causal explanation of (1) proceeds by deriving the trajectory followed by the device and then locating it in the collection of paths of minimum length out of the building from the initial position. It does not purport to offer an informative account of why that trajectory should fall into that class.

I now want to suggest that we can arrive at a satisfactory explanation of (1) in terms of a rudimentary semantic description of Karl's program P. Suppose that P incorporates markers $p_1, ..., p_n$ which, under a certain correspondence, call it f, represent positions in the building, and markers $s_1, ..., s_m$ which, under another correspondence, call it g, represent Karl's basic actions (for example, 'move one unit forward/backward/left/right'). We think of these actions as requiring the same time to perform and as moving Karl the same distance from his initial position. The program incorporates two data structures: first, an *exit graph*, a list of the position-markers p_i such that $f(p_i)$ is an exit-position; second, a *tracking graph*, which pairs each position-marker p_i and action-marker s_j with the marker representing the position that would be occupied by the device if it were to execute $g(s_j)$ when occupying $f(p_i)$.[37] Thus, for example, in the particularly simple case of this situation with a single corridor with four positions $p_1, ..., p_4$, where the exit graph is given, say, by the singleton $\{p_1\}$, if s represents the action taking the device one space forward and s^{-1} the reverse action, the tracking graph might be given as follows:

[37]Note that this graph may describe only a partial function on position-action pairs, since for some positions the building layout may not permit certain actions.

s	p_2	p_3	p_4	—
s^{-1}	—	p_1	p_2	p_3
	p_1	p_2	p_3	p_4

Consider now a possible explanation of (1) in terms of these materials. We must first give some information about the operation of the program P. P is assumed, first, to incorporate an algorithm that computes the current position of the device by reference to the tracking graph. Given any initial position p, then, the tracking and exit graphs fix the set Σ_p of all finite sequences $\langle z_1, q_1, ..., z_{k-1}, q_{k-1}, z_k \rangle$ such that $z_1 = p$, and

(a) For any positive integer i, if $i \leq k$, $z_i \in \{p_1, ..., p_n\}$ and if $i < k$, $q_i \in \{s_1, ..., s_m\}$;

(b) For any positive integer $i < k$, the tracking graph pairs $\langle z_i, q_i \rangle$ with z_{i+1};

(c) For any integers $i, j \leq k$, $z_i = z_j$ iff $i = j$;

(d) z_k codes an exit.

Because of the condition (c), Σ_p is finite and effectively computable from p, and we suppose that P contains an algorithm that does just that for any position p. Third, the program selects a sequence $\langle z_1, q_1, ..., z_{k-1}, q_{k-1}, z_k \rangle$ of minimum length from the set Σ_p . The device then executes the actions coded by $q_1, ..., q_{k-1}$ in order.

If the program P functions in the indicated way, then starting from the given initial position in the relevant initial state Karl will traverse a minimal path to an exit. Let us see why. Under the correlations f and g, a sequence σ satisfying the conditions (a) and (b) represents a possible history of the device starting from the initial position: taken in order, the even-numbered components of σ represent successive basic actions of the device, and the odd-numbered components its resulting positions. The condition (d) narrows this class to the histories that terminate at an exit-position, and the condition (c) to those histories wherein Karl never occupies the same position twice. The successive position-components of the sequences satisfying all four conditions thus describe *direct paths* out of the building from the given initial position. The third step in the program selects a sequence σ_0 of minimum length from this set; the odd-membered subsequence of σ_0 then describes an optimal path to an exit from the initial position, and the even-membered subsequence actions that when performed in the specified order take Karl through that path.

This sketch explains the fact that Karl follows an optimal egress from the initial position in terms of a correspondence relation between the program P and a causal structure linking possible basic actions of the device to changes in its position, and the fact that Karl *instantiates P*. The availability of the notion of Karl's 'instantiating' or 'following' an algorithm or effective procedure is of course crucial here, and will come in for detailed treatment below.[38] Anxiety about this matter need not, however, detain us for the purposes of the present example, which will serve as a simple prototype for interpretational explanations in which, I wish to argue, semantical notions play an essential role. In the interpretational version, 'correspondence' will be explicated in terms of reference, the descriptive devices in P will correspond to a fragment of the belief-specifying component of an appropriate interpretation, and accurate representation will be interpreted in terms of truth under the associated scheme of reference. But we will need a general term covering all cases of the sort of correspondence-based explanation just illustrated. I shall call them **conformal explanations**.

The conformal explanation I have sketched above targets an exemplification of a property (optimality, in the relevant sense) by a particular event (Karl's trajectory). By generalizing the explanation, we may explicate the capacity described by (2). I said above that even if satisfactory causal explanations of sentences like (1) could be given, it would not follow that we can obtain a fully satisfactory explanation of (2) by simply compiling these explanations. The difficulty is that the explanations may have so little in common in terms of structure and content that even when these are fully assembled it may yet remain quite mysterious that each explanandum attributes *the same* property to Karl's trajectory. The suggested conformal explanation of (1), however, makes no use of special properties of the given initial position; a parallel explanation may be given for any initial position. What makes these explanations possible is the fact that the program P incorporates a unified strategy that, for each instance of the capacity described by (2), generates a representation of a causal structure underlying that instance. This feature of P affords a type of explanatory unification that eludes the strategy of compiling causal explanations referred to earlier.

A conformal explanation, then, explains a capacity or its instances in terms of a 'correspondence' relation. The *existence* of such a relation, of course, is a suprising fact, something we might also want to explain. That, however, is a separate issue. In the case of the robotic Karl, such an explanation might appeal to the intentions of its designers. One could imagine a biological analogue of robotic Karl for which the existence of the relation is explained, in part, in evolutionary terms. But for my purposes it is important to stress that the adequacy of a conformal explanation in no way depends on the availability of a special sort of explanation of the underlying correspondence relation. Suppose, for example, that the robotic

---

[38]See the postscript to this chapter.

device finds itself in another building that happens to have the same layout as the building in our story. Precisely analogous conformal explanations apply to the analogues of (1) and (2) in this situation, but in this case the relevant correspondence relation may be purely fortuitous.

2.4.2   Interpretive Conformal Explanations

I now return to the original Karl, leaving the robotic simulacra of the last section behind. I now want to ask how broadly linguistic representation can contribute to explanations built on the pattern illustrated above in subsection 2.4.1.

Thus, suppose we are given an interpretation of Karl containing a specification **A** of Karl's attitudes in terms of semantic representations of the sort it associates with sentences of his language (we continue to call it 'L'), and a scheme of reference **R** for L. Suppose that, under **R**, a subset K of the belief-fragment of **A** expresses the relevant tracking and exit graphs, so that it is effectively determinable from $K + \mathbf{R}$ what the paths out of the building from any starting point are.[39] Suppose further that the belief-fragment of **A** correctly specifies Karl's initial situation, and that **A** equips Karl with a standing desire to exit the building via an optimal path when in that situation. Finally, suppose that Karl's inductive method incorporates a strategy corresponding to the program P. We can then assemble an explanation of (1) that is analogous to the one just sketched. Karl will be represented as inferring in the indicated way from K a description of the ways in which his basic actions bring about changes in his position relevant to the desired outcome of following an optimal path to an exit. In general, then, if o is an outcome that Karl desires according to the interpretation in question, by a 'conformality property' for o in that interpretation we will understand roughly a subset of the belief-fragment of **A** that, under **R**, describes an explanatory relation between basic actions available to Karl and the outcome o. A conformality property for o is thus the basis of a conditional explanation connecting his prospective basic actions to o that Karl can frame himself: and such an explanation is in turn the basis of a conformal explanation that we can frame of Karl's capacity to bring about that outcome.

---

[39] Corresponding to the tracking graph, for example, K might be supposed to contain conditionals, one for each entry pairing a position, action pair $\langle p_i, a \rangle$ with a position p_j, which says that a is an action type and p_i, p_j positions such that if Karl performs a while occupying p_i, he will move from p_i to p_j; see below for a more detailed implementation of this idea.

I can now proceed to some fundamental definitions. In each case the definition is relative to an assumed interpretation of Karl, and in particular to the scheme of reference associated with that interpretation; but to avoid clutter this relativity will be largely suppressed.

Let A be a sentence of L that specifies a basic action a and E a set of sentences of L.[40] We say that the pair $\langle E, A \rangle$ is a **projective explanation** of an outcome o if $E \cup \{A\}$ explains o by explaining a's bringing about o. Some comments are in order.

A sentence of the form

[i] a brought about o.

is intended to capture a broad sort of causal-explanatory connection between actions and outcomes. When combined with an appropriate specification of a, a description of such a connection can be used to explicate o, by delineating a mechanism by which o arises from a. The locution 'explains o by explaining a's bringing about o' is intended to convey that the sentence A provides such a specification of a and the set E a description of such a mechanism: if we idealize the situation somewhat, we might think of the set $E \cup \{A\}$ as generating a deductive-nomological derivation of a sentence reporting o that describes the mechanism by which a brings about o. Such an explanation, of course, need do nothing by itself to explain A (that is, why Karl performs a). It should be clear that this is not a contradistinction to the claim that $E \cup \{A\}$ explains o: we can explain why o comes about in terms of Karl's performing a without explaining that performance as, for example, when we explain Socrates' demise in terms of the fact that he drank the hemlock, without explaining why he drank the hemlock.

Finally, the property of being a projective explanation of an outcome can be defined only against the background of an interpretation of Karl with certain properties. It must be determinate when sentences in L specify actions and outcomes, and it must be determinate when constructions in L describe explanatory mechanisms by which actions generate outcomes. If, as on the deductive-nomological model, such a description is deductively organized, then the interpretation in question must provide a characterization of logical relations in L. The concepts of causal possibility and necessity may also come into play. In general, the repertoire of semantic structures in Karl's language required to support the concept of projective explanation is rather thick.[41]

---

[40]See n. 19 for a definition of 'specifies'.

[41]The problem of characterizing logical relations in Karl's language is taken up in chapter 4, as is the problem of interpreting modalities.

By a **conformality property** for an outcome o we understand a set K of semantic representations of beliefs ascribed to Karl by the interpretation in question such that, under the semantic description supplied by that interpretation, a basic act-specifying sentence A can be chosen so that $\langle K, A \rangle$ is a projective explanation of o. In this case, if a is the action thus specified, we say that K **connects** a to o. If K is a conformality property for o, then, under the interpretation in question, K describes a mechanism by which the action specified by A brings about o, and is thus the basis of a conditional explanation of o relative to A that Karl can frame himself. In particular, Karl will hold a conditional belief to the effect that o will obtain if he performs the action specified by A.[42] Finally, against the background of that interpretation, a **conformal explanation** of Karl's bringing about the outcome o is a pair $\langle K, E \rangle$ wherein

(a) K is a conformality property for o;

(b) Karl performs a basic action a such that K connects a to o;

(c) E is an intentional explanation of a in terms of the beliefs ascribed to Karl in K and an ascription to Karl of the desire that o obtain.

An interpretation-based conformal explanation of Karl's bringing about o, then, is a rationalizing explanation of a basic action available to Karl together with a projective explanation of how that action brings about o which, in an epistemic sense, is also available to Karl.[43] In the context of the given interpretation of Karl, then, we are able to recover Karl's projective explanation of o in terms of an appropriate description of a and thus, via the assumed intentional explanation of A, an explanation of Karl's doing something that brings about o. This last observation points to a pragmatic role of the notion of conformal explanation: if we are prepared to ascribe truth, or approximate truth, to the relevant beliefs, building conformal explanations within an interpretation of an agent allows us to use the beliefs of the agent as a guide to explanatory mechanisms in the world. This of itself, I think, gives a minimal rationale for the deployment of a semantical characterization of Karl's language and attitudes.[44] But that is not the end of the matter. I want to claim that a conformal explanation of Karl's bringing about an outcome can at least in some cases *amplify* the explanatory content of Karl's account of how his actions bring about that outcome.

Consider, for example, an analogue of the conformal explanation of the

---

[42]I am here assuming the epistemic idealization described in 2.2.2.

[43]There is an obvious generalization of the notions of projective and conformal explanation that allows each to make use of finite sets of basic act-specifying sentences. I shall assume this when needed.

[44]I took this line in "Representation, Intentionality, and Quantifiers," sec. 3.

path-optimality of the robotic device above, based on an interpretation of Karl that affords him information about the building layout and a standing desire to exit the building efficiently in case of an alarm.[45] The information is given in terms of an assignment of semantic representations to a subset of Karl's beliefs. The explanation makes use of finitely many basic act-specifying predicates $A_1(n), ..., A_k(n)$, each saying, under the semantic description of Karl's attitudes associated with the interpretation in question, and under an appropriate *de se* specification of Karl, that Karl performs a certain action a_i at the time n. Similarly, for each position in the tracking graph, there will be a specification p of that position in L such that for a certain predicate $Loc(x, y)$ the sentence $Loc(p, n)$ says that Karl occupies the location coordinated with p at the time n. The tracking graph then corresponds to the set of all true conditionals of the form

$$(\forall n)((A_i(n) \ \& \ Loc(p, n)) \ \rightarrow \ Loc(q, n + 1)).^{46}$$

The exit graph corresponds to the set of true sentences $Ex(p)$, where Ex is a predicate whose extension in L consists of precisely the exit-positions. If '0' represents the initial time, an effective pattern of first-order inference, analogous to the strategy of robotic Karl in 2.4.1, leads from any sentence of the form $Loc(p, 0)$ to the collection of all true sentences

[ii] $(Loc(p, 0) \ \& \ A_{i_1}(1) \ \& \ ... \ \& \ A_{i_n}(n)) \ \rightarrow \ (Loc(p, n + 1) \ \& \ Ex(q))$,

where n is minimal. By acting in the ways specified by the sentences $A_{i_1}(1), ..., A_{i_n}(n)$, then, Karl will be led to an exit via an optimal path; and if the sentences corresponding to the tracking and exit graphs specify a subset of Karl's beliefs within the interpretation in question, Karl can infer that by acting in these ways he will generate that outcome. (A complete decision-theoretic explanation of Karl's performing such a set of basic actions will appeal to a preference ordering defined on conjunctions of action sentences derived from conditionals of the form [ii]. Karl will be represented as assigning maximal expected utility to an outcome including his exiting the building, and as preferring no course of action to realize this outcome to the basic actions specified by a minimal conjunction of this sort.)

---

[45] I stress at the outset that the present example is not intended as a serious model of human navigation, but as a conceptual experiment intended to illustrate the potential explanatory relevance of semantic notions.

[46] For simplicity I assume a discrete temporal ordering of actions whereby each basic action consumes one unit of time; the indicated conditional then provides that if at a given stage Karl finds himself at the location p, by performing the action specified by A_i he will arrive at location q at the next stage.

This story constitutes an informative answer to the question of why Karl follows a path of minimal length out of the building from the initial position, in terms of the fact that Karl instantiates an effective procedure for arriving at representations of minimal paths. In the present example, Karl's explanation of his egress may be imagined to be analogous to the direct combinatorial explanation considered earlier: his strategy is simply to select, via a suitable preference-ordering, a path of minimal length from the collection of possible egresses. But by exhibiting Karl's procedure as an instance of the combinatorial explanation, we make possible an answer to the question of why Karl's egress is minimal which is more informative than that of the combinatorial explanation itself. It is one thing to say that Karl's path is minimal because he performs a certain sequence of basic actions and to explain why, either in physical or intentional terms, he performs that sequence of actions, and then to observe that when performed in that sequence the relevant actions generate a minimal path. It is another, and something more, to explain those actions in intentional terms that exhibit them as a realization of a strategy that draws on just this sort of information. That is what the indicated conformal explanation does, and it is in this sense that the conformal explanation amplifies the combinatorial one.

2.4.3 The Object of Conformal Explanation

We are now in a position to provide one answer to the question of what it is that ascriptions of semantic properties explain. Semantic data contribute to interpretation-based conformal explanations. Such an explanation explains how something that Karl does basically brings about an outcome that Karl desires; and it explains, in intentional or broadly decision-theoretic terms, the relevant basic action(s). In the case of a single action, if a is the action and o the outcome, the object of explanation may then be expressed

[iii] $By(a, Karl)$ & a brought about o,

where $By(e, x)$ says that e is an action and x an agent such that e is performed by x; or, equivalently, in terms of a corresponding sentence

            $By(a, Karl)$ & a brought it about that p,

wherein 'p' represents a sentence of which 'o' is a gerundive nominal.[47] The

---

[47]The 'By-' locution originates with Donald Davidson, "The Logical Form of Action Sentences," in *Essays on Actions and Events* (New York: Oxford University Press, 1980). For helpful discussion of the notion of performance, see George M. Wilson, *The Intentionality of Human Action* (Stanford: Stanford University Press, 1989), pp. 44–52. There is an obvious extension of the present observation to locutions of the form [iii] in which 'o' represents a set of outcomes and 'a' a *course* of action.

state of affairs reported by such a sentence might be called a *second-order action*, for that state of affairs consists in the fact that a certain basic action of Karl's exemplifies a certain property, namely, bringing about the outcome *o*. Of course, a construction that explains [iii] also explains its existential closure, the sentence

[iv] $(\exists e)(\text{By}(e, \text{Karl}) \ \& \ e$ brought about $o)$,

which says that Karl did something that brought about *o*. But to say that Karl did something that brought about *o* is to say that *Karl brought about o*. That is not by itself, of course, to say that Karl brought about that outcome intentionally, which is another way of saying that the modifier 'intentionally' in a sentence of the form

Karl brought about *o* intentionally.

is not generally otiose. The present object of explanation, then, is Karl's bringing about, in a sense not requiring intentionality, a certain state of affairs in the world. I think there is a natural way to generate the intentional from the nonintentional ascription: Karl brings about an outcome intentionally if he brings it about, and there is a conformal explanation of his doing so. In subsection 2.4.6, I shall present some evidence relevant to this claim.

The objects of conformal explanation have so far been restricted to states of affairs reported by sentences of the form [iii] or [iv]. However, the present account in fact captures a somewhat broader range of explananda. Let '*V*' represent a verb of the sort linguists call 'causative', of which the following sentences contain typical examples:

    (a) Karl *tamed* a lion;
    (b) Karl *raised* his glass;
    (c) Karl *demolished* the Pont Neuf.

On the assumption that a sentence of the form

[v] a V-ed b

is equivalent to a corresponding sentence of the form

[vi] $(\exists e)(\text{By}(a, e) \ \& \ e$ brought it about that $V(b))$,

the account of conformal explanation just rehearsed for the form [iv] transfers, via [vi], to [v]. However, it is by no means clear that the construction [v] generally admits the reading [vi]. On such a reading, (a) would say that

Karl performed an action that brought it about that the lion was tamed, and (b) that Karl did something that brought it about that his glass was raised.[48] The difficulty arises from the fact that these readings can hold without the indicated outcomes being precipitated 'in the normal way', and that at least in some cases the relevant outcome's being brought about in the normal manner seems to be implied by the causative construction. Thus, for example, there is a reading of (b) on which it would not be rendered true by Karl's flipping a switch that caused the glass to be raised by a pulley and cable across the room.

One case that does not resist such a reading is the sentence (c): to say that Karl demolished a certain bridge in central Paris is to say that Karl did something that brought about the demolition of the bridge. He could do it by throwing a hand grenade, or by fusing a delayed-action detonating device. Or, as commander of a resistance cell, he could do it by ordering subordinates to perform such an action. Or he could do it in any number of unintentional ways, for example, by issuing an instruction that is mistakenly interpreted as an order to blow up the bridge. There seems to be no linguistic requirement in this case of a normal mechanism or causal path through which that outcome must be generated. The sentence (a) is something of an intermediate case, though on the whole I think it is more plausibly assimilated to (c) than to (b).[49] In any case, in what follows I will occasionally avail myself of examples for which the [v]/[vi] equivalence is uncontroversial.

2.4.4 Conformal Explanation and Success

I wish to pause at this point to interpose a brief comparison of the present account of the explanatory role of semantic notions with a related account once proposed by Hilary Putnam.[50] Putnam suggested that a theory of

---

[48]I am using the quantified form 'Karl did something that ...' as a variant of 'Karl performed an action that ...', ignoring some complexities about 'did something'.

[49]The problem of causatives has been extensively treated in the linguistic literature, in which the equivalence of [v] to something like [vi] is not infrequently defended. For two classic discussions, see James McCawley, "Prelexical Syntax" in *Semantic Syntax* edited by Pieter Seuren (London: Oxford University Press, 1974), and George Lakoff, "On Generative Semantics" in *Semantics: An Interdisciplinary Reader*, edited by D. Steinberg and L. Jacobovitz (Cambridge: Cambridge University Press, 1971). My complaint about the [vi]-type analysis of (b) is similar to an objection raised by Chomsky to a parallel reading of 'x killed y'; see N. Chomsky, *Studies on Semantics and Generative Grammar* (The Hague: Mouton, 1972), p. 72. See also Wilson, *Intentionality of Human Action*, ch. 4 for a helpful discussion of this issue.

[50]See Hilary Putnam, "Reference and Understanding," in *Meaning and the Moral Sciences* (London: Routledge and Kegan Paul, 1978), especially pp. 100–103.

reference for Karl's language can help to explain the *success* of Karl's behavior. In capsule, the idea is that Karl's behavior in a certain situation is successful because (i) Karl acts in that situation in order to obtain a goal; (ii) acts on beliefs given by sentences which are *true*; and (iii) under the relevant interpretation, these beliefs imply that by acting in this way Karl can achieve his goal. This suggestion is connected to the present account in ways that I shall now briefly consider. But it is not at all the same account.

The success of an action consists, roughly, in its actualizing the content of a desire. However, Stephen Schiffer has objected that, if success if understood in this way, then it seems circular to rationalize the explanatory role of semantic properties by pointing out that they are required in order to explicate the success of Karl's behavior.[51] For, any description of Karl's behavior as *successful* must assume a notion of *satisfaction* for Karl's desires, and satisfaction is a reference-dependent notion: to say that a desire given by a sentence of Karl's language is *satisfied* is to say that the sentence is *true*. Schiffer argued that it is circular to rationalize the introduction of semantic properties by invoking a class of explananda for them specified in terms of those same semantic properties. It is circular, in any case, from a standpoint that questions the need to invoke such properties at all: and the rationale for semantic description that I aim to provide here is directed to precisely that standpoint.

The explanatory rationale for the notions of reference and truth I have described escapes this criticism, for the objects of conformal explanation are actions that, for the purposes of the explanation, *are* generally described in non-semantic terms. Thus, to take just one case, in the preceding example we explain Karl's effecting an efficient egress on a particular occasion. There is no use of semantic notions in our specification of this explanandum or, in general, in sentences of the form [iv]. Say that an outcome is an **accomplishment** of Karl relative to a given interpretation if the outcome is brought about by Karl's basic actions, and this fact is conformally explicable in the interpretation. Karl's accomplishments relative to an interpretation are thus connected to basic actions that are successful against the background of attitudes it ascribes to Karl: an accomplishment is *generated* by a successful basic action or actions. But it does not follow that what a conformal explanation *explains* is the *success* of that action.

2.4.5 Two Extensions

In this section I shall consider two related generalizations of the model of

---

[51]See "Truth and the Theory of Content," in *Meaning and Understanding*, edited by H. Parrett and J. Bourveresse (Berlin: de Gruyter, 1981).

interpretive conformal explanation developed in subsection 2.4.2. A sentence of the form [i] reports what might be called a *generative* relation between the action a and the outcome o: the fact that a brings about o. Part of what the schema of 2.4.2 explicates is a generative relation between basic actions available to Karl and an outcome desired by Karl by reference to the fact that, under the interpretation in question, Karl's beliefs provide him with a guide to connections between his prospective basic actions and the relevant outcome. There is a companion account of conformal explanation for what might be called **generative capacities**. A generative capacity of an agent is a capacity or ability of the agent to bring about an outcome of a certain type under suitable conditions. We speak, for example, of Karl's capacity to exit the building efficiently, Karl's ability to tame lions, or of Karl's ability to blow up the Pont Neuf. These formulations refer back to conditionals which say that, if suitable conditions are present, then Karl will act in such a way as to bring about the relevant outcome; thus, for example, the first capacity mentioned might refer to the fact that, when suitably prompted, Karl acts in such a way as to effect an efficient egress. Alternatively, a generative capacity may be described by the collection of its *possible manifestations*, consisting in a range of possible exemplifications of the relevant generative property by a basic action or by a set of such actions. Formally, then, a generative capacity might be identified with a relation between possible worlds and exemplifications of a generative property.[52] Each such exemplification is in turn associated with a basic action and an outcome such that the action brings about the outcome at the possible world in question. A conformal explanation of a generative capacity will appeal to an interpretation of Karl over each of the relevant possible worlds. If $\mathcal{R}$ is the manifestation relation describing the capacity to be explained, the sentences of L giving Karl's beliefs in the interpretation will incorporate a set that is simultaneously constitutive of a conformality property for the outcome associated with each event α paired with some world by $\mathcal{R}$, and that underlies a conformal explanation of α in that world.

---

[52]Where by an *exemplification* of a property (or relation) designated by a predicate A I will mean the state of affairs specified by a gerundive nominal of the form 'x's being A/A-ing at t' where t designates a time (or interval) and x an object (or n-tuple). The ontological status of property exemplifications has been discussed at length by Jaegwon Kim in, for example, "Causation, Nomic Subsumption and the Concept of Event," in *Supervenience and Mind* (Cambridge: Cambridge University Press, 1993), 3–21. My primary role for them will be as objects of explanation, and for this purpose indicative sentences corresponding to gerundive phrases would for the most part serve as well. Following Kim, I will sometimes refer to such structures as 'events', or 'event-structures'.

A conformality property for one of Karl's generative capacities, then, embodies a model of a generative connection between Karl's prospective basic actions and the relevant type of outcome that plays the explanatory role described above for each manifestation of that capacity.[53]

To briefly return to the question raised earlier concerning explanatory unification: I said that even if we had acceptable explanations of each manifestation of a capacity, we need not obtain a satisfactory explanation of the capacity simply by compiling them. How does the suggested explanatory strategy for capacities address this problem? The adequacy of a conformal explanation of a particular nonbasic action is in part a function of the adequacy of the underlying object-language explanation to which it refers; similarly, the degree of unification of a collection of such explanations is a function of that of the associated object-language explanations, where the latter sort of unification is to be assessed in standard ways. A collection of conformal explanations of the manifestations of a capacity will exhibit the relevant sort of unification if the associated object-language explanations are similar in structure and content, which is to say that they deploy largely overlapping resources in largely similar ways. The condition imposed earlier, that there exist a *single* set of semantic representations underlying a conformal explanation of each manifestation of the capacity, is clearly relevant to such a requirement.

I now turn to a second extension of the account of 2.4.2. I have described a framework for the conformal explanation of actions and capacities of individual agents. There are social analogues of both of these models. The social models make use of a semantic description of the attitudes of social groups of agents sharing a common language, as well as the atti-

---

[53]The sentences comprising this unitary model need not exhaust the conformality properties for the various world-indexed outcomes; we should allow for some contextual variation in these properties. Consider, for example, a conformal explanation of Karl's ability to exit the building via an optimal path from any initial position. A conformality property for such an explanation will comprise sentences describing the pertinent aspects of the building layout, but these must be combined with a specification of Karl's initial situation in order to give a conformality property for a specific egress; and these initial situations are variable. It is, however, inappropriate to require that the stable conformal features explain why the context-sensitive ones lead to the outcome in question when combined with the relevant set of basic actions. Thus, we may formally take a conformality property for the relation R to be a set T of semantic representations such that for each $\langle w, \alpha \rangle \in R$, there is a set S of context-specifying sentences such that:

(a) $T \cup S$ is a conformality property for the outcome associated with α in w;
(b) Under the interpretation in question, T explains why the contextual features specified by S lead to the outcome associated with α when combined with the action(s) associated with α.

tudes of individual agents. The social analogue of the model for actions, for example, would explain a generative relation between a set of collectively undertaken basic actions and a collectively desired outcome. The required semantic characterization of the attitudes of the group would be determined by an interpretation of the population in question, that is, a set of simultaneous interpretations of the members of the population that assign the same semantic description to their common language. Such an interpretation would fix the relevant collective attitudes on the weak reductive assumption that the attitudes of a social group are determined by a complete specification of the attitudes of its members.

We can distinguish two concepts of collective intentionality. The first might be called 'summative'.[54] On the summative construal, a collective attitude toward p consists in the fact that each member of the relevant collective bears that attitude toward p. There is a corresponding social model of conformal explanation that I shall also call 'summative'. On the summative model, there is a fixed conformality property that underwrites a set of accomplishments within an actual population in much that same way that a conformal explanation of a capacity provides a unitary account of its manifestations in different possible worlds. The object of such a summative explanation is the fact that agents in the population have individually brought about a type of outcome in accordance with a shared understanding of how to bring about outcomes of that type. By generalizing along both the social and modal dimensions, one arrives at a summative model of the conformal explanation of social capacities.

The summative conception of conformal explanation is limited, for accomplishments of a social group do not generally consist in the fact that several individuals in it have each brought about an outcomes of the same type, that type being constitutive of the social accomplishment in question.[55] Thus, the construction of the Verrazano Narrows Bridge, the first lunar landing, and the outcome of the battle of Kursk are each nonsummative collective accomplishments. A nonsummative conformal explanation of such an outcome will appeal to appropriate nonsummative notions of collective belief, desire and action, but is otherwise characterized in analogy to the individual concept considered above. In particular, if G is the relevant social group and o an outcome brought about by G, a conformality property for o is a set of sentences in the language of G that express a conception held by G of a generative connection between basic actions available to G and the outcome o, where by a 'basic action of G' we understand a set of

---

[54]This term is from Margaret Gilbert, *On Social Facts* (Princeton: Princeton University Press, 1992), p. 241.

[55]This observation goes along with a parallel limitative observation about the summative account of social attitudes; see Gilbert, pp. 257–312.

basic actions of one or several members of G. I shall have occasion to recur to the nonsummative social notion of conformal explanation in the account of reference to natural kinds developed in the following chapter.

2.4.6 Conformal Explanation and Intentionality

I want to conclude this section by commenting briefly on some connections of the foregoing with some topics in the philosophy of action. The outcomes of Karl's conformally explicable second-order actions have been described as Karl's 'accomplishments' (2.4.4); these are the states of affairs that are brought about through such an action or, a bit more explicitly, the outcomes whose bringing about such an action consists in. The word 'accomplishment' is ambiguous in English as between the outcome and the action, and so I will sometimes speak of Karl's conformally explicable actions themselves as accomplishments. Still, the entire terminology may seem puzzling. The concept of accomplishment is connected to that of intention: Karl's accomplishments are things that Karl brings about intentionally. And so one should expect a reasonably tight connection between the concepts of conformal explanation and intentional action.

The preceding examples, of which we may take the sentence

(c)   Karl demolished the Pont Neuf.

to be typical, have nonintentional constructions of the form [iv]. On the other hand, these sentences are sometimes used to report that Karl brought about a certain outcome intentionally. On their intentional construals, sentences like these notoriously resist a certain avenue of analysis. If understood to report an intentional action, (c) obviously requires at least, but clearly more, than that Karl's actions bring about the demolition of the bridge. That, after all, could be true without Karl's having any intention or desire to destroy the bridge. The next move would be to add to the condition just indicated the requirement that Karl wants to destroy the bridge and believes, correctly, that by performing certain basic actions he can effect this outcome. But there is still the problem of 'deviant causal chains'. Suppose that Karl places his explosive device under the bridge and activates it by setting a timer for five minutes. The fuse malfunctions, and the bomb fails to explode, but an alarm attached to the timer does sound after five minutes. An unrelated saboteur, Pierre, hears the alarm from across the Seine and mistakenly thinks it a signal from a coconspirator to activate his own fully functional explosive device. Pierre sets the fuse of his device, which duly explodes, destroying the bridge.

Karl didn't intentionally demolish the bridge, Pierre did. Yet, Karl acted as he did because he correctly believed that acting in this way would bring about the destruction of the bridge. The problem is that although this is true the causal chain by which the desired outcome is effected is 'deviant'. It realizes Karl's desire, by happenstance, as we might say, but it is not of Karl's design. At a first approximation, my suggestion is that it is deviant, in the relevant sense, *because* it is not of Karl's design. The action is intentional only if its outcome is realized by a causal path that is, in a certain not-too-clearly understood sense, 'of the agent's design'. What might this mean?

Of course, Karl does have a slight conception of how the causal path goes; it is:

(P)   sets timer → a bomb explodes → bridge collapses

where the arrows represent causal transitions. The difficulty seems to be that the first transition indicated is generated by a mechanism that is not 'of Karl's design'. In particular, the bomb that Karl thinks will explode as a result of his actions is not the bomb that in fact does so. Of course, to require the complete etiology underlying the first transition to have been plotted by Karl would be absurd; Karl need not have complete information about the mechanism underlying the first transition. So it seems that an intentionality-underwriting design for the causal path in question requires more information than (P) but less than that of the complete explanatory text for the outcome in question. How is the required sort of information to be characterized? It is at this point that the technical notion of 'accomplishment' introduced earlier may be of some help. In the story I have told, the destruction of the Pont is Pierre's accomplishment, not Karl's. This is owing to the fact that there is a conformal explanation of Pierre's bringing about this outcome, whereas no such explanation is applicable to Karl. This asymmetry is in turn derivative from the circumstance that Pierre is in possession of at least a sketch of a projective explanation of that outcome whereas Karl is not. Pierre's explanation is assembled from the following beliefs: he has placed a bomb in proper working order under the bridge; the bomb is of a certain size; that if detonated a device of this sort will explode with sufficient force to destroy the bridge; that under the circumstances if activiated by setting a timer the device will detonate in five minutes; and finally that, under the same circumstances, a basic action available to him suffices to set the timer.

Pierre's account is explanatory because the indicated beliefs are true. Karl, of course, has an exactly parallel story to tell. But it isn't explanatory because it isn't true; in particular, Karl's assumption that his bomb is properly fused and detonates is false. Moreover, there is no other subset of Karl's beliefs that would generate a projective explanation of the outcome in question. Karl has no *projective understanding* of how his setting the timer leads to the destruction of the bridge. It is in this sense that Karl lacks a design for that outcome. I now suggest that this distinction is constitutive of a minimal conception of the intentionality of at least a certain range of actions, those described by sentences of the form

Karl brought about *o*.

or

Karl brought it about that *p*.

The second-order action consisting in Karl's bringing about an outcome is intentional if and only if that action can be explicated in conformal terms (this criterion being relative, of course, to an assumed interpretation of Karl; 'explanation in conformal terms' refers to conformal explanation within such an interpretation). Equivalently, the outcomes that Karl brings about intentionally are precisely Karl's accomplishments in my technical sense. These are the outcomes that Karl brings about through a mechanism of his own design.

Does this proposal afford a generally adequate analysis of the intentionality of an agent's bringing about an outcome? I am unsure. There are special factors that bear on whether to call the bringing-about-of an outcome intentional in a given situation. These contextual items are variable. The present conception of intentional action relativizes the ascription of intentionality only to a semantical description of the agent's language and attitudes, ignoring special contextual considerations. It is for this reason that I called the conception 'minimal'. Nevertheless, with that qualification I believe that the suggested criterion of intentionality does a rather good job of sorting the cases. Objections to the criterion are likely to come from two directions. First, it might be suggested that the requirement of conformal explanation is not a necessary condition for the intentionality of action, for it does not seem to be generally true that agents act intentionally to bring about an outcome only if they can frame an explanation of how their actions bring about that outcome. Second, it might be suggested that what makes the action intentional is not the ability of the agent to explain how what he does brings about the desired outcome but rather the fact that the agent's belief that his action will bring about that outcome is appropriately grounded. That, it might be claimed, is the relevant asymmetry between Karl and Pierre in the preceding story. Pierre *knows* that his fusing his device will result in the destruction of the bridge; Karl does not, although it may be imagined that in the indicated situation Karl has good reasons to believe that his action will bring about this outcome. I shall consider these objections in turn.

It seems that agents intentionally bring about many outcomes through mechanisms they cannot informatively describe. I bring about various outcomes by means of technologies that I don't understand at all. Thus, for example, I contacted my wife by cellular telephone earlier this afternoon, but I have no conception of how my dialing the number brought about that outcome. That is true in one way, but false in another. It is true in the sense that I have no understanding of the inner workings of cellular telephones. But I do have a rather thick repertoire of beliefs about the causal powers of such objects. That is all that is required for the purposes at hand. For the purpose of framing the required sort of explanatory sketch, instances of a technology may be treated as black boxes, characterized in terms of their causal capacities. These would normally be specified by means of rudimentary 'phenomenological' generalizations through which I could verbalize, for example, my beliefs about the causal powers of cellular telephones. Pierre in the case described might be supposed to have just this sort of understanding of his explosive device.

My claim is that if, through a series of basic actions, an agent intentionally brings about an outcome, that agent must have at least a rudimentary conception of how those actions brought about that outcome. He must, I suggest, be able to frame at least a sketch of a projective explanation of that outcome. But it may seem that it makes a difference to the intentionality of the action how that conception was formed. Suppose that Karl can frame an explanation of how a prospective basic action will bring about an outcome he desires, but that the beliefs from which this explanation can be assembled are epistemically ungrounded.[56] Would this circumstance undercut the intentionality of Karl's bringing about the outcome in question? I will briefly consider a test case.

Suppose that a notorious prankster tells Karl, as a joke, that the basement of a certain building is filled with an explosive gas. Karl gullibly believes the story and uses it in a plan to fulfill a desire he secretly harbors to destroy the building. Karl acts to bring about a circumstance that would ignite such a gas were it present in the building. But in fact, unknown to the prankster (and to Karl), an accident has occurred that has resulted in precisely the state of affairs he has described to Karl. Karl is successful; the building is demolished. Has Karl brought about that outcome intentionally? I believe that we would say that he has. But in the imagined situation Karl doesn't know that his action will bring about that outcome. Nor, if Karl has antecedent knowledge of his informant's unreliability, is his belief

---

[56] I am being deliberately vague about what notion of grounding is in question here, because I think that no condition of this sort is required for the intentionality of action. On one interpretation of grounding, a belief is grounded if it constitutes knowledge; on another, if it is justified.

that his action will precipitate that outcome justified. But his bringing about this outcome seems intentional nonetheless. Notice that this second-order action is counted as intentional on the suggested criterion, for in the imagined situation Karl can frame a rudimentary causal explanation of how his behavior brings about the destruction of the building in terms of his for-tuitously correct beliefs about the presence of an explosive gas. This causal explanation underwrites a conformal explanation of his bringing about that outcome.

I believe that examples such as the one just rehearsed can be used to de-feat the claim of any strong epistemic grounding requirement to constitute a necessary condition for the intentionality of an agent's bringing about an outcome. I have suggested that it is rather the fact that the agent is in possession of a minimal causal explanation of how his basic actions bring about the desired outcome, where there is an intentional explanation of the actions referring in an appropriate way to the beliefs constitutive of that causal explanation, that makes his actualizing that outcome intentional. I have touched on this matter in part because its intrinsic interest; but it is also relevant to the main themes of this discussion. Properties of an inter-pretation of Karl phrased in terms of the conditions under which conformal explanations flow from it can normally be rephrased in terms of the condi-tions under which it renders Karl's second-order actions intentional. Such such a rephrasal is sometimes suggestive, as will be seen in 2.5.1 below.

2.5   Conformal Interpretation

2.5.1   The Principle of Conformality

The foregoing was directed toward capturing the connection between content-ascription and conformal explanation. I now want to ask how this account of the explanatory role of reference may help fix a scheme of ref-erence for Karl's language. My suggestion is roughly this: the acceptable schemes of reference for Karl's language are those that, ceteris paribus, best play this explanatory role. I shall thus supplement the Minimal Framework by adding to the suggested constraints on radical interpretation a require-ment to the effect that an acceptable interpretation of Karl must be the one, or one of the ones, that best explicates Karl's nonbasic actions in conformal terms. I call this constraint the **Principle of Conformality** (PC). This principle may be phrased concisely by use of the notion of 'ac-complishment' introduced earlier: since the accomplishments of an agent relative to an interpretation are outcomes associated with the nonbasic ac-tions which are conformally explicable therein, (PC) says roughly that a good interpretation must optimize Karl's accomplishments. I shall call the set of constraints that results by combining (PC) with the principles of the Minimal Framework the **Conformal Framework** for radical interpretation.

The Principle of Conformality, then, is an optimizing constraint, but it is not yet clear how to gauge what is to be optimized. In what follows, and in particular in chapter 3, I shall describe a number of strategies for implementing this idea. But two preliminary comments about how to assess interpretations with respect to (PC) are in order. First, it is clear that 'optimizing accomplishment' must not be understood simply in terms of the *number* of Karl's accomplishments, but also in terms of the variety and importance of his accomplishments. That is to say that an interpretation that renders Karl's activity broadly intelligible in conformal terms will be preferable under (PC) to one that explicates a greater number of actions in an artificially limited context. The goal is to explicate Karl's overall generative role within his natural and social context.

Second, under (PC) the adequacy of an interpretation of Karl is determined, in part, by the adequacy of the conformal explanations it generates. In turn, I have observed that a conformal explanation of Karl's bringing about an outcome presupposes an object-language explanation, or explanatory sketch, that Karl himself might give of a generative relation between a set of prospective basic actions and that outcome. The adequacy of the conformal explanation is determined, in part, by that of the associated object-language explanation: other things equal, the better Karl's explanation, the better our conformal one. The 'average value' of the underlying object-language explanations is largely a matter of the goodness of fit between Karl's beliefs and the causal structure of his context, or that part of it that is relevant to the interests ascribed to him by the interpretation in question.

As it is currently put, the Principle of Conformality applies to interpretations of individuals. Earlier I alluded to a social analogue of the suggested model of conformal explanation, targeting actions and capacities of groups; and I will argue that interpreting the language of an individual in fact generally requires interpreting the language of a population of which that individual is a member.[57] In that context, we shall require a social analogue of (PC). An interpretation of a population P, I said, comprises a semantic

---

[57] A recurring theme of chapter 3.

interpretation of the language of P and a simultaneous specification of the attitudes of each member of P. The targets of explanations characterized by the social model of conformal explanation are generative connections between group actions in P and socially desired outcomes; the social version of (PC) would then say that a good interpretation of P should optimize the conformal explanation of these connections.

The relation between conformal explanation and intentional action described in 2.4.6 makes possible an alternative formulation of the Principle of Conformality in terms of the concept of intentionality. It would say roughly that an adequate interpretation of Karl should as far as possible represent the outcomes that Karl desires as states of affairs that he brings about intentionally. It is of course not required that an adequate interpretation of Karl will represent him as fulfilling all, or even most, of his desires. This formulation of (PC) is to be understood as requiring rather that the exceptional cases, Karl's 'misses', be situated against a background of unexceptional cases, Karl's 'hits'. This way of viewing (PC) makes it possible to nuance that requirement in a way only hinted at thus far. I said earlier that (PC) should not be understood simply to say that an acceptable interpretation should generate more conformal explanations than otherwise equally acceptable competing interpretations; that what we seek is an interpretation that renders Karl's activity broadly intelligible in conformal terms. I can now put this goal in a somewhat different light.

What is basically at issue is the ability of an acceptable interpretation of Karl to underwrite a connected narrative of Karl's intentional activity in the world. Such a narrative is assembled from clauses that specify instrumental connections among outcomes that Karl brings about intentionally. Karl brings about some things *by* bringing about others, a relation between outcomes whose converse is normally indicated by the phrase 'in order to'.[58] Thus, for example, in the foregoing story we may suppose that Pierre thwarted the advance of a German armoured column by demolishing the bridge, that he demolished the bridge by detonating the bomb, that he detonated the bomb by setting the fuse, and that he set the fuse by pressing a button. Such a sentence conveys, first, that the pair of outcomes described in it are intentionally brought about by the agent in question and,

---

[58] In combination with an infinitive form of the outcome-describing phrase; for example, 'Karl turned on the light by flipping the switch' would correspond to 'Karl flipped the switch in order to turn on the light'. I say 'normally indicated' rather than 'described' here because of course these two forms are not equivalent. Karl may flip the switch in order to turn on the light and yet not turn on the light. Conversely, there is a broad nonintentional use of the 'by'-construction on which Karl can turn on the light by flipping the switch but not turn on the light intentionally. In this context, we are concerned with the intentional use only; but the first observation still stands.

second, that there is an explanatory connection between the two outcomes. The sentence is true in virtue of a conformal explanation of Karl's bringing about the first outcome that incorporates a conformal explanation of Karl's bringing about the second outcome, an overall explanation that ascribes to Karl a conception of the explanatory connection between them. Such nesting of conformal explanations generates one sort of connectedness in an intentional narrative, illustrated by the chain of by-sentences considered earlier. Another is represented by the interlocking of such chains, arising from many-one or from one-many explanatory relations between outcomes specified in the narrative. The connectedness in this sense of an intentional narrative of Karl's activity corresponds broadly to the information Karl's beliefs afford about the complete explanatory text underlying his accomplishments. The degree of connectedness of the intentional narrative generated by an interpretation of Karl is thus an index of the conformal-explanatory depth of that interpretation.

2.5.2   Conformality and Indeterminacy

I shall now look preliminarily at the ways in which the Conformal Framework allows us to address the problem of referential indeterminacy. There are various dimensions of appraisal relevant to this question, but a good litmus test is the ability of (PC) to resolve the impasse between a given interpretation and its Quinean alternatives. Suppose, then, that $\mathcal{I}$ is a given interpretation of Karl acceptable under the Conformal Framework, which construes Karl's language L to be an elementary first-order language. Quinean alternatives to $\mathcal{I}$ may be defined as above in terms of permutations of the ontology ascribed to L by $\mathcal{I}$. If π is such a permutation, $\mathcal{I}(\pi)$ will be the corresponding reinterpretation of Karl. In order to ensure that $\mathcal{I}(\pi)$ satisfies (PC), we must show that conformal explanations in $\mathcal{I}$ correspond, under the induced reinterpretation of Karl's language and attitudes, to conformal explanations in $\mathcal{I}(\pi)$; and such a correspondence requires causal explanations in L that support conformal explanations in $\mathcal{I}$ to be mapped onto parallel explanations in $\mathcal{I}(\pi)$ by the induced reinterpretation of L.

That this sort of explanatory symmetry will not generally obtain may be seen by considering a simple example. Suppose that π maps each object α onto an object 50 miles due North of α.[59] Suppose further that the initial interpretation $\mathcal{I}$ generates a conformal explanation of Karl's extracting a frozen cork from a bottle of Chateau Lafite-Rothschild that appeals to

---

[59] Obviously, if according to the given interpretation Karl's ontology contains polar, extraterrestrial, or nonspatial objects, the permutation π cannot be specified in quite this way. But the definition of π may be modified to deal with these cases, while preserving the point of the example that follows.

his belief that bottle-necks expand when put in hot water. Underlying the conformal explanation is a conditional causal explanation that can be assembled from the beliefs ascribed to Karl by $\mathcal{I}$. In typical D-N form, the explanation might be expressed as follows:

(E)

> L: Bottle-necks expand when put in hot water.
> P: b is a bottle-neck placed in hot water.
> C: b expands.

The sentence (L) expresses one of Karl's beliefs, and (P) specifies a state of affairs that Karl can bring about by means of a basic action. To ensure the required sort of explanatory invariance, we must obtain a parallel explanation in $\mathcal{I}(\pi)$ by substituting the relevant alternative contents. We obtain the following, wherein $b^\#$ is the object correlated with b:

$(E^\#)$

> $L^\#$: $(\forall x)(x$ is 50 miles due North of a bottle-neck placed in hot water $\rightarrow$ $(\exists y)(y$ is 50 miles due South of x and y is expanding)).
> $P^\#$: $b^\#$ is 50 miles due North of a bottle-neck placed in hot water.
> $C^\#$: There is an object 50 miles due South of $b^\#$ that is expanding.

But $(E^\#)$ is notoriously unexplanatory. The problem with $(E^\#)$ is that, while (L) expresses a causal generalization (albeit a low-level one), $(L^\#)$ does not. This example (Kim's, nearly enough) is an instance of the familiar problem of 'parasitic constant conjunctions' affecting regularity analyses of the role of laws in causal explanation.[60]

The present example clearly illustrates one way in which the reinterpretation of Karl's language induced by a permutation of his ontology may fail to preserve explanatory relations among sentences of *his* language, and thus may also fail to preserve conformal explanations in *our* language. We see from such examples that the transition from a given interpretation of Karl to one of its Quinean alternatives may destroy virtually *all* of the conformal explanations available in the initial interpretation. Which permutations 'work'?

Think of a permutation of Karl's ontology as inducing a mapping of states of affairs described by sentences of his language to other states of

---

[60]See Kim, "Causation, Nomic Subsumption, and the Concept of Event," for a discussion of this and related examples.

affairs. Thus, for example, if α is an object in Karl's environment, the mapping just considered takes the state of affairs consisting in α's falling under a property F onto $\alpha^{\#}$'s falling under the property of being 50 miles due North of something exemplifying F. To generally ensure conformal-explanatory symmetry, the generating function for a Quinean alternative to a given interpretation of Karl must preserve causal-explanatory relations among states of affairs specifiable in Karl's language, and in particular between Karl's prospective basic actions and outcomes that Karl desires according to the interpretation. It may immediately be seen that the functions generating the 'Pythagorean' indeterminacies adduced by Quine (functions, for example, mapping physical objects to numbers or pure sets) will fail this requirement. There are no explanations linking Karl's prospective basic actions to outcomes in the Pythagorean realm.[61]

2.5.3 Rigidity Revisited

Other cases may fare better. For example, if we can explain Karl's catching a rabbit in conformal terms, then by slightly revising his attitudes we shall be able to explicate his bringing himself into an allied relation with a rabbit-stage, and this suggests that the function mapping each object onto the mereological sum of its time-slices may be the basis of a reconstrual of Karl's language and attitudes that preserves conformal explanations. I argued in subsection 2.3.3 that this and similar indeterminacies may be resolved if the generating functions for Quinean alternatives are required to preserve the *existence-conditions* of objects. If Γ is a collection of possible worlds, the *rigidity condition over* Γ is the requirement that the generating function for a Quinean alternative map each item in the initial ontology onto an object with which it coexists at each world in Γ.[62] The aforementioned 'stage-fusion' function will fail to satisfy this condition if, for example, Γ includes possible worlds that omit stages of actual objects. The possibility of deploying such an observation to defeat a putative indeterminacy of this

---

[61]See "Ontological Relativity," p. 55. Recall that the generating function for such an example must be altered somewhat to coincide with the identity function on Karl's basic actions; see 2.3.1. Another example of conformal asymmetry is afforded by the Twin Earth case described earlier. Here the generating permutation exchanges objects on Earth other than Karl's basic actions and their constituents with their counterparts on Twin Earth. In this case, the asymmetry arises precisely because the permutation in question disturbs causal-explanatory relations between basic act-specifying sentences of L and sentences describing outcomes that are brought about by such actions: Karl's actions are followed by, but do not bring about, the counterparts on Twin Earth of the outcomes they generate.

[62]The requirement, then, is that if x is the initial item and y its image, x and y both exist or both fail to exist at each world in Γ; not that both exist at each such world.

sort is thus bound up with the question of motivating cases of the Rigidity Condition.

The main argument of subsection 2.3.3 shows that a correlation f defined on the ontology ascribed to Karl by a given interpretation will fulfill the Rigidity Condition over a chosen set Γ of worlds if

(a) according to the initial interpretation, Karl's language contains a necessity operator, interpreted in the standard way in terms of Γ (or some superset of Γ);

(b) the initial interpretation and the alternative to it generated by f assign the same truth-value to each sentence of Karl's language at each world in Γ ;

(c) the condition (b) remains satisfied if Karl's language is supplemented with additional predicates.

Suppose, then, that condition (a) is satisfied by the interpretation in question. What reasons have we to require that conditions (b) and (c) be fulfilled for some suitably robust choice of Γ? We are now in a position to suggest one answer to this question.

We have seen that if the transition from a given interpretation of Karl to one of its Quinean alternatives is to generally preserve conformal explanations, the alternative contents assigned to Karl's beliefs by the two interpretations must play parallel causal-explanatory roles. On the wide focus of subsection 2.4.5, we would wish this sort of symmetry to obtain not only for conformal explanations of individual second-order actions, but also for conformal explanations of capacities, both individual and social. Recall from 2.4.5 that if E is a conformality property for a capacity, then E enables conformal explanations of each manifestation of that capacity. Accordingly, any sentence belonging to E must hold in each world in which the capacity is exercised. Beyond a handful of rather banal constraints, there are no prior restrictions either on the sentences of Karl's language that can play such an explanatory role, or the possible situations in which a conformally explicable capacity is exercised by a member of Karl's kind.[63] Thus in order to generally ensure the present sort of explanatory symmetry in the context of a reinterpretation of the Quinean type, we must require that the reinterpretation preserve truth with respect to the initial interpretation for arbitrary sentences at each of the worlds in question. This requirement, in effect, just *is* the condition (b), where Γ is specified as the collection of all possible situations in which some capacity conformally explicable in the initial interpretation is exercised. Condition (c) is pertinent

---

[63] Clearly, we should be prepared to require, for example, the sentences in question to be true with respect to the initial interpretation, and the worlds in question to be causally possible and to contain agents relevantly like Karl.

when we broaden our perspective further to consider conformal interpretations based on extensions of the given scheme of reference; the condition is motivated, in the same way that (b) is motivated, by the requirement of conformal-explanatory symmetry, but in this case with reference to situations in which Karl's language is equipped with additional descriptive resources.

To sum up: the requirement of conformal-explanatory symmetry allows us to motivate a reasonably strong form of the Rigidity Condition, and that condition significantly reduces the indeterminacies arising on the Quinean schema. Of course, the present argument bears on only one strategy for constructing examples of indeterminacy. It says nothing about indeterminacies which are not of the distinctively Quinean sort; it also does nothing to limit the Quinean indeterminacies infecting the interpretation of classical mathematics, since the generating functions for many of these satisfy any rigidity condition. However, the examples involving ordinary physical objects are perhaps the most familiar, and troubling, apparent cases of referential indeterminacy, and it is for these cases that I believe the present argument has force.

2.6 Conclusion

The framework for radical interpretation developed in this chapter combines a number of features that reflect our interests in framing an interpretation of an idealized agent whom I have been calling 'Karl'. One thing we wish to do is to explicate Karl's raw behavior in intentional terms: to exhibit his basic actions as being the things which are rational for him to do against the background of his beliefs and desires. To this end, we wish to know what his beliefs and desires are; more than that, however, we wish to know how he has formed those attitudes. We shall thus try to exhibit Karl as a realization of an inductive method, that is, roughly, a rule-based conception of epistemic rationality, and an analogue of this for desires. Finally, we wish to frame a semantic description of Karl's language and attitudes.

A central theme of this chapter was structured around a skeptical question: why do we require such a description in the first place? My answer to this question attempted to define an explanatory role for the notions of reference and truth. I have argued that a scheme of reference for Karl's language can help to explicate Karl's *non*basic actions, in particular, the fact that Karl's behaviors bring about outcomes relevant to his interests; and although the specification of Karl's interests is an interpretation-relative matter, the specification of the relevant outcomes need not be. The correctness of a semantic description of Karl's language and attitudes is to be judged, in part, in terms of its suitability for such an explanatory role.

That is largely a matter of the goodness of fit between Karl's beliefs and causal structures in the world relevant to his interests.

It may finally seem that I have arrived, via a route somewhat different from those considered earlier, at a form of the Principle of Charity. Satisfaction of the Principle of Conformality is a matter of degree. I have not required any particular subset of Karl's beliefs to be true; but it is still correct to say that, on the account of the explanatory role of reference defended in this chapter, to the extent that Karl is massively in error about the causal-explanatory structure of his contexts of interest, referential interpretation loses its point. I must therefore contend with the arguments of a number of philosophers who have maintained that the semantic characterization of Karl's language and states of thinking should allow Karl any possibility of error however radical. The following chapter will address a number of cases of this issue.

PROBLEMS OF APPROXIMATE REALIZATION

A. Introductory Remarks

Karl has so far been construed to be an idealized cognizer, in that the beliefs ascribed to him in any situation are assumed to be in an idealized sort of reflective equilibrium with respect to his inductive method. It is the purpose of this postscript to spell out the relevance of such a conception to the interpretation of actual systems by explaining how an actual system can be related to an idealized one to which the account of this chapter applies directly. That account may then be said to be *approximately* satisfied by the epistemic profile of an actual agent. The main task of this postscript is to explicate the relevant notion of approximation.

It might be thought that the idealized model of belief ascription developed in subsection 2.3.2 could be adapted to the situation of an actual cognizer by relatively minor modification. Recall that the ideal Karl holds a sentence of L to be true if and only if it appears in $\Phi^{(n)}(\sigma, \pi)$ for each sufficiently large n, where σ and π comprise Karl's basic and prior beliefs respectively, and $\Phi^{(n)}(\sigma, \pi)$ is the state of information resulting after n steps in the inductive evaluation of the initial epistemic situation given by $\langle \sigma, \pi \rangle$. Part of the difficulty here is that an actual agent can compute $\Phi^{(n)}(\sigma, \pi)$ only for $n \leq n_0$, where n_0 is some (relatively small) upper bound. The obvious suggestion would then be to say that an actual agent's beliefs should coincide, more or less, with $\Phi^{(n)}(\sigma, \pi)$ for some suitable bound n.

The difficulty with this suggestion is that if Karl is an actual cognizer, the cognitive procedures he employs in any epistemic situation depend on the *goals* he is pursuing in that situation. The evaluation function in the ideal case describes Karl's entire repertoire of epistemic procedures. If Karl is an actual agent, he can apply only a limited number of these in any epistemic situation; and in any case only a fraction of them will generally be *relevant* to the goals that he is pursuing in that situation. This suggests that in the actual case Karl's evaluation function is not defined independently of his desires.

If Karl is an actual subject, then, Karl's evaluation function Φ will take as arguments triples $\langle \beta, \sigma, \pi \rangle$, where as before σ and π comprise Karl's underived and prior beliefs, and β is a specification of the desires ascribed to him by the interpretation in question. Karl's rule of revision will be similarly relativized: $\Phi^{(n)}(\beta, \sigma, \pi)$ will be the set that results after n steps in the inductive evaluation of $< \sigma, \pi >$ against the background of the desires specified by β. The beliefs to be ascribed to Karl in the given situation are obtained by applying the rule of revision ascribed to him to a suitable modulus of iteration.[1] The problem of describing Karl's rule of revision is an analogue of a question in cognitive science that has become known as 'the frame problem'.[2] An automated reasoning program incorporates a large number of inference routines. The question is how such a program selects, for the purpose of effecting a specified goal, just the inferences relevant to achieving that goal. Thus broadly defined, it is clear that the frame problem is not a problem about specifically *artificial* intelligence but a problem about *intelligence*. We have put no prior constraints on a solution to the problem; the adequacy of a proposed solution is to be judged in terms of its contribution to the success of our overall interpretation of Karl, which in turn is to be assessed in terms of the constitutive principles described in the body of this chapter. The suggested modification of our framework for describing Karl's inductive method is intended to ensure that an acceptable interpretation incorporate *some* solution to the problem. However, any solution at all presupposes that it makes sense to ascribe a set of epistemic rules to an actual agent, in that the agent can in some suitable sense be said to instantiate rules for making certain inferences or computing certain functions. Skepticism about this matter threatens to unravel much of the framework developed in the body of this chapter. I shall now turn to what I take to be the most serious skeptical argument concerning instantiation. The argument is that of Kripke's Wittgenstein.

---

[1] There is an element of residual idealization even here, of course: to within the chosen modulus of iteration, Karl is represented as applying his rule of revision without error. However, in the account developed in what follows of what it is for Karl to approximately instantiate such a rule, the possibility of misapplication is recognized. The beliefs of an ideal cognizer described by that rule relative to a fixed choice of β, σ, and π would be given by the limit of the sets $\Phi^{(n)}(\beta, \sigma, \pi)$.

[2] See Patrick Hayes and John McCarthy, "Some Philosophical Problems from the Standpoint of Artificial Intelligence," *Machine Intelligence* 4 (Edinburgh: Edinburgh University Press, 1969), and Patrick Hayes, "The Frame Problem," in *Artificial and Human Thinking* (Elsevier, 1971). I am grateful to Hayes for discussions of the Frame Problem, though I don't know what he would make of my present formulation of it.

B.   Kripke's Problem

Our question, then, concerns first *what we are saying* in claiming that Karl instantiates an effective procedure, and second the determinacy of Karl's inductive method as described in terms of his instantiation of such procedures. An explanation of Karl's inductive performance in these terms may be seen as a special case of a scheme for explaining capacities familiar from the writings of functionalists.[3] Suppose we wish to explain the capacity of a system to produce an output of type *A* given an input of type *B*. One way of doing so is to represent the system as a realization of a program that computes a mapping of *B*s to *A*s. Thus, for example, a stimulus-response relation in an organism may be explicated by representing the organism as a model of a program, the inputs for which represent stimuli and the outputs responses. Configurations in the program correspond to physical states of the organism, and transitions of configuration to causal relations between states of the organism. These relations may themselves admit an explanation of this sort, leading to a nested ensemble of programs, terminating with algorithms whose constituent transitions correspond to relations between physical states of the organism that are explained directly in biophysical terms.

The application of this conception to the problem of what it is for a system to be following a rule has been sharply criticized by Saul Kripke in his book *Wittgenstein on Rules and Private Language*.[4] Kripke asks us to consider the following 'dispositional' account of what it is for an agent to understand the meaning of the addition symbol '+': if queried under appropriate circumstances about any sentence of the form '*a* + *b*', the agent would respond with the appropriate sum. In other words, the agent means addition by '+' if she has a *disposition* to respond with (a representation of) the sum of two arguments given, under appropriate conditions, (representations of) those arguments. On the model of explanation described above, such a disposition might be explicated by showing that the agent instantiates a program for the addition function (in the relevant notation); for example, a Turing machine that, given any two numerals k_n and k_m as inputs, generates a computation yielding k_{n+m} as output.[5]

Kripke points out that the indicated dispositional account is subject to the apparently crippling objection that there simply *are no dispositions*,

---

[3]See, for example, Robert Cummins, "Functional Analysis," *Journal of Philosophy* 72 (1975): 741–65, and "Programs in the Explanation of Behavior," *Philosophy of Science* 44 (1977): 269–87.

[4]Cambridge, Mass.: Harvard University Press, 1982. Page references in this postscript will be to this work.

[5]If n is an integer, k_n is the corresponding numeral.

in the sense required by the account; nor can an actual agent literally *instantiate* an algorithm for the addition function. For the dispositional account requires the agent's dispositions to determine a value for each of infinitely many distinct inputs. But the dispositions of an actual finite system are finite in extent; they determine a response for only finitely many arguments of the addition function. In short, an actual finite agent has only a *finite* computational capacity:

> The dispositional theory attempts to avoid the problem of the finiteness of my actual past performance by appealing to a disposition. But in doing so, it ignores an obvious fact: not only my actual performance, but also the totality of my dispositions, is finite. It is not true, for example, that if queried about the sum of any two numbers, no matter how large, I will reply with their actual sum, for some pairs of numbers are simply too large for my mind-or my brain-to grasp. (pp. 26–27)

These observations lead naturally to the skeptical objection that the dispositional account cannot decide between rival hypotheses about which arithmetical function an agent means by '+' that agree for all arguments for which the agent is disposed to give a response. Kripke puts the objection as follows:

> Let 'quaddition' be redefined so as to be a function which agrees with addition for all pairs of numbers small enough for me to have any disposition to add them, and let it diverge from addition thereafter. Just as the skeptic previously proposed the hypothesis that I meant quaddition in the old sense viz., as defined to agree with addition on all arguments I have *actually* considered, he now proposes the hypothesis that I meant quaddition in the new sense. A dispositional account will be impotent to refute him. As before, there are infinitely many candidates the skeptic can propose for the role of quaddition. (p. 27)

Consider how Kripke's problem might arise within the interpretive framework described earlier. If Karl is an actual agent, we wish to describe Karl's inductive method in terms of a set of cognitive procedures applied against the background of his prior beliefs, basic beliefs, and desires. Let us suppose that the these procedures include the familiar rule

$$[\text{i}] \qquad \frac{\phi \to \psi \quad \phi \to \chi}{\phi \to (\psi \& \chi)}$$

from sentential logic. Clearly, there is a finite upper bound M on the length of sentences of the form $A \to B$ that can serve as inputs in an actual application of this rule. We can then consider a quus-like alternative to [i] which discharges the conclusion of [i] given premises for it of length $\leq M$ and an arbitrarily chosen sentence otherwise. The skeptical challenge here would be to say why Karl cannot equally well be said to be 'following', or to 'instantiate'–to just the extent to which he instantiates [i]—the alternative rule. In the absence of an answer to this sort of question, we must view Karl's inductive method as being radically indeterminate.

In what follows, I shall develop a response to Kripke's indeterminacy argument. The idea is briefly this. An actual system does not literally instantiate any program computing the addition function, for, as Kripke stresses, the dispositions of such a system extend to only finitely many cases. However, I shall characterize a relation, to be termed **partial realization**, holding between finite systems and certain abstract automata. An agent may *partially* realize a program for a function, in the sense to be specified, even though the agent's dispositions fix only a finite initial segment of the function. Now suppose that the dispositionalist, armed with our definition, claims that part of what constitutes the fact that Karl understands '+' to express addition is the fact that he is a *partial* realization of a suitable program for the addition function. To make his case, Kripke's skeptic must respond by claiming that if Karl partially realizes an algorithm for +, then he partially realizes an algorithm computing any function that agrees with + on those arguments to which his computational dispositions extend. I shall argue that this claim is false, so that the skeptical argument described above does not apply, at least in full generality, to the present modification of the dispositional analysis.

Residual indeterminacies will appear. However, my claim will be only that *part* of what constitutes Karl's relation to his inductive method is that he is a partial realization of a computational scheme describing it. What makes a particular such program *constitutive* of that method is the role that it plays in explaining Karl's inductive performance, and in what follows I will be concerned to show that the residual alternatives are ill-suited to such a role. Thus there may indeed exist several computational descriptions of Karl's performance if there are any at all, but not all of these need adequately explain it. My suggestion will be that it is the fact that Karl can be related to a computational scheme that plays such an explanatory role that grounds our ascription to Karl of the inductive method described by that computational scheme. I shall describe a further constraint on partial realization motivated by some reflections on what this requirement means. It will finally be easy to see that thus supplemented the definition of partial realization excludes, on rather trivial grounds, all but finitely many 'skeptical' alternatives of the sort typified by Kripke's function *quus*.

C.   Turing Machines and Their Realizations

I shall describe and illustrate a definition of partial realization for *Turing machines*. Turing machines are only one of many classes of algorithms which could have been considered. However, the skeptical objection to computational models of dispositions or capacities is quite general; it should apply to Turing machine based models if it applies anywhere, and a response to it in this case will suggest a parallel response for any class of programs of a certain not-very-special sort. Thus it is not implied that the inductive capacities of an actual agent can be adequately modeled by a Turing machine, but only that a satisfactory response to Kripke's problem for this case should be readily generalizable. I begin, then, with a review of some basic notions from the Turing model of computability.

A Turing machine is usually pictured as a device that can assume finitely many machine states and is equipped with a (potentially) infinite tape and a printer/scanner that can execute instructions of the following two types: (a) the scanner can move one unit left or right on the tape and the machine change state when it is scanning a given symbol and is in a specified state; (b) the machine can replace a symbol S with another symbol and change state if it is scanning S and in a specified state. The symbols are chosen from a finite alphabet $\{S_0, ..., S_{n-1}\}$, the **machine alphabet**. Turing thought of his 'machines' as characterizing certain ideal clerical routines, or mechanical procedures.[6] A **machine word** for a Turing machine M is a finite string of symbols from its alphabet, and a function f mapping a set W of machine words for M to machine words for M is said to be **computed** by M if, when any word $\alpha \in W$ is inscribed on the tape for M and a computation is initiated (say, by placing the printer/scanner over the first symbol of α and the machine in a chosen initial state), the computation terminates at a time when $f(\alpha)$ appears on the tape. Such a function is said to be **Turing computable** if some Turing machine computes it.

Turing machines are of course not physical but abstract automata. Physical devices are not equipped with infinite computational space or time (this is a form of Kripke's 'finiteness' problem); and in any actual physical system the possibility of machine malfunction must be taken account of. Turing machines possess various mathematical representations. For example, let $S_0, ...S_{n-1}$ be the alphabet symbols of a Turing machine M, and let $q_0, ..., q_{m-1}$ be distinct symbols representing its states. Let 'L' and 'R' represent the operations *move one space left* and *move one space right*, re-

---

[6]See A. M. Turing, "On Computable Numbers, with an application to the Entscheidungs problem," *Proceedings of the London Mathematical Society* 42 (1938): 230–65, reprinted in *The Undecidable*, edited by M. Davis (New York: Chelsea, 1958).

spectively. Then in a familiar representation the instructions of M may be described by a set of quadruples of the following types:

(1) $\qquad\qquad\qquad\qquad (q_i, S_k, L, q_j)$

(2) $\qquad\qquad\qquad\qquad (q_i, S_k, R, q_j)$

(3) $\qquad\qquad\qquad\qquad (q_i, S_k, S_p, q_j).$

These instructions determine the computational transitions of M: (1) and (2) say "when in stage q_i and scanning a locus with content S_k, move the scanner to the next locus left (right) and assume state q_j"; (3) says "when scanning S_k in state q_i, print S_p and assume state q_j." The **computations** of M arise by applying the instructions of M to initially given machine words.

Two simple examples of Turing algorithms will be useful. Both concern computation over a set N of words generated from an initial word '1' by concatenation. The elements of N represent, in the obvious sense, positive integers, and we sometimes speak of functions from N to N as functions of positive integers. The *successor function* on N associates any numeral $\mathbf{k}_n$ with $\mathbf{k}_{n+1}$. The machine computing it is described as follows. At any input, the computation is initiated on the left most locus on which a symbol is printed with the machine in an initial state q_0. The monitor moves stepwise to the right until it reaches an unoccupied locus. It then prints '1' and the computation halts. This action may be represented by the following quadruples:

$$(q_0, 1, R, q_0)$$
$$(q_0, e, 1, q_1),$$

where 'e' represents a blank (regarded as associated with every alphabet) and 'q_1' a halting state.

A second example is the addition function $+$. Its arguments are pairs of positive integers, which may be represented on the tape by two numerals punctuated by a blank. The computation proceeds by replacing the blank separating the two numerals with a ' 1' and erasing the terminal '1' on the right, an action that is described by the following program:

$$(q_0, 1, R, q_0)$$
$$(q_0, e, 1, q_1)$$
$$(q_1, 1, R, q_1)$$
$$(q_1, e, L, q_2)$$
$$(q_2, 1, e, q_3).$$

A **configuration** of a Turing machine M is a complete specification of the contents of its tape, its machine state, and the locus being scanned at a time. Given any configuration of M, the instructions of M determine the next configuration. The computations of M may be identified with finite sequences of configurations of M arising from initial configurations by successive application of the instructions of M. An **interpretation** of M in an idealized physical system S is a mapping of configurations of M onto states of S that arises by assigning physical significance to the relevant machine data (for example, 'M is in state q', 'M is scanning locus l', etc.). An interpretation f of M in S is said to be a **realization** of M in S if, under f, the computations of M correspond to causal chains in S, and S is said to **instantiate** M if there exists a realization of M in S. A disposition or capacity of S may be explained by exhibiting a realization of M in S that associates the initial and terminal configurations of M with the properties of S that are causally linked, as 'inputs' and 'outputs', by that disposition or capacity. Our question arises precisely because this model of computational explanation does not apply to actual physical systems but only to their idealized analogues; for the reasons Kripke adduces, no actual system literally instantiates any nontrivial Turing machine. At best, an actual system may *approximately* instantiate a Turing machine. Our problem is to explicate what we are saying when we claim that an actual system and a Turing machine are related in this way.

Before moving on to the solution to the problem I have to offer, it is worth pausing to briefly consider a solution that naturally presents itself. It might be suggested that a system approximately instantiates a Turing algorithm if the system would instantiate that algorithm if its computational capacity were appropriately enhanced: for example, if limitations of computational space and time were removed that prevent its executing computations of arbitrary complexity. While something like this proposal may seem very natural, there are two difficulties with it which appear fatal. One is that the idea of *supplementing the computational capacity of the system* makes sense only if we already know *which* physical limitations stand in the way of its realizing a Turing algorithm; for example, one would need to know which properties of the system define its computational "space," and more generally which physical changes in the system count as *extensions* of its computational capacity. However, the answers to these questions are not given in advance, and different answers will lead to different answers to the question of which machines the system approximately instantiates. Consider, for example, an attempted approximate realization of the Turing machine for the successor function in terms of a mechanical device equipped with a finite tape, a printer and a scanner which are set up to behave according to the successor algorithm for inputs that can be inscribed on the tape. We increase its computational capacity by adding more tape. But is this all we must do? Suppose, for example, that the motors in the machine break down if the length of its inputs becomes too great. If we do not increase the capacity of the motors at the same time, we will not get a better approximate realization of the successor algorithm: but we may get an excellent realization of a different algorithm. Let K be the least upper bound of the arguments for which the motors do not break down. What is to prevent us from saying that the device instantiates a machine that computes the function that coincides with the successor function on all integers $\leq K$, and that coincides with the identity function on larger arguments? This example suggests that we will not know *which* adjustments in the device are relevant to applying the suggested criterion of approximate instantiation *unless we already know what algorithm we are trying to approximate.* In that case, of course, the criterion is superfluous.

However, suppose that we know *in advance* what modifications are to be carried out in applying the criterion in a given case. There is still an obvious difficulty: no matter what adjustments we make, we will still be left with a finite physical system. It is implausible that any such system can literally instantiate a Turing algorithm; that was where we started. The obvious, but quite useless, reply is that for our present purposes we need not talk of 'instantiation' but only of 'increasingly good approximate instantiation'. The problem with this reply is that it assumes that we already understand what it is for a one physical system to be a *better* instantiation of a Turing machine than another. But the problems to be solved in characterizing this relation seem not unlike those of explicating the original relation of approximate instantiation.

D. Partial Realization

In this section I shall characterize a notion of approximate instantiation for Turing machines. I begin with a rough sketch of the idea behind the definition.

Let M be a Turing machine. A configuration of M, I said, is a complete description of the contents of the tape, the space being scanned, and the machine state at some time. The **configuration space of** M is the collection of all configurations of M, which we denote by 'cnf(M)'. Where M is fixed, a **path in** cnf(M) is a finite sequence of configurations of M that arises by iterated application of the instructions of M, beginning with an initial configuration. A **computation** of M is a maximal (inextendible) path in cnf(M). My suggestion for capturing the required concept of approximate instantiation arises from a natural generalization of the notion of realization introduced in section C. A **partial interpretation** of a Turing machine

M in an actual system S is a *partial function* mapping the configuration space for M into the collection of states of S, that is, a function mapping a subset of $\mathrm{cnf}(M)$ to states of S. The domain of such a function consists of all configurations of M satisfying a fixed bound p on computational space, that is, the number of machine-spaces specified in a configuration. A partial interpretation f of M in S is extended to paths sequentially; that is, if $\sigma = \langle \sigma_1, ..., \sigma_n \rangle$ is a path in $\mathrm{cnf}(M)$, $f(\sigma) = \langle f(\sigma_1), ..., f(\sigma_n) \rangle$. Finally a partial interpretation f of M in S constitutes a **partial realization** of M if any path of less than a fixed length q lying in the domain of f corresponds, under f, to a stable sequence of causal transitions in S. The number q may be thought of as a bound on the *time* of computations. Thus the idea is that, under a partial realization, paths in the configuration space of M satisfying fixed bounds on space and time correspond to *causal paths* in S. We will then say that S approximately instantiates M if there exists a partial realization of M in S; the associated numbers q and p give measures of the degree of approximation. The remainder of this section is devoted to making the present suggestions precise.

Some additional notions will be useful. If S is a physical system, by '$\mathcal{P}(S)$' we denote the collection of all causally possible states of S. I shall use Kim's notation $[S, \psi, t]$ to express S's falling under the property ψ at a time t, suppressing reference to time when possible. The items so described will be called **event-structures over S.**[7] An **etiology** of an event-structure **e** in a possible world w is a finite sequence $\langle \mathbf{e}_1, ..., \mathbf{e}_n \rangle$ of event-structures such that $\mathbf{e}_n = \mathbf{e}$ and for each $i < n$, $\mathbf{e}_i$ exists and causes $\mathbf{e}_{i+1}$ in w. A computational capacity of S is characterized by its possible manifestations, which in turn may be described by a relation holding between possible worlds and pairs of event-structures. Thus, Karl's capacity to add may be described by the collection of couples $\langle w, \alpha \rangle$ such that w is a world and α a pair $\langle \mathbf{e}_1, \mathbf{e}_2 \rangle$ of event-structures that specify an input-state and an output-state for an addition in w; $\mathbf{e}_1$, for example, might be the event-structure consisting in Karl's being queried about the sum of two integers, and $\mathbf{e}_2$ an event-structure configuring his response.

I have been developing the idea that an actual system approximately instantiates a Turing machine M by literally instantiating a structure that arises from M by imposing limitations on the complexity of computations of M. Call such a structure an 'elementary restriction' of M. A partial realization of M in S may then be thought of as a realization of an elementary restriction of M in S. Thus, let p and q be positive integers which as before we think of as giving bounds on the space and time used

---

[7]See Kim, "Causation, Nomic Subsumption, and the Concept of Event," in *Supervenience and Mind* (Cambridge: Cambridge University Press, 1993), sec. 1.

by computations of M. The **elementary restriction** $M_{p,q}$ of M is the set of all computations of M of length $\leq q$ which involve $\leq p$ machine loci. By an **interpretation** of $M_{p,q}$ in S we understand roughly a mapping of machine data in $M_{p,q}$ to states of S; such a mapping induces a physical interpretation of each computation of M of length $\leq q$ involving at most p machine loci. Formally, we may identify an interpretation of $M_{p,q}$ in S with a triple $\langle f, g, h \rangle$ of functions such that (a) f maps the state symbols of M to $\mathcal{P}(S)$; (b) g maps $\{1, ..., p\}$ to $\mathcal{P}(S)$; and (c) maps the set of all pairs $\langle x, n \rangle$ such that x is a machine symbol and n a positive integer $\leq p$ to $\mathcal{P}(S)$. For each state symbol y, $f(y)$ is the state associated with y in S; for each $n \leq p$, $g(n)$ is the state interpreting 'is scanning locus n' in S; and for each machine symbol x and each integer $n \leq p$, $h(x, n)$ is the state interpreting 'x is inscribed in space n' in S.

For any integer $p > 0$, we denote by $\mathrm{cnf}_M(p)$ the set of all configurations of M involving at most p machine loci. If J is an interpretation of $M_{p,q}$ in S, J^* is the mapping of $\mathrm{cnf}_M(p)$ into $\mathcal{P}(S)$ induced, in the obvious way, by J. Thus, for each configuration $z \in \mathrm{cnf}_M(p)$, $J^*(z)$ is the conjunction of the properties in $\mathcal{P}(S)$ corresponding, under J, to the machine description specified by z. An interpretation J of $M_{p,q}$ in S will be said to **realize** $M_{p,q}$ over a collection of possible situations if, roughly, computations of $M_{p,q}$ correspond, under J, to causal etiologies in those situations. A bit more precisely, if H is a set of possible worlds, J realizes $M_{p,q}$ over H if, for each computation $\langle y_1, ..., y_k \rangle$ in $M_{p,q}$ and each world $w \in H$, if S exemplifies $J^*(y_1)$ in w, then the sequence

$$\langle [S, J^*(y_1)], ..., [S, J^*(y_k)] \rangle$$

is an etiology in w. A **partial realization of M over H** is then officially a realization of an elementary restriction of M over H.

These materials enable us to answer the question of what it is for a capacity of S to have a computational explanation in terms of the Turing machine M. Let R be the relation between possible worlds and pairs of event-structures representing the capacity we wish to explain. We define $\mathcal{W}_R$ to be the set of worlds at which that capacity is exercised:

$$\mathcal{W}_R = \{w | \ (\exists \alpha) \langle w, \alpha \rangle \in R\}.$$

If $M_{p,q}$ is an elementary restriction of M, then, an interpretation J of $M_{p,q}$ in S will be said to constitute a **basis** for the capacity described by R if

(a) J is a realization of $M_{p,q}$ over $\mathcal{W}_R$;
(b) For any world w and any pair $\alpha = \langle \mathbf{e}_1, \mathbf{e}_2 \rangle$ of event-structures, $\langle w, \alpha \rangle \in R$ iff there exists a computation $\langle z_1, ..., z_n \rangle$ of $M_{p,q}$ such that $\mathbf{e}_1 = [S, J^*(z_1)]$ and $\mathbf{e}_2 = [S, J^*(z_n)]$.

This is roughly to say that an interpretation of an elementary restriction of M is a basis for a capacity of S if, under the partial mapping of configurations of M to states of S induced by the interpretation, computations of M correspond to causal paths underlying the possible manifestations of that capacity. The idea is that, under the interpretation in question, the relevant restriction of M describes the causal structure of the capacity.

E.   Indeterminacies of Partial Realization

What is accomplished by these definitions? I have attempted to say when an architecture of the sort described by a Turing machine constitutes a computational basis for a capacity of a finite system in terms of the conditions under which the system instantiates a Turing machine to within fixed bounds of computational complexity. How does this story assist us with problems of interpretation?

Consider an actual physical system that we wish to interpret as computing a function mapping a set W of words from a finite alphabet to W. We begin, first, with a construal of the states of the system that constitute inputs and outputs for finitely many words in W, and second with a rough conception of the circumstances of normal function. In the most favorable case, these data together will fix a description of a certain capacity: its manifestations will be given by the pairs $\langle w, \alpha \rangle$ such that w is one of the normal worlds in which the capacity is exercised, and α is a pair coupling the system's exemplifications of the relevant input and output states in w. What then are the functions on the total set W of words that the system may be correctly said to compute? At a first approximation, they are the mappings computed by the Turing machines in an alphabet for W which are a basis for the capacity in question.[8] Of course, there are ways in which the actual circumstances of interpretation may fall short of the 'best possible' case just .described. This is owing to the possibility of miscomputation, even under circumstances of normal function. These circumstances fix at most a *propensity* of an input to generate a fixed output. In this case, the worlds w aforementioned will be restricted to a representative subset of the situations that embody manifestations of the propensity in question.

Under what conditions is such a propensity uniquely characterized by a

---

[8]Notice that the set W of words may be syntactically generated by more than one alphabet. For example, let W be the set of words that represent even integers less than 10^{10}. Then the usual alphabet consisting of the single stroke symbol 1 generates W, but so does the alphabet consisting of the single dyad 11, as well as the alphabet consisting of the words of W itself. Thus the underlying machine alphabet is not fixed in advance; this lends another dimension of indeterminacy to the problem of computational interpretation.

Turing machine of which the system is a *partial* realization? I shall consider two questions. Say that two Turing machines are **congruent** when their instructions can be identified by a correlation of their alphabets and state symbols. First, assuming a fixed representation of a capacity of a system, does there exist a basis for that capacity in terms of a Turing machine that is unique up to congruence? The answer (not surprisingly, from Kripke's point of view) will be that there generally does not. We may then ask, second, whether there are further constraints on partial realization which could be used to motivate the choice of one such basis over any other.

The intuitive force of the requirement of partial realization can be illustrated by revisiting Kripke's example *quus*. Imagine a system that returns (notations for) sums of integers given (notations for) integers of bounded size as inputs. Recall that the function *quus* is defined by setting a quus b equal to $a + b$ on all arguments a, b for which the system has a disposition to return a value and equal to 5 otherwise. The question was why such a system might not properly be said to be computing *quus* as well as $+$. For concreteness, we think of the system as a physical device equipped with a printer/scanner that moves back and forth over a segmented track. The device is a partial realization of the addition machine in virtue of a partial mapping of the configurations of the machine onto states of the device under which the computations of the machine describe the workings of the device to within fixed bounds of space and time, the bound on space being given by the length of the track. Consider now a Turing machine computing *quus*. How might it work? Given a pair of integers as input, the machine might first execute a subroutine that *counts* the numbers represented. If for both numbers the answer is less than the relevant bound, the machine adds the numbers. If, on the other hand, the answer exceeds that bound, the machine prints '5'.

It is easily seen that the machine just described will *not* generally constitute a partial realization of such an algorithm for *quus*. The reason is simply that there is no reason to expect that the device will instantiate, for example, the counting subroutine. If it did, one could identify a process in the device that precedes the mechanism executing the addition algorithm for each pair of arguments which the device has a disposition to add, a process that can be interpreted as counting the length of the inputs. This is owing to the fact that, given any pair of inputs, the indicated algorithm for *quus* (one is tempted to suppose, *any* Turing algorithm for *quus*) must *first* determine the size of the inputs, and *then* execute one of a pair of alternative subprograms. There need be nothing in the workings of the machine I have imagined that corresponds to such a branching procedure.

The question is now whether, up to congruence, there is a *unique* Turing machine which is a basis for the computational capacity of such a device. In this case, one could say that the device's dispositions uniquely determine a certain function. However, it is not difficult to see that the answer is in the negative. I will describe the problem as it arises for the successor machine, but the difficulty is quite general. Let T be the Turing machine described earlier for the successor function, and suppose that a partial realization of T in a system S accounts for S's capacity to compute finitely many values of that function. Let N be the least number greater than all those arguments for which the system will return a value; we suppose that, for inputs $\geq N$, the device breaks down in a certain state with the input still inscribed on the tape. Then S must also be a partial realization of a Turing machine computing the function f on positive integers defined by

$$f(n) = \begin{cases} n+1, & \text{if } 1 \leq n < N \\ n, & \text{if } n \geq N \end{cases}$$

Similarly, consider the function g whose domain consists of positive integers $< N$ and is defined for each n in that domain by $g(n) = n + 1$. T computes g: for g is simply the restriction of the successor function to numerical arguments $< N$. But it is easily seen that S is also a partial realization of a rather less informative Turing machine computing g. First, the machine for g:

(α) *The Rote Machine.* The alphabet of this Turing algorithm consists of two sets of symbols $a_1, ..., a_{N-1}$ and $b_1, ..., b_{N-1}$; its states are given by $\{q_0, q_1\}$ where q_0 represents the initial state and q_1 the halting state. The algorithm is

$$(q_0, a_1, b_1, q_1)$$
$$(q_0, a_2, b_2, q_1)$$
$$\vdots$$
$$(q_0, a_{N-1}, b_{N-1}, q_1).$$

Intuitively, the rote machine is just a catalogue of the responses that the system gives for the positive integers $n < N$. For each such n, a_n is interpreted in S as the input state associated with the argument n, and b_n is the corresponding output state. The state symbols q_0 and q_1 are mapped onto the same states of S with which they are associated by the given partial realization of T; S is then a realization (and thus, to within the relevant bounds on space and time, a partial realization) of the Rote Machine.

Next, the machine for f:

(β) *The Tracking Machine* has the alphabet of T and state symbols

$q_1, ..., q_N, \bar{q}$; q_1 represents the initial state. Its instructions are

$$(q_1, 1, R, q_2) \qquad (q_2, B, 1, \bar{q})$$
$$(q_2, 1, R, q_3) \qquad (q_3, B, 1, \bar{q})$$

$$\vdots \qquad\qquad \vdots$$

$$(q_{N-1}, 1, R, q_N) \qquad (q_N, B, 1, \bar{q}).$$

The Tracking Machine behaves like the canonical machine T except that its state symbols are indexed in such a way that in the course of a computation it keeps track of the number of right-translations it executes, and thereby tracks the length of its input. When in a computation the index of the state symbol reaches the bound N and a '1' is being scanned, no instructions apply, and the computation terminates. We now specify an interpretation θ of the Tracking Machine in S; θ coincides with the given partial interpretation of T in S on all data except the state symbols $q_1, ..., q_N, \bar{q}$. The interpretation θ maps each state symbol q_i onto the property that the given partial realization associates with q_0, and maps $\bar{q}$ onto the property thus associated with q_1. θ is then a realization of the Tracking Machine in S.

F.   Other Conditions

It is clear that analogues of the examples just considered arise quite generally, and constitute 'skeptical alternatives' with which Kripke may confront a hypothesis about the computational underpinnings of a propensity of an actual system. These examples provide only rather limited support for the skeptic: they are based on quite special tricks, and do not lead to the open class of indeterminacies suggested by Kripke's argument; but they do exist.

A possible response to these examples begins by drawing a distinction between uses of Turing machines or other computational models to describe a capacity of a system and uses of such a model to explain that capacity. (In the same way, we can distinguish between computational models that can be used to predict the performance of a system and those that can be used to explain it.) Talk of 'the function computed' by a system should be referred, it may be argued, to the computational model that best explains the capacity in question. Can the explanation/prediction asymmetry drive a wedge between a preferred computational scheme and its skeptical alternatives?

As a test case, let us reconsider the Rote Machine. The Rote Machine is on a par with the initial machine T as regards prediction but scores very poorly in point of explanatoriness. It is, in effect, simply a catalogue describing a repertoire of responses. Both the canonical machine T and the Tracking Machine do better in this regard, for each describes to some degree the causal structure underpinning those responses. An explanation of a capacity in terms of a Turing machine is not a causal explanation, but its explanatory content is in part a function of the information it conveys about the *structure* of a satisfactory causal explanation of that capacity; in conjunction with a partial realization of the machine, it should determine such an explanation. The Rote Machine specifies no such information; it is simply a list that correlates inputs to outputs.

The Tracking Machine does better, but is in other respects systematically misleading about the causal structure of its models. A partial realization of the Tracking Machine may assign distinct physical interpretations to the state symbols $q_1, ..., q_N$; it is only by identifying each of the states $q_1, ..., q_N$, that we recover the canonical machine. The Tracking Machine by its very design lacks the essential recursive feature of the canonical one, which returns the machine to the *same* state each time a right-translation is effected that begins and ends with the machine scanning a '1'. These observations about the Tracking Machine suggest the rule that for a Turing Machine to be fully informative about the causal structure of its approximate physical models, the partial realization of the machine that describes such a model should correlate the relevant machine states with states of that system in a one-to-one way, and more generally that the induced partial function mapping computations of the machine to causal chains in the model should constitute an isomorphism. The contemplated realization of the Tracking Machine in models of the canonical one manifestly violates this rule, which might be called the **isomorphism condition**.[9]

It is interesting that combining the isomorphism condition with the definition of partial realization leads immediately to a response to one blanket indeterminacy claim. One form of Kripke's skeptical thesis held that any actual system which can be regarded as computing a given number-theoretic function f can also equally be regarded as computing any recursive function that agrees with f on a sufficiently long finite initial segment. Transposed to our present setting, that claim would be understood to say that any actual system that approximately instantiates a machine computing f also and equally approximately instantiates some machine computing any recursive function that agrees with f on a sufficiently long finite initial segment.

---

[9]The natural way to ensure that a partial realization of a Turing machine meets the isomorphism condition is to require the interpretative functions that generate it to be one-to-one. But the requirement is meaningful in any situation in which we have a concept of instantiation for whole configurations of the machine, independently of how that relation is defined. The requirement is that configurations map in a one-to-one way onto the realizing states for them, and that under this map computations correspond to causal paths.

On essentially trivial combinatorial grounds, however, this claim is false if 'approximate instantiation' is interpreted in terms of *isomorphic partial realization*.[10] If S is an actual finite system, then the collection $\mathcal{P}(S)$ of causally possible states of S is, presumably, finite. It then follows easily that, up to congruence of machines, S can constitute an isomorphic partial realization of only finitely many Turing machines over any fixed alphabet. Distinct number theoretic functions cannot be computed by congruent machines over the canonical alphabet N. Thus there are only finitely many functions computed by some machine over that alphabet of which S constitutes an isomorphic partial realization. All but finitely many 'skeptical alternatives' to f can thus be excluded.

The general constraint suggested by the preceding examples is that, for the purpose of construing a system as computing a given function, we shall consider only machines which are *relevantly informative* about the structure of a causal explanation of the system's propensity to produce values of the function given its arguments as inputs. Both the Rote Machine and the Tracking Machine infringe this rule, in rather different ways. Such requirements might be considered for roles as constraints on radical interpretation, providing that a proper specification of Karl's inductive method in terms of a Turing machine or other computational model should be relevantly informative about the causal structure of the propensity, in this case an epistemic one, that it describes. Such a requirement would be understood to constrain the use of the notion of partial realization in the context of radical interpretation: in particular, its use in characterizing Karl's relation to his rule of evaluation. However, a constraint of this sort must be applied with two cautionary notes in mind. First, as an interpretive constraint, a causal informativeness requirement functions in concert with the other principles explored in the body of this chapter. It would say that, other things equal, an interpretation is the more satisfactory the more of the relevant sort of information it provides; but of course other things need not *be* equal. Thus, for example, the possibility exists, though it seems rather unlikely, that no interpretation satisfying the isomorphism condition adverted to above very well fits the other interpretive constraints I have suggested. In this circumstance, we would normally prefer an interpretation that meets the other constraints well to one that does not but meets the isomorphism requirement.

Second, we want a proper specification of Karl's inductive method to provide the *right sort* of information about the explanation of Karl's inductive performance. I said in 2.2.2 that what is wanted in the interpre-

---

[10]That is to say, as requiring a partial realization of the machine in the system in question that satisfies the isomorphism condition.

tive context is not information about the neurophysiological explanation of
Karl's belief-states nor one couched in noncognitive computational terms,
but one framed in terms of Karl's instantiation of epistemic rules. Just
what this means is difficult to crystallize into a concise constraint, but the
following observation can be made. Recall from 2.2.3 that it is part of our
understanding of the Rationalization Principle that Karl's attitudes can be
mapped onto states of Karl as a physical system in such a way that intentional explanations of his basic actions correspond to causal explanations of
those events. The idea behind the second caveat is that the relevant belief-
states should be the primary locus of the required partial realization of a
computational description of Karl's inductive method. The requirement of
causal informativeness should be understood to enjoin such a description to
reflect the structure of a causal explanation of Karl's belief-states in which
other such states play the primary causal roles. We are interested in a level
of description for which beliefs are represented as being generated by other
beliefs; from the point of view of interpretation, the doxastic sphere is in
that sense autonomous.

G.   Concluding Remarks

My main aim in this postscript has been to describe a concept of imperfect
or approximate instantiation. Such a concept is required for my purposes
in this chapter, since on my account it is part of the aim of an interpretation of an agent to describe the agent's inductive method, which in turn
is represented in terms of a set of belief-forming procedures which are, in
an appropriate sense, *instantiated* by the agent. I have suggested that a
concept suitable for this purpose is that of the *partial realization* of a program embodying those rules, that is, roughly, a realization of a restriction
of that program to fixed bounds of computational complexity. By way of
illustration, I have spelled out this idea in reasonable detail for the case of
Turing algorithms; but extending it to other computational models would
seem to present no serious difficulty.

Suitably generalized, the notion of partial realization acquires a very
wide significance, and is applicable to many of the computational architectures usually considered.[11] The corresponding notions of partial realization
are coarse: the primary units of interpretation are whole configurations for
the architectures in question; in particular, it is worth noting that in the
general case we can get along without a structural distinction between phenomena in the interpreting systems that correspond to *computations* and
those that constitute *data* or *representations computed*. But the discussion

---

[11]In particular, those of the von Neumann type.

of the case of Turing machines shows that the notion of partial realization is strong enough to render the computational basis of an actual disposition or capacity at least substantially determinate. These considerations are readily generalizable. Indeterminacies of a limited sort survive; but I argued that we have good reasons, at least in the case of the Turing machine based models, to set aside two sorts of residual indeterminacy that naturally present themselves. I do not know if there are other types of indeterminacy of partial realization. But with reference to Kripke's problem, enough has been said, I believe, to show that a finite propensity of an actual system may at least largely determine a computational scheme with an infinite domain of definition.

THREE

THE ROOTS OF REFERENCE

The previous chapter developed a set of constitutive constraints on radical
interpretation that together comprise what I have called 'the Conformal
Framework'. However, it did not answer the question of how, within this
framework, the reference of expressions in specific categories is determined.
In the present chapter I address this question for the following sorts:

(1) N (proper names);
(2) Obs (observational predicates, broadly construed);
(3) NK (natural kind terms, broadly construed).

One point of addressing these cases together is that our account of reference
for expressions of these sorts exhibits a feature that might aptly be called
'local holism'[1]: in each case the answer provided takes the form of saying
how the reference of expressions of the given sort is fixed relative to the
interpretations of expressions in one or both of the other sorts. In each case,
the answer given is justified directly in terms of the Conformal Framework.
The mechanisms of reference to be suggested in this chapter have the status
of enabling proposals with respect to the satisfaction of the constitutive
principles suggested earlier, in particular the Principle of Conformality.

3.1 Naming and Conformality

A noteworthy fact about the Conformal Framework is that it appears to
sanction a scheme of reference for the language of an agent or population without regard to the *origin* of the correspondence relation which that
scheme of reference describes. This aspect of the present framework con-
trasts strikingly with various forms of the causal theory of reference. In the
broadest possible terms, for the causal theory the reference of an expression
on a given occasion of its use is fixed by a certain type of causal chain connecting that occasion to an original occasion (or occasions) of its use, which
generally involves an appropriate sort of direct contact with the extension

---

[1]This term is due to Christopher Peacocke, *Thoughts*, Aristotelian Society Series 4
(Oxford: Blackwell, 1986).

of the expression. This idea has been developed primarily for proper names and natural kind terms.[2] It is therefore natural to ask whether, in the first place, there are cases where the conclusions of the account of the reference of proper names and natural kind words to be suggested in this chapter diverge from those of the causal theory, and second, if so, whether these cases cut for or against the present account. It will be seen that there are such cases; and I will argue that they support the present account.

3.1.1   The Conformal Criterion

How might the Principle of Conformality help fix the reference of proper names in a fragment of English, assuming that the reference of descriptive predicates of the fragment has been fixed. The question is how the selection of one object rather than another as the reference of a proper name contributes to conformal explanations. Suppose, for example, that 'Karl' and 'Mary' are proper names of the fragment. Consider the following sketch of a conformal explanation of Mary's ability to contact Karl by telephone. Let $\mathcal{F}$ be an interpretation of Mary, $\mathbf{R}$ the scheme of reference associated with $\mathcal{F}$ and $\mathbf{A}$ the description of Mary's attitudes provided by $\mathcal{F}$ in her language. Let $\mathbf{A}$ ascribe to Mary a set of beliefs that, under $\mathbf{R}$, constitute an accurate description of Karl's location over time, and a set of beliefs that specify the number of a functioning telephone at each location. In addition, according to $\mathbf{A} + \mathbf{R}$, Mary has the normal repertoire of beliefs about telephones, and is capable of telling time. Thus at any time, Mary can determine a sequence of basic actions that constitute dialing the number of a phone in Karl's vicinity at that time. These observations are the basis of a conformal explanation of Mary's capacity to contact Karl under suitable circumstances.

This entirely commonsense account is a typical conformal explanation-sketch. We may imagine Mary's beliefs about Karl's location to be given by sentences of the form

$$\text{Karl is at } p \text{ at } t,$$

---

[2]The literature on the causal theory of naming is large, and I have made no systematic attempt to canvass it here. I will consider mainly Kripke's original formulation in *Naming and Necessity* (Cambridge, Mass.: Harvard University Press, 1980). An excellent elaboration of the basic account considered here may be found in Michael Devitt, *Designation* (New York: Columbia University Press, 1981), who also considers some problems similar to those discussed hereafter. The corresponding view for natural kind terms was first developed by Kripke, *Naming and Necessity*, lecture 3, and Hilary Putnam in, among other places, "The Meaning of 'Meaning'" and "Explanation and Reference," in *Mind, Language and Reality, Philosophical Papers*, vol. 2 (Cambridge: Cambridge University Press, 1975).

where 'p' and 't' represent singular terms that, according to **R**, specify a location and a time. Clearly the conformal explanation of the fact that Mary can contact Karl by telephone will be destroyed if the reference of the name 'Karl' is shifted. The efficacy of that explanation depends on the correctness of the causal story Mary can assemble about the result of her using the telephone at different times; and this story may go seriously wrong if the referent of the name 'Karl' is shifted. From the standpoint of (PC), such a shift is acceptable if and only if it generates a comparable explanation; but we will not obtain another explanation if the new referent of the name 'Karl' does not have the causal powers ascribed to Karl in the original explanation. If the interpretation of the other referential devices in the explanation is held fixed, no one will serve unless he would pick up a telephone connected to Mary in the circumstances in question.

On the individualistic version of (PC), the admissible schemes of reference for Mary's language pair names with objects in such a way that Mary's accomplishments are maximized. (Recall from the previous chapter that a second-order action is an *accomplishment* relative to an interpretation if it is conformally explicable therein.) Thus it is normally the case that a proper name of Mary's language refers to the object that best fits Mary's beliefs about the causal role of its bearer, where the beliefs in question are weighted according to their relevance to Mary's interests. It is not, however, the fact that the object in question satisfies a certain subset of Mary's beliefs that *makes* it an admissible referent on (PC); otherwise, this account would collapse into a form of the 'cluster' version of the description theory. The point here is that the assignment that best satisfies Mary's beliefs about the causal role of the referent of the name which are most relevant to her interests will normally be the one that optimizes the availability of conformal explanations of her actions; for these explanations trade on the accuracy of the picture that Mary has of the causal connections between her prospective basic actions and desired outcomes.

The obvious objection to this idea is that Mary may acquire the name 'Karl' without possessing the information required for explanations of the sort illustrated above. An important insight of Kripke's discussion of naming is that a name may possess a determinate reference in the language of an agent in virtue of the fact that the agent is embedded in a social context in which its reference is determined.[3] That insight may be adapted to the present account in the following way. The social version of (PC) helps fix the reference of the name 'Karl' in the language of a population of which Mary is a member. It is the individual who best fits a socially defined conception of Karl's causal role, where the elements of that con-

---

[3] See Kripke, *Naming and Necessity*, lecture 2.

ception are weighted according to the interests of individuals and groups across the community. The idea is that 'Karl' refers to Karl in Mary's language in virtue of the fact that sufficiently many individuals or groups in her community exercise capacities which are conformally explicable by assigning Karl to that name in *their* dialects. Thus, as in Kripke's account, the work of fixing the reference of proper names is socially shared. This is one reason why a complete interpretation of Mary normally requires an overall interpretation of Mary's community. We will find others.

The proposal, then, is roughly this. In framing a complete interpretation of the population in question, we will assign to a name in the language of the population that reference which best fits the causal role ascribed to the bearer of the name by individuals and groups within the population as a whole, where the various elements of this *causal profile* are weighted according to their relevance to the goals of these individuals or groups. This is a proposal as to how the reference of names is fixed: as in Kripke's account, a distinction is to be maintained between fixing the reference of a proper name and giving its meaning. In any counterfactual situation, the referent of the name is that object that meets the indicated requirement in the *actual* world. As in Kripke's account, then, the reference of names is rigid.

Two points of a preliminary nature deserve comment. First, it should be fairly obvious that the suggested criterion does not account for the reference of *all* proper names. It is intended to explicate the contribution (PC) can make the settling the reference of proper names, where it can make a contribution at all. It does, I believe, fix a best candidate for the reference of most proper names, but there is a minority for which it doesn't apply simply because their referents don't figure in conformal explanations at all. For example, if Kripke is correct in holding that names can be introduced purely by means of definite descriptions, we might introduce a name by means of a description that specifies such an object; for example, 'the last surviving dinosaur', 'the youngest Roman to fight at the battle of Actium', and so on. Another family of such cases arises from the possibility of introducing a name demonstratively to refer to a fleeting or momentary object. Such an object may be of too transient a character to acquire the sort of causal role that grounds conformal explanations. My suggestion is that we should look to (PC) to settle the reference of a name where it can; otherwise, we shall have to make other arrangements.

The second point concerns time. It should be clear that the object that best satisfies the suggested criterion for the reference of a name at one time need not do so at another; we will see examples below. The criterion must therefore be understood as saying that the reference of a proper name *over a fixed interval* is that object which best fits the relevant causal profile *over that interval.* In that case, however, there seems to be a problem about reference to nonexistent objects: when *nothing* even approximately fulfills the causal profile for a name (as will generally happen when its referent ceases to exist), the name will cease to fulfill the suggested criterion of reference to anything at all.

But the objection rests on a misunderstanding. Again, fitting a fixed causal profile for the referent of a name is not the fundamental criterion of its reference; it is, so to speak, a (rough) *criterion for* satisfying the criterion. The criterion is that an acceptable referential interpretation over an interval must optimize conformal explanations over that interval. We expect an interpretation that assigns an object fitting the relevant causal profile to the name to satisfy the criterion, if there exists such an object over the interval in question; but that is quite compatible with the possibility of an object's satisfying the criterion that does not exist over the interval. For example, Sitting Bull is the individual who best satisfies the causal profile for the name 'Sitting Bull' within the population of the United States during his lifetime; but he is *currently* the individual who if taken as the referent of the name 'Sitting Bull' optimizes conformal explanations over the entire interval from 1800 to the present.

3.1.2   Conformality and the Causal Theory

The suggested picture of reference for proper names is motivated directly in terms of the Principle of Conformality, but it is worth noting that it agrees with Kripke's account and disagrees with the description theory (and the cluster-of-properties view) as applied to some now familiar cases. Consider, for example, the Gödel/Schmitt case.[4] For this case, we imagine that all speakers of English (or German) believe that Gödel alone first proved the incompleteness of arithmetic, and that no further individuating beliefs about Gödel are common property. However, in the imagined situation, not Gödel but Schmitt actually first proved the incompleteness result. Gödel appropriated this discovery, disposing of Schmitt. The description view would suggest that Schmitt is the bearer of the name 'Gödel', but this is clearly not the case: Schmitt would have been an unsung hero of modern logic, but on the description view his most important achievement would be universally attributed to him. Kripke's mechanism fixes Gödel as the referent, since Gödel, not Schmitt, stands at the end of the relevant chain of referential transmissions.

How does the present account deal with this case? The question is whether the suggested criterion for the reference of proper names favors

---

[4]*Naming and Necessity*, pp. 83–84.

Gödel as the referent of the name 'Gödel' as opposed, for example, to Schmitt. As Kripke has described the case, the answer is that it does. There are many conformal explanations that arise from the assignment of Gödel to the name 'Gödel' that are in no way duplicated under the assignment of Schmitt arising from the description theory. Consider, for example, a variation on the case of Mary and Karl described earlier. The context is Princeton in the late forties. Gödel plays the role of Karl, and the role of Mary is played by someone (say, Einstein) with whom Gödel was in regular telephone contact at that time. We explain, on the model described above, various manifestations of Einstein's capacity to contact Gödel by telephone. This sort of example can obviously be multiplied *ad libitum*, and the explanations in question lapse if the reference of the name 'Gödel' is shifted from Gödel to Schmitt. This consideration might be offset if the contemplated reference-shift generated sufficiently many new explanations; but this is evidently not the case. Indeed, as we are conceiving the example, it is difficult to think of *any* conformal explanation that would be generated by shifting the reference of the name 'Gödel' from Gödel to Schmitt.

The suggested model of reference for N, then, agrees with Kripke's account in at least one sort of thought-experiment. However, despite the points of agreement, there are cases where the object nominated by the social version of (PC) as the referent of a proper name will diverge from the object determined by Kripke's account. The question is then whether such cases cut against the present proposal or against the causal theory. I will describe two thought-experiments that, I believe, support the present account.

For the first case, we suppose that at the end of the eighteenth century, the planet Mars was surreptitiously replaced with a similar body, call it 'Twin Mars'.[5] In the imagined situation, Twin Mars plays the role previously played by Mars in the solar system: it thus plays just the same role in astronomy, navigation, and so on as did Mars. Consider the referential behavior of the name 'Mars' under these circumstances. If we suppose that, prior to the exchange, 'Mars' referred to Mars on Kripke's account, it would have done so thereafter: the object of reference is fixed by the terminus of the Kripkean chain of referential transmissions, and it makes no difference to where the chain terminates that the exchange has taken place. It terminates in the 'baptismal' situation, and the referent of the name is the object associated with it in that situation, which in this case is the planet Mars.

---

[5]This case is similar to some considered by Gareth Evans in "The Causal Theory of Names," *Procedings of the Aristotelian Society supplementary,* vol. 47 (1973); see also the discussion of naming in *The Varieties of Reference* (Oxford: Clarendon Press, 1982). I discuss Evans's view in subsection 3.1.3.

At first, this seems to be just what we should say. It is implausible that at the moment of the exchange the reference of the name 'Mars' shifts from Mars to Twin Mars (this would, presumably, be the prediction of the 'cluster' version of the description theory: at the moment of the exchange, the object that satisfies most of the *properties* associated with Mars shifts from Mars to Twin Mars). But this intuition is not, I believe, stable through time. Twin Mars plays the role in the theoretical and practical activities of the nineteenth century that Mars played in those of the eighteenth; from the standpoint of a nineteenth century interpreter, it is *as if* these agents use 'Mars' to refer to Twin Mars. But it seems increasingly plausible to regard Twin Mars as the actual referent the more embedded this object becomes in that role. Suppose that we were to discover that an exchange of the sort described had actually taken place. How would we describe the situation? If we were to follow Kripke's original proposal, we would say that we had discovered that Mars does not now exist, and that most of the statements we have been making using the name 'Mars' are either false or lack truth value. But it does not seem to me that this is what we would say. We would say rather that the body that we are now calling 'Mars' is not the body that that name designated originally. The 'original Mars', as we might say, no longer exists, but the body we now call 'Mars' has most of the properties of the original Mars. If this is right, both the cluster-of-properties view and the causal theory on Kripke's original formulation get this case wrong. The cluster view predicts a reference shift prematurely; the causal theory predicts no reference shift at all. But there is a reference shift, over time.[6]

To apply the present account to this case: again, (PC) tells us to look for that scheme of reference which optimizes the *accomplishments* of individuals or groups from the population in question; for an accomplishment is just a conformally explicable second-order action. As applied to a proper name (again, holding the reference of other expressions fixed), we shall look for the assignment that best realizes the causal profile of its referent within that population, where the various elements of that profile are weighted according to their involvement in explicating the actual accomplishments of indivudals and groups in the population. As noted, the assignment that best satisfies this criterion at one time need not do so at another. In this case, the accomplishments of the English-speaking population in the eighteenth century are best explicated by the standard scheme of reference that

---

[6]The same conclusion is reached by certain refinements of Kripke's account, in particular Devitt's (see *Designation*). On Devitt's model, the reference of a name is (typically) *multiply* grounded by 'dubbings' that accumulate over time. This model leaves open the possibility of the sort of reference shift just described. I consider Devitt's account in 3.1.3.

assigns Mars to the name 'Mars'. On that scheme, for example, the beliefs of seafaring subsets of the earlier population include approximately correct representations of the relative positions of salient celestial objects, including Mars, by reference to which we may explicate actual navigation in conformal terms; and we can similarly explain why astronomers in the earlier period were able to obtain telescopic images of Mars under various circumstances. The analogous conformal explanations for the nineteenth century population require the hypothesis that Mars then refers to Twin Mars.

The Principle of Conformality, then, counsels a reference shift. Moreover, the principle allows us to explicate the intuition that the correctness of the ascription of reference in this case is a matter of degree: that it is increasingly right to say that the name 'Mars' refers to Twin Mars as Twin Mars becomes increasingly embedded in the matrix of causal-explanatory relations that previously connected uses of the name 'Mars' to Mars. My suggestion is that the causal-explanatory relations *relevant* to ascribing reference are precisely the relations reported by the projective explanatory stories that underlie successful conformal explanations. In the situation described, these relations multiply with time under the revised scheme of reference, and thus the number of available conformal explanations similarly increases. Since the social form of (PC) tells us to optimize the availability of conformal explanations for the population over any interval, the fit of the reference-shifted interpretation will also increase with time.

3.1.3   Dubbings and Dossiers

I shall now briefly compare the result in the present case of the suggested model of reference for N with those of two alternatives to Kripke's view. On the alternative to the 'pure' causal theory advocated by Gareth Evans, a name **n** in the language of a population P refers to an object x if the members of P intend to refer to x by using **n**, where an individual (say, Karl) *intends to refer* to x by using **n** when x is the *dominant source* of the information Karl associates with **n** (beliefs that would be represented in Ak by sentences of the form 'F**n**').[7]

Although Evans's theory is motivated, in part, by a consideration of some examples similar to the one presented earlier, I do not think that it deals satisfactorily with this case. It might be suggested that as we acquire more information in our dealings with Twin Mars, this body is increasingly a 'source', in Evans's sense, of our information or 'dossier' for 'Mars', and eventually achieves dominance in the sense required by Evans's account. In

---

[7] Evans, "The Causal Theory of Names."

this case, that account can explain the reference-shift described above; it can also explicate, in a natural way, the intuition that the shift is gradual, and that the correctness of the shifted ascription of reference is a matter of degree.

However, although my story can be filled out in this way, it does not have to be. Let us imagine that most of the information the agents in the story have about the referent of the name 'Mars' was acquired prior to the substitution of Twin Mars for Mars. In this case, *Mars* is the dominant source of the dossier indexed to 'Mars' after as well as before the exchange, whence the name 'Mars' will unwantedly designate Mars throughout. An advocate of Evans's view can avoid this problem only by a suitable weighting of the elements of the dossier for 'Mars'. If that dossier includes pieces of information spread through the population at any time, such items as 'Mars is in position p at time t', where 't' represents a time in the nineteenth century when Twin Mars is observed, may count. If you weight that sort of thing sufficiently heavily, Twin Mars may dominate after all. But the weighting seems inexplicable in isolation from something like the account I have suggested. The reason we want to say the name 'Mars' in this case *comes to refer* to Twin Mars is not, at least primarily, because this object stands in a special causal relation to beliefs given by sentences of the form '$F(\text{Mars})$' within the population in question, but rather because it plays a special role in certain practices in which the use of the name 'Mars' is embedded. The strategy I have suggested for fixing the reference of proper names operates in this case by directing us toward the assignment that best enables us to make sense of the accomplishments of such practices.

Similar conclusions can be reached on certain refinements of the causal theory. Michael Devitt has described a variant of Kripke's picture on which the reference of a name is *multiply* grounded.[8] By a 'dubbing' of an object by a name, Devitt understands an occasion on which the use of a name stands in the same sort of causal relationship to the object as an ostensive use of a name stands to its referent in Kripke's 'baptismal' situations. On the multiple grounding model, the reference of the name over an interval is fixed by a majority, or a weighted majority, of the dubbings involving the name over that interval. On this conception, the possibility of reference-change is apparent: the object fixed by such a majority vote over one interval need not be over another. The multiple grounding model then accounts for a form of the Twin Mars case, for we can imagine the case in such a way that over time dubbings accumulate that favor Twin Mars as the referent of 'Mars'.

Again, however, it is not necessary to imagine the case as developing

---

[8]See Devitt, *Designation.*

in this way. In order to test the multiple grounding conception against the conformality criterion, imagine that in the nineteenth century the population in question is not perceptually related to Twin Mars at all. The question would then be whether the case can be described in such a way that the availability of conformal explanations based on the shifted ascription of reference can be used to justify that ascription. Thus suppose that the main role of reference to Mars within the population is to facilitate the location of other celestial objects, and that because of the existence of a scheme for predicting the position of Mars on the basis of information about its orbit, this practice gets along without any *observations* of Mars. The original scheme of reference may be imagined to facilitate conformal explanations of activities, such as navigation, that depend on the ability of members of the earlier population to locate celestial objects. In the subsequent situation, the corresponding explanations require the shifted assignment of reference to 'Mars'. The rationale for a reference-shift in this situation seems to me quite comparable to that of the original version of the case, but to be independent of the assumption of direct contact with the referent of the name that is required to explain the reference-shift on the multiple-grounding model.

3.1.4 Another Thought-Experiment

To indulge in another bit of science fiction: in this story, Karl is lost in space. After years of fruitless searching, he encounters a planetary system that he believes to be our solar system. Unfortunately, however, Karl is mistaken. This planetary system is not our solar system but an exact copy of it that has arisen through a remarkable case of parallel evolution. Within this parallel system, then, there is an exact duplicate of Earth, which, following the previous chapter, we again call 'Twin Earth'; and on Twin Earth there is, or rather was, a copy or *doppelganger* of Karl (who at this moment, we might suppose, is similarly encountering our solar system). The question is what to say about the reference of names in the languages of these agents after their interchange. Suppose, for example, that the name 'Mary' refers to Mary in Karl's language before the exchange. Kripke's original picture would suggest that this name should retain its initial reference: the relevant causal chain still connects Karl's uses of 'Mary' to the situation on Earth in which Mary was named. However, the more thoroughly Karl is assimilated into the population of Twin Earth, the more reasonable it seems to say that, in his language, the name 'Mary' refers not to Mary but to her *doppelganger*. If Mary's double is a person who plays a regular part in Karl's life on Twin Earth, after a point it seems to me very implausible to say that the name 'Mary' in Karl's idiolect retains its original reference.

One response to this case available to the causal theory appeals to the distinction between Karl's language and those of the various populations of which, at various times, he is a member. Kripke's mechanism fixes the reference of a proper name in the language of a historical population: the question of what a name refers to in the language of an *agent* makes sense in general only if we place the agent in the context of such a population. The relevant populations here are those of Earth and Twin Earth, and the corresponding languages are English and a language that might be called 'Twinglish'. On both planets, it might be claimed, the name 'Mary' refers to that object standing at the end of the relevant sort of causal chain. Thus in English it refers to Mary, and in Twinglish it refers to her *doppelganger*. If Karl is regarded as a member of the English-speaking population of Earth, then the name 'Mary' in Karl's language refers to Mary; regarded as a member of the Twinglish-speaking community of Twin Earth, it refers to Twin Mary. We might then explicate the intuition that on Twin Earth the name 'Mary' in Karl's language refers to Twin Mary by reference to his membership in the population of Twinglish. We may perhaps also make sense of the idea that the name refers *less* to Twin Mary earlier than later by reference to the fact that Karl only gradually acquires membership in that population.

But of course this response will not survive a simple change in the example. Suppose that Karl's entire language group is exchanged with the corresponding population on Twin Earth. Let **R** be the initial scheme of reference for the language of Karl's population (the scheme, that is, which is appropriate to the terrestrial context), and consider the alternative $\mathbf{R}^\pi$ to **R** generated by the permutation π that exchanges terrestrial objects with their Twin counterparts and that leaves all else fixed.[9] Call $\mathbf{R}^\pi$ the 'Twin scheme' to **R**. It is clear that the initial scheme of reference fails to be a basis for any conformal explanations at all of accomplishments of Karl's population in the Twin environment. However, as that population becomes increasingly embedded in that environment, the Twin scheme is increasingly a basis for conformal explanations of its accomplishments therein. Accordingly, the conformal framework will come to favor the Twin scheme over the initial one in the Twin environment. That seems the right outcome.

An objection is likely to arise to the present case. The objection is that, although the 'Twin' correspondence relation helps explain Karl's nonbasic actions on Twin Earth, the *existence* of that correspondence relation is left utterly unexplained. The causal theory of reference is intended by some of its proponents to fit into an explanation of the existence of the correspondence relation between the beliefs and the environment of an agent, in

---

[9]For the exact definitions of 'alternative' and 'generated by', see 2.3.1.

part by enabling a causal explanation of reliability properties of the inductive method of the agent. It might be claimed that the proper explanation of Karl's accomplishments in the Twin context appeals not to the 'Twin' correspondence relation but to the *old* relation—the relation appropriate to the initial context—and the fact that the initial and Twin environments are isomorphic.

There are two points to be made in reply to this line of argument. The first is that an explanation of an action arising in the Twin context in terms of the alternative strategy just indicated is no more satisfactory than a conformal explanation that appeals directly to a correspondence between Karl's beliefs and the Twin environment. The objection to the latter was that it appeals to an unexplicated correspondence relation; but the contemplated alternative explanation *also* appeals to an unexplicated correspondence relation, namely, *the isomorphism between the initial and Twin contexts.* The detour through the initial correspondence relation and back again through the isomorphism between the initial and Twin environments adds nothing to the explanatory content of the direct conformal story.

The second point is that the two interpretive strategies appear to afford symmetrical explanations of reliability properties of Karl's inductive method. Consider a typical case of such an explanation for the initial context. Suppose we wish to explain the fact that under a certain set C of perceptual circumstances, Karl holds a sentence S true according to the initial interpretation if and only if S *is* true according to that interpretation. We might use a causal account of vision to explain why under circumstances C the state of affairs described by S covaries with a perceptual state that causes Karl to believe S.[10] Under the Twin interpretation, the state of affairs described by S is the counterpart, in the Twin environment, of the state of affairs on Earth grounding the given explanation of Karl's reliability in the circumstances C. Our assumption is that there is a complete symmetry between the causal roles of the correlative states of affairs in the two contexts. There will thus exist a parallel causal story showing how, under the corresponding circumstances in the Twin context, the state of affairs described by S under the Twin interpretation is causally connected to the belief in question. In general, the 'correspondence relation' between

---

[10]Recall from 2.2.3 that it is a constraint on an interpretation of Karl that the attitudes it ascribes to him can be mapped onto states of Karl as a physical system in such a way that intentional explanations of basic actions correspond to causal explanations of those actions. In saying that the relevant perceptual state causes Karl to believe S we mean that the perceptual state brings about the state of Karl as a physical system that realizes, in the present sense, the belief expressed in Karl's language by S. This is the state that underlies, among other things, sincere manifestations of belief in S.

Karl's beliefs and any environment can be resolved into two parts: an internal component, consisting in Karl's instantiating a set of belief-forming procedures, and an external component, characterized by reliability properties of those procedures, assessed in terms of a given interpretation of Karl relative to that environment. I just observed that in the Twin Earth cases, there appears to be a thoroughgoing symmetry between the initial and Twin interpretations vis-à-vis the explanations they make available of reliability properties of Karl's inductive method. The fact that Karl instantiates that method, on the other hand, is an autonomous psychological property of Karl that is to be explicated in nonsemantic terms.[11]

In this section, I have considered the 'local' problem of fixing the reference of names within the Conformal Framework. That is to say, holding the semantic properties of other expressions fixed, we look for referential interpretations of proper names that optimize the conformal explanation of second-order actions of individuals and groups within the population in question. I have described a number of variations on two cases in which the reference for a proper name suggested by the Conformal Framework diverges from the reference for it determined by the causal theory of naming. These cases rely on rather bizarre thought-experiments. However bizarre, it seems to me that the examples I have described support the referential assignments arising within the Conformal Framework over those of causal theories. I shall now go on to apply that framework to two broad classes of general terms.

3.2   Observation Terms

Traditionally, an observation term is roughly a predicate expressing some observable trait of an object or ordered 'n-tuple of objects. I shall develop an account of observational predicates within the present framework in the spirit of the traditional idea, but which counts a somewhat broader range of expressions as observational. It also deals, I believe, with a number of objections to positivist (and more recent) implementations of the traditional conception.

3.2.1   Positivist Interpretation

A central feature of the positivists' conception of the observational is the idea that an observation term is associated with an *observational procedure*,

---

[11] A property of Karl is 'autonomous' in the present sense if it is shared by each of his (possible) physical replicas; the property of instantiating, or approximately instantiating, a computational scheme is autonomous in this sense. See Stephen Stich, "Autonomous Psychology and the Belief-Desire Thesis," *Monist* 61 (1978): 571–91.

or a set of such procedures, that serves as a *criterion of application* for the term. I wish to take the notion of 'observational procedure' broadly, so that essentially any operational test - any structured set of operations that in each case generates an observable outcome - will count. In its crudest form, the positivist idea is that an object falls under an observation term if and only if it would pass the associated test(s): that the application condition of the term is given by the bare counterfactual saying that if the associated procedure were applied to the object, it would indicate that the object falls under the term.

In this form, the positivist construal is subject to a number of objections. One problem concerns the background conditions that must be assumed in applying the relevant observational procedures. If the lighting is not right, an object that is in fact red may appear to be some other color; retinal abnormalities may cause cubic objects to look otherwise; and so on. The relevant ancillary conditions concern, on the one hand, the condition of the observer, and on the other the conditions in the environment of the observer. Both sets of conditions must in some sense be *normal* if the test is to give the right answers. The obvious remedy is to restrict the indicated counterfactual to normal conditions, both of the observer and of the environment of the observer. One then gets such familiar formulae as 'to be red is to look red to normal observers under normal circumstances'.

But this will not do. One problem is that (for example) some *cubic* objects are not *observable* in the required sense, for example, because they are too small to see; they are *inaccessible* to observation. Another is that we have no non-circular characterization of the relevant conditions of normality. There is, however, an even more fundamental problem, which has been pointed out by Christopher Peacocke.[12] Even under normal conditions, a noncubic object can *look* cubic. Suppose, for example, that a noncubic object systematically changes shape, so as to present a cubic profile to any observer. One can imagine a skeptic who believes that for a given noncubic object this always happens. The skeptic's view would be incoherent on the modified positivist suggestion; but it is not incoherent. Peacocke's suggestion is to modify the positivist criterion by requiring that "it has to be the object's *actual* shape in present circumstances which is responsible in the [appropriate] counterfactual circumstances for the [relevant] perceptual experiences."[13] Such a criterion of application for 'cubic' does not apply

---

[12] Peacocke, *Thoughts*, ch. 2, pp. 18–20.
[13] Peacocke, p. 18.

directly to perceptually inaccessible objects, but as restricted to accessible objects we may express it as follows: for any object x and time t, x falls under 'cubic' at t if and only if for any time $t' > t$, if the relevant observational test(s) were applied to x at t' and the shape of x was invariant between t and t', the test(s) would indicate at t' that x falls under 'cubic'.[14]

One stumbling block encountered in applying this idea in the context of radical interpretation is that we have no way of knowing in advance that a given predicate is to designate a *shape*. The difficulty is that if another class of properties is substituted for shapes in the indicated criterion, it will lead to a different conclusion about the reference of 'cubic'. For example, for any shape S, define an alternative property $S^{\#}$. $S^{\#}$ applies to an object just in case it fulfills the observational criteria for S under normal circumstances. If S is the shape of x, call the corresponding $S^{\#}$ the *quape* of x. If quapes were substituted for shapes in our formulation of Peacocke's criterion, it would indicate that 'cubic' refers to (cubic)$^{\#}$, that is, to the property of being disposed to pass the observational tests for 'cubic' under normal circumstances. Since the question of whether to construe 'cubic' as designating a *shape* is not settled prior to interpretation, we are unable explain why Peacocke's criterion for that predicate should be taken to refer to shapes rather than, for example, quapes. A bit of ingenuity will suggest further classes of properties that could play such a role.[15] But if in the context of radical interpretation we have no way of saying, in advance, what *type* of property a given predicate should be taken to designate, the application condition delivered by the present criterion is left indeterminate.[16]

---

[14]This is something of a gloss. Peacocke does not, in fact, give general conditions for the ascription of the predicate '(is) cubic', but truth conditions for contents of the form 'a is cubic' where 'a' represents a singular term referring to an accessible object. Peacocke deals separately with the problem of inaccessible objects. One virtue of the approach suggested below is that it avoids the need for a separate account of the contents of observational predications for inaccessible objects.

[15]Why not simply take the invariant properties in Peacocke's criterion to be *all* (nonrelational) properties exemplified by the object? The difficulty is then that it is not causally possible to fulfill the conditions required for the application of the criterion. Any procedural interaction with the object will involve disturbing it in some ways, and so it is not possible to suppose that all of the nonrelational properties of the object will be stable over the interval of the interaction. We should allow for the disturbance of properties of the object *which are independent of the property being tested for*; but this condition is patently circular in the present context.

[16]This is not to say that in a particular interpretive situation we could not have good reasons to fix on one class of properties rather than another: only that the account now being considered does not, by itself, suggest such reasons.

3.2.2   The Present Proposal

Rather than pursue this and other modifications of the positivist's idea in a similar spirit, I shall develop an account of the reference of observation terms within the Conformal Framework that leads, I believe, to a satisfactory solution to the problems confronting the positivist conception. It was seen that what makes an object fall under 'cubic' is not the fact that the relevant observational tests would indicate that it does, even if applied under normal circumstances. However, what *explains* the fact that these procedures generate positive answers for the cubic objects actually encountered under typical circumstances is the fact that they are cubic. My suggestion will be roughly this: an observation term refers not to those items that would, under normal circumstances, pass the relevant observational tests, but to those objects falling under a property that explains why typical instances of the term normally pass those tests. To make this a little more explicit, say that a **paradigm** for an observation term is an object in the environement of the population in question which within that popoulation has been stably and conclusively taken to fall under the term; and call the circumstances of the population that, in conjunction with properties of the paradigms, explains their passing the relevant observational tests, the **paradigmatic circumstances** for the term. The suggestion is then that the reference of such a term is fixed by a property φ such that all, or most, of its paradigms exemplify φ, and their exemplification of φ explains their disposition to pass the observational tests associated with the term under the relevant paradigmatic circumstances.

One difficulty with this proposal is that there are typically various properties that could play such an explanatory role. Suppose, for example, that the perceptual criteria for an observation term P coincide with those of the color term 'is blue', but that the paradigms for P happen to be copper sulphate crystals. Both properties then explain why the paradigms have the relevant observational profile. There are good reasons to resist identifying the reference of P with that of 'copper sulphate crystal', however. The latter is a substance term; P, we are supposing, is an observation term. It might perhaps be claimed that the fact that all of the local instances of P share a common chemical nature shows that P has been *mis*classified as observational, and should rather be taken to designate a chemical kind. In the imagined case, such a move would have some unpalatable consequences. The assumption was that the criterion of application of P is just that of 'is blue'. The decision to thus count P as designating a chemical kind would render the procedure for applying P pathological; any blue object that presented itself would be classified as falling under that kind.

We are left in any case with the problem of saying which of the properties playing the required explanatory role should be taken to determine the reference of P. My suggestion is roughly that it is the *weakest* among all *surface* properties of the paradigms that explain why they fall under the relevant observational profile. These properties can be characterized in the following way. Recall that an **event-structure** is a state of affairs consisting of one (or several) objects falling under a property (or relation) at a time (or over an interval); the sort of thing that Jaegwon Kim has called a *property exemplification*.[17] Let e and f be two event-structures, e consisting in the exemplification of a property φ by an object x and f consisting in the exemplification of a property ψ by y (at some time). We say that e and f are **grounded in** x and y and **constituted by** φ and ψ. Define two orderings, $<$ and $\subset$, on event-structures: e $<$ f holds if and only if x's exemplification of φ causally explains y's exemplification of ψ; and let e $\subset$ f hold if $x = y$ and φ is included in ψ. For our present purposes, we can operate with a weak notion of property-inclusion, on which one property is included in another if the converse extensional inclusion between them is causally necessary. That is to say, we will take it that

$$P \subseteq Q \ =: \ \Box(\forall x)(Q(x) \rightarrow P(x)),$$
$$P = Q \ =: \ P \subseteq Q \ \& \ Q \subseteq P,$$
$$\text{and } P \subset Q \ =: \ P \subseteq Q \ \& \ P \neq Q,$$

where '$\Box$' signifies causal necessity. I will then say that e is a **proximate cause** of f if e $<$ f, and there is no event-structure g grounded in x such that e $<$ g $<$ f; e is a **minimal** proximate cause of f if *bolde* is a proximate cause of f, and there is no proximate cause g of f such that g $\subset$ e.

On the present usage, an event may have more than one proximate cause. The proximity condition says that an exemplification e of a property by an object counts as a proximate cause of an event-structure f only if there is no structure *grounded in that object* that is causally explained by e and that causes f. Thus there is no event-structure grounded in the subject of e that is intermediate between e and f in the order of causal explanation; but there may be structures not so grounded which are. For example, *the flag's being red* may, proximately, cause the bull to charge, but *the bull's being in a certain retinal state* may also be such a cause. The minimality condition eliminates, in effect, causally superfluous content: a proximate cause of f that properly includes another such cause will not count as a minimal proximate cause of f.

On this proposal, then, the reference of an observation term is determined by a property whose exemplifications by its paradigmatic instances

---

[17]See *Supervenience and Mind* (Cambridge: Cambridge University Press, 1993), ch. 3.

bear the minimal proximate causal-explanatory relation to their disposition to pass the observational tests associated with the term (under the relevant paradigmatic circumstances). For example, in the preceding case, the fact that the paradigms for P are blue, that is, instantiate a certain reflectance property, is proximately responsible for their tendency to appear blue under normal conditions, though the fact that each is a copper sulphate crystal also explains this fact. It does so, however, by explaining the fact that they are blue (by explaining that reflectance property), which shows that their being instances of copper sulphate is not a *proximate* cause of their tendency to appear blue. Moreover, their being blue is the weakest property of the paradigms playing such an explanatory role, so that their exemplification of this color property is a *minimal* proximate cause of their exemplifying that disposition.

3.2.3   Observational Criteria and Conformal Relevance

The present proposal solves the problems raised earlier for the positivist model. The problems were, first, that an object's passing all the tests associated with an observational predicate should be compatible with its not falling under that predicate; and second that an object may fall under the predicate and yet not be accessible to such a test. On the suggested criterion, an observation term designates a property that explains why its typical instances are disposed to pass the relevant tests under normal ('paradigmatic') circumstances, but this is quite compatible with the possibility that an object fulfills all of the relevant observational criteria and yet fails to fall under the term. Thus, in Peacocke's example, an item that systematically changes shape may pass all the tests for 'is cubic' and yet not *be* cubic. It is still true that the fact that explains, in the relevant proximate way, why typical cubic objects pass these tests is their being cubic. This proposal thus explains the intelligibility of skepticism, at least of a limited sort, about the tests. Second, the suggested criterion is able to deal easily with the problem of inaccessible instances. The property that is constitutive of the minimal proximate cause of the fact that a local instance of an observation term is disposed to pass the observational tests associated with it may also be exemplified by inaccessible objects. For example, it is again the fact that the paradigms for the term 'cubic' are in fact cubic that explains, in the relevant way, why they appear cubic under the relevant paradigmatic circumstances, but this property is exemplified by cubic microscopic objects.

Finally, this construction allows us to explain a reliability property of the criterial procedures for observation terms: of all the properties of the local instances of the term which causally explain their disposition to pass the relevant observational tests, the hypothesis that the term refers to the property selected in the suggested way renders those tests *most* reliable. For, suppose that φ is the property selected by the present account in a particular case. Then φ is weakest among the superficial properties of the paradigms that play the required explanatory role; it is the causally most proximate such explanatory property, stripped of causally irrelevant detail. The tests, if applied under paradigmatic circumstances, detect φ directly, and for this reason are more reliable indicators of φ than any property whose exemplification by the paradigms *explains* their exemplification of φ. For an extreme example, suppose again that the paradigms for the predicate P above happen to be copper sulphate crystals, and that the observational criteria for P coincide with those for the predicate 'is blue'. Although their being instances of copper sulphate explains why the paradigms for P pass the observational test associated with 'is blue', this test is an absurdly unreliable indicator of their underlying chemical nature.

From the standpoint of optimizing the reliability of the criteria of application for an observation term, then, we will want to assign it a property of its paradigms playing the required explanatory role that is maximal with respect to the causal basis ordering $<$. Having selected such a property, however, we shall want to strip it of content that plays no role in explaining why the paradigms for the term pass the relevant observational tests. Thus, for example, since the likelihood of an object's falling under the conjunction of the color *blue* and any unrelated nonvacuous property is less than the probability of its exemplifying *blue*, the criterion for 'is blue' more reliably indicates an object's being blue than its falling under any such conjunctive property. Thus from among the explanatory properties maximal with respect to $<$, we will want to select the one (or one of the ones) minimal with respect to the inclusion ordering $\subset$. That is precisely what the suggested mechanism of reference does.

These observations go some way toward showing how this interpretation of observation terms may be justified in terms of the Principle of Conformality. It is evidently relevant to an agent's ability to frame causal-explanatory sketches that he instantiates reliable procedures for ascribing observational properties; for ascriptions of such properties quite generally appear as initial or boundary conditions in causal explanations. Since this ability determines, in part, the conformal explanations that we can giv of Karl's behavior, the present characterization of reference for observational predicates has a clear rationale within the Conformal Framework. However, it might seem that it would have been even better from the standpoint of the Principle of Conformality if Karl's ascriptional procedures for observation terms were *perfectly* reliable, at least under local circumstances. In that case, it might seem that the following naive positivist construal would be preferable to the indicated one on the suggested interpretive story: simply say that an object falls under an observation term if it would pass the relevant observational tests under local circumstances.

But in fact the suggested account fares significantly better under the Principle of Conformality than the naive positivist one. Karl's observational reliability contributes to conformal explanations by affording him access to exemplifications of observational properties. But access to these contributes to conformal explanations only if they are causally operative in the world; sheer dispositions to pass observational tests are not. Suppose, for example, that we wish to give a conformal explanation of Karl's ability to get bulls to charge by reference to the fact that he believes that bulls charge when confronted, in normal daylight, with red placards. The conformal explanation presupposes a causal explanation that Karl can frame himself (at least in outline). Karl's explanation requires that a placard's being red *causes* bulls to charge under certain circumstances. It is hard to see, on the naive positivist construal, how this could be the case. On that account, being red is a purely dispositional property: the placard is red in virtue of the fact that it appears red to normal observers under normal conditions of observation. But how is this supposed to explain its characteristic effect on bulls? Perhaps it is the fact that it 'looks red to bulls' that prompts them to charge, but this is no part of Karl's explanation. What is needed is a property that simultaneously explains the placard's satisfying our observational criteria, *and* its looking red to or having whatever relevant effect on bulls. Its *being red* is the causally most proximate property of the object playing such an explanatory role.

By thus targeting the reference of an observation term of Karl's language on the proximate *cause* of the satisfaction of the observational criteria for the term by its local instances, this model equips Karl with a source of information about the causal powers of objects in his environment. It is this sort of information that determines, in part, the causal stories that Karl can frame, and thus the conformal explanations that we can frame. By selecting the *weakest proximate cause*, the model makes his observational criteria optimal in terms of reliability: optimal, that is, within the class of interpretations of the term that assign it any such causally relevant property. The aim of the model, then, is to strike a balance between two sorts of optimization: we wish to optimize the reliability of the relevant observational procedures; but we also wish to optimize the causal relevance of the sort of information they afford.

3.3   Homogeneous Natural Kind Terms

The semantic category NK of natural kind terms I am about to consider cuts across mass nouns such as 'gold' or 'water', and count-nouns such as 'fish' or 'neutron star'. One way of smoothing out the categorial differences is to treat the interpretation of a mass noun as derivative from that of an associated count-noun along something like the following lines: Putnam's account (described hereafter), for example, would apply directly to the fused count-nouns 'piece-of-gold', 'portion-of-water', and so on, whose extensions in any possible situation comprise sets of objects. The denotation of a mass term would be obtained by mereological aggregation from the items in the extension of the corresponding count-noun. However, count-nouns do not form a homogeneous semantic category; 'electron', 'tiger', 'baseball', 'chair' and 'lump' are each nouns of this sort, but only the first two are natural kind terms. The question, then, is how the words to which such an account of reference applies are to be identified: when is a term a natural kind term?

This is not, I believe, a question that needs to be settled at the outset; eventually, however, it will have to be. One difficulty is that the model of reference I shall develop for NK can be also applied in certain cases to which the model for observation terms applies. This would not be a problem if the two accounts gave the same answers in these cases, but they do not. Thus we will require a characterization of the range of applicability of the separate accounts. The characterization is given in subsection 3.4.4, concomitantly with an answer to the question of how the suggested mechanism of reference for NK is justified within the Conformal Framework for radical interpretation.

3.3.1   The Kripke-Putnam Model

I begin with a brief overview of the related accounts of Saul Kripke and Hilary Putnam, concentrating for definiteness on Putnam's formulation. Putnam holds: (1) A natural kind term of our language (say, 'tiger') refers to just those organisms that have the same underlying 'structure' or 'nature' as the animals which are called 'tigers' within our own linguistic community, and analogously for other natural kind terms. (2) Although the instances of such a term may be locally identified by a set of qualitative properties, this 'stereotype' does not constitute a necessary and sufficient condition for an item to fall under the term, but only a means by which its instances are normally recognized in the local situation.[18] (3) Each natural kind term is

---

[18] "Explanation and Reference," 204–5; "The Meaning of 'Meaning'," 235–38; also

associated with an equivalence relation: objects are *equivalent* if they agree in certain (relevant) natural properties. To be an instance of a natural kind is to stand in that relation of equivalence to the 'paradigms' of that kind, that is, (roughly) its typical local instances.[19] Thus, for example, an animal falls under the term 'tiger' if it stands in the relation *same animal as* to the local tigers, and a liquid falls under the term 'water' if it stands in the relation *same liquid as* to local instances of water. (4) In both cases, the equivalence relation consists in agreement in important structural properties; but in neither case is it supposed that a competent speaker can *specify* those properties. For example, 'water' will refer in English to just the liquids exemplifying the molecular structure of the instances of water accessible to speakers of English; but a speaker need only intend to apply the word to those liquids which are relevantly similar to the local instances of water.[20]

All of this is by now familiar. In this section, I shall discuss some difficulties with this account, some of which are also familiar. Others will emerge hereafter.

On Putnam's account, I said, a natural kind term refers to exactly those objects that stand in an appropriate relation of equivalence to the local paradigmatic instances of the kind it designates; in each case, equivalence consists in agreement in certain important properties: normally, (micro)structural properties. The difficulty is that these instances will typically share *many* such properties. For example: (a) Suppose that biological sorts could be characterized by more or less definite genetic properties, specifiable ultimately in terms of the molecular structure of the genetic material.[21] The organisms in any sample of tigers will almost always happen to exemplify genetic properties more specific than the property shared by exactly the tigers, as well as a number of more inclusive ones such as prop-

---

Naming and Necessity, 115–18.

[19] "The Meaning of 'Meaning'," 224–55, 230–32.

[20] I am here sliding over Putnam's distinction between arbitrary speakers of the language in question and those who are in some sense linguistically responsible for the application of the term. In Putnam's discussion, an arbitrary speaker is not in general assumed to have special knowledge of the paradigmatic instances of the term. Putnam stresses that a typical speaker normally intends to apply a natural kind term in conformity with *expert* usage (see "The Meaning of 'Meaning'," 227–29). But the reference of such a term must then be grounded in the usage of the *experts,* who are assumed (collectively) to have access to the relevant paradigms and intend to apply the term to whatever stands in the relevant equivalence relation to them. However, not even the experts need be in possession of the structural characterization of the kind.

[21] That is to say, as we now know, in terms of the polynucleotide sequencing of DNA. This supposition is in fact false (see sections 3.5.3–3.5.4 for more on this issue). But suppose that it holds at least approximately for the purposes of this example.

erties common to all mammals or to all cordates. On Putnam's account of the reference of the term 'tiger', then, which of these properties determines its extension? (b) Some chemically homogeneous samples of a sugar are instances of a single *isomer* (their constituent molecules are composed of atoms of the same elements in the same stereographic conformation); but they share many weaker structural properties, such as being instances of the same molecular formula, all isomers considered. On the suggested mechanism of reference, then, will a term introduced with reference to these as paradigms refer to that molecular type or to a particular isomer of that type? (c) Some samples of a single *isotope* of helium (composed of atoms exemplifying the same atomic number and mass number) share not only the property of being instances of that isotope but other structural properties as well; for example, they are instances of the same element (helium), and the same periodic family (inert gases), and so on. Again, which natural kind does the suggested mechanism associate with a term for which these samples are the paradigms?[22]

Notice that it will not do in general to answer these questions to appeal to disambiguating linguistic *intentions* on the part of the speakers of the language. We can't solve the problem in the isotope/element case, for example, by reference to explicit intentions on the part of the relevant speakers to use the term in question to designate an *isotope*, say; for such intentions presuppose information that these agents cannot generally be supposed to possess. For example, the term 'helium' was introduced into English before detailed ideas about atomic structure were developed, and I take it that part of the point of the Kripke-Putnam account is to explain how this can be the case. However, it now seems apparent that that account does not unambiguously pair a natural kind with a natural kind term *if nothing more* is said about the equivalence relation that generates the natural kind from its paradigms than that equivalent objects share the same 'hidden structure', or that equivalent objects 'agree in important physical properties'.[23] I shall call the present difficulty with the Kripke-Putnam account the *disambiguation problem*. It is essentially the question of *which*

---

[22]The same sort of question has been raised before, for example, by Keith Donellan, "Kripke and Putnam on Natural Kind Terms," in *Knowledge and Mind*, edited by C. Ginet and S. Shoemaker (Cambridge, Mass.: Harvard University Press, 1983), pp. 84–105; Kim Sterelny, "Natural Kind Terms," *Pacific Philosophical Quarterly* (1983): 294–313; and Mark Wilson, "Predicate Meets Property," *Philosophical Review* 91 (1982): 549–89.

[23] "The Meaning of 'Meaning'," 232, 235. None of this is to deny that a natural kind term *could* be introduced by reference to an explicitly characterized equivalence relation. Indeed, in mature science, such introductions are common. The preceding considerations arise from the observation that some natural kind words have not been introduced in this way, and it is for these that we are seeking a mechanism of reference.

of various possible relations of equivalence are relevant to the mechanism of reference Putnam and Kripke have described.

The second question I want to raise about the Kripke-Putnam view concerns the possibility of reference failure. One of the merits of that view is that it seeks to explain how we can succeed in talking about a natural kind while not knowing the structural properties that determine it, and while in the grip of quite a lot of misinformation about it. I shall take it as a condition of adequacy on any account of the matter that it should do this. The difficulty is that some errors *do* abort reference in such cases, and the unmodified Kripke-Putnam account will have trouble in dealing with these. Consider two examples.

Imagine the following set of circumstances surrounding the origin of the term 'witch' (OE: *wicce*) in English. Authorities introduce the term to designate a *kind* of person that is thought to be exemplified by certain paradigmatic instances. The kind is believed to be characterized by a relation of its members to a supernatural realm. This relation is thought to explain capacities (for example, casting spells) that are attributed to witches. The difficulty I find in this for the Kripke-Putnam account lies in the fact that the paradigms for the term 'witch' *may in fact exemplify a natural kind*; indeed, they exemplify many. But this fact seems to me to have no tendency to show that in the imagined circumstances the term 'witch' is nonempty.

To make the case a bit more vivid, suppose that the paradigms for the term 'witch' share psychological properties that are causally responsible for the socially held beliefs about them. We might, for example, suppose this common property to underly the alienation of the paradigmatic 'witches' from certain social institutions, and that the exemplification of this property by these individuals explains socially prevalent beliefs about them. The paradigms then do instantiate a psychological kind; moreover, their exemplification of that kind explains their classification under the term 'witch'. But we would not wish to say that under these circumstances the term 'witch' would have referred to that kind.[24]

For a second case, consider a speculative explanation of the origin of the

---

[24]This case undercuts a certain response to the disambiguation problem. One might suggest that a natural kind term refers to the *intersection* of the natural kinds exemplified by its paradigmatic instances, the items falling under each kind exemplified by its locally typical examples. But in this case, the intersection of the kinds instantiated by the paradigms for the term 'witch' is non-empty, whereas the reference of that term *is*, presumably, empty. In other cases, for example, 'tiger', the intersection is nonempty but is plausibly narrower than the correct reference: as noted earlier, the paradigmatic tigers will almost certainly happen to exemplify various genetic properties which are not shared by all tigers.

term 'vampire'. Porphyria is a disease resulting in toxic accumulations of certain substances (porphyrins), an acute form of which has symptoms including some of the behavioral and morphological characteristics associated in folklore with the term 'vampire'. Let us imagine that the beliefs about vampires actually originated with certain sufferers from this disease being taken to fall under the relevant (fictive) properties, and that the supernatural elements in this story arose, in part, to explain the natural ones. These persons were then the original paradigms for the term 'vampire'. Moreover, there *is* a property common to the paradigms that explains their classification under that term, by way of being a causal basis for their actual exemplification of certain properties socially associated with it. In this situation it is not clear why, on the Kripke-Putnam model, falling under the term 'vampire' does not consist in being afflicted with acute porphyria. I take it, however, that in the situation described the extension of this term is empty.

3.3.2   The Present Proposal

Consider yet another case of abortive reference. Suppose we have introduced the word 'tiger' by Putnam's procedure, but suppose also that the paradigmatic tigers are not biologically homogeneous but are rather a curious ensemble of specimens from quite divergent animal groups that happen to have a common appearance, behavior, and morphology. In this situation, the word 'tiger' would fail to refer to a natural kind; perhaps it would fail to refer at all.[25] As usual, however, the paradigms coexemplify many natural kinds. What is it about this case that prevents the word 'tiger' from referring to one of them?

What seems to be missing here is a property exemplified by the paradigms that *explains* certain biologically important facts about tigers. Although each of the paradigms falls under the phenotypic traits normally associated with tigers, these characteristics are exemplified for different biological reasons by the different paradigms. That is to say, although the paradigms exemplify a common phenotype there is no invariant explanation of why they do.

---

[25]The conclusion that the term is vacuous is not mandated in the indicated circumstances. Putnam considers the example of 'jade'. Jade consists of two structurally distinct substances that give rise to the same appearance, texture, and so on; the same observational profile. In this case we do not say that the term 'jade' is empty (that 'there is no such thing as jade'), but rather that 'there are two kinds of jade'. The term 'jade', then, does not designate a natural kind, but this, by itself, does not imply that the term is empty. Similarly, the agents in the imagined case might say that there have turned out to be several kinds of tiger. I take up this sort of case in 3.4.3.

In the 'witch' case, there are a number of 'paradigms' for the term that, in its context of introduction, are believed to be responsible for certain phenomena (for example, casting spells). The term 'witch' did not refer to a natural kind; but its paradigms coexemplified many natural kinds. My question was why the term 'witch' does not refer to one of these. In this case, the difficulty is that the term 'witch' is in some sense *linguistically associated* with certain properties, most of which are not even approximately exemplified by its paradigms. Thus there can be no question of *explaining* their exemplification of these properties. It is a property or properties appropriately figuring in such an explanation that would ground the reference of the term, if the term referred to a kind at all.

These examples suggest that it is not only its paradigms but also certain *properties* associated with a natural kind term that play a role in fixing its reference. In conjunction with its paradigms, such a set of properties fixes a kind if there is a property exemplified by the paradigms that plays an appropriate role in explaining why they exemplify the properties in the set (or exemplify most of these properties, suitably weighted); it is this explanatory property that delimits the relevant kind. I will call the explanandum-properties *saliencies* for the term in question. The formal properties of the notion of explanation then account for the cases of reference failure I have discussed. If a property is to figure in explanations of why the paradigms for a natural kind term exemplify its saliencies, it must be the case that its paradigms *do* exemplify its saliencies.[26] Otherwise, no such explanations exist, and on the suggestion being considered, the term will fail to refer to a kind. Alternatively, the paradigms associated with a word may exemplify the relevant salient properties, but there may be no uniform explanation of why they do. Since, on the present suggestion, the term in question designates a natural kind only if that kind is made up of just the objects falling under a property shared by the paradigms for the term that explains why they exemplify its saliencies, that term will again fail to refer to a kind.

The present proposal also makes possible a natural explanation of reference *change*. At different times, a natural kind word may be associated with different saliencies.[27] Accordingly, different properties may characterize the kind designated by the term at different times, depending on which properties must be invoked to explain the exemplification of its saliencies by its paradigms. Thus, for example, suppose that at one time the term 'hy-

---

[26] Or do so approximately, in some suitable sense.

[27] Of course, it may also be associated with different paradigms, and this is another source of referential variation. The following remarks make clear, however, that referential variation is still possible even in the presence of paradigmatic stability. I will consider some effects of paradigmatic variance later.

drogen' is saliently associated with chemical properties of its local instances that can be explicated by reference to atomic number. On the present proposal, then, it will refer at that time to just the items exemplifying that atomic number (that is, to instances of the element hydrogen). However, suppose that the paradigmatic instances of hydrogen exemplify the predominant *isotope* of hydrogen, characterized by both atomic number 1 and mass number 1, and suppose further that, at a later time, the term 'hydrogen' acquires saliencies (such as ratios of combination by weight) whose local exemplifications require reference to the mass number of the predominant isotope for their explanation. On the suggestion being considered, the extension of this term will then narrow so as to encompass just that isotope.

As a second example, consider a substance term that designates, at an initial time, a chemical compound such as a sugar. Such a compound can be described by a structural formula that does not distinguish between a molecule and its mirror image. The subspecies of a compound composed of stereographically superimposable molecules comprise the *optical isomers* of that compound. The terminology is due to the fact that when plane polarized light is passed through solutions of the separate isomers, one causes the plane of polarization to rotate around the axis of the beam in one direction, whereas the other causes the plane to rotate equally but in the opposite direction. One says in this case that the isomers are *optically active*. On the present model, at the initial time, the term in question will designate the totality of optical isomers of the compound in question, provided that the exemplification of its saliencies by its paradigms is explicable in terms of the molecular structure of the compound without reference to isomerism. Suppose, however, that in fact the local instances of the term are instances of a single optical isomer. If, at a later time, the term acquires a saliency, such as the relevant optical activity property, whose exemplifications must be explained in terms of a particular isomeric structure, the extension of the term will narrow so as to comprise only instances of that isomer.[28]

This proposal has a natural semantical implementation. Putnam characterized the semantic role of the paradigmatic instances of natural kind words by interpreting them as *indices* in a relativized theory of satisfaction of Montague's sort:[29] a natural kind term refers to an item at a possible world just in case that item has the same nature as the indexical paradigms for the term *in the actual world*. The difficulty with this idea, it was seen, is that the notion of *sameness of nature* or *structure* is not generally well de-

---

[28] It should be noted that the two examples just presented are somewhat fictive in character, since elements and compounds normally occur in nature as *mixtures* (of their isotopes or isomers). I study the case of mixtures in 3.3.4.

[29] "The Meaning of 'Meaning'," pp. 229–35.

fined. However, the role of the properties I have called 'saliencies' allows one to *define* the equivalence relation relevant to Putnam's suggestion: objects are *equivalent* in the relevant sense if they exemplify the properties of the paradigms for the term that stand in the appropriate causal-explanatory relation to their exemplification of its saliencies. Thus, for example, the equivalence relation for *metals* would consist in agreement in the physical properties underlying exemplification of certain properties associated with metals.[30] In terms of Montague's framework, the present proposal may then be described as follows: take as indices for a natural kind term pairs $\langle X, P \rangle$ such that X is a set of objects and P a set of properties. The elements of X are the **paradigms** for the term and the elements of P its **saliencies**, relative to that index. If $\langle X, P \rangle$ is the index for the term associated with a given point of its utterance, then the term refers to an object α at a world w at that point if and only if, at w, α falls under the properties that play the appropriate role in explaining why the elements of X exemplify the properties in P (or a weighted majority of these properties) *in the actual world*.[31]

Of course, at this point the suggested mechanism of reference for natural kind words is seriously underdescribed; this formulation is no more than a framework for an account of such a mechanism. Its main unexplicated features are the (relevant) notion of explanation and the notion of *salience*. To fill out the framework, we will thus require a characterization of the sort of explanation that is in question here, and of the conditions under which a property is a saliency for a natural kind term. I discuss these issues in the following subsections. I then take up the question of how the suggested mechanism of reference is justified within the Conformal Framework for radical interpretation.

3.3.3   Structural Explanation

Putnam wanted to say roughly that a natural kind term designates those objects *relevantly like* its local paradigmatic instances, and I have suggested that an object is relevantly like those instances when it falls under the properties that contribute in an appropriate way to an explanation of their

---

[30]Suppose, for example, that the saliencies for '— is a metal' are thermal conductivity and electrical conductivity. Then the present proposal would generate the correct extension for this term; for the physical properties underlying the exemplification of thermal and electrical conductivity by paradigmatic metals are just those which are characteristic of all metals. See Linus Pauling, *The Nature of the Chemical Bond*, 3rd ed. (Ithaca: Cornell University Press, 1960), pp. 393–442, for a classical discussion.

[31]Equivalently: when α at w stands in the relevant form of Putnam's equivalence relation, as defined in terms of P, to the paradigms for the term in the actual world.

exemplification of the saliencies for the term. This subsection is largely devoted to unpacking 'contributes in an appropriate way to an explanation of', and thus to the question of what a kind-delimiting property is.

In the required explanations of why the paradigms for a natural kind word exemplify its saliencies, the properties that characterize the kind are *intrinsic* properties of those objects. A property is 'intrinsic' in the present sense if it is invariant under the relation of physical indiscernibility: that is, it applies to any possible physical replica of an object to which it applies.[32] The notion of 'intrinsic property' thus incorporates two other property-concepts: first, an intrinsic property is *nonrelational*, for 'relational' properties (for example, being equidistant from the sun and the moon) are not preserved under replication of objects to which they apply. Second, an intrinsic property is *generic*, in the sense that it may be specified in such a way as not to involve ineliminable reference to individuals. The intrinsic properties of objects which are fundamental in causal explanations of their physical properties are generally structural, or mereological; for fundamental explanation generally proceeds by showing how a property of the physical system in question is brought about or determined by properties and relations of parts of the object which, for the purposes of the explanation, need be specified only in terms of those properties and relations. Thus, for example, 'solid composed of atoms with atomic number 3' is a structural characterization of a piece of lithium at room temperature. In this description, reference to the parts of the object enters only existentially; what matters are the physically basic properties and relations of those parts.

The kind-delimiting properties associated with a natural kind word, then, are intrinsic properties of its paradigms that explain their exemplification of its saliencies. But we need to be careful about how the requirement of explanation is understood. Consider a property ϕ, which the paradigms for a natural kind term happen to have in common, and let χ be a property of those objects that explains their exemplification of the saliencies for the term. Then their exemplification of $\chi \& \phi$ *also* explains why the paradigms for the term exemplify its saliencies, but we should not for that reason wish

---

[32]It is doubtful that the present definition is really a noncircular characterization of the notion of 'intrinsic property', since the relation of physical indiscernibility arguably presupposes the concept of 'intrinsic property'. Although I think the notion is clear enough for present purposes, one can perhaps arrive at a more informative characterization as follows: an intrinsic property is one that is invariant under *isomorphisms* of systems to which it applies, where an isomorphism of physical systems S and S' is a one-to-one correspondence mapping the physically basic constituents of S onto the physically basic constituents of S' that preserves fundamental physical properties and relations. The latter are to be specified simply by enumeration.

to treat $\chi\&\phi$ as constitutive of the relevant kind if ϕ plays no role in the explanations. As in the discussion of observation terms, we wish to strip the relevant explanatory properties of superfluous detail. We cannot, however, as in the case of observation terms, accomplish this aim by requiring that no property properly included in a kind-delimiting property play such an explanatory role. This move was appropriate in the observational case precisely because what we sought were the *surface* properties of instances of the term responsible for certain dispositions. In the case of a natural kind word, however, a property explaining exemplifications of its saliencies by its paradigms might well be included in another such property on the conception of property-inclusion adverted to in 3.2.2. Thus, for example, suppose that the saliencies for a term designating a kind of animal are explicable in terms of a *functional* architecture common to its paradigms, and that the biological properties delimiting that kind give rise to the relevant functional architecture in each causally possible situation. On the criterion of property-inclusion with which we have been operating, then, the property of instantiating that architecture is included in the conjunction of the properties characterizing the relevant biological sort. The appropriate criterion of explanatory relevance is not that no trait properly included in a property characterizing the extension of a natural kind term also explains why its paradigms exemplify its saliencies, but rather that *that* the paradigms exemplify any such trait is *explained* their exemplification of the relevant kind-delimiting property.

These observations lead to the following definitions. Let Q be an intrinsic property of an individual a. The property P will be said to be a **structural basis** for a's exemplification of Q if

(a) P is an intrinsic property of a;
(b) $[a, P] < [a, Q]$;
(c) For each event-structure $\mathbf{e}$ such that $\mathbf{e} \subset [a, P]$, if $\mathbf{e} < [a, Q]$, then $[a, P] < \mathbf{e}$.[33]

The present proposal, then, is that a kind-delimiting property for a natural kind term is a structural basis for the exemplification of one or more saliencies for the term by its paradigms. The conjunction of the kind-delimiting properties for a term will be called the **characteristic property** for that term. The extension of the term in any possible world consists of just the objects therein exemplifying its characteristic property. Two comments may be useful.

First, the condition (b) obtains when a's falling under P causally explains its exemplification of Q. If a is a paradigm for a natural kind term ζ and Q a saliency for ζ, then, the condition (c) expresses the requirement of

---

[33] For the definitions of '$\subset$' and '$<$' see 3.2.2.

explanatory relevance described earlier: if P is a kind-delimiting property for ζ by virtue of being a structural basis for $[a, Q]$, then $[a, P]$ explains a's exemplification of any weaker property that explains a's exemplification of Q. The conjunction of an arbitrary property ϕ of a with the given structural basis P for $[a, Q]$ thus generally fails to constitute such a basis, for we have $[a, P] \subset [a, P\&\phi]$ and $[a, P]$ explains $[a, Q]$, but $[a, P\&\phi]$ does not explain $[a, P]$ (a's falling under $P\&\phi$ entails, but does not explain, a's falling under P).

Second, if the intrinsic properties of objects which are fundamental in the order of causal explanation are microstructural properties, the suggested mechanism of reference functions to ensure that the instances of a natural kind term will exemplify the most basic structures underlying paradigmatic exemplifications of its saliencies. But the model does not assume a most fundamental level of structural explanation; it is compatible with the possibility of the indefinite extendibility of structural explanations. This possibility is, of course, intuitively unappealing; we expect explanations to come to an end somewhere. In this case, the term in question will refer to the most fundamental basis for the exemplification of its saliencies by its paradigms: the basis, that is to say, that is determinative of every other. The reason for this is that the conjunction of a finite chain of properties ordered by the causal-determination relation coincides with the minimal element in the chain. However, if in fact there is an unfounded descending chain of structural explanations for the relevant saliency-exemplifications (or if there is genuine causal overdetermination), the members of the kind will fall under each explanation in the chain (or each determining property).

The suggested account of kind-delimitation may be illustrated by considering an example that has figured repeatedly in the literature. One of Putnam's first examples of the operation of his model was the case of *acids*. Putnam believed that his model explained how it is possible that Lavoisier or Dalton ca. 1800 were referring to the same substances as Linus Pauling or Robert Woodward in 1960, and that this case typified the mechanism of reference for natural kind terms he wished to suggest. The various items which over time were taken as paradigmatic instances of the term 'acid' fall under a natural kind. Putnam recognized that taking 'acid' to designate that kind renders many beliefs at the earlier period mistaken: but he believed that since the paradigmatic instances satisfy a unitary structural characterization, the word 'acid' referred at both periods to just the items falling under that characterization.

Ian Hacking has described a problem for this seeming success-story.[34]

---

[34] Hacking, *Representing and Intervening* (Cambridge: Cambridge University Press, 1983), pp. 84–87.

It has nothing to do with the problem of identifying the saliencies for the term acid; we may suppose, for the purposes of the objection, that just *the same* saliencies were associated with this term in 1800 and in 1960, and that these were given by what Hacking calls the 'professional stereotype' for the term: acids taste sour in water solution, turn blue litmus paper red, and so on.[35] The difficulty is that *two* explanations of these facts are available for the paradigmatic acids. They stem from the two competing twentieth-century structural characterizations of acids. According to the definition proposed by J.N. Brønsted and T.M. Lowry, an acid is a *proton donor*, that is, a substance that has a tendency to loose protons, while a base is a proton-acceptor. But there is an alternative definition due to Gilbert Newton Lewis: an acid is a substance that can accept an electron pair to form a covalent bond. The difficulty is that these definitions are not equivalent; Lewis's definition is marginally the more general, subsuming somewhat more substances under the term 'acid' than the Brønsted-Lowry characterization. Hacking writes: 'Still, the philosopher of naming must ask if Lavoisier meant Brønsted-Lowry acids or Lewis acids when he spoke of acids. Obviously he meant neither. Must we now mean one or the other? No, only for certain specialized purposes.'[36]

One confusion that is apt to arise from these remarks stems from the fact that it really *is* obvious that Lavoisier *intended* to refer neither to the species given by the Brønsted-Lowry definition nor to the one given by Lewis's. But that is not the question. The question is, even if neither referential intention was present, he actually *did* refer to one or the other species. I take Hacking's claim to be that it is *pointless* to give *either* answer. But here, I think, we need to be careful. In 1800 all paradigmatic acids satisfied both structural definitions, and that is still so: the substances that are now presented as typical acids fall unproblematically under both the Brønsted-Lowry and the Lewis characterizations. Which kind would the present model select as referent for the term 'acid', assuming the saliencies for the term to comprise the 'professional stereotype'? The answer is surprisingly unequivocal: it is the species picked out by the Brønsted-Lowry definition. This outcome would be unwelcome if Hacking were right in supposing any such answer to be ungrounded. But there is, in fact, a nonarbitrary basis for the present answer. That typical acids satisfy the Brønsted-Lowry definition explains why they also satisfy the professional stereotype. Their falling under Lewis's definition does so as well. But there is an asymmetry between the two definitions, an asymme-

---

[35] It will be seen later that this picture of salience is not in general quite right, but that will not matter for the purposes of the present example.

[36] *Representing and Intervening*, p. 85.

try that bears on the decision which definition to count as circumscribing the acids. The Brønsted-Lowry account explains why the paradigmatic acids satisfy Lewis's, not conversely. The property in terms of which the Brønsted-Lowry story picks out the acids is in fact what we have termed the 'characteristic property' for the term 'acid': it is constitutive of an explanation of the exemplification of the supposed saliencies for that term by its paradigmatic instances that underlies *other* such explanations, and is in this sense the fundamental causal-explanatory basis of the information saliently associated with the term. It is this fact, I suggest, that rationalizes the choice of this property as constitutive of the kind designated by the term 'acid'.

A natural objection to this line of thought is that although these considerations show the suggested assignment of extension to 'acid' to be in a certain sense nonarbitrary, it would also appear to be implausibly anachronistic.[37] It would pick out the reference of the French term 'acide' in Lavoisier's idiolect, for example, by reference to a microstructural property of acids that was unknown to Lavoisier, and that was to remain unknown for well over a century. That property figures in the *grounding* explanation of why the substances Lavoisier took to be acids exemplify properties that he took to be typical of acids. But what, one might ask, has this grounding property to do with Lavoisier's linguistic situation, or with that of Lavoisier's community? Why is the *most fundamental* explanatory property the uniquely appropriate candidate to determine the reference of the term in that situation? A framework for radical interpretation can answer this question in terms of an interpretive role that the suggested assignment of reference can play that alternative assignments cannot, or cannot play as well. Within the present framework, I shall argue in section 3.4 that such a role can indeed be defined for the suggested mechanism of reference in terms of the Principle of Conformality.

3.3.4 Salience

Whatever saliencies are going to turn out to be, it is clear that the properties saliently associated with a natural kind term must generally outrun the properties that *any speaker* associates with the term (and it will shortly be clear that they may also *under*-run these properties). Thus the saliencies for a term are not simply what Putnam called 'stereotypes'.[38] The stereotype of a natural kind term consists of information shared by all speakers, and

---

[37]This line of objection is forcefully pressed in connection with Putnam's view by Mark Wilson in "Predicate Meets Property." A similar question was raised by Keith Donellan; see "Kripke and Putnam on Natural Kind Terms," p. 103.

[38]See "The Meaning of 'Meaning'," pp. 247–51.

as such it is extremely thin in many cases. For example, perhaps the only properties of cadmium that every speaker of English who competently uses the word 'cadmium' know follow from the fact that cadmium is a *metal*. On the other hand, there is nothing in Putnam's discussion to prevent a property shared by the local instances of a term, but having no special causal-explanatory connection at all to the kind it designates, from constituting part of the stereotype of the term. But there is such a connection between the kind designated by a term and its saliencies.

Saliencies, then, are not captured by Putnam's stereotypes. However, there is an aspect of Putnam's account not yet touched on that provides a point of departure for the characterization of salience. Putnam introduces the idea of the 'division of linguistic labor'.[39] The idea is that a natural kind term ξ in the language of a population P is normally associated with a subpopulation P_ξ of P such that (i) it is generally recognized within P that members of P_ξ know operational or descriptive criteria for membership in the extension of ξ, and (ii) members of the population at large apply ξ in conformity to its usage within P_ξ. Call P_ξ the **canonical subpopulation of P for ξ**. Putnam argued on plausible sociolinguistic grounds that natural kind words can generally be associated with such subpopulations; it is less plausible, however, that this association is independent of context. The question is in part when, within P, it would be generally recognized that a claim that an instance of ξ exemplifies a property is authoritative. When would we accord this status to such a claim about *lions*, for example? Depending on the context, one might defer to an ethologist, a veterinarian or a lion-tamer. The appropriate locution, then, is not 'P_ξ is the canonical subpopulation of P for ξ', but rather 'P_ξ is the canonical subpopulation of P for ξ in circumstances C', where C specifies a context in which a question about the behavior of instances of ξ arises. My aim is to characterize the conditions under which a predicate expresses a saliency for ξ in such a context; these contexts will then play a quasi-indexical role in fixing the reference of ξ.

It might be suggested that the saliencies for ξ in such a context comprise just the 'thick' stereotype for ξ possessed by the relevant canonical subpopulation. We would then say that the saliency-cluster for the term in that context is made up of those properties in terms of which the 'experts' therein would normally identify an instance of the term. But this is not quite right. The thick stereotype comprises those properties by which the experts make local identifications. But these properties might, like those in the ordinary stereotype, be entirely contingent to the relevant kind. Suppose, for example, that zoologists have spotted no albino tigers. They might

---

[39] Ibid., pp. 227–29.

then identify local tigers in part by their orange-yellow and black stripes. In that case, having orange-yellow and black stripes is part of the 'thick' stereotype of the word 'tiger' for zoologists, and hence, on the present proposal, is a saliency for it in any context in which the zoologists constitute the relevant canonical subpopulation. But this property is not a saliency for that term in any normal context of its use. Otherwise, the genetic properties of the local tigers responsible for their orange-yellow and black stripes would, on the suggested model, be constitutive of the kind *tiger*. They are not, for albino tigers are causally possible, even under local circumstances.

At a first approximation, I suggest that the saliencies for a natural kind term $A(x)$ in a context for the population P are given by those predicates $B(x)$ such that the extensional generalization

[i] $$(\forall x)(A(x) \rightarrow B(x))$$

is in a very strong sense *held to be lawlike* within the canonical subpopulation associated with that context. Though not analytic, these extensional connections, in a memorable phrase of Putnam's, are *treated as analytic in the actual practice* of the subpopulation in question. Thus, let P_0 be that subpopulation. That [i] has this epistemic status within P_0 is manifested by the fact that members of P_0 satisfy a certain counterfactual: if an agent in P_0 were to come to believe that an object falls under $A(x)$, she would believe it to fall under $B(x)$. This is intended to include the circumstance that the agent in question believes that an object a has come to fall under $A(x)$, and requires, in case the agent antecedently believes a to fall under $\neg B(x)$, that she will come to believe a to fall under $B(x)$. Thus, consider a generalization that we may suppose the agents in P_0 to treat as accidental, for example, 'Everyone in this room owns a copy of *The Critique of Pure Reason*'. Under normal circumstances, even if such an agent believes this generalization to be extensionally correct, if she were to come to believe that an unphilosophical person has entered the room, she would not on that account come to believe that person to own a copy of *The Critique of Pure Reason*; she would rather give up the generalization.

Part of what is missing in this case is that the indicated extensional connection is not treated as a law within P_0. But to be treated as lawlike in P_0 is not, by itself, quite the condition we require, for [i] could be treated as lawlike in P_0 and yet $B(x)$ not express a saliency for $A(x)$. If, for example, the sentence 'All tigers have yellow and black stripes' has been inductively well confirmed in P_0, it could be treated as lawlike. Still, if an albino tiger were presented to P_0, this generalization may simply be given up. In this case, having yellow and black stripes would not constitute a saliency for the term 'tiger'. If, on the other hand, this property were a saliency for 'tiger', the albino specimen would not be taken to fall under that term. It would rather be taken to fall under a closely related but distinct natural kind. The predicate $B(x)$ expresses a saliency for $A(x)$ if and only if, within P_0, an object would not be taken to fall under $A(x)$ unless it were taken to fall under $B(x)$, so that if an object were presented to P_0 as falling under $\neg B(x)$, it would not be taken to fall under $A(x)$.[40] Somewhat misappropriating a term of Goodman's, I shall say that an extensional generalization satisfying the indicated condition is **entrenched for** P_0.

In sum, then, the saliencies for a natural kind term ξ in a given context of its utterance are those properties designated by an observation term φ such that the generalization subsuming instances of ξ under φ is entrenched for the subpopulation associated with that context.[41] It is then roughly correct to say that, on the present proposal, the instances of a natural kind term comprise those objects falling under the structural properties exemplified by its paradigms which, if *taken* as constitutive of the kind designated by the term, render the entrenched generalizations concerning it lawlike.

With the characterization of salience, the basic structure of the present model of reference for natural kind terms is before us. Not all natural kind terms are satisfactorily described by the model, as I will show; but it does plausibly characterize the extensions of many such terms. The lawlike generalizations about many natural kinds are explicable in terms of structural properties that characterize the instances of the kind. Thus, for example, entrenched scientific and commonsense generalizations about chemical substances are explicable in terms of their molecular structures; thus it is those structures that circumscribe chemical kinds on the present model. Moreover, the model leads to plausible answers to the questions about referential ambiguity and stability with which we began. Typical of a whole family of cases is the example of optical isomerism introduced

---

[40]Christopher Peacocke has attempted to use something like the foregoing condition in saying what it is for an agent to treat an extensional generalization as a law. The direct attempt founders on the sort of consideration just rehearsed. Peacocke addresses the problem by placing restrictions on the mode of presentation of the objects in question; see his "Causal Modalities and Realism," in *Reference, Truth and Reality*, edited by Mark Platts (London: Routledge and Kegan Paul, 1979). It seems to me that the features of the original condition that obstruct its constituting a satisfactory criterion of perceived lawlikeness make it quite plausible as a criterion of salience. The saliencies for a natural kind word are connected with it by extensional generalizations that are not only treated as lawlike within the relevant canonical subpopulation; this attitude is stable under the introduction of certain sorts of information. An account of causal necessity in terms of a related notion of epistemic stability has been suggested by Brian Skyrms in *Causal Necessity* (New Haven: Yale University Press, 1979).

[41]Saliencies, then, constitute observational qualities (in my very broad sense). Still, this restriction seems overly confining in some contexts; see 3.3.5 for a discussion of this issue.

earlier. Certain organic compounds exist in multiple isomeric forms that are distinguished from one another only by a property of the way in which solutions of the separate isomers transmit polarized light. Different optical activity properties characterize different isomers. Suppose that in fact only one isomeric form of such a substance is found locally. Would a natural kind term introduced by reference to local samples of the substance refer to the local isomer, or to the totality of isomers?

On my view the answer would depend on whether the relevant form of optical activity is a saliency for the term. Some optically active compounds are historically exemplified in only one isomeric form; but terms for these compounds may have been introduced before the relevant optical activities were known (much less salient). The exemplification of its nonoptical saliencies by the paradigms for such a term is explicable in terms of molecular structure without reference to isomerism. Thus, on the present proposal, the term in question would have designated the totality of isomeric forms. If such an optical property were to have *become* salient, on the present model the term would have undergone a reference shift, and would have subsequently designated the locally exemplified isomeric form. A similar story can be told for certain cases of the isotope/element example.

However, the situation envisioned in the preceding paragraph seems rather uncommon. Most compounds exhibiting optical isomerism occur in nature as *mixtures* of the relevant optical isomers (just as most chemical elements occur as mixtures of their isotopes). I shall examine a particular but rather typical such case that affords a good illustration of the role of the notion of salience. The case involves tartaric acid, a compound that naturally occurs as a mixture of two isomeric forms. Some background will be useful.

In the simplest cases, optical isomers occur in two forms which are nonsuperimposable reflections of each other. The chemical and physical properties of the two forms are identical, except that they rotate the plane of plane-polarized light passed through solutions of the separate isomers equally but in opposite directions. Mirror image forms of the same compound are called *enantiomers*. A compound, like tartaric acid, that occurs as a mixture of roughly equal numbers of molecules of each enantiomer, is optically inactive because the net optical rotation is zero. Such a mixture is called *racemic*. Although the ordinary physical properties of pure enantiomers (apart from their optical properties) are identical, they frequently differ from those of the racemic mixture. In such cases, the mixture has a crystal structure different from those of the pure enantiomers and may therefore differ in melting point, solubility, and density. Tartaric acid is a case in point: for example, the racemic tartaric acid has a higher melting point and lower solubility than the component enantiomers. This is explained by the fact that the racemic acid has a more stable crystal structure than either of the component enantiomers.

Equivalents of the term 'tartaric acid' were in use before any of this was known. The question is what we should say about the reference of such a term in the prior situation. The possibilities are these: it referred to

(a) one of the enantiomers;
(b) the compound;
(c) the racemic mixture;
(d) none of the above.

Option (d) would be appropriate for someone who denied that the term had a definite reference at all, say, in the early nineteenth century; that was Hacking's conclusion about 'acid'. I shall try to avoid that conclusion, at least for the moment. Option (a) can also be set aside, for the reason that for any rationale that might be produced for regarding the term as referring to one enantiomer, there is a symmetric story that would rationalize its referring to the other. I take it, then, that the real choice here is between (b) and (c), the compound and the racemic mixture.

We know what the term refers to now: in the lexicon of contemporary chemistry, the term 'tartaric acid' refers to the compound, comprising all instances of either enantiomer *and* the racemic mixture. That is the conclusion of the present model. The present paradigms comprise instances of each of the three species: the two enantiomeric forms and the racemic mixture, and the properties in common to these are explicable in terms of structural invariants common to these forms, that is to say, in terms not requiring reference to structural properties of any particular isomer. These structural invariants pick out the compound. However, all of the paradigmatic instances of tartaric acid at some point in the nineteenth century would have been instances of the *racemic mixture*. The melting point and solubility of the accessible samples would have been common currency, and presumably attributed to *tartaric acid* by generalizations that were confirmed, to some extent, and may even have been treated as lawlike. It may then seem that the best candidate for the reference of the term 'tartaric acid' at that period is the racemic mixture, not the compound. In that case, one would be led to the somewhat implausible conclusion that the term 'tartaric acid' has undergone a reference shift, referring earlier to the racemic mixture, and subsequently to the compound.

But it did not happen that way. For the fact that the melting point and solubility ascriptions were treated as lawlike does not mean that these properties were *saliencies* for the term 'tartaric acid'. If they were, when the pure enantiomeric forms were isolated and shown not to have the solubility and melting point of the racemic mixture, they would not have been taken to be instances of tartaric acid. The new samples would rather have been taken to be instances of two new species, in many respects similar to tartaric acid, but in crucial respects not. But that is not in fact what happened. Instead, the relevant generalizations seem simply to have been *given up* (compare the case of albino tigers earlier). The situation could be accurately described by saying that it had been discovered that there are several forms of tartaric acid, each with a different solubility and melting point. What properties *were* then the saliencies for the term 'tartaric acid'? Broadly chemical ones: patterns of reactivity, approximate ratios of combination by weight, the 'empirical formula', or ratios by weight of the elements into which tartaric acid can be resolved. Failure to exemplify any of these would in fact have disqualified an item from falling under the term 'tartaric acid'. These are explicable in terms of the structural characterization of the compound, and, indeed, only in terms of that characterization, and so on the present model the term referred at the earlier period to the compound, and has done so ever since. This is a good example of the possibility of referential stability in the presence of significant variance in the class of paradigms for a natural kind word over time.

3.3.5   Saliencies and Law Clusters

The discussion of the isomerism case suggests a difficulty for the notion of salience. I said at one point that substance terms may be saliently associated with patterns of chemical reactivity. The difficulty is that such a property, for example, 'combines with oxygen in a ratio of 2:1', is not observational even in our rather extended sense, and so cannot by the letter of the definition qualify as a saliency for such a term. Reactivities are nonobservational in two ways: first, such properties are dispositional, and would normally be expressed in terms of a universally quantified conditional of some sort; second, specifying such a property involves reference to other natural kinds. Solubilities constitute another class of such properties. Against the background of the characterization of logic in chapter 4, we could safely expand the notion of salience to allow predicates whose only nonlogical terms are observational to specify saliencies; this would allow us to express saliencies involving extensional relationships between observational properties.[42] But there is still the problem of accommodating saliencies for natural kind terms specified in terms of *other* natural kind words.

It might be suggested that this problem be solved by means of an inductive stratification of saliencies and natural kind terms. The idea would be

---

[42] Or even relationships between such properties involving certain modalities.

to allow previously accumulated natural kind terms to figure in the spec-ification of saliencies at the next level up. A bit more explicitly, for any natural number n, we may say that a natural kind term is of level n if its saliencies are of level n. We now specify when a predicate expresses a saliency of level n by induction on n: a predicate expresses a saliency of level 0 if its only nonlogical terms are observational; and for any n, a predicate expresses a saliency of level $n + 1$ if its only nonlogical terms are either natural kind terms of level n or express saliencies of level n. Thus, for example, if the word 'water' is of level 0, then solubility in water would be a saliency of level 1. But the inductive stratification idea, while applicable in some cases, does not apply in many situations in which the determination of saliencies seems to run in a circle. Thus, for example, while 'combines with oxygen in a ratio of 2:1' arguably expresses a saliency for 'hydrogen', 'combines with hydrogen in a ratio of 1:2' has an equal claim to express a saliency for 'oxygen'. On the mechanism of reference I have described, then, to determine the reference of either term we must suppose that the reference of the other has been fixed.

The way out of this impasse begins with the observation that relations may be saliently associated with ordered sets of natural kind words in much the same way that properties are saliently associated with individual natural kind words. Thus the relational phrase 'combine in a ratio of 2:1', under some suitable operational specification of 'combines with', may be taken to express a saliency for the pair

$$\langle \text{'hydrogen'}, \text{'oxygen'} \rangle.$$

In general, then, a saliency-ascription for an n'tuple of terms $\langle A_1, ..., A_n \rangle$ is a sentence of the form

[i] $(\forall x_1)...(\forall x_n)((A_1(x_1) \text{ \& } ... \text{ \& } A_n(x_n)) \rightarrow B(x_1, ..., x_n))$

where B is assembled from observational lexicon, which satisfies the en-trenchment requirement. The story of section 3.3.4 is now generalized in the obvious way: we look for a simultaneous assignment of properties to $A_1, ..., A_n$ that appropriately explains why n'tuples of paradigms for $A_1, ..., A_n$ fall under the relation given by B.[43]

There is still one difficulty. Say that a set of such generalizations is a **law cluster** for the context in question, and that a law cluster is **solvable** if it is possible to assign properties to the relevant terms in such a way as to satisfy the explanatory grounding requirement. Such an assignment will be

---

[43] Here 'appropriately explains' is to be understood in terms of the direct analogue for the relational case of the definition of 'structural basis' introduced in 3.3.3.

called a **solution** for the cluster. The natural suggestion for implementing the idea of the previous paragraph is to take the term A_1, say, to refer to the kind delimited by the property assigned to it by a solution for the law cluster consisting of all generalizations of the form [i] (or most of them, suitably weighted) that satisfy the entrenchment requirement in the context in question. The problem is that this cluster may be unsolvable through no fault of A_1: in such a case, although we should wish to say that A_1 has a definite reference, it is associated in this way with so many empty terms that the entire law cluster for it is unsolvable.

One might ask why, under these circumstances, we should not prescind from ascribing reference to any of the terms figuring in the cluster. But such a policy would be too restrictive. Consider the case of ethnobotany. Ethnobotanists have studied plants used by various societies for medicinal purposes. The populations in question have terms that have been construed as referring to certain rather narrow taxa. These terms resemble natural kind words against the background of the mechanism of reference I have described: there is a canonical subpopulation (healers) who associate the terms with paradigmatic instances (local specimens of the relevant taxa) and with salient properties. The difficulty is that typically a good many of these properties are fictive. But others are not. For example, in many cases, compounds derived from such plants have real medicinal powers which are saliently associated with the terms within the population in question. At the same time, the terms are associated with a number of empty terms by a law cluster that expresses, as we might put it, a mistaken theory about the mechanism underlying the causal powers of their instances. In such cases, we will look for the best partial solution for the relevant law cluster, the partial assignment of explanatory properties that provides a basis for the largest number of saliency-ascriptions, weighted according to their actual frequency of projective use. It is entirely possible that there will be more than one optimal partial solution, in which case we would have what Lewis called an 'indeterminacy of compromise'.[44] The terms that are unevaluated in such a partial solution will count as empty.

There is a reasonable strategy for effecting such a partial solution. The strategy must be suitably nuanced in order to lead in each case to an outcome optimal in the spirit of the previous paragraph, but the procedure I shall sketch generally leads, I believe, to a good approximation to such an outcome. Let C be a law cluster for a set K of natural kind terms. If S is a subset of K, by C/S we denote the collection of all members of C containing no occurrences of members of S. Say that S **defeats** C if

---

[44]See "Radical Interpretation," in *Philosophical Papers*, vol. 1 (New York: Oxford University Press, 1983), p. 118.

C/S is solvable but C is not. If S defeats C, then, the unsolvability of C is representable as being due in some way to the terms in S. A natural first suggestion would be to take the admissible partial solutions for C to be total solutions for C/S for *minimal* defeaters S for C, that is, defeaters for C containing no proper subset that is also a defeater for C. But this will not quite do. Imagine a language with a term for a kind of witch who are believed to cast spells by means of ritual interactions with a certain kind of orchid, beliefs that are expressed by a small number of saliency-ascribing generalizations for both the witch-term and the orchid-term. The law cluster, call it W, consisting of just these generalizations is unsolvable, but the cluster that results by excising W from the collection, call it C of all entrenched generalizations in the language may be imagined to be solvable. (For this, we need only suppose that the given witch-term is the only fictive predicate in the language, and that the saliency-ascribing generalizations for it are included in W.) The set consisting of just the witch-term is thus a minimal defeater for C. The difficulty is that in this case, the set consisting of just the orchid-term is *also* a minimal defeater for C, and thus on the present proposal a partial solution for C that results by simply omitting all saliency-ascribing generalizations for the orchid-term will be as suitable as any other. That is implausible: the unsolvability of the overall cluster, we want to say, stems from the nonexistence of the witches, not the orchids. The question is how to represent this insight within a description encompassing only the notions of a law cluster, a defeater for a law cluster, and so on. In the imagined case, the term putatively designating orchids has a prima facie claim to refer. The problem was that this term is connected to an empty term by an unsolvable set of saliency-ascribing generalizations. But these, we may suppose, comprise only a proper subset of the set of saliency-ascribing generalizations for the orchid-term. Omitting either term would restore solvability, but omitting the orchid-term would violate a principle of least disturbance: the resulting disturbance is greater because the law cluster associated with the orchid-term is *larger*. In general, then, let

$$S_1, S_2, ..., S_n$$

be the alternative minimal defeaters for C. The acceptable partial solutions for C will be solutions for *maximal* restrictions C/S_m; such a partial solution will assign properties to the terms in the sets S_m such that C/S_m is not properly included in any alternative restriction C/S_k. In the present case, the collection that results by omitting from C all saliency-ascriptions for the witch-term may be imagined to have this property. The residual set still incorporates a thick saliency-profile for the orchid-term, which for that reason will be associated with a definite reference by the relevant partial solution.

3.4 Grounding the Model

3.4.1 Natural Kinds and Conformal Explanation

The model of reference to natural kinds I have just sketched satisfies our judgments about what the extensions of many natural kind terms should be. But that is not enough. For it is not yet explicit how, within the framework for radical interpretation described in the previous chapter, the present account of the reference of natural kind terms is to be motivated. It must be shown how the suggested strategy for assigning extensions to natural kind terms contributes to the construction of interpretations which are acceptable within the Conformal Framework. My goal in this section will be to show how the present strategy facilitates interpretations which are best candidates from the standpoint of the social version of the Principle of Conformality.

I begin with a somewhat simplified example. Suppose we wish to explain in conformal terms the fact that Karl has frequently tamed lions. We may do so, in terms of Karl's standing desire to tame lions in a set of frequently encountered situations, if we can explicate Karl's ability to tame lions in conformal terms. Karl might have general information about lions expressed by semantic representations of the form

(1) $(\forall x)(\text{LION}(x) \to (\forall t)(R(x,t) \to \text{TAME}(x, t + \epsilon)))$,

where according to the interpretation in question, $\text{LION}(x)$ designates lions, $R(x,t)$ says that x fulfills certain conditions at the time t, and $\text{TAME}(x,t)$ says that x is tame at t. If Karl is generally in a position to bring it about that a presented lion fulfills the conditions described by $R(x,t)$, then we can explicate Karl's ability to tame lions in conformal terms. The explanation refers to a causal-explanatory strategy by which Karl himself might give conditional explanations in terms of (1) of how he would tame one or another lion should the need arise. The question, then, is the extent to which the requirement for such conformal explanations constrains us to assign the correct extension to $\text{LION}(x)$.

I have observed that the adequacy of a conformal explanation is in part a function of the adequacy of the causal explanation that underlies it: Karl's explanation. Thus we shall look for the interpretations of $\text{LION}(x)$ that render (1) the best ground for the explanation of instances of lion-taming.

Such an explanation is more adequate the more resolution the interpretation assigned to LION(x) affords of the causal basis of the items explained. The best resolution arises, one might suppose, in part from a structural specification of a genetic property of lions; it is such a property that might be supposed to be ultimately responsible for the disposition of lions to become tame under the circumstances described by $R(x, t)$, and in that case it is this property that is selected as characteristic for LION(x) in Karl's language if (1) expresses the sole saliency for this term therein. If there is such a property, common to all lions, then it is plausible that it constitutes at least a good approximation to the genotype of a typical lion.[45] The genetic structure in question must account for the responsiveness of the local lions in the training-situation. That would include any gene responsible for essential biological functions making possible *any* pattern of responsiveness. That is rather a lot of structure; moreover, the structures underlying these functions in lions are likely to distinguish lions from other animal groups.[46]

For the purposes of the present example we needn't claim that the relevant explanatory property in this situation picks out exactly the lions; but the example is instructive in showing how, in fulfilling the individual version of (PC) in this case, we might be led to *something like* the actual extension of the term 'lion'. The setting of the suggested social model of reference for natural kind terms is essentially that of the present example writ large. That model would generate precisely the foregoing observations if the relevant subpopulation for the term 'lion' consisted of Karl alone and the only generalization about lions that is entrenched for Karl was expressed by (1). In the general case, the model directs us to the grounding structural explanations of why the local instances of a natural kind term exemplify the properties associated with the term by the generalizations concerning it that are entrenched in the relevant subpopulation. The reference of the term will consist of those objects falling under the structural properties introduced by these explanations. In general, the canonical subpopulation for a natural kind term associated with a typical context of its utterance will have a more or less thick portfolio of saliencies for it; in this way, a natural kind word occurring in Karl's language may inherit a well-defined exten-

---

[45]In fact, such a disposition cannot plausibly be explained *solely* in terms of the genotype of a typical lion, for the required explanation will have to implicate mechanisms whose expression in the phenotype of a lion depends on the developmental or environmental background. In that case the structures responsible for such mechanisms would be partly constitutive of the relevant characteristic property.

[46]One question that arises at this point is whether there is any reason to suppose that there *is* an invariant genetic basis for these functions *within the class of lions*; this is connected to the question of whether 'lion' is an inhomogeneous natural kind term in the sense of 3.5. For the purposes of this example, I am simply assuming that there is such a basis. See 3.5.1–3.5.3 below for a discussion of this issue.

sion, rationalized by the maximizing role of that extensional assignment in enabling conformal explanations of actions within Karl's population. Thus, for example, electrical conductivity plausibly constitutes a saliency for the word 'copper' figuring in innumerable conformal explanations of successful circuit design or repair; and the capacity to neutralize acids is a saliency for substance-terms designating bases invoked in many conformal explanations of purposive neutralizations of acids by bases. It is the ubiquity of such commonsense conformal-explanatory stories that largely rationalizes the suggested mechanism of reference for natural kind terms.

In broad outline, that is the story I wish to tell. Still missing, however, are some crucial details. To adequately justify the present model of reference for NK within the Conformal Framework, we need to more fully exhibit the interpretive role of some fine-structures in that model, in particular, the account given in 3.3.3 of kind-delimiting properties and the demarcation of saliencies suggested in 3.3.4. It needs to be explained why that demarcation is especially appropriate to the purpose of optimizing conformal explanation. (Why restrict the saliencies for a term to properties associated with it by *entrenched* generalizations? Couldn't many weaker associations play a role in conformal explanations?) Something must be said about how the explanatory levels of the properties determining natural kinds have been located. (Why are the properties fixing the reference of a natural kind term the ones introduced by the *grounding* explanations of why its paradigms exemplify its saliencies?). And we must attend to the question of anachronism mentioned at the conclusion of 3.3.3. (Isn't it simply implausible that the extension of a noun in middle English should be exactly fixed by a microstructural property?) These problems of justification turn out to be connected.

I will first deal with the question about explanatory levels. Consider some plausible saliencies for the word 'copper': for example, thermal conductivity, electrical conductivity, and malleability. Suppose that these were the only saliencies for that term. Each of these features is explained by the electronic structure of copper, and that structure is in turn explained quantum mechanically in terms of the fact that copper has atomic number 46. That is the grounding explanation of why local instances of copper exemplify these properties, and so having atomic number 46 is the characteristic property for the term 'copper', even if just these properties are identified as its saliencies. However, the fact that specimens of copper exemplify that atomic number also explains why they fall under other properties which, though not saliencies for 'copper', may yet be associated with this term by means of inductively confirmed generalizations (in the present case, for example, melting point, hardness, patterns of reactivity, and so on; each of these is explicable in terms of the atomic number). Such generalizations may in turn figure in projective explanations in the object language that in turn underwrite additional conformal explanations. The characteristic property for a term, then, is ascribed to its local instances by the explanation most fundamental in level of why those objects exemplify its saliencies, but that property will typically stand in a causal explanatory connection to many other properties besides.

However, in the imagined situation, having atomic number 46 is not the only explanation of the relevant saliency-exemplifications. Each of the properties saliently associated with 'copper' in that situation is exemplified by *all metals*. This is explained by a feature of the electronic structure of metals: the outer electrons of atoms of a metallic element are not localized in orbitals but are free to roam about randomly (or will do so directionally, in the presence of an electric potential). But the reason why a particular metallic element exemplifies the delocalization property is that it exemplifies the atomic number that it does; that is why the suggested mechanism of reference identifies the atomic number of copper and not the delocalization property as the determining property for the reference of 'copper'. One good interpretive reason for this assignment is the conformal-explanatory benefit indicated above: even though in this situation few empirically important properties are saliently associated with the term 'copper', others may be inductively associated with it that are not explicable in terms of the delocalization property but that are explicable in terms of atomic number. Assigning the standard reference to 'copper' renders these extensional connections lawlike and thus available for a role in causal explanations in the object language.

There is a second, related respect in which the goal of constructing conformal explanations favors the standard assignment over the alternative construal of 'copper' as designating metals. It is a consequence of the idea, noted earlier, that other things equal, conformal explanations are better the better the object-language explanations that support them. The fact that a specimen, c, of copper exemplifies a property P (say, electrical conductivity), which is explained by the fact that c is a metal and a lawlike generalization subsuming metals under P, is normally better explained by the fact that c is copper and the lawlike generalization subsuming copper under P. The second explanation is more informative, locating the subject of the explanation in a narrower reference-kind. But informativeness is not, by itself, the issue. The point is that the information conveyed is information about the structural basis of the state of affairs to be explained. One reason why c falls under P is that c is metallic; but the reason why c is metallic is that it is made of stuff with atomic number 46. The explanation in terms of atomic number, then, cites the more fundamental reason, which is also the more specific reason, why c falls under P, and a lawlike generalization connecting the property constitutive of that reason to P, the property constitutive of the object of explanation. It is for this reason that the second story scores higher in point of explanatoriness. The present benefit is conferred quite systematically by the policy of taking the reference of a natural kind term to be fixed by its characteristic property.

I have just considered two ways in which the suggested mechanism of reference facilitates conformal explanations by generating causal-explanatory structures in the object-language: the second of these concerns the adequacy of the explanations thus generated, the first the availability of such explanations. In light of these observations, I want to return to the charge of anachronism raised earlier. It has seemed to some philosophers quite implausible that the use of the term 'gold', say, in Locke's community could determine a highly specific reference for it, characterized in terms of a microphysical trait utterly unknown at the time, the very trait, indeed, in terms of which contemporary chemistry characterizes that reference. Thus, Mark Wilson writes:

> While we can safely assign samples of the stable isotope of Au to Locke's 'gold', there is no reason to insist that the 12 radioactive forms of Au be so apportioned. For convenience, we will prefer to assign *is Au* to Locke's 'gold' because that particular property, among all its interchangeable indices, has the shortest label in present-day English. But the convenience of this description should not bewitch us into historical parochialism.[47]

On the view I have advocated, the extension of 'gold' is fixed by its characteristic property, and so the question becomes how the use of the term in Locke's situation determines its characteristic property. But that property is simply the basis for a grounding explanation of why certain objects exemplify certain properties associated with the term 'gold' *in that situation*. It is the interpretation of the term that makes the agents' ascription of membership in the kind it designates the best answer to the question of why its paradigmatic instances exemplify its saliencies. These traits have a clear claim to be considered the most important properties associated with the term in that context. There is then a rather natural sense in which a body of information about the use of the term *in this situation* determines its characteristic property, and thus its extension, therein. Having said this, however, it should be acknowledged that there is one way in which the charge of 'historical parochialism' seems correct but, I would argue, harmlessly so. The interpretive rationale for the suggested mechanism of reference lies not within the time-line of the relevant population but outside it: *we* want to construct a connected set of conformal explanations that render the causal-historical role of these agents broadly intelligible in con-

---

[47] "Predicate Meets Property," p. 580.

formal terms. I argued in subsection 2.4.6 that this aim is equivalent to the goal of rendering the same data broadly intelligible intentional terms, and so the interpretive purpose may be seen throughout to be to understand the activity of the population in its natural and social context in terms of the notions of belief, desire and intentional action. But the semantical devices by which we arrive at that understanding are our own.

3.4.2   Salience and Stability

I now want to consider a problem raised by the possibility of extensional generalizations which, though not entrenched for the community in question, are yet in a weaker sense treated as lawlike. These express connections of a natural kind term with other predicates that have been confirmed to some extent, but not in the way required for those predicates to express saliencies for the term. There is no difficulty if the relevant extensional inclusion is already explicable in terms of the characteristic property associated with the term; this is the sort of explanatory dividend referred to previously in which the characteristic property fixed by a given set of saliencies for a term explains further properties of its instances. When it exists, such a connection can normally be discovered by empirical means. However, there are cases in which this procedure misfires: the association in question has been inductively confirmed in the local situation, but there are causally possible counterinstances.

An example of this situation is afforded by the case of tartaric acid considered earlier. Recall that this compound occurs in two optically active forms (enantiomers) or as a mixture of the two, such a mixture being called 'racemic' when it consists of roughly equal numbers of molecules of each enantiomer; and recall that the racemic mixture has physical properties such as melting point and solubility that differ from those of its component isomers. Consider a situation in which only instances of the racemic mixture are paradigms for 'tartaric acid', but in which only properties common to all forms of tartaric acid are saliencies for it.[48] However, suppose also that the melting point of the racemic tartaric acid comes to be inductively ascribed to tartaric acid on the basis of tests conducted on its local instances. The difficulty is this. On the mechanism of reference I have described, we have seen that the term 'tartaric acid' designates the compound tartaric acid, and so on that criterion of reference the indicated ascription of melting point is false. But it might seem even better from the standpoint of the Principle of Conformality if that ascription had been

---

[48]The situation of chemistry at some point in the nineteenth century might be a good example.

rendered true: for we can certainly imagine that the generalization about melting point figures in *some* attempted projective explanations that the relevant agents frame, and in this case additional conformal explanations may well be forthcoming if the semantical construction of 'tartaric acid' were to render that generalization lawlike (and thus true). In other words, from the standpoint of the interpretive *rationale* I have given for the suggested mechanism of reference, it is not clear why *all* properties inductively associated with such a term should not have a claim to count as saliencies for it. In that case, the extension of the term would be given by a structural trait that best explains paradigmatic exemplifications of all such properties, perhaps weighted according to the actual frequency with which the corresponding generalizations occur in projective explanations framed within the community.

Such a policy would be at odds with our judgments of sameness of extension in some cases. We are disinclined, for example, to view the term for 'tartaric acid' as undergoing a reference shift in the situation described earlier. On the suggestion I am now considering, we would be forced to look for a more specific referential assignment each time a generalization about tartaric acid came to be confirmed that is not explicable in terms of the antecedently given reference of that term. We would in effect have to give up any distinction between *discovering* a regularity about the stuff designated by 'tartaric acid' and *stipulating* a certain sort of constitutive condition of membership in its extension. In the 'tartaric acid' case, for example, the liberalized criterion of salience will shift the reference of that term in such a way as to build into the characteristic property for it the properties of its local instances responsible for their melting point; that term will then subsequently designate the racemic form of tartaric acid. It will seem to the chemists in this situation that they are making an empirical discovery, but on the mechanism of reference I am now considering this is an illusion. They would describe the situation by saying that they had 'discovered the melting point of tartaric acid'. But if the melting point ascription is interpreted with respect to the prior reference of the term, it is simply false; if interpreted with respect to the subsequent reference, it is true, but the truth it expresses is not appropriately described as having been discovered. Rather, the reference of the term in this situation automatically shifts in such a way as to accomodate the projected melting point. The demarcation of salient properties I have suggested on the basis of the entrenchment requirement avoids this outcome by drawing a distinction between variations in the properties associated with a term that should lead us to expect an accompanying variation in its reference and those that should not. The question, however, continues to be what interpretive justification can be given for drawing the distinction in just this way.

The alternative construction of 'tartaric acid' just rehearsed differs from the one I have suggested by enabling, at least potentially, some additional conformal explanations at the margin, but at the cost of a structural sort of referential instability. One possibility of addressing the predicament described in the previous paragraph would be to adopt an additional constraint on interpretation. We might call it the 'Principle of Stability'. It would say that, other things being equal, an interpretation of a population should minimize referential variance of terms over time. Such a constraint would limit the operation of the Principle of Conformality in cases where the unrestricted application of that principle would result in excessive referential instability. Besides the obvious problem of deciding how much instability is excessive, however, it is not clear what interpretive rationale could be given for such a requirement as a *further* constraint on radical interpretation. Rather, I now want to argue that a form of the Principle of Stability is a byproduct of the present framework for interpretation. In brief, I shall argue that a policy favoring the stability of the reference of natural kind terms over time may considerably enhance the conformal explanation of accomplishments and capacities of *groups*.

Let P be a population that we wish to interpret over an interval $[t_1, t_2]$. Let P_1 and P_2 be the restrictions of P to the times t_1 and t_2; that is, P_1 and P_2 are respectively the stages of P at t_1 and t_2. Finally, let C be a class of outcomes. Consider the problem of explaining in conformal terms the fact that agents in P_1 and P_2 have separately produced outcomes of type C. At issue are two interpretations of P which are candidates for such an explanatory role. Both interpretations give, separately for P_1 and P_2, conformal explanations of how outcomes of type C are realized in the two situations. The difference is that on one interpretation the reference of terms in the language of P relevant to the explanations is shifted over $[t_1, t_2]$ whereas on the other the reference of these terms is stable. There is an obvious respect in which, other things being equal, the present circumstance favors the second interpretation over the first on grounds of simplicity: the first interpretation uses two ascriptions of reference to generate the desired explanations, whereas the second interpretation deploys only one. A consequence of this asymmetry is that the second interpretation provides a somewhat more unified semantical underpinning for the separate conformal explanations.

The point about explanatory unification is connected to the possibility of explaining accomplishments and capacities of groups in conformal terms. In subsection 2.4.5 I alluded to a social analogue of the suggested model of conformal explanation of actions and capacities of individuals. I distinguished summative from nonsummative social actions. A summative accomplishment of a group consists in accomplishments of the same sort of several individuals comprising the group. Thus, for example, the effective treatment of a disease in a society consists in a certain range of successful individual outcomes, and one can explain this social accomplishment by explicating the relevant individual outcomes in conformal terms. However, recall that such a set of conformal explanations does not constitute a conformal explanation of the summative group action unless the conformality properties associated with the explanations substantially coincide; that is, there must exist a single set of interpreted semantic representations grounding the projective explanations by which the individual agents bring about the outcomes in question. These representations describe collective beliefs in the summative sense. If the individual accomplishments are scattered through time, the summative conception of social belief requires the relevant semantic representations to be stably interpreted over the interval in question. The assumption of referential stability, then, is built into the very idea of a conformal explanation of a summative social action extended over time. The corresponding constraint in the nonsummative case is in essential respects similar. A nonsummative group action consists in the structured exercise of a set of individual capacities; a conformality property underlying such an action is a set of semantic representations that express nonsummative collective beliefs of the group (or its subgroups). The requirement of referential stability for these representations is relevant in cases where the group action in question takes place over an extended temporal interval.

The foregoing observations make the point that referential stability of terms facilitates conformal explanations of social actions, a point that places some interpretive premium on minimizing referential variance. Of course, the stability condition is defeasible: we should expect to countenance referential variance under some circumstances. My proposal has been roughly that the reference of a natural kind word is given by a property that in an appropriate sense *grounds* the saliency-ascribing generalizations associated with the term. These generalizations have a claim to express, more than any other body of information associated with it, the *point* of the term. A change in the properties saliently associated with such a term thus reflects a fundamental change in its theoretical and/or practical role, and it is not surprising that such a change will in many cases be accompanied by a perturbation of its reference.

3.4.3 Ensemble Terms

I am at the end of my account of reference for what might be called 'well-behaved' natural kind terms. I take up the miscreant cases in the following section. However, I still have to attend to two questions about the range of applicability of the present model. First, we need to be somewhat more careful about cases of reference failure. If the reference of a natural kind term is fixed by a property that is a suitable causal-explanatory basis for the exemplification of its saliencies by its paradigms, what of the case in which there is no such basis? In such a case the paradigms for the term exemplify its saliencies, but there is no invariant structural explanation of why they do. As it is currently formulated, the present model assigns the empty extension to a term in this situation; but I noted earlier that I would want to qualify this conclusion somewhat.

Suppose that the number of explanatory bases is small, say, two. I said that it is not a good explanation of why an object falls under a property P to appeal to the fact that it falls under the disjunction of several properties whose exemplification by the object would separately explain its exemplification of P. However, if we know that the object falls under the disjunctive property, we have been given *some* information about what the explanation is. If the disjunction is bipartite, we can identify two potential explanatory stories, one of which we know is correct. It seems right to say that this circumstance confers *some* explanatory relevance on the disjunctive story; and this suggests a somewhat more charitable construction of the extension of the term in the preceding situation.

Peter Railton has suggested an information-theoretic account of the explanatory relevance of noncausal explanations. In the broadest possible terms, Railton's idea is that a derivation of an event-describing sentence that is not itself a causal explanation may yet have explanatory content if it conveys *information about* the causal explanation of that event.[49] Railton used this idea to describe the explanatory content of certain probabilistic inferences, but I think it can be equally well used to motivate the explanatory relevance of the sort of disjunctive account considered above. If you know that an object falls under one of a small class of properties the exemplification of each of which would explain an outcome, you know that an explanation of that outcome can be located within a small number of explanation-candidates. In a quite straightforward sense, then, this gives you *information about* the explanation of that event. This information decreases with the *number* of explanatory properties which are considered, of course; and this means that the present rationale for the explanatory relevance of 'disjunctive' stories will deteriorate as the disjunctions get longer.

Consider a generalization of the form

[i] $(\forall x)((A_1(x) \lor ... \lor A_n(x)) \to B(x))$,

where each sentence obtained from [i] by deleting all but one of the disjuncts $A_i(x)$ is a causal law. My suggestion is that the model of conformal

---

[49] Peter Railton, "Probability, Explanation, and Information," *Synthese* 48 (1981): 233–56.

explanation I have given may be stretched to allow such disjunctive generalizations to play something like the role causal generalizations play in its original formulation. But it is important to see that this sort of stretching may be accomplished without sacrificing the original aim. What drives the original model is the idea that the semantic representations accorded to Karl's beliefs generate a map of the causal structure of a space of outcomes in which his basic actions are embedded. That map in turn allows us to explain how Karl actualizes various outcomes. We may use essentially the same idea if the semantic representations accorded to some of Karl's beliefs constitute disjunctive-causal generalizations of the form [i], although in this case we cannot recover a fully determinate map. In a particular case, we can only locate a set of such maps within which the explanatory map must reside. The smaller the set, the more information we will have about what the relevant map might be.

Against the background of such a generalized picture of conformal explanation, the suggested mechanism of reference for natural kind terms operates essentially as before, except that the reference of a term need not be univocal: its semantic correlate is no longer a natural kind, but an ensemble of kinds. For this reason I shall call such an expression an **ensemble term**. I suggest that it is this sort of picture that is appropriate to cases like Putnam's example of 'jade'. Here there are two natural kinds associated with just the same qualitative saliencies. I believe that our inclination in this case is to say *both* that 'there are two kinds of jade' *and* that 'jade is not a natural kind'; we do not say 'there is no such thing as jade'. The suggested extension of the preceding model to this case allows us to make sense of these intuitions. The term 'jade' is not empty: it designates, on the present suggestion, a disjunction of two kinds, jadeite and nephrite. But the disjunction of these kinds is not itself a natural kind. The divided semantic interpretation of 'jade' may yet play a limited conformal-explanatory role. It is in terms of this role that the interpretation may be justified within the Conformal Framework.

3.4.4   NK Circumscribed

I have now developed two models for the reference of predicates: the model of section 3.2, directed toward observation terms, and the model of section 3.3, targeted on certain natural kind words, which I shall call the *NK*-model. We shall subsequently extend the *NK*-model to cover a broader range of natural kind words, but in such a way that the interpretive rationale for it will be largely preserved. However, we have not, as yet, given a non-circular characterization of the classes of expressions to which the separate models apply. This is a problem, for there are cases to which the two models can both be applied, with different results. In this section, I shall take up the question of when an expression of Karl's language falls into one of these semantic categories. For this purpose, two additional concepts will be useful.

Call a term of Karl's language **weakly observational** if Karl, or Karl's kind, has local observational criteria of application for it. The notion of 'observational criterion' is here to be understood in the broad way indicated in section 3.2: any critieral procedure available to the relevant agent(s) for determining, of a locally encountered object, whether it falls under the term, is a candidate. As before, these criteria are not indefeasible; they are procedures that normally, but need not always, indicate whether local objects fall under the term in question. Moreover, the relevant criteria may be context-dependent, and the contexts may refer criteriological questions to specialized subpopulations. Thus natural kind terms, as well as observation terms, may count as weakly observational. In that case, however, there is a problem when a natural kind term is weakly observational, for if one were to suppose that the given natural kind word is in fact an observation term, the suggested account of reference for the observational case will count an object as falling under the term just in case it exemplifies the relevant observational properties. However, the object may exemplify these properties and yet not fall under the natural kind designated by the term. The question is: what tells us that the term is to be *treated* as a natural kind term and *not* as an observation term?

The second concept we shall require is that of a 'causally projective' notion. Say that a predicate $A(x)$ is **causally projective** for a population if there is a set of generalizations of the form $(\forall x)(A(x) \to B(x))$ in the language of the population that satisfy the requirement of entrenchment described in 3.3.4, and that have actually been instantiated sufficiently often. The second condition is understood to require that in a large number of cases such a generalization is actually a basis, in conjunction with a singular belief of the form $A(c)$, for the corresponding singular belief of the form $B(c)$.[50] Causal projectivity is then a matter of degree in two ways: first, other things being equal, a term is more projective the greater the number of entrenched generalizations associated with it; second, it is more

---

[50]The concept of a causally projective predicate, as well as that of a weakly observational term, is clearly implicitly relational; an expression falls under either concept only in relation to a background interpretation, assumed fixed. For the purpose of assessing whether a generalization of the indicated form is entrenched for a population, we require an interpretation of the population over a certain range of counterfactual situations in which (relevant) agents acquire information of the form $A(c)$ (see 3.3.4). The assertion that one set of beliefs is the basis of another for an agent is to be evaluated in relation to the inductive method ascribed to the agent by the interpretation in question.

projective the more frequently those generally generalizations have actually been applied. An important distinction between natural kind words and observation terms is that natural kind terms are causally projective; observation terms are not, or only weakly so. I have discussed the first prong of this bipartite claim in 3.3.4; here I shall comment on the second.

The discussion of section 3.2 attempted to define a tolerably clear sense in which the semantic correlates of observation terms are *surface* properties of objects. It did so by means of the notion of causal proximity: of the various properties of the local instances of an observation term that explain why they satisfy the observational criteria associated with it, the property it designates is the proximate one in the order of explanation. It is this characteristic of observational predicates that renders them only weakly causally projective. Surface properties underwrite few, if any, lawlike universal generalizations. Consider, for example, the stock example 'cubic', designating a typical primary quality. There are few lawlike generalizations about all cubic things. There are a handful of exceptions having to do with observation (for example, 'cubic objects look cubic to normal observers under normal circumstances'), geometric mechanics ('cubic objects of volume x^3 don't fit into round holes of diameter less than $x\sqrt{2}$'), and so on. Moreover, few if any of these generalizations satisfy the requirement of instantiation. Generalizations about purely observational properties are not frequently applied; they are normally too trivial to be useful. Thus observation terms score poorly on both measures of causal projectivity alluded to: they are associated with few substantive generalizations, and of these few if any are projectively deployed.[51]

Natural kind terms, then, are causally projective; observation terms are not, or only weakly so. I propose to use this distinction to segregate the cases to which the two models apply. My suggestion is simply that a predicate be subsumed under the NK-model just in case it is causally projective. This proposal solves, by arbitration, the problem that as things stand the suggested models of reference for observation terms and natural kind words apply simultaneously, and incompatibly, to some weakly observational predicates. However, the suggested demarcation of targets for the NK-model is not simply a device brought in to resolve some conflicts

---

[51]The claim that observational predicates are not causally projective is quite compatible with the assumption that observational properties are causally relevant or operative; it was in part in terms of this assumption that the suggested account of the reference of observation terms was justified. The claim that observational predicates are not causally projective is essentially the assertion that there are few if any nontrivial causal generalizations about the items falling under observational predicates. But such predicates can and frequently do figure in specifications of initial and boundary conditions within causal explanations, and this is all that is required for the claim of causal relevance.

between the two models and to rid the observational model of certain coun-
terexamples. The demarcation has a rationale in terms of the Principle of
Conformality, which tells us to optimize the availability of conformal explanations within an interpretation of an agent or population. The suggested
criterion functions, in effect, to maximize NK: for the NK-model *can* be
applied to any causally projective predicate, and the suggested demarcation mandates that it be applied to any term meeting this condition. From
the standpoint of optimizing the availability of conformal explanations, this
is just what we should expect. The indicated pattern of conformal explanation involving natural kind terms trades on the fact that the suggested
mechanism of reference pairs a natural kind term with a property of its local instances that best explains their exemplification of its saliencies; these
are the properties associated with the term by the most firmly entrenched
generalizations concerning it. The model thus functions to ensure that
these generalizations will as far as is possible actually count as causal laws.
Other things being equal, the more such generalizations count as causal
laws, the more causal explanations, or causal-explanatory sketches, will be
available to the agent(s) in question; the more causal explanations they can
frame, the more conformal explanations we can frame. By contrast, on an
observational interpretation of the relevant terms, these generalizations are
trivial and quite uninformative. Thus the imperative to optimize conformal explanations will prompt us to subsume as many causally projective
expressions as possible under the semantic category of natural kind terms.

3.5   Reference to Inhomogeneous Kinds

3.5.1   Essence and Archetype

The model of reference to natural kinds I have developed in sections 3.3 and
3.4 does not apply to all natural kind words. It does not, for it is implausible that all natural kinds are characterized by definite structural properties
(what I have called 'characteristic properties'); and the suggested mechanism fixes the reference of a natural kind term by locating such properties.
Call a kind that is circumscribed in this way **homogeneous**. A homogeneous kind, then, is one for which there exists a characteristic property
that picks out the items belonging to the kind in each possible world: its
instances at any world are just the objects therein exemplifying the property. My claim is then that not all natural kinds are homogeneous, and
that therefore terms for these kinds cannot be described by the suggested
model. In this section, I will begin by presenting some evidence relevant
to this claim. I will then go on to sketch a model of reference for the

inhomogeneous case.

The natural kind words that fall under the suggested model have two distinctive traits: first, they are socially associated with clusters of regularities that, in conjunction with their paradigmatic instances, determine their characteristic properties; second, within the limits of precision of the classes of regularities and paradigms, the extension of such a term is definite. Substance terms seem good candidates for homogeneous natural kind terms on these criteria, as some of the preceding examples suggest. However, neither of these features are exhibited by many natural kind terms. The most obvious problem is that many natural kind words, particularly those for wide biological sorts, are hard to associate with saliencies. Thus, for example, the terms 'bird', 'mammal', 'fish', and so on are associated with few if any substantive generalizations of the sort required for the homogeneous model to operate. Perhaps there are terms designating narrow subkinds of these sorts that can be viewed as designating homogeneous natural kinds; but the present examples cannot plausibly be so construed. I believe that the same point can be made about many natural kind terms in ordinary language and in biology: in these cases, the terms of application of the model for the homogeneous case are abrogated more often than not.

It might be suggested that the saliencies for the preceding terms are quite general morphological and behavioral characteristics. A possible difficulty with this response is that the morphological and behavioral properties common, for example, to all dogs are exemplified by other animals (for example, certain wolves). Stephen Schiffer has observed that any phenotypic property common to any two dogs is plausibly common to any dog and a timberwolf.[52] This would not be a problem if the exemplification of these properties by dogs and by wolves had different explanations, explanations that appeal to properties that distinguish dogs and timberwolves, say, in genetic terms. But suppose that the explanations do not differ in the required way. In that case the *genetic* structure relevant to these explanations common to any two dogs is common to any dog and any timberwolf, and on the homogeneous analysis 'dog' would incorrectly apply to timberwolves.

There is an obstruction to extending the model for the homogeneous case to 'broad spectrum' natural kind words, particularly those for wide biological taxa, which runs in the opposite direction to that of the previous observation. It arises from the fact that an exemplification of even a weak saliency for such a term may require a highly specific genetic basis for its complete explanation. Suppose, for example, that the generalization 'mam-

---

[52]Stephen Schiffer has forcefully criticized the assumptions of the Kripke-Putnam account along lines that overlap those developed here; see *Remnants of Meaning* (Cambridge, Mass.: Bradford, 1987), pp. 60–71. See also John Dupré, "Natural Kinds and Biological Taxa," *Philosophical Review* 90 (1980): 66–90, for some similar cases.

mals suckle their young' expresses a saliency for the word 'mammal'. It is implausible that this property has precisely the same genetic basis in all mammals. The activity of innumerable genes would enter into a complete causal explanation of any complicated behavior pattern such as suckling. There is little reason to suppose that the genetic properties responsible for these functions in one animal group are exactly the same as those responsible for the same functions in another. The same reflection, however, suggests that the model of reference for the homogeneous case applies at most to terms for quite narrow biological taxa. And it suggests that the situation described in the preceding paragraph is rather uncommon.

One reply to these considerations that might occur to a defender of homogeneous account would be to say that although there is no invariant *genetic* explanation of the fact that mammals suckle their young, there may be a *functional* architecture common to all mammals that explains this property. In that case mammals would have a functional, not a genetic characterization. But this is very implausible. A *machine* constructed to instantiate the relevant architecture would not be a *mammal*.[53] Mammals do not form a genetic *equivalence*-type, but they do plausibly form a genetic *similarity*-type. A genetic equivalence type, in the sense in which I am using the phrase, is delimited by a well defined genetic property that picks out all and only its possible instances. A genetic similarity type is characterized only by a more or less loosely defined cluster of such properties.[54]

Thinking of a biological sort as being characterized by a more or less loose relation of structural similarity helps us to make sense of a feature of the behavior of the corresponding kind terms that is puzzling on the

---

[53]Dupré has claimed that "higher taxa, having no real existence, are defined in scientific vocabulary by nominal essences. Thus I would hold that such statements as that birds have feathers, mammals suckle their young, or spiders have eight legs are analytic." ("Natural Kinds and Biological Taxa," p. 87.) If the relevant nominal essences are characterized in purely descriptive terms, and conjointly supply sufficient conditions for membership in the kind, then Dupré's analysis seems to have the consequence that a machine constructed to resemble a hummingbird in respect of the properties that define the order *Trochilidae* would be a hummingbird. Another difficulty with Dupré's account is that the indicated generalizations are not, in fact, analytic. The statement 'Mammals suckle their young', for example, does not even appear to be necessary. It would seem that either mutation within the class of mammals or developmental/environmental abberations could produce a (female) mammal that does not have the disposition in question.

[54]Richard Boyd has argued for such a conception of natural kinds in a number of articles in terms of the technical notion of a 'homeostatic property cluster'. See, for example, "How to be a Moral Realist," in *Essays on Moral Realism* edited by G. Sayre-McCord (Ithaca: Cornell University Press, 1988), and "Realism: What It Implies and What It Does Not," *Dialectica* 43 (1989): 5–29. The account presented hereafter does not depend in any direct way on the notion of homeostasis.

homogeneous analysis. Many biological sortals are essentially *vague*; for example, the extensions of many terms for animal groups, both in ordinary language and in biology, fail to be exactly defined. Thus it is not determinately true or false of any biologically possible organism that it falls under the terms 'reptile', 'bird', or 'fish'; evolution has in fact produced indefinite instances of each of these kinds. But the extension of a homogeneous natural kind word does not exhibit this kind of looseness: if the paradigms and saliencies of such a term are fixed, the extension of the term is definite (even if empty). A manifestation of this sort of indefiniteness is that many natural kind terms for animal groups exhibit an analogue of the sorites-like behavior that is characteristic of vague descriptive predicates. For example, it may seem reasonable to suppose that an organism whose genetic map differs from that of a given lion in a sufficiently small way (say, by a single nucleotide pair) must also be a lion. It follows via mathematical induction that the property of being a lion is preserved by any rearrangement of the genetic code, which is evidently false.

Not all natural kind terms, then, designate homogeneous natural kinds. I now wish to sketch a generalization of the model of section 3.3 to the inhomogeneous case. It would be a good approach to a model of reference for this case to attempt to specialize a satisfactory general semantics for vague predicates. Unfortunately, we possess no agreed-on general semantics. But there is a loose framework that fits the two most prominent alternatives, and that it is plausible to suppose would be instantiated by any reasonable alternative. Its leading idea is that the extension of a vague general term is determined in some way by a 'cluster' of exact predicates, call them *archetypes* for the term, and a relation of comparative similarity between properties, defined at least for properties designated by archetypes for the term, that determines its semantic role outside the class of its positive definite instances. These are the objects falling under one of its archetypes.[55]

That is about as far as one can go without prejudging substantive issues. The rough idea is that an object *more or less* falls under a vague predicate if it exemplifies a property that is *more or less similar to* the property designated by one of its archetypes; to fall under its complement is to instantiate a predicate sufficiently dissimilar from each such property. The best cases of the term are those things falling under one of its archetypes. This picture clearly allows for the possibility of indeterminate cases, that is, for objects that definitely exemplify neither the term nor its complement. My suggestion is that the extension of an inhomogeneous term is fixed by a set

---

[55] In the postscript to this chapter, it is shown that a formal realization of this general idea can be implemented within both the fuzzy set and the supervaluationist approaches to the semantics of vague terms.

of *homogeneous* natural kind predicates, and that these are related to the given inhomogeneous term in roughly the way in which an exact descriptive predicate is related to a vague descriptive term of which it is a definite case; the relevant homogeneous terms are the archetypes for the given inhomogeneous one. To articulate this suggestion, we need to characterize the conditions under which a homogeneous predicate constitutes an archetype for such a term, and the relevant relation of comparative similarity between properties.

I first suggest that the **archetypes** for an inhomogeneous kind term P in Karl's language L are those homogeneous terms A such that the inclusion

[i] $$(\forall x)(A(x) \to P(x))$$

is entrenched in L. The concept of an 'archetype' for P thus refers, at least implicitly, to a group of individuals within Karl's community that can play the role of a canonical subpopulation in the definition of entrenchment. The archetypes for P, then, are the homogeneous predicates A such that the inclusion [i], in Putnam's phrase, is *treated as analytic in the actual practice* of the relevant subcommunity. The archetypes for P thus determine a cluster of definite cases, each delimited by a characteristic causal-explanatory property.

The relevant similarity relation among characteristic properties concerns, in part, overall resemblance in the roles that they play in explicating the saliencies for these archetypes. A property closely approximates the characteristic property for an archetype in this respect if it is a causal basis for most of the saliencies associated with that archetype in the same way (by participating in the same sort of mechanism) as that characteristic property itself. But there is an aspect of the relevant similarity relation that is missed by this description of the situation. Recall Schiffer's example. Think of German shepherds and timberwolves as forming homogeneous kinds, and of the term 'German shepherd' as providing an archetype for the inhomogeneous term 'dog'.[56] The characteristic property for 'timberwolf' is a causal basis for most of the saliencies for the term 'German Shepherd' in the same way as the characteristic property of that term itself. But we do not for that reason wish to say that timberwolves are dogs. The characteristic property for timberwolves is structurally very similar to that of a dog-archetype and plays a very similar causal role, but this close causal-explanatory resemblance is not, in the present case, relevant. It has no tendency to show that timberwolves are dogs.

---

[56]This assumption is not exactly correct (see 3.5.3); but this will not matter for the purposes of this example.

A significant moral flows from this observation. There is no difficulty in thinking of a possible inhomogeneous term that would possess the same archetypes as the word 'dog' but of which timberwolves *would* be good instances: the word 'canine', on one reading, might be an example of such a term in English. What this shows is that the relation of comparative similarity in the present model must itself be interpretively plastic; it is not the same for all inhomogeneous natural kind terms. In general, it seems clear that inhomogeneous terms could share the same archetypes—roughly, the same definite positive cases—and yet be semantically distinguishable. (One way in which this might come about is that terms could have the same archetypes and yet be of differing *degrees of vagueness*). A pair of inhomogeneous terms will not be thus distinguishable within the preceding framework if the notion of comparative similarity is not itself variable. The problem is then to define, for each inhomogeneous term of Karl's language, the required relation of similarity between properties on the basis of the sort of information provided by an interpretation of Karl or of his community.

In the case of dogs and timberwolves, one way to separate the dogs from the more general class of canines is in terms of the pure or definite *negative* instances of the term 'dog'. The word 'timberwolf' is what we might call an **antiarchetype** for the term 'dog', in that the exclusion relation between these terms is entrenched in English: timberwolves just aren't dogs. The antiarchetypes for an inhomogeneous term P in L may be characterized as those homogeneous terms A such that the inclusion

[ii] $$(\forall x)(P(x) \ \rightarrow \ \neg A(x))$$

is entrenched in L. The suggestion I shall explore is that the similarity relation coordinated with P is determined jointly by (i) the neutral relation of similarity among properties adverted to earlier, (ii) the archetypes for P, and (iii) the *anti*archetypes for P. The rough idea is to allow the relation for P to coincide with the neutral relation on the class of all homogeneous kinds sufficiently close to archetypal properties for P and on the class of homogeneous kinds sufficiently remote from such properties, but to weight the relation in such a way as to widely separate properties in the intermediate case.

To make this idea a little more precise, define the **vicinity** of P to be the collection of all homogeneous kind-specifying properties Q such that Q (neutrally) resembles the characteristic property of some archetype for P more closely than Q resembles the characteristic property of any antiarchetype for P. Let R be the neutral similarity-relation between kind-specifying properties. The special similarity relation R_P for P may then be characterized as follows. For the purposes of the definition, we say that objects in the field of R are *alike in type* if they both belong to the vicinity of P or they both belong to its complement. If x, y are alike in type, then $R_P(x, y, z)$ holds iff $R(x, y, z)$ holds provided that y, z are alike in type and holds outright if y and z differ in type; $R_P(x, y, z)$ fails when x, y differ in type. If we let '1' represent falling into the vicinity of P and '0' falling into its complement, then this definition may be nicely expressed in terms of the following table.

x	y	z	$R_P(x, y, z)$
1	1	1	$R(x, y, z)$
0	1	1	$\bot$
1	0	1	$\bot$
0	0	1	$\top$
1	1	0	$\top$
0	1	0	$\bot$
1	0	0	$\bot$
0	0	0	$R(x, y, z)$[58]

The present construction fixes the semantic role of P in terms of the archetypes for P and the relation R_P of comparative similarity between properties coordinated with P. The positive definite instances of P are the items falling under one of its archetypes. But we need to make sense of the possibility that an object may not fall under any archetype for P and yet be a good instance of P. Suppose, for example, that the archetypes for the word 'dog' comprise finitely many homogeneous terms for specific kinds of dog. By breeding individuals from two of these, we may obtain a dog that falls under none of the relevant archetypes. So far, however, all that we can say is that such an offspring exemplifies a property that falls in a particular similarity ordering, resembling the characteristic properties of certain archetypes for P more than some properties but not as much as others. The question is whether there is an acceptable way of characterizing

---

[58]The only cases of this construction that might seem to require comment are rows 2 and 7. In the case where y and z lie in the vicinity of P and x lies outside it, it might be suggested that whether $R_P(x, y, z)$ holds should be determined by the neutral relation $R(x, y, z)$ and similarly for the case where x lies in the vicinity of P and y and z lie outside it. However, the idea here is that $R_P(x, y, z)$ says that x more closely resembles y than z, all things considered, in respect of the properties relevant to falling under P. If y and z agree in type with respect to P but x differs from both, then the dissimilarity of x from y and z should be considered maximal from the standpoint of P. In particular, x cannot resemble y more than z with respect to P.

an absolute concept of being a *good instance* of an inhomogeneous term that falls short of being a (positive) *definite* instance of that term.

There would in fact appear to be at least two natural ways of doing this. One makes use of the concept of the 'vicinity' of P introduced above. The vicinity of P consists of properties that neutrally resemble some positive definite case of P more than any negative definite case of P.[59] That is not, however, in all situations enough to make an item falling under such a property a very strong instance of P. Such an object may resemble some positive definite instance of P more than any negative one, but only slightly more than it resembles some definite negative instance of P. In that case, the object should be only a marginal instance of P. A stronger notion of instantiation arises by considering a narrower collection of properties. That narrower collection consists of all properties in the vicinity of P that neutrally resemble the characteristic property of some archetype of P more than that property resembles any *other* positive definite case of P. An object that falls under some property in this set might be called a **nearly definite** instance of P. Thus, for example, in many cases a hybrid of two homogeneous kinds designated by a pair of archetypes for the word 'dog' will exemplify a property that neutrally resembles the characteristic properties of those terms more than those properties resemble the characteristic property of any other archetype. Such a hybrid property will then constitute a nearly definite case of the inhomogeneous term 'dog'.

We have, I believe, come pretty much to the end of what can be said about inhomogeneous kind terms in the absence of an agreed-on account of vagueness. But I can still give a general idea of how the approach to the semantics of inhomogeneous terms outlined in this section can be justified within the Conformal Framework, and by so doing amplify the present suggestions somewhat. This I attempt in the following section. But advocates of particular models of vagueness will be dissatisfied. They will want to know how the present general proposal is to be implemented in their models. In the postscript to this chapter, I will sketch answers to this question for the two leading theories of vagueness.

3.5.2 *Grounding the Inhomogeneous Model*

I shall now consider how the present model of reference for inhomogeneous natural kind terms might be justified within the Conformal Framework. The central question is how assigning interpretations to such terms in the

---

[59] Where by a positive (negative) definite *case of* P we mean the characteristic property of an archetype (antiarchetype) for P. A positive (negative) definite *instance* of P is then an object falling under a positive (negative) definite case of P.

indicated fashion can contribute to conformal explanations. On the present account, an inhomogeneous kind is *locally approximately homogeneous*: each instance of an inhomogeneous term *approximately* instantiates one of its archetypes (even though different instances may approximate different archetypes); and its archetypes are homogeneous terms. There are few properties nomothetically associated with inhomogeneous terms; and those which are need have no invariant causal-explanatory basis within the corresponding kinds. Thus there are few if any causal generalizations about them to play the role in projective explanations envisioned by the account of reference I have suggested for homogeneous terms. In many cases, however, there are *probabilistic* generalizations that can play an analogous role. Let me explain.

I have suggested that the extension of an inhomogeneous kind term be viewed as being fixed by the characteristic properties for its archetypes, together with a relation of comparative similarity between properties: an object falls under such a term to the degree that it exemplifies a property sufficiently close to the characteristic property of an archetype for it. I shall say that an inhomogeneous term P is **regular** if, (a) under the actual circumstances of the population in question, the degree to which a nearly definite instance of P approximates an archetype for P increases with the number of saliencies for that archetype that it exemplifies, and (b) such an instance falls under a property that closely resembles the characteristic property of an archetype for P in terms of the relevant similarity-ordering if it exemplifies most of the saliencies for that archetype. Clearly, the regularity condition is defeasible. One can easily imagine kinds for which it would fail: for example, an inhomogeneous kind containing structurally diverse homogeneous subkinds whose paradigms display identical surface characteristics.[60] However, the regularity condition is satisfied in many cases; and where it is satisfied, it makes possible a type of probabilistic explanation that underwrites a corresponding sort of conformal explanation. Let us consider an example.

Birds form a good case of an inhomogeneous kind. There are few properties nomothetically associated with all birds; and there is little reason to suppose that the properties which are have an invariant basis in all birds. But specific sorts of birds do constitute homogeneous kinds, and terms for these specific kinds may constitute archetypes for the term 'bird'.[61] Under the regularity condition, the saliencies for the various archetypes are connected in such a way that if a reasonablly good instance of the term

---

[60]See 3.5.3.

[61]In fact I think the relevant archetypes are only approximately homogeneous, in the sense defined in 3.5.3. But we can ignore this complication here.

'bird' exemplifies most of the saliencies for such an archetype, then it is
more or less likely to exemplify others. For an object that exemplifies most
saliences for such an archetype must, on the regularity condition, approximately exemplify the characteristic property for that archetype, and so is
more or less likely to exemplify other saliencies for it.

This example illustrates one sort of probabilistic connection between
saliencies: if an item falls under a regular term, its exemplification of sufficiently many saliencies for an archetype for the term favors its exemplification of others. This is a type of connection that may be exploited in
a probabilistic style of conformal explanation. In this sort of explanation,
the role played by ascriptions of attitudes toward causal laws is taken over
by ascriptions of attitudes toward certain probabilistic generalizations. In
conformal explanations grounded in the homogeneous model, the relevant
causal generalizations subsume instances of a natural kind term under its
saliencies. In the probabilistic analogue, the generalizations would say that
any instance of an inhomogeneous kind term that exemplifies certain saliencies for one of its archetypes is likely to exemplify others.

What is the explanatory significance of such generalizations? One answer emerges from the account of the explanatory relevance of probabilistic
explanations abstracted from Railton in 3.4.3: a probabilistic explanation
that utilizes such a generalization affords *information about* the casual explanation of the state of affairs described in the explanandum. For example,
here is a partial phenotype for the hummingbird family (*Trochilidae*) due
to the ornithologist Charles Sibley:

> Schizognathous anisodatyle Apodiformes with 8 pairs of ribs; bill long
> and slender, gape not deeply cleft; tibial bridge absent; nostrils lateral,
> broadly operculate; tongue extensile; secondaries 6-7; alular feathers 0-1;
> aftershaft small or absent; 14-15 cervical vertabrae; syrinx with 2 pairs of
> special intrinsic muscles, nestling with spherical crop; caeca rudimentary
> or absent; no adult down; no claw on manus.[62]

Suppose that hummingbirds form a homogeneous kind, and that the indicated characteristics are saliencies for the word 'hummingbird'. The word
'hummingbird' would then constitute an archetype for the term 'bird'.[63]
Now suppose a given specimen exemplifies these characteristics. There is
an element of the hummingbird-phenotype that has been omitted here:
birds in this family do not have gall-bladders. There is then a probabilis-

---

[62]Quoted in C. Greenwaldt, *Hummingbirds* (New York: American Museum of Natural History Publications, 1958), pp. 17–18.

[63]Again, this seems somewhat unrealistic. It is questionable that hummingbirds,
comprising 116 genera and 341 species, form a homogeneous natural kind. It is rather
plausible that hummingbirds are best viewed as forming a quasi-homogeneous kind in
the sense of 3.5.3.

tically correct generalization that says that it is more or less likely that a bird falling under the indicated phenotype will lack a gall-bladder. Let Q represent the conjunction of the phenotypic properties mentioned above, and consider the following inductive-statistical explanation, where '$P(A|B)$' expresses conditional probability:

$$P(x \text{ lacks a gall-bladder} \mid x \text{ a bird and } Q(x)) >> .5$$
$$\underline{\alpha \text{ is a bird and exemplifies } Q(x)}$$
$$\alpha \text{ lacks a gall-bladder}$$

This probabilistic inference conveys, in the presence of the regularity condition, some substantive information about the complete explanation (the 'ideal explanatory text', in Railton's phrase) of the state of affairs described by its conclusion. We know, in particular, that α instantiates a genotype *close* to that of a hummingbird, and thus that the genetic properties of hummingbirds that account for their lacking gall-bladders will probably be duplicated in α. The inference conveys the probable existence of a particular causal-explanatory structure underlying the explanandum.

I now want to consider a certain sort of anamolous case. In responding to it, I will be led to another species of probabilistic explanation. The explanations I have just described are ill-adapted to explain properties of 'intermediate' cases of an inhomogeneous kind, for example, of instances of a wide biological sort which are phenotypically intermediate between two of its archetypes. Suppose, for example, that we are presented with a bird that is intermediate in phenotype between a hummingbird and a crested swift (family *Hemiprocnidae*). Both swifts and hummingbirds, which together comprise the order Apodiformes, are small birds with tiny feet and similar wing morphologies. These morphologies are characterized by bone structures which are adaptations for flight. In the crested swifts, the bill is short and the gape wide to aid in catching insects in flight; in the hummingbirds, the gape is small and the bill slender, adapted to feeding at flowers. Hummingbirds have long and extensile tongues for accessing nectar; swifts lack this feature. The nostrils of swifts are rounded and exposed, but are slitlike and covered by an operculum in hummingbirds. Swifts are generally dull colored; hummingbirds are brightly colored and iridescent. Suppose these features to constitute saliencies for the terms for the respective families.[64] The intermediate case (call it 'β') is a bird sharing the typical characteristics of the crested swifts with the exception of the fact

---

[64] Notice that in this case the families in question are described both by commonsense terms ('hummingbird', 'crested swift') and biological terms ('Trochilid', 'Hemiprocnid'). These are unusal cases in this respect.

that β has the bill morphology and extensile tongue of hummingbirds: β, like the hummingbirds, is adapted to feeding at flowers.

The genetic map of β resembles those of both hummingbirds and crested swifts, but is rather more similar, overall, to that of a swift. Let $P(x)$ be a predicate specifying the saliencies for crested swifts, omitting the bill morphology and the property of lacking an extensile tongue. Since β is a bird falling under $P(x)$, assuming again that the regularity condition is satisfied by the term 'bird', β will exemplify a genotype close to that of the crested swifts, and will thus probably *lack* an extensile tongue. Thus we obtain the following probabilistic explanation:

$P(x$ lacks an extensile tongue $\mid x$ a bird and $P(x)) >> .5$

β is a bird and exemplifies $P(x)$

β lacks an extensile tongue

The explanation misfires, of course, because β does in fact possess an extensile tongue. This is not, by itself, a problem, precisely because the purported explanation is probabilistic. But now consider the following probabilistic inference, wherein $A(x)$ is the conjunction of $P(x)$ and the bill morphology of hummingbirds:

$P(x$ has an extensile tongue$\mid x$ a bird and $A(x)) >> .5$

(E) $\quad$ β is a bird and exemplifies $A(x)$

β has an extensile tongue

I want to claim that (E) is a good probabilistic explanation of why β *has* an extensile tongue. But (E) does not fall under the explanatory pattern in terms of which we previously rationalized the inhomogeneous construction of the term 'bird'. That pattern explains why an instance of this term exemplifies a saliency for one of its archetypes by reference to the fact that the instance exemplifies other saliencies for that archetype. Thus on this model we would explain the fact that β exemplifies one saliency for the hummingbirds, or for the crested swifts, in terms of the fact that it exemplifies other saliencies for these terms. The difficulty is that in (E) we are appealing to the fact that β exemplifies an ensemble of properties that are saliencies for *no* archetype for the term 'bird'. $A(x)$ expresses a combination of properties, most of which are exemplified by swifts, but not by hummingbirds, but some of which are exemplified by hummingbirds, but not by swifts.

Why then is (E) a good explanation? Under the conjunction of the regularity condition and the suggested semantic construal of the term 'bird', a bird's falling under $P(x)$ is a reasonably good indication that it does *not* have an extensile tongue. But the situation changes when we add the piece of information that it exemplifies the bill morphology of a hummingbird. Relative to this information, it is probable that the specimen does have an extensile tongue. This is so because the properties in question are associated in nature. Both characteristics are adaptations for a form of feeding behavior. But the bill morphology would be quite useless without the extensile tongue. An instance of 'bird' rather like a crested swift but exemplifying the bill morphology of a hummingbird is likely to exhibit the feeding behavior of hummingbirds, and is thus likely to possess an extensile tongue.

I have argued that the suggested semantic interpretation of inhomogeneous natural kind words may be justified in terms of its role in generating one type of probabilistic explanation in the language of the agent or population in question, which in turn can underwrite probabilistic-conformal explanations within an interpretation of that agent or population. The example I have just considered exemplifies another type of probabilistic explanation that can also play such a role. The general situation may be described as follows. If P is an inhomogeneous kind term and S a collection of saliencies for its archetypes, say that S is a **net for** P if the exemplification of some elements of S by an instance of P favors its exemplification of others, at least under the local circumstances of the population in question. A bit more explicitly, the probability that an instance of P falls under a property in S relative to its falling under P and a subset S_o of S not containing that property increases as the size of S_o increases, and is close to 1 when the size of S_o is near that of S. Note that the regularity condition implies that the collection of *all* saliencies for any archetype for P is a net for P: for, by regularity, the greater the number of saliencies for such an archetype an instance of P exemplifies, the greater the degree to which that instance approximates the characteristic property for that archetype, and thus the more likely it is to exemplify any of the saliencies generated by that property. In the second type of probabilistic explanation I described, other groupings of saliencies become relevant. The example correlated the property of having an extensile tongue with the properties making up the hummingbird bill-morphology in birds. In that example, then, the set

$$\text{hummingbird bill morphology} \cup \{\text{extensile tongue}\}$$

constitutes a net for the term 'bird'.

If S is a net for P, Karl may obtain a probabilistic inference to the conclusion that an object falls under a member of S by appealing to the fact that it is an instance of P and exemplifies other members of S. The explanatory relevance of such an inference on the interpretation of statistical explanation borrowed from Railton earlier may be seen against the background of a generalization of the regularity condition to arbitrary nets. As applied to any net S for P, it would say that there is a *uniform* causal-explanatory basis for the exemplification of the properties in S by any nearly definite instance of P that does in fact exemplify each of them, and that the degree to which any such instance of P approximates this basis increases with the number of properties in S it exemplifies.[65] Call this requirement the **generalized regularity condition**. The ordinary regularity condition for P, then, provides that the saliency-cluster for any archetype for P satisfies the generalized regularity condition. By reference to the fact that it satisfies the generalized regularity condition, we can explain why a net S for P *is* a net for P: the exemplification of sufficiently many members of S by an instance of P favors its exemplification of others, because it favors its approximate exemplification of a property that is simultaneously a causal explanatory basis for *each* member of S. The same observation allows us to locate the sort of information that a probabilistic explanation of the second sort considered provides about the causal-explanatory text of the item explained.

3.5.3 Quasi-Homogeneous Terms

In the previous two subsections, I have made use of the simplifying assumption that the archetypes in the examples considered are homogeneous terms. This assumption must now be exposed as fictive: in fact, none of these archetypes are strictly homogeneous terms, but they are, in a sense I shall now try to explain, approximately homogeneous. Few of our terms for biological sorts, either in science or in everyday life, are homogeneous natural kind words for two reasons. First, even where such a term is associated with a more or less thick descriptive profile, these properties do not normally constitute saliencies for the terms in question. They are only statistically typical characteristics comprising what might be called the *sortal phenotype* for the term, the markers by which members of the canonical subpopulation for the term would pick out its local instances. But there can be and normally are exceptional instances. Second, even within the class of typical instances, the explanation of the sortal phenotype is variable. For example, the complete explanation of any complex behavioral

---

[65]Here as earlier the notion of 'degree of approximation' of a property by an *object* is short form for a condition phrased with reference to the similarity-ordering among properties associated with P. For any objects x and y, to say that x better approximates such a basis than y is to say that x falls under a property that resembles that basis more than any property exemplified by y in terms of the relevant ordering.

capacity must rely on a description of physiological and biochemical details that may be variable even within a species.

On the other hand, if most of our commonsense and scientific terms for biological sorts fail to be homogeneous, then neither are they inhomogenous in the sense required by the model of 3.5.1. For that model works by imputing archetypes to an inhomogeneous term, and archetypes have so far been construed to be homogeneous terms. There simply are, in general, no archetypes for our commonsense or scientific terms for biological sorts. And so we shall require a different basis for the operation of the preceding model in these cases, if it is to operate at all.

Thus consider a natural kind term, again call it 'P', which is neither homogeneous, nor associated with homogeneous definite cases. P may yet, in a weaker way, be associated with certain properties. For the idea of a 'sortal phenotype' readily generalizes: it is just the idea of a statistically stable profile for the typical instances of P, the 'thick' stereotype by reference to which the community, perhaps by deference to a canonical group, would normally identify instances of that term. We are supposing that, for the reasons rehearsed earlier, P is not homogeneous with respect to the choice of these properties as saliencies; but I will argue that they still play a substantive role in fixing its reference. It will be convenient to have a general name for this sort of statistically typical property, the analogue in the general case of the sortal pheotype for a biological term. I shall call the properties in question **nuclear** for P: the local instances of P that exemplify these properties are its *typical* instances in the local situation. A nuclear property for a term is associated with it at least by a rough statistical generalization that is accepted by the relevant canonical subpopulation, and that is actually the basis for beliefs within that population that particular instances of the term fall under the property in question. The fact that a term is associated in this way with a more or less thick portfolio of nuclear properties is thus a probabilistic analogue of causal projectivity. In the case of a causally projective notion, there is a set of nomological generalizations constraining the extension of the term which are obligatory information for members of the relevant canonical group and which are actually applied in a significant range of cases. The situation is similar for an inhomogeneous term of the present type, except that the generalizations in question are statistical, not nomic. I will say that a term of this sort is **typically projective**.

Imagine a set of potential or implicit homogeneous terms that are cases of our target term P. The saliencies for each of these are just the nuclear properties for P. Their paradigms comprise maximal subsets of the paradigmatic instances of P for which there exists a *common* structural explanation of their exemplification of those properties. These explanations

will, as indicated, differ in detail, and will invoke a correspondingly var-
ied range of grounding explanatory properties. These grounding properties
will be the characteristic properties for the relevant implicit homogeneous
terms. Now suppose that these various implicit terms are related to one
another in the way that the archetypes of an inhomogeneous term are connected on the semantic construction of such terms described in 3.5.1. In this
case, I shall say that the virtual homogeneous terms constitute **implicit
archetypes** for the term P. The implicit archetypes for P, then, specify
a family of structurally connected properties that underlie exemplifications
of the nuclear properties for P by its typical instances.

I now suggest that where possible the implicit archetypes for a typically
projective term be taken to define its semantic role in just the way the
archetypes for an inhomogeneous term characterize its semantic interpretation on the model of 3.5.1. Within that model, the semantic role of an
inhomogeneous natural kind term is fixed by its definite positive cases (the
characteristic properties for its archetypes) and a relation of comparative
similarity between properties; and I argued at the conclusion of 3.5.1 that
the relevant similarity relation is in turn fixed by the definite positive and
negative cases of the term. On the present suggestion, the definite positive cases of the target term P are described by the implicit archetypes
for P. The definite negative cases of P will in turn be specified by the
implicit archetypes for those typically projective terms $A(x)$ such that the
relation [ii] is entrenched for the community in question. That is to say
that the definite *negative* cases of P are the definite *positive* cases of those
terms whose instances are excluded from the extension of P on the basis
of an entrenched generalization. A term P characterized in this way will
be said to be **quasi-homogeneous**. A quasi-homogeneous term is then
a non-homogeneous term that may be viewed as *approximately* homogeneous. First, as noted, the nuclear properties associated with such a word
are not saliencies for it, if only for the reason that not all of its local instances need exemplify them. But most do: these are what I have been
calling the 'typical' instances of the term. Second, even within the class of
its typical instances, there need be no invariant basis for exemplifications of
its nuclear properties; but there is a connected family of overlapping bases.
Quasi-homogeneous terms for these reasons approximate an explanatory
role of homogeneous ones. Consider an inductive-statistical explanation of
the fact that a local instance α of P falls under one of its nuclear properties
in terms of the fact that α falls under P and a statistical generalization
saying that most instances of P fall under the property in question. Such
an inference is a direct inductive analogue of a deductive explanation of the
fact that a local instance of a homogeneous term exemplifies a saliency for

it in terms of a universal generalization subsuming instances of the term under that salient property.

These observations afford an avenue of justification for the suggested interpretation of quasi-homogeneous terms within the Conformal Framework. As usual, what needs to be shown is how the interpretation in question contributes to conformal explanations of second-order actions within the population in question, and for this it is sufficient to show how that interpretation generates a significant class of object-language explanations of outcomes relevant to the goals of these agents on the basis of their beliefs. The form of explanation just described is, as noted, a statistical analogue of a type of D-N explanation subsuming the instances of a homogeneous term under one of its saliencies: and it was this type of explanation that grounded the conformal-explanatory role of the suggested semantic interpretation of such terms. The statistical counterparts of these D-N stories are invoked in a corresponding analogue of the conformal explanations in the homogeneous case. It is this class of explanations that rationalizes the suggested model of reference for quasi-homogeneous terms within the Conformal Framework.

The robust sortals ('hummingbird', 'crested swift') in the examples of subsection 3.5.2 are not homogeneous terms, but they are, I suggest, perfectly reasonable examples of quasi-homogeneous terms. Sibley's profile of a hummingbird quoted earlier does not constitute an enumeration of saliencies for the word 'hummingbird', for the relevant traits are not in fact exemplified by all hummingbirds. They are only statistically typical characteristics of hummingbirds. These are what I have called 'nuclear' properties for the term 'hummingbird', and they enable the present model of reference for quasi-homogeneous terms to apply in this case. Within that model, the term 'hummingbird' designates an inhomogeneous kind whose positive definite cases consist of a family of structural properties underlying exemplifications of the relevant nuclear characteristics by its typical instances. My suggestion is that the role of archetypes in the model of 3.5.1 can only rather infrequently be played by strictly homogeneous terms, and that quasi-homogeneous terms can naturally play that role in many situations. Because quasi-homogeneous terms are approximately homogeneous in the sense described earlier, the justification I suggested in 3.5.2 for the initial model of reference for the inhomogeneous case may be extended to the present situation in which that model is allowed to operate with this more flexible class of archetypes.[66]

---

[66]One objection to this story as an account of the reference of a word like 'hummingbird' is that by thus tying the reference of such a term to mechanisms underlying typical manifestations of the nuclear properties for it, we make it difficult to account

3.5.4   Species as Kinds

I have suggested that many of our general terms applying to living organisms can be naturally interpreted as quasi-homogeneous terms. In this section I shall explore, briefly and somewhat speculatively, an interpretation of species names as inhomogeneous kind terms, and thus define a conception of species as natural kinds. However, on what probably deserves to be called the 'standard' conception of the nature of species in evolutionary theory, species are not kinds at all but individuals.[67] There is some disagreement about higher biological taxa, but as characterized within evolutionary biology species are items that come into being, evolve, and pass out of existence (extinction). Kinds, it would seem, do none of these things.

That is a bit too fast. We do speak, for example, of the origin of a chemical element such as oxygen, meaning thereby to indicate the processes that first gave rise to oxygen in the universe. Similarly, one could conceive of a cosmological outcome (for example, the 'big crunch') that could naturally be described as involving the *extinction* of oxygen. Usages like these suggest

---

for instances of the term that significantly diverge from typical ones with respect to these mechanisms and properties. The key to answering this worry is to recall that a quasi-homogeneous term is an inhomogeneous term, and that as interpreted on the model described in 3.5.1, 'satisfying' a term of this sort is a matter of degree. The *most* definite instances of the term 'hummingbird' will indeed be specimens falling under the properties grounding the nuclear phenotype in one or more typical instances, and will thus exemplify that phenotype under developmental and environmenal circumstances sufficiently similar to the local situation. But an atypical specimen may yet be a nearly definite instance of that term. Thus, for example, *hybridization* of two 'hummingbird' archetypes will normally result in an organism falling under a property resembling the characteristic property of at least one of the parental archetypes more closely than those characteristic properties resemble the characteristic property of any other archetype, and more closely than that of any antiarchetype. Moreover, this circumstance should be preserved under small—or sometimes even relatively large—perturbations within the parental genotypes, which could easily result in an organism exemplifying a phenotype that omits one or more nuclear properties for the term 'hummingbird'.

[67] A prominent advocate of this point of view is Ernst Mayr; see, for example *Animal Species and Evolution* (Cambridge, Mass.: Harvard University Press, 1963). Others include M. T. Ghiselin, for example, in "A Radical Solution to the Species Problem," *Systematic Zoology* 23 (1974): 536–44 and David Hull, "Are Species Really Individuals?" *Systematic Zoology* 25 (1976): 174–91, and *The Metaphysics of Evolution* (Albany: State University of New York Press, 1989), among other publications. There are, however, many incompatible forms of species-nominalism, the thesis that species are individuals. On Mayr's version, species are reproductively isolated populations of interbreeding individuals. On other species concepts, species are individuated in terms of certain lineages, on still others in terms of the evolutionary mechanisms that give rise to those lineages. For comparative overviews of alternative species concepts, see *Species: The Units of Biodiversity*, edited by M. F. Claridge et al. (London: Chapman and Hall, 1997).

the familiar point that substance terms like 'hydrogen' and 'oxygen' have a dual semantic status: in some contexts they are general terms referring to a kind; in others they are singular terms ('mass' nouns) designating a particular chunk of the material content of the actual world. The question is whether species terms might not have a similarly ambiguous status. I suggested at the outset of section 3.3 that the mass noun interpretation of a substance term might be derived from its reading as a general term by taking the denotation of the mass noun to arise by mereological aggregation from the extension of the corresponding general term. By contrast, in this section I shall sketch an interpretation of species names as inhomogeneous kind terms that is derived from data about the corresponding species as individuals. These data are assumed to be specified in other terms.

There are two objections to the possibility of such a bipartite conception of species that naturally flow from the standard conception of species as individuals. The first is that there is a theoretical obstruction to such a dual conception presented by essentialist commitments of any representation of species as kinds.[68] I will argue that this concern can be answered if species are interpreted as suitable *inhomogeneous* kinds. The second objection is more fundamental. The second objection is that there is no theoretical point to such an interpretation. The theoretical role of species terms in biology, it is claimed, is that of singular nouns referring to spatiotemporal particulars. There would be no evident use for an interpretation of species terms as natural kind words even if one could be coherently specified. The problem facing us, then, is not only to show how such an interpretation can be given in such a way as to avoid objectionable metaphysical commitments; it is to explain what theoretical interest the interpretation might have.

The source of the first objection mentioned is a widely accepted anti-essentialist conviction about species. It is sometimes incautiously expressed as the claim that there is no *biological property* that is shared by all and only the members of a species. But it would appear that 'is a member of *Drosophila melanogaster*' is a predicate of biological theory, and thus expresses what is in a broad sense a 'biological property', which is exemplified by exactly the members of a common species of fruit flies. The claim might then be qualified to say that there is no general, nonrelational property—no *intrinsic* property, in the sense of 3.3.3—that picks out exactly the members of a species. A property is intrinsic when it is coexemplified by physically indiscernible individuals. Of course, on what I have been calling the 'standard' conception of species, species membership need not be like that: a purely synthetic or an extraterrestrial organism does not fall into *Drosophila melanogaster* no matter how much it may resemble

---

[68] See Hull, *The Metaphysics of Evolution*, for a detailed discussion of this objection.

the fruit fly on the wall. On the dominant view, the fact that a synthetic individual is physically indiscernible from a specimen of *D. melanogaster* has no more tendency to show the synthete to be a member of that species than the fact that a very successful reproduction is physically indiscernible from a painting of the Elyére atelier shows that the reproduction is in fact a painting of the Elyére atelier. That is an observation about what obtains within the standard interpretation: it is not a premise that can be used in an argument in favor of that interpretation. On this construal of what the essentialist is after, what is required is a mapping of species-individuals to intrinsic properties that associates any such concrete species with a property that is exemplified (normally, barring cases of synthetic organisms, parallel evolution and the like) by just the members of that species.

But that cannot be quite what the antiessentialist is denying either. Unfortunately, such a mapping is easily specified: for example, for any concrete species σ, take the corresponding property to be the disjunction of the genotypes of the members of σ. Rather, what is fundamentally denied by the antiessentialist is that there is an intrinsic *explanatory* property common to all members of σ, a property that explains important facts about σ that might be codified in a species phenotype for σ. The evidence against this version of the essentialist thesis is very strong. One problem concerns the idea of a 'species phenotype' itself. It is very implausible that a substantive species phenotype should consist only of properties exemplified by all members of the species; variation can and normally will present exceptional instances. This is a point we have seen before: the species phenotype will consist only of statistically typical properties. It is thus inappropriate to require of a structural characterization of the species that it incorporate properties whose role is to generate all elements of the species phenotype. But set that point aside. Suppose there exists an exceptionless species phenotype. It is still normally not the case that the elements of this phenotype have *the same* explanation across all members of the species. This is also a point we have seen before: I have already noted the fact that the causal basis of any complex phenotypic marker is likely to involve essentially mechanisms which are variable even within a species.

On its present construal, then, the antiessentialist thesis is true. And it effectively undercuts one conception of species as kinds: species names cannot plausibly be construed as *homogeneous* natural kind terms. The dossier of phenotypic properties that could constitute the *saliencies* for such a term is extremely thin if it exists at all; and there is no reason to suppose that such properties as may happen to be common to all members of the species will be exemplified by those organisms for just the same reasons. But these considerations do not at all undercut the possibility of interpreting species words as *inhomogeneous* natural kind words; indeed, it was in terms of such observations that the conception of inhomogeneous natural kinds was motivated in the first place. In what follows, I shall describe a class of hypothetical quasi-homogeneous kind terms that play a certain role in explicating an idealized ecology of a system of species-individuals. Both the ecology and the species-individuals are supposed to be fixed by the biological facts. All that ultimately has to be assumed here is that, although the relevant species may be characterized in any number of different ways, the object thus characterized is a genuine individual, and that it makes sense to inquire into the conditions underlying the persistence of that individual through time. Species words will then be interpreted as inhomogeneous kind terms whose *archetypes* are quasi-homogeneous terms of the present sort.

First consider an attempted direct characterization of species as quasi-homogeneous kinds. What is required for such a characterization on the model of subsection 3.5.3 is a demarcation of the definite positive cases of the species and of its definite negative cases. I will construe the latter to be the definite *positive* cases of *other* species kinds represented in the biological environment of the given species-individual. And so the problem becomes that of simultaneously specifying an ensemble of homogeneous definite positive cases for each of the species exemplified in the relevant environment. Recall that in the quasi-homogeneous case these are determined by *typical* properties of local instances of the kinds in question. But there are various properties that might be singled out as typical. Which are relevant to a demarcation of species as kinds? They are, I suggest, the phenotypic properties of members of a concrete species that underly its identity as an individual through time, that is, that explain the persistence of the relevant species-individual over the interval through which it endures. These are the phenotypic properties which are relevant to a minimal success story for the species, a story that will be told largely in ecological terms. For many species they include:

(a) dispositions or capacities of members of the species relevant to patterns of individual survival;
(b) properties of members of the species that contribute to reproductive success;
(c) properties of members of the species that underly its reproductive isolation.

The properties in these classes are not exemplified by all members of the concrete species, but they are widely exemplified. The members of the species falling under them are the individuals which for my purposes here will be classified as its *typical* members. Typical members of mammalian species, for example, instantiate characteristic strategies of survival; they mate with other typical individuals to produce fertile offspring that also instantiate these strategies; and a typical individual will mate only with conspecifics.[69] The present suggestion is roughly that a species-kind is characterized by the mechanisms that underly these properties in typical cases. A bit more explicitly, on this suggestion the homogeneous positive definite cases of the kind corresponding to a concrete species σ are characterized by properties that explain why a range of typical individuals in σ fall under traits whose exemplification by those individuals underlies (that is, in conjunction with environmental conditions, explains) the persistence of σ as an individual through time. Its homogeneous negative definite cases are characterized by properties which are associated in the same way with other species in the biological environment of σ. Under favorable circumstances, these positive and negative cases determine a quasi-homogeneous kind.[70] It is this kind with which, at a first approximation, I propose to identify the species-kind instantiated by the members of σ.

The intention here is that a species-kind be characterized by the most informative description of the cluster of mechanisms underlying the persistence of the species as an individual that is satisfied at least approximately by each member of the species. The optimal satisfiers instantiate one set of mechanisms generating the phenotype responsible for the persistence of the species, but there can be and normally are suboptimal satisfiers that instantiate some but not all of those mechanisms. In any case the basis of our theoretical interest in such an inhomogeneous kind is not difficult to locate. One of the most important biological facts about a species is its persistence (in a certain range of environments), and a species-kind is described by the widest demarcation of the mechanisms responsible for its persistence. The implicit archetypes for a hypothetical term designating such a quasi-homogeneous kind are associated with characteristic properties that explain (in conjunction with developmental and environmental boundary conditions) the expression of the relevant partial phenotype, the properties of typical members of the species that enter into the explanation of its persistence as an individual. Such an explanation is largely ecological in the sense that a large part of what normally has to be explained is the fact that the species successfully occupies a particular niche. It has sometimes been claimed that ecological units such as niche should be conceptually segregated from evolutionary ones. Thus, David Hull: "Species

---

[69]These points apply to many animal species. But the reference to sexual reproduction is inessential: as long as the idea of a species individual persisting over time makes sense, it is meaningful to ask what properties of members of the species contribute to that outcome; a suitable answer to that question is all that is required for the present construction.

[70]See 3.5.3.

is strictly a geneological unit, niche an ecological unit. Mixing the two together is sure to cause problems."[71] John Dupré has responded that "surely ecologists will be in trouble if they cannot intelligibly claim that some particular species currently occupies some niche in some ecological system."[72] At its present level of articulation, the suggestion I am exploring is that a species-kind is determined by an indefinite microcharacterization of a particular concrete species that explains its persistence as an individual largely *in terms of* its ecological role. But the ingredients in such a characterization are neither functional/ecological nor phenotypic. They are rather structural properties of a wide range of individuals in the species that underly phenotypic properties of these individuals making possible the ecological role of the species, and which are otherwise responsible for its persistence as an individual through time.

However, this description of the present proposal shows what is wrong with the proposal. First, there is, in general, no *single* phenotypic profile of individuals in a concrete species that accounts for its persistence even within a fixed ecological system. Typical species members can generally be partitioned into several sorts, each with a characteristic phenotypic profile that contributes to the success of the species within such a system. Sex distinction is the most obvious example of this sort of partition; but for many purposes finer partitions are required.[73] Second, a single species can occupy different niches in several different ecological systems, and the phenotypic properties underlying those divergent roles need not be the same in each case. These observations show that what the foregoing construction characterizes is not a *species*-kind, but rather a more limited natural kind that we may call a **species-form**. A species-form is determined by a more or less loosely defined family of explanatory properties that underly *one* typical phenotype within the species which in turn enters into the explanation of the persistence of the species in *one* of its biological enviornments.

We have thus arrived at the following point of view. Let σ be a concrete species. A species-form of σ is a certain quasi-homogeneous kind. The partial phenotypes associated with alternative forms of σ will more or

---

[71] *The Metaphysics of Evolution*, p. 122.

[72] *The Disorder of Things* (Cambridge, Mass.: Harvard University Press, 1993), p. 43.

[73] As, for example, in the case of social insects, wherin a single sex may be partitioned according to caste. The present example also shows, incidentally, that in the foregoing construction the relevant characteristic properties cannot comprise *only* partial genotypes. For in social insects, caste distinctions are drawn ultimately in physiological, not genetic terms; precisely the same genotype could under different circumstances be exemplified, for example, by female ants differing in caste. See E. O. Wilson and B. Holldobler, *The Ants* (Cambridge, Mass.: Harvard University Press, 1990), p. 348 for a discussion of caste determination in ants.

less strongly overlap, as will the mechanisms responsible for the expression of those phenotypes. The relationship of these alternative forms to one another and to the forms of other species may be described in terms of a certain inhomogeneous kind. The archetypes for a term designating that kind are just hypothetical designators for the species-forms associated with σ; its antiarchetypes will be designators for species-forms associated with other actual concrete species. It is this derived inhomogeneous kind with which I finally propose to identify the species-kind corresponding to σ.[74]

This construction of species-kinds out of species-forms has a status similar to that of the suggested construction of species-forms out of homogeneous kinds. A species-form for σ is characterized by the most informative specification of the properties underlying a certain phenotype that is approximately satisfied by each member of the species approximating the phenotype; these properties characterize a family of connected homogeneous kinds. Our interest in a quasi-homogeneous kind circumscribed by these properties was the role played by that phenotype in explaining the persistence of σ in one of its biological environments. Similarly, the species-kind associated with σ is characterized by the most informative specification of the properties underlying the totality of these explanatory phenotypes that is approximately satisfied by all members of the species.

This semantic interpretation of species-terms does not, of course, apply directly to an actual language; the linguistic background assumed in it is largely if not entirely hypothetical. The construction of species-forms applies to the language of an idealized ecology in which all species-individuals in the relevant biological environment have been described and in which the phenotypic markers of broad types of individuals in each species responsible for its persistence in that environment have been identified. The supervening interpretation of species names as ntural kind terms presupposes an epistemic context in which these factors have been specified for each biological environment of the species. My suggestion is that a species term in an actual language be construed as inheriting its reference from this idealized situation. But this will mean that the interpretive rationale for the suggested semantic description of species terms will apply directly only to the idealized situation, and at best approximately to the actual one.

The very ideality of that description allows it to escape a type of relativity affecting previous cases. To fix the reference of a quasi-homogeneous term, we require a background of typification. The question of which objects and which properties are taken as typical for the term is quite sensitive to the cognitive background of the agents in standard contexts of use of

---

[74]I have thus used in an essential way the broadened conception of archetypes introduced at the conclusion of 3.5.3.

the term. Species-forms have been construed as quasi-homogeneous kinds, but the typical properties and paradigmatic instances associated with these kinds have been fixed, so to speak, by nature: the relevant instances are just the members of a given concrete species, and the properties comprise a phenotypic profile that plays a certain role in an explanation of the persistence of that species in a chosen environment. Species-kinds are in turn fixed via the mechanism of 3.5.1 by the totality of actually exemplified species-forms. It is tempting to say that for this reason the present application of that mechanism delivers kinds that are in some sense *more* natural than cases in which the background of typification is more strongly conditioned by the epistemic situation and interests of the agents in question. The crucial fact responsible for this enhanced naturalness is of course the assumed objective existence of species as individuals. This observation suggests the possibility of an analogous construction of an inhomogeneous kind corresponding to any population that may similarly be said to constitute a real individual. And it suggests that such a construction is unlikely to apply generally to higher biological taxa.

INHOMOGENEOUS KIND TERMS
AND MODELS OF VAGUENESS

Inhomogeneous natural kind words are vague terms. My aim in this postscript is to indicate how the general approach to the interpretation of inhomogeneous terms described in this chapter may be realized within the two leading formal semantic models of vagueness. These are the supervaluation model proposed by Fine, and the 'fuzzy set' model of Zadeh.[1]

Both of my adaptations will presuppose that the notion of comparative similarity for kind-determining properties that figures in the sketch presented earlier is representable by a normalized metric, d, on such properties. To say that d is a *metric* is to say that d is a nonnegative-real-valued function such that for each pair (p, q) of relevant properties, the following conditions are satisfied:

(1) $d(p, q) = 0$ iff $p = q$
(2) $d(p, q) = d(q, p)$
(3) For any r, $d(p, q) \leq d(p, r) + d(r, q)$.

The metric d is **normalized** if in addition $d(p, q) \leq 1$ for each p, q. To say that d 'represents' the relevant notion of similarity between properties is to say that a property p is more similar to property q than a property r iff $d(p, q) < d(p, r)$.

We shall also require d to satisfy two natural *continuity conditions*:

(C1) For any family $\{p_n\}$ of properties for which d is defined and any object x, if q is a property such that

$$\lim_n d(p_n, q) = 0,$$

and x exemplifies p_n for each n, then x exemplifies q.

Condition (C1) says that if an object exemplifies properties that are *arbitrarily close* to a given property in the metric, then it exemplifies that

---

[1] Kit Fine, "Vagueness, Truth and Logic," *Synthese* 30 (1975): 265–300, and L. A. Zadeh, "Fuzzy Sets," *Information and Control* 8 (1965): 338–53. The supervaluationist view seems to have been formulated by a number of authors.

property. The other continuity condition says that if a sequence of properties converges to a property q in the metric, the sets of properties for which they are a causal basis also 'converge' (in an appropriate sense). Say that a sequence of sets A_n **converges** to a set B (written $\lim_n A_n = B$) if $B = \{x : (\exists n)(\forall m > n)\ x \in A_m\}$. For any property p, let $G(p)$ be the set of all properties for which p is a causal basis; that is, the set of those properties q such that exemplifications of p by an object bring about exemplifications of q by that object.[2] The second continuity condition may now be expressed as follows:

(C2) For any family $\{p_n\}$ of properties for which d is defined and any property q,

$$\lim_n d(p_n, q) = 0 \Rightarrow \lim_n G(p_n) = G(q).$$

There may be, and probably are, various normalized metrics that represent, in the sense described, the relevant similarity relation among homogeneous-kind-specifying properties. The continuity conditions, I believe, further and significantly constrain the choice of such a metric. Still there may be more than one acceptable choice. In that case, to the extent that the semantic models considered hereafter reflect the specific choice of a metric, we have another source of indeterminacy.

A.   The Fuzzy Set Model

A subset S of a domain D is representable by its characteristic function, the function which is valued 0 at an element of D if that object belongs to S, and 1 otherwise. The characteristic function provides a sharp demarcation of the elements of the set. Suppose, however, that we think of the set as admitting *degrees* of membership. We might then represent S by a function f mapping D into the unit interval $\{x : 0 \le x \le 1\}$. $f(x) = 0$ if x is definitely in S, $f(x) = 1$ if it is definitely out; intermediate values reflect intermediate degrees of membership. Let us identify a **fuzzy set** with such a function. The fuzzy set model of vague terms attempts to explain the characteristic semantic role of vague predicates in terms of the hypothesis that the extension of such a predicate is a fuzzy set.

The explanation is based on a recursive characterization of degrees of truth. For an ordinary first-order language L, the characterization proceeds

---

[2]This definition could be understood in two ways, one as requiring that $G(p)$ consist of those q such that exemplifications of p cause exemplifications of q in all causally possible situations, the other as requiring of q only that this causal relation obtain in certain circumstances. It depends somewhat on the application being considered which interpretation is relevant.

as follows. An interpretation M of L will consist of a domain D and an assignment to each n'ary predicate P a function P^* mapping the collection of n'tuples over D into the unit interval. (For simplicity, let's suppose that L lacks constants and function symbols.) For any formula $A(\mathbf{x})$ of L in the variables $\mathbf{x} = x_1, ..., x_n$, the degree of truth $\|A(\mathbf{c})\|_M$ of $A(\mathbf{c})$ in M for a selection of parameters $\mathbf{c} = c_1, ..., c_n$ from D is defined recursively as follows. If $A(\mathbf{x})$ is an atomic formula in the predicate P, then $\|A(\mathbf{c})\|_M = P^*(\mathbf{c})$. If $A(x)$ is $P(\mathbf{x}) \vee Q(\mathbf{x})$, then

$$\|A(\mathbf{c})\|_M = \max\{\|P(\mathbf{c})\|_M, \|Q(\mathbf{c})\|_M\}.$$

If $A(\mathbf{x})$ is $P(\mathbf{x}) \& Q(\mathbf{x})$, then

$$\|A(\mathbf{c})\|_M = \min\{\|P(\mathbf{c})\|_M, \|Q(\mathbf{c})\|_M\}.$$

If $A(\mathbf{x})$ is $\neg B(\mathbf{x})$, then $\|A(\mathbf{c})\|_M = 1 - \|B(\mathbf{c})\|_M$. For any set S of real numbers, if S is bounded above, we let sup S denote the least upper bound of the members of S, and if S is bounded below we let inf S be the greatest lower bound of S. Then, if $A(\mathbf{x})$ is $(\exists y)B(\mathbf{x}, y)$, we set

$$\|A(\mathbf{c})\|_M = \sup\{\|B(\mathbf{c}, a)\|_M \mid a \in D\};$$

and if $A(\mathbf{x})$ is $(\forall y)B(\mathbf{x}, y)$,

$$\|A(\mathbf{c})\|_M = \inf\{\|B(\mathbf{c}, a)\|_M \mid a \in D\}.$$

The question is now how to characterize degrees of truth for predications of inhomogeneous natural kind predicates. It is for this purpose that we shall invoke a normalized metric d of the sort adverted to. Let P be such a predicate. I shall define a function $|\ |_P : D \rightarrow [0, 1]$, where we now think of D as the range of significance of P. For any $x \in D$, $|x|_P$ is to be thought of as the degree to which x falls under P. Let $\mathrm{Hom}(P)$ denote the collection of all characteristic properties for the archetypes of P. We now define:

$$|x|_P = \sup\{1 - d(F, G) : Fx \ \& \ G \in \mathrm{Hom}(P)\}.$$

Then $|x|_P$ is maximized when $|x|_P = 1$ and is minimized when $|x|_P = 0$. The **definite** cases of P are those objects x such that $|x|_P = 1$.

This is a reasonable definition. The number $d(F, G)$ reflects the degree to which the property F of x diverges from the property G. So the definition says that the degree to which x exemplifies P measures the degree to which properties exemplified by x approximate the characteristic properties for the archetypes for P. Since this is a natural measure of the *extent* to which an item falls under an inhomogeneous term, we have accomplished the minimum required to implement suggested conception of reference for such terms within the fuzzy set framework.

In this context, I shall not go much beyond this minimum. But we need to show what was claimed at the outset, that the definite cases of an inhomogeneous term are just those things falling under one of its archetypes. Granted the explicit constraints adopted above, we can be exact.

PROPOSITION 1. *For any x, $|x|_P = 1$ iff x exemplifies some member of* Hom(P).

PROOF. Suppose, for the right-to-left direction, that x exemplifies an archetype for P. If Q is the characteristic property for this archetype, then since $d(Q, Q) = 0$, $\sup\{1 - d(F, G) :\ Fx\ \&\ G \in \text{Hom}(P)\} = |x|_P = 1$.

Suppose, for the other direction, that $|x|_P = 1$. If the set

$$M_x = \{d(F, G) :\ Fx\ \&\ G \in \text{Hom}(P)\}$$

is finite, the least upper bound defining $|x|_P$ is a maximum of a finite set of numbers and there is a characteristic property G for an archetype for P and a property F exemplified by x such that $d(F, G) = 0$. By the condition (1), then, $F = G$ and so x exemplifies G. On the other hand, suppose that the set M_x is infinite. Then there exist two sequences $S_1 = \langle F_n \rangle$, $S_2 = \langle G_n \rangle$, where each F_n is exemplified by x, each G_n is designated by an archetype for P, and such that $\lim_n d(F_n, G_n) = 0$. Since the set of archetypes for P is finite, there exists an e such that $G_n = G_e$ for infinitely many n. There must then exist a subsequence $\langle F_{n_i} \rangle$ of S_1 such that $\lim_i d(F_{n_i}, G_e) = 0$. Thus, by the continuity condition (C1), x exemplifies G_e, and thus falls under an archetype for P.

B.   The Supervaluation Model

The supervaluation approach starts with the idea that to be a definite case of a vague predicate is to fall under each property that constitutes an acceptable 'precisification' of the predicate, an acceptable way of making it precise. To be a definite noncase is to fall under none of its acceptable precisifications. This leaves room for the possibility that an item may fall under some acceptable sharpenings of a vague term but not under others; these are the indeterminate cases of the term. On this view, then, we might identify an extensional interpretation of a vague term P over a domain D with a collection $\{S_i\}$ of subsets of D, I being a suitable index set. The S_i's represent the acceptable precisifications of P on the given interpretation. The **extension** of P on such an interpretation is $\bigcap_{i \in I} S_i$, and its **antiextension** is $\bigcap_{i \in D} D\backslash S_i$. The extension of P on an interpretation consists of its definite cases therein, and its antiextension of its definite noncases.[3] Typically there will be indeterminate cases, items, that is to say, falling in some but not all of the S_i.

There is a natural adaptation of the supervaluation approach to inhomogeneous natural kind terms. Again, fix a suitable normalized metric d on the collection of homogeneous-kind-specifying properties. If P is such a term, let $P_1, ..., P_n$ be the archetypes for P, and let $K_1, ..., K_n$ be the corresponding characteristic properties. For any real number $r > 0$ and any property Q, let $N_r(Q)$ be the neighborhood of Q consisting of all properties F such that $d(F, Q) < r$ and let $|N_r(Q)|$ be the set of objects exemplifying a property in $N_r(Q)$. Say that r is **acceptable for** P_i if each property in $N_r(K_i)$ is a structural basis for most of the saliencies associated with P_i. It follows from the continuity condition (C2) that for each i there exists some $r > 0$ such that r is acceptable for P_i. Then the initial probabilistic-explanatory rationale for the suggested interpretation of inhomogeneous terms holds good if we assign to P any extension of the form

$$(\#) \qquad |N_{z_1}(K_i)| \cup \ ... \ \cup \ |N_{z_n}(K_n)|,$$

where z_i is acceptable for P_i for each i, $1 \leq i \leq n$. For, on any such interpretation, if an object falls into one of the sets $N_{z_i}(K_i)$, it will exemplify a property that is close enough to the characteristic property for P_i to account for *most* of its saliencies. Thus, on the regularity condition, the exemplification of suitably many saliencies for an archetype for P by that object will favor its exemplification of others. And this was the minimum required for the applicability of the model.

Call the set of properties $N_{z_1}(K_i) \cup ... \cup N_{z_n}(K_n)$ generating an extension of the form (#) an **admissible cluster** for P. The suggestion, then, is that the acceptable precisifications of P are obtained by disjoining the elements of admissible clusters for P. Thus, on the supervaluation model, the extension of P consists of those things that exemplify some element in any admissible cluster for P, and its antiextension is made up of those things that fall under *no* element in any admissible cluster for P. I can now show, as I did for the fuzzy-set model, that the positive cases of P are precisely the items falling under one of its archetypes:

---

[3]In general, the extension of any formula φ of the language under such an interpretation of all of its terms will be the set of sequences from D satisfying φ in any classical model that assigns to each term some extension acceptable for it with respect to that interpretation; similarly for the antiextension.

PROPOSITION 2. *For any x, x falls under each admissible precisification of P if x falls under some archetype for P.*

PROOF. Again, let $P_1, ..., P_n$ be the archetypes for P and $K_1, ..., K_n$ the corresponding characteristic properties. The right to left direction is clear, since if x falls under an archetype P_i, it exemplifies some element in any neighborhood of K_i, namely K_i itself. For the other direction, suppose that x does not exemplify any archetype for P. We show that there is an admissible cluster for P such that x exemplifies no element of the cluster. For each $i \leq n$, there exists a number $l(i) > 0$ such that x exemplifies the complement of each property in $N_{l(i)}(K_i)$. Otherwise, for each $r > 0$ there exists a property Q in $N_r(K_i)$ such that x exemplifies Q, whence by the continuity condition (C1) x would fall under P_i. Set $z_i = \min\{l(i), r(i)\}$ where for each i ($1 \leq i \leq n$), $r(i) > 0$ is a number acceptable for P_i. Then the collection

$$N_{z_1}(P_1) \cup ... \cup N_{z_n}(P_n)$$

is an admissible cluster for P wherein no property is exemplified by x.

FOUR

THE GROUND OF LOGIC

4.1 Introduction

In framing a semantic description of Karl's language, it is customary to divide his vocabulary into 'descriptive' and 'logical' expressions. The observational predicates and natural kind terms considered in the previous chapter are typical descriptive expressions. Logical expressions are typified by the connectives and quantifiers of elementary quantification theory. Some philosophical logicians consider these to exhaust the logical constants.[1] Many are more liberal, but all would construe the first-order logical terms to be paradigms of the logical.

In this chapter, I shall take up the problem of interpreting logical expressions within the present framework for radical interpretation. The questions are these: (1) What data in an interpretation of Karl allow us to distinguish the logical terms from other expressions of Karl's language? (2) With what sort of semantic interpretation is such an expression to be associated? (3) On what empirical basis is an expression of the relevant type to be assigned a particular interpretation of this sort? Finally, (4) what is the range of expressions that count as 'logical'? Together, these questions constitute what I shall call 'The interpretation problem for logic.'

4.1.1 Method

My procedure will be as follows. As earlier, I distinguish constitutive principles from enabling proposals: a constitutive principle is a fundamental constraint on radical interpretation; an enabling proposal with respect to that principle is a construction designed to show how the constitutive principle may be satisfied. For example, the Principle of Conformality is a constitutive principle, which says roughly that part of the aim of interpretation is to facilitate the understanding of Karl's activity in conformal

---

[1] Quine is the most prominent example. See, for example, his discussion of first-order logic in *Philosophy of Logic* (Englewood Cliffs, N.J.: Prentice-Hall, 1970).

terms. The accounts suggested in the previous chapter of the reference of proper names, observational predicates, and natural kind terms were enabling proposals to this end.

What constitutive principles are relevant to the interpretation problem for logic? A choice of logical constants is preparatory to a model-theoretic definition of logical consequence and logical truth for Karl's language. The fundamental constraint I wish to suggest is that the model-theoretic consequence relation, characterized with reference to a given choice of logical constants, should be a case of a more general entailment relation for Karl's language: in the usual notation, that $A \models B$ only if A entails B. For this to make sense as a constitutive requirement of interpretation, of course, it must be shown that the data in a complete interpretation of Karl determine the relevant entailment relation in Karl's language. I shall argue that a representation of Karl's inductive method of the sort described in chapter 2 does indeed generate a natural entailment relation for Karl's language. Alternatively, it is natural to say that a set of sentences Σ entails a sentence ϕ if ϕ obtains in every possible world that realizes each member of Σ. To follow this line within the present framework, it must be shown how a complete interpretation of Karl fixes a specification of the relevant possibilities. In section 4.5, these will be identified roughly with maximal consistent descriptions of the world which are closed under the entailment relation generated by Karl's inductive method. Call these descriptions Karl's **epistemic alternatives**, or, simply, Karl's **alternatives**. Under quite natural conditions, the two characterizations of entailment may be shown to be equivalent.

I suggested in chapter 1 that the delineation of Karl's alternatives is an independently defensible goal of radical interpretation. It is essentially the goal of providing, in addition to a model of Karl's inductive method, a demarcation of the descriptions of the world that are *epistemically possible for Karl*. It seems natural and desirable that such a demarcation should *follow* from a proper specification of Karl's inductive method, and hereafter I will be concerned to show that this is the case. With or without this connection, however, a demarcation of the states of affairs which are *thinkable for Karl* tells us *something about* Karl as a person, and should be a byproduct of a complete understanding of Karl as an intentional system.

Such a demarcation would afford another means of describing Karl's attitudes, in terms of sets of alternatives. Within the framework of chapter 2, Karl's attitudes are specified by semantic representations of the sort accorded to sentences in his language. On this alternative representation, they would be given by the set of epistemically possible worlds in which the sentences are true. The familiar objection to possible worlds-based representations has been that they describe Karl's attitudes too coarsely, and

are subject to rather implausible conditions of closure. I shall argue that
this outcome is avoided if, as on the description I will suggest, a sufficiently
comprehensive system of worlds is employed: this construction will require
only that Karl's beliefs be closed under the relation of entailment generated
by his inductive method. In effect, this is to say that, within the suggested
description of Karl's attitudes, Karl is represented as applying his inductive
method ideally; but this is an assumption already in place.

I will call the indicated constitutive requirement the **Completeness
Principle**. The terminology here is suggested by an analogy to *completeness theorems* in logic, the idea that a model-theoretic entailment relation
be coordinated with a syntactic one. In this case, in place of syntactic
deducibility, we have the entailment relation generated by Karl's inductive
method; the Completeness Principle says precisely that this entailment relation should subsume the model-theoretic one. The enabling proposal I
have to suggest that is relevant to the Completeness Principle arises by
asking what property of the logical constants *explains why* a sentence ϕ is
a model-theoretic consequence of a set Σ only if Σ entails ϕ. The logical
constants will then be characterized as just the expressions that exemplify
that property. The main task, then, is to identify the relevant property,
and to show how it leads to the required explanation.

Before proceeding, however, it is prudent to sound one cautionary note.
It should not be expected that there is a single characterization of the logical constants adequate for all purposes of theoretical logic. In a thoughtful
and useful article, Leslie Tharp distinguished two broad designs for the
nature of logic.[2] One design sees logic as a part of the theory of *demonstration*. This is the design that best fits my project. Indeed, as noted, the
entailment relation defined with reference to the totality of Karl's alternatives corresponds to an idealized sort of demonstrability in Karl's language.
But there is another design for logic, one that conceives it as an *instrument
for characterizing structure*. On this conception of the nature of logic, the
goal, or one of them, will be to supply, for various isomorphism types of
mathematical interest, a set of logical devices enabling a natural categorical
description of that isomorphism type, that is, a theory in the logic whose
models are precisely the members of that type.

It is obvious that these two conceptions of logic are quite different.
Indeed, it is commonplace to hear that they are, at least to some extent, at
odds with one another: that the expressive capacity required of a logic in
order for it to categorically describe mathematically interesting structures
makes it implausible that the corresponding consequence relation can be

---

[2] "Which Logic Is the Right Logic?" *Synthese* 31 (1975): 1–21.

coordinated with a reasonable notion of demonstration.[3]   However, the framework developed in this chapter makes it possible to describe a general connection between the two conceptions of logic. I shall return to this matter in subsection 4.6.4 below.

4.1.2 Prospect

I shall first discuss the conditions under which a model-theoretic characterization of validity for a simple extensional language leads to a class of logical truths that exemplify certain modal properties. The question is this. Think of a notion of possibility as being characterized by a collection $\mathbf{M}$ of sets of sentences in a suitable extension of the language. A statement of the language is said to be *possible over* $\mathbf{M}$ if it occurs in some set in $\mathbf{M}$ and to be *analytic over* $\mathbf{M}$ if its negation is not possible over $\mathbf{M}$. Under what conditions will the model-theoretically valid statements be analytic over $\mathbf{M}$? This question will receive a general answer in terms of certain properties of the expressions that are treated as constants in the characterization of validity. Each notion of possibility $\mathbf{M}$ of a certain not-very-special sort will be associated with a property, *invariance over* $\mathbf{M}$, defined for expressions of the language in question. It may then be shown that if the logical expressions of the language are invariant over $\mathbf{M}$, then a sentence is model-theoretically valid only if it is analytic over $\mathbf{M}$. Similarly, a sentence ϕ is a model-theoretic consequence of a set Σ of sentences only if ϕ belongs to each member of $\mathbf{M}$ realizing Σ. This is then an abstract completeness result that can be expressed in the familiar form

$$\Sigma \models \varphi \;\Rightarrow\; \Sigma \vdash_{\mathbf{M}} \varphi,$$

where we write '$\vdash_{\mathbf{M}}$' to indicate the entailment relation generated by $\mathbf{M}$.[4]

My account of the logical constants in the extensional case will emerge from a specialization of this abstract completeness result. For this purpose, I will take $\mathbf{M}$ to comprise complete specifications of all of Karl's

---

[3]This view is suggested by Tarski's indefinability theorem. If an axiomatic T theory in a given logic is categorical, and entailment in the logic coincides with demonstrability (in some sense), then the sentences true in the models of T are precisely the sentences demonstrable in T. If, by means of a suitable coding, the proof-relation for T can be identified with a relation on the natural numbers, and the natural numbers can be embedded in models of T, then any language in which that relation is definable will enable a definition of the truth-predicate for the models of T. It follows by Tarski's theorem that the proof-relation for T is not itself definable in the language of T over any of its models. However, one would expect any reasonable notion of proof to be thus definable if T is of sufficient strength.

[4]See my "Modality, Invariance, and Logical Truth," *Journal of Philosophical Logic* 16 (1987): 23–43. A version of this result is given in postscript B to this chapter.

epistemic alternatives. My suggestion will be that the logical constants of Karl's language are the expressions that exemplify the invariance property with respect to this choice of **M**. The indicated result then says in this case that the model-theoretically valid sentences of Karl's language are analytic over the collection of all of his epistemic alternatives, and that the model-theoretically characterized consequence relation for that language is a species of the entailment relation generated by Karl's inductive method. This is the connection we sought.

My account of the logical constants also bears directly on the question of the determinacy of Karl's logic. If Karl speaks a simple extensional language, the invariance or non-invariance of an expression of that language over the entire collection of his epistemic alternatives are properties that can be 'read off' the structure of those alternatives; in fact, I will argue that the semantic interpretation of any logical expression is determined by the truth-values of sentences containing it over all of Karl's alternatives. Those alternatives are in turn fixed, or so I will argue, by a suitable description of Karl's inductive method. I will thus arrive at a relative determinacy result: in the extensional case, both the *character* of an expression as logical or nonlogical, and its *semantic interpretation* if it is logical, are settled once a suitable description of Karl's inductive method is given. Parallel observations are available for the intensional case (see 4.8–4.12).

4.2   Framework 1

4.2.1   Valuations

In this subsection, I will set up a framework within which to discuss logical relations in extensional languages. As earlier, L will be the formal language that comprises the semantic representations of the sentences of Karl's language in the context of a complete interpretation of Karl, assumed fixed. The interpretation will incorporate both a syntactic and semantic description of L, and for the purposes of the next few sections suppose that these descriptions assume an especially simple form. Specifically, assume that L is a language containing two categories of **formulas** and **terms**, and two subcategories of syntactically primitive terms, **variables** and **individual constants**. The **descriptive constants** of L comprise its formulas and terms, and are built up from the primitive terms by operators that apply to cartesian products of the four categories. Thus, n-place predicates map n-tuples of terms to formulas, unary quantifiers map variable-formula pairs to formulas, and n-place function symbols map n-tuples of terms to terms.

Second, L is assumed to have a simple extensional semantics of the sort described in subsection 2.2.1. If τ is a category in L and D is a nonempty set, we characterize the class $\mathcal{E}(\tau, D)$ of extensions appropriate for type τ over D. If τ is the category of formulas, $\mathcal{E}(\tau, D) = D^\omega$, and if τ is the category of terms, $\mathcal{E}(\tau, D)$ is the collection of all functions from D^ω to D.[5] If τ is the subcategory of individual constants, $\mathcal{E}(\tau, D)$ is the collection of constant functions from D^ω to D, and if v is the n'th variable in a standard enumeration, the unique extension appropriate for v over D is the projection function π_n^D on D^ω, $\pi_n^D(\mathbf{s})$ for any $\mathbf{s} \in D^\omega$ being the n'th component of $\mathbf{s}$. If Q is an operator in L that applies to a cartesian product $\tau_1 \times ... \times \tau_n$ of categories to yield expressions of a category σ, then an extension appropriate for Q over D is a function from $\mathcal{E}(\tau_1, D) \times ... \times \mathcal{E}(\tau_n, D)$ to $\mathcal{E}(\sigma, D)$. A **valuation** for L is a pair $\mathfrak{A} = \langle |\mathfrak{A}|, F_\mathfrak{A} \rangle$ such that $|\mathfrak{A}|$ is a nonempty set, the **domain** of $\mathfrak{A}$, and $F_\mathfrak{A}$ is a function that assigns an extension of the appropriate sort to each lexical primitive in L over $|\mathfrak{A}|$. A valuation $\mathfrak{A}$ for L thus determines an extension for each formula or term of L inductively in the obvious way.[6] A sequence from $|\mathfrak{A}|$ that belongs to the extension of a formula in $\mathfrak{A}$ will be said to **satisfy** that formula in $\mathfrak{A}$, and a formula is **true on** $\mathfrak{A}$ if it is satisfied therein by all sequences.

Finally, we give definitions of consequence and validity relative to a variable base of logical constants. A **logic** $\mathcal{L}$ for L will be a collection of operators from L. These are the expressions of L whose interpretations are, in some sense, to be held fixed in characterizing a corresponding model-theoretic consequence relation for L. Thus, let ϕ be a sentence and Σ a set of sentences in L, and let $\mathcal{L}$ be a logic for L. Then ϕ will be said to be an $\mathcal{L}$-**consequence** of Σ in L if ϕ holds in each valuation $\mathfrak{A}$ of L such that (i) every sentence of Σ is true in $\mathfrak{A}$, and (ii) $\mathfrak{A}$ respects each member of $\mathcal{L}$. Similarly, ϕ is said to be $\mathcal{L}$-**valid** if ϕ holds in every valuation that respects each member of $\mathcal{L}$. To say that a valuation $\mathfrak{A}$ 'respects' an operator $Q \in \mathcal{L}$ is roughly to say that $\mathfrak{A}$ assigns the correct extension to Q over $|\mathfrak{A}|$. For this to make sense, it is assumed, as provided in section 2.2, that the semantic rule assigned to any operator Q of L defines a mapping J_Q that for any nonempty set D returns an extension $J_Q(D)$ of appropriate type for Q over D. Formally, then, a valuation $\mathfrak{A}$ is said to **respect** a logic $\mathcal{L}$ if

$$\mathfrak{A}(Q) = J_Q(|\mathfrak{A}|)$$

holds for each operator $Q \in \mathcal{L}$.

---

[5]If D is a nonempty set, D^ω is the collection of all infinite sequences $\langle a_0, a_1, ... \rangle$ such that $a_n \in D$ for each n.

[6]A bit more explicitly, if $\mathbf{e}$ is a constant or variable, the extension of $\mathbf{e}$ in $\mathfrak{A}$ is $F_\mathfrak{A}(\mathbf{e})$, and if Q is an operator mapping $\tau_1 \times ... \times \tau_n$ to σ, and $E_1, ..., E_n$ are the extensions in $\mathfrak{A}$ of expressions $\mathbf{e}_1, ..., \mathbf{e}_n$ of types $\tau_1, ..., \tau_n$, then the extension of $Q(\mathbf{e}_1, ..., \mathbf{e}_n)$ in $\mathfrak{A}$ is $F_\mathfrak{A}(Q)(E_1, ..., E_n)$.

4.2.2   Quantifiers

The framework just described may be illustrated by considering some cases of quantificational operators Q that apply to variables and formulas to yield formulas.[7] The most familiar examples are the elementary quantifiers $\exists$ and $\forall$. Thus, let Q be $\exists$. For each domain D, π_n^D is again the n'th projection function on D^ω; for any $s \in D^\omega$, we have $\pi_n^D(s) = s(n)$. Define

$$s \equiv_n s' \;\leftrightarrow\; (\forall k)(k \neq n \rightarrow s(k) = s'(k)).$$

Then if $f = \pi_n^D$ and $E \subseteq D^\omega$, set

(1) $J_Q(D)(f, E) = \{s \in D^\omega | \ (\exists s')(s' \equiv_n s \ \& \ s' \in E)\}.$

Thus, pick $\mathfrak{A}$ such that $|\mathfrak{A}| = D$. If v is the n'th variable and ϕ is a formula such that $\mathfrak{A}(\phi) = E$, since $\mathfrak{A}(v) = \pi_n^D$, (1) implies that a sequence s from D^ω satisfies $(\exists v)\phi$ in $\mathfrak{A}$ if some sequence differing from s in at most its n'th component satisfies ϕ in $\mathfrak{A}$. This is, of course, the standard Tarskian truth clause for $\exists$. A similar story holds for $\forall$.

As another example, consider the quantifier Q_0 characterized as follows. For a fixed domain D, if $f = \pi_n^D$ and $E \subseteq D^\omega$, we have for any $s \in D^\omega$ that

$$s \in J_{Q_0}(f, E) \;\leftrightarrow\; \{s' \in D^\omega | s' \equiv_n s \ \& \ s' \in E\} \text{ is infinite.}$$

If Q_0 is so construed, $(Q_0 x)P(x)$ holds in any valuation if infinitely many items fall under $P(x)$ therein: Q_0 thus expresses 'for infinitely many'.[8]

There is an alternative semantical characterization of quantifiers familiar from generalized model theory. The idea is that a quantifier refers to class of relational structures, where by a relational structure we understand a finite sequence $\langle D, R_1, ..., R_n \rangle$, where D is a nonempty set and $R_1, ..., R_n$ are relations on D.[9] Thus, for example, $\exists$ would express $\{\langle D, A \rangle | \ A$ is a non-empty subset of $D\}$. If Q is $(1,1)$-ary (applying to one formula and binding one variable), the idea is that Q refers to the class of all structures

---

[7]In the general case, there are positive integers n and m such that Q applies to any choice of variables $v_1, ..., v_n$ and formulas $\varphi_1, ..., \varphi_m$ to give a formula $Qv_1...v_n[\varphi_1...\varphi_m]$.

[8]The credentials of Q_0 and other cardinality quantifiers as logical expressions are discussed in 4.6.2.

[9]This idea goes back to Mostowski, "On a Generalization of Quantifiers," *Fundamenta Mathematicae* 44 (1957): 12–36; for a good general discussion, see H.-D. Ebbinghaus, "Extended Logics: The General Framework," in *Model-Theoretic Logics*, edited by S. Feferman and J. Barwise (Berlin: Springer Verlag, 1987), 25–76. Mostowski puts some constraints on the notion of a quantifier that I will consider later.

$\langle D, A \rangle$ such that the sentence $(Qx)P(x)$ is true on the assignment of A to $P(x)$ over the domain D; and analogously for quantifiers of other types.

The two semantical characterizations of generalized quantifiers are interconvertible, where the alternative characterization applies at all.[10] Nevertheless, there are some reasons for treating J_Q as the more fundamental semantical correlate of Q. First, the alternative characterization does not apply without modification to nonquantificational operators; the proposed characterization applies quite generally. Second, from my modestly Fregean perspective, the reference of an operator of any sort should be a transformation that maps extensions of the sort possessed by expressions to which it applies onto extensions appropriate for the items it returns, and that is just what J_Q is designed to do for any operator Q.

4.2.3   Which Logic Is the Right Logic?

What is the interest of a model-theoretic characterization of logical consequence for Karl's language? The obvious question concerns the choice of the logic, call it '$\mathcal{L}$', underlying the characterization. Depending on how inclusive $\mathcal{L}$ is taken to be, the consequence relation will be wider or narrower. If $\mathcal{L}$ comprises all primitives of L, the consequence relation will almost but not quite subsume any pair of sentences alike in truth-value.[11] If, on the other hand, no expressions at all of L are counted as logical constants (that is, if $\mathcal{L}$ is empty), the consequence relation will be vacuous. Between these

---

[10]For any domain D and $A \subseteq D$, set

$$\text{CON}(D, A) = \{\langle a \rangle^\frown s | \ a \in A, s \in D^\omega\}$$

where for any a, s, $\langle a \rangle^\frown s$ is the sequence on D such that $(\langle a \rangle^\frown s)(0) = a$ and $(\langle a \rangle^\frown s)(n+1) = s(n)$ holds for each n. Let Q^* be the class of relational structures associated with the quantifier Q (again, for simplicity, consider only the unary case). Then we have:

$$\langle D, A \rangle \in Q^* \ \leftrightarrow \ J_Q(D)(\pi_o^D, \text{CON}(D, A)) = D^\omega.$$

Conversely, given Q^*, we may recover J_Q via the equivalence

$(\forall s)(s \in J_Q(D)(f, E) \ \leftrightarrow$
$\qquad (\exists n)(f = \pi_n^D \ \& \ \langle D, \{a \in D| \ (\exists s' \in E)(s' \equiv_n s \& f(s') = a)\}\rangle \ \in \ Q^*).$

---

[11]This is owing to the fact that we must still take account of variation of domains. Thus, for example, the sentence '$(\exists x)(\exists y)x \neq y$' would not follow from '$(\exists x)x = x$', since the former is false and the latter true in all unit domains; nor would '$(\exists x)x$ is red' follow from '$(\exists x)x$ is square', since the former is false and the latter true in all domains containing some square objects and no red ones, and so on.

two extremes, we find various choices of logical constants, and correspondingly many possible consequence relations. In a semantical definition of 'logical consequence', the logical constants are given simply by a list. The question, as Tarski stressed long ago, is whether there are objective grounds for preferring one such list to any other.[12]

However, the choice of logic is not ultimately *arbitrary* if the point of the definition is to explicate the intuitive notions of logical consequence and logical truth. Both notions are connected to certain modal and epistemic concepts, and it is a reasonable constraint on an account of what it is to be a logical constant that it explicate these connections. Thus, for example, a sentence of an elementary language is logically true only if it is necessarily true. But the requirement that our account of the logical constants fit into an explanation of the necessity of the logical truths places constraints on the demarcation of the constants. For example, suppose that L is an elementary language containing two predicates, F and G, the extensions of which contingently coincide. That is, imagine that the statement

[i] $(\forall x)(Fx \leftrightarrow Gx)$

is true in L, but contingently so. In this situation, then, F and G cannot *both* be counted as logical constants: otherwise, [i] would incorrectly be counted as valid. Care must be exercised in choosing the logical constants, then, if the connection between logical truth and necessity is to be explained.

A related question has been discussed by John Etchemendy.[13] Etchemendy questions the claim of Tarski's definition to lead to a notion of logical consequence that satisfies the requirement that sentences should be *necessary relative to* sets of which they are logical consequences. Etchemendy attributes to Tarski something like the following modal fallacy: using a bit of set theory, Tarski deduces from the hypothesis that a sentence ϕ is a logical consequence of a set K ($K \models \phi$) a sentence which says that ϕ is true if K is. According to Etchemendy, Tarski then concludes that

(N1) $K \models \phi \ \Rightarrow \ \Box(K \text{ is true} \Rightarrow \phi \text{ is true})$

holds. However, what follows from Tarski's argument is only that

(N2) $\Box(K \models \phi \ \Rightarrow \ (K \text{ is true} \Rightarrow \phi \text{ is true}));$

---

[12]Tarski, "On the Concept of Logical Consequence," reprinted in *Logic, Semantics, and Metamathematics* (Oxford: Clarendon Press, 1956).

[13] *The Concept of Logical Consequence* (Cambridge, Mass.: Harvard University Press, 1990).

but, as Etchemendy points out, (N1) does not follow from (N2).

I do not wish here to enter into the lively dispute over whether Etchemendy has Tarski right here.[14] Simply consider what would be required to fill the lacuna that Etchemendy has identified, whether or not the lacuna is Tarski's. If the modality represented by '$\Box$' respects the distribution principle

(S) $$\Box(A \to B) \to (\Box A \to \Box B),$$

we could derive (N1) from (N2) if we could assume

(N3) $$K \models \phi \;\Rightarrow\; \Box(K \models \phi).$$

For, by (N2) and (S), we have

$$\Box(K \models \phi) \;\Rightarrow\; \Box(K \text{ is true} \Rightarrow \phi \text{ is true}),$$

which with (N3) yields (N1). The difficulty is that, in the absence of substantive constraints on the logical terms, (N3) is sometimes *false*. For example, let $ be a binary connective defined by a rule saying that $A\$B$ is valued true if A and B are both true and Galileo believed that the earth moves, and is valued false otherwise. Since Galileo did in fact believe that the Earth moves, $ is extensionally equivalent to conjunction. Thus, if $ were treated as a logical term, setting $K = \{\phi, \psi\}$, we would have $K \models \phi\$\psi$; but this relation fails in any possible situation in which ϕ and ψ are true and in which Galileo does not believe that the Earth moves. Etchemendy's objection thus stands. However, notice that the connection between the concepts of necessity and logical consequence expressed by (N3) would be ensured by any definition of $\models$ satisfying the Completeness Principle if '$\Box$' is interpreted with reference to a collection of possible worlds that are epistemically possible for Karl; Etchemendy's necessitation requirement simply *is* the Completeness Principle, if these worlds *coincide* with Karl's epistemic alternatives. In what follows, we shall address Etchemendy's problem by placing constraints on the logical terms that suffice to ensure that the Completeness Principle is satisfied.

---

[14]See, for example, Gila Sher, "Did Tarski Commit 'Tarski's Fallacy'?" *Journal of Symbolic Logic* 61 (1996): 653–86. For a helpful recent discussion of the whole issue, see Scott Soames, *Understanding Truth* (New York: Oxford University Press, 1999), especially pp. 117–36.

4.3   Invariance 1

4.3.1   *Mostowski's Condition*

In 1957, Mostowski suggested a constraint on generalized quantifiers that I have elsewhere argued to be relevant to a demarcation of the logical constants.[15] One succinct statement of Mostowski's condition is that the interpretation of a generalized quantifier should be *invariant under isomorphism*. For this to make sense, of course, it must be assumed that the interpretation of the quantifier symbol in question is defined for each domain: but this assumption was in any case required if such an expression is to play the role of a constant in a model-theoretic characterization of validity for a language containing it. Thus, for example, suppose that Q is a quantifier symbol that combines with a variable v and a formula ϕ to yield a formula $(Qv)\phi$. The extension of v over a domain D is a projection function mapping D^ω to D, the extension of ϕ over D a subset of D^ω . Thus, in the notation of the previous section, the extension of Q over D is a function $J_Q(D)$ mapping each pair $\langle f, E \rangle$, where f is a projection function for and E a subset of D^ω, to another such subset. Mostowski's requirement, slightly reformulated to fit the present context, is that any isomorphism of the structures $\langle D, f, E \rangle$ and $\langle D', E', f' \rangle$ also maps $J_Q(D)(f, E)$ isomorphically onto $J_Q(D')(f', E')$. That is to say if λ is any one-to-one correspondence mapping D onto D', f is the projection function π_n^D, f' is $\pi_n^{D'}$, and $E' = \lambda(E)$, then

$$J_Q(D')(f', E') = \lambda(J_Q(D)(f, E)).^{16}$$

What this means, then, is that if f and f' are alike the n'th projection functions for their respective domains, if the items satisfying a predicate $A(x_n)$ on the interpretation described by $\langle D', f', E' \rangle$ are just the images under λ of the sequences satisfying $B(x_n)$ on $\langle D, f, E \rangle$, then the same relationship obtains between the extensions of $(Qx_n)A(x_n)$ and $(Qx_n)B(x_n)$ in the respective interpretations. The invariance requirement for operators of other types is described analogously: if α is any operator, the idea is that no matter what the interpretation of a sequence of expressions $e_1, ..., e_n$ to which α applies, any function mapping the extensions of $e_1, ..., e_n$ isomorphically onto the extensions of a corresponding sequence $e'_1, ..., e'_n$ also maps the extension of $\alpha(e_1, ..., e_n)$ onto the extension of $\alpha(e'_1, ..., e'_n)$.

It is easy to see that the elementary quantifiers satisfy this requirement. For example, let Q be $\exists$, and let f be π_n^D for a fixed domain D. Consider a

---

[15]Mostowski, "On a Generalization of Quantifiers"; for my argument, see "The Idea of a Logical Constant," *Journal of Philosophy* (1981), 499–523, especially 507–510.

[16]Where if $E \subseteq D^\omega$, we write $\lambda(E) = \{\langle \lambda(a_n)\rangle | \langle a_n\rangle \in E\}$.

function φ mapping the structure $\langle D, f, E \rangle$ isomorphically, onto the structure $\langle D, f', E' \rangle$. Then $f' = \pi_n^{D'}$, whence, since $\varphi(E) = E'$, we have for any $s \in D^\omega$ that $s' \in E$ holds for some sequence s' such that $s' \equiv_n s$ iff $s' \in E'$ holds for some sequence s' such that $s' \equiv_n \varphi(s)$. But this is to say precisely that

$$\varphi(J_Q(D)(f, E)) = J_Q(D')(f', E'),$$

as required by Mostowski's condition. It may similarly be seen that the cardinality quantifiers 'for at least κ x', where 'κ' denotes an arbitrary cardinal number, satisfy Mostowski's requirement.

I argued in the article cited in note 15 above that it is natural to require the logical constants to satisfy Mostowski's condition, on roughly the grounds that we should expect the semantic role of a logical constant in a sentence to be determined solely by the *structure* of the subject matter of the sentence, independently of features specific to the objects constituting that subject matter. However, using something like Etchemendy's requirement I also argued that Mostowski's constraint does not, as it stands, ensure that a quantificational expression satisfying it is a logical constant. The problem is that there can be accidental invariance. Consider, for example, a quantifier symbol Q of Karl's language L translated into English by the phrase 'for some $-$, if P, and for all $-$, if $\neg P$', where P represents a contingent truth of English. The quantifier Q extensionally coincides with $\exists$ on any domain; thus if Q were treated as a logical constant, for any predicate $A(x)$ the formula $(Qx)A(x)$ would be a logical consequence of $(\exists x)A(x)$ in L. However, the truth of $(\exists x)A(x)$ does not *necessarily ensure* the truth of $(Qx)A(x)$ in L, for in any possible situation in which the extension of $A(x)$ is non-empty but non-universal, and in which the condition represented by 'P' fails to obtain, $(\exists x)A(x)$ will be true but $(Qx)A(x)$ false. Another example is afforded by the deviant connective \$ considered in 4.2.3. The connective \$ coincides extensionally with & on any domain and so fulfills Mostowski's requirement. But for the reasons already indicated, \$ is not a logical expression.

To arrive at a demarcation of the logical terms that excludes such cses, it is natural to consider a modal generalization of Mostowski's condition. The idea is in effect to apply the suggested invariance constraint *across all possible situations*. We would then require of the quantifier Q that, for any pair of worlds α, β and any pair of predicates A and B, any function mapping the extension of A at α isomorphically onto the extension of B at β also maps the extension of $(Qx)A$ at α onto the extension of $(Qx)B$ at β, no matter what the interpretations of A and B at the respective worlds. This condition will be violated if α and β are worlds such that P holds at α, P fails at β, and A and B are monadic predicates in x such that the extension of A in α is nonempty, nonuniversal, and isomorphic to the extension of B in β. The quantifier Q thus fails the generalized invariance requirement; a similar argument shows that such a requirement would also rule out the connective $. If an operator of L fulfills this generalization of the Mostowski property with respect to a chosen collection of possible worlds, I will say that the operator is *rigidly invariant over* that collection. To anticipate the main criterion I have to propose, my suggestion will be that the logical constants of Karl's language are those operators therein which are rigidly invariant over the entire collection of his epistemic alternatives.

4.3.2 Modalities and Modal Invariance

I shall now characterize this property a bit more fully. To do this, it will be necessary to be somewhat more explicit about how Karl's alternatives are to be represented. For my purposes here, it will be sufficient to deploy a set of syntactic representations that specify an epistemically possible situation in terms of a state description phrased in some extension of Karl's language L. By a **frame** for L, I will mean a pair $\mathcal{F} = \langle T, \Gamma \rangle$, where T is a collection of sentences in some extension of L and Γ is a collection of individual constants in the language of T; T is subject to certain conditions of completeness, consistency and closure to be described hereafter. By the **language of** $\mathcal{F}$ I mean that of T. Frames (under suitable restrictions) will be my preferred candidates for syntactic representations of Karl's epistemic alternatives. The constants in Γ are to be regarded as correlated in a one-to-one way with the individuals in the possible situation described by T, and the sentences of T as the sentences in the language of $\mathcal{F}$ which are true in that situation. If ϕ is a sentence in the language of $\mathcal{F}$, we sometimes write '$\mathcal{F} \models \phi$', or 'ϕ holds in $\mathcal{F}$', to mean that ϕ belongs to T, and '$|\mathcal{F}|$' to denote Γ.

Frames, I said, will be required to satisfy certain conditions of completeness, consistency, and closure. I shall assume that under the interpretation in question Karl's language L incorporates expressions corresponding to the logical particles of elementary quantification theory, interpreting these in the standard way, and that frames are closed under first-order deducibility if the relevant expressions in L are identified with the elementary constants.[17] If $\neg$ is the device of L interpreted as negation, then for any frame $\mathcal{F} = \langle T, \Gamma \rangle$ and any sentence ϕ in the language of T, we require that either

---

[17]I shall frequently represent these expressions of L by the standard expressions $\neg$, &, ∃, and so forth. The present assumption means only that there is some set of particles in Karl's language that behave extensionally and inferentially like the first-order constants. It will be seen below that in conjunction with the other constraints on a modality this is enough to ensure that any two expressions that both play the role of an elementary constant in this sense are rigidly equivalent over the modality in question; see 4.4.2.

ϕ or $\neg\phi$ belong to T (the **Completeness Condition**) and that not both belong to T (the **Consistency Condition**). Next, it is assumed that the formula $\neg a = b$ appears in T for each pair a, b of distinct constants in Γ (the **Diversity Condition**); this reflects the fact that the constants in Γ are regarded as correlated in a one-to-one way with the individuals in the situation described by $\mathcal{F}$. To state the next constraint, we require a notion of equivalence for expressions of L over a frame. If Γ is a collection of individual constants and ϕ is a formula, a Γ-**instance** of ϕ is a sentence that results by substitution of members of Γ for free variables in ϕ. If $\mathcal{F} = \langle T, \Gamma \rangle$ is a frame, two formulas of the language of $\mathcal{F}$ are said to be **equivalent in** $\mathcal{F}$ when their Γ-instances co-occur in T; terms s and t are equivalent in $\mathcal{F}$ when the formulas $v = s$ and $v = t$ are equivalent in $\mathcal{F}$ for a chosen variable v occurring neither in s nor in t. Finite sequences of expressions are equivalent in $\mathcal{F}$ when they are of the same type and are componentwise equivalent in $\mathcal{F}$.[18] The required constraint, then, is that operators behave extensionally within frames, in the sense that if $\mathcal{F}$ is any frame and Q is an operator that is defined for a product Π of syntactic categories, then the expressions that result by applying Q to sequences from Π which are equivalent in $\mathcal{F}$ are also equivalent in $\mathcal{F}$. I shall call this constraint the **Extensionality Condition**.

The Extensionality Condition has two consequences worth noting briefly. First, if $\langle T, \Gamma \rangle$ is a frame and $\phi(x)$ is a one-variable condition in the language of T, then $(\forall x)\phi(x)$ belongs to T if $\phi(c/x) \in T$ for each $c \in \Gamma$. For in this case, $\phi(x)$ is equivalent to $x = x$ in $\mathcal{F}$, by first-order closure. For the same reason, the sentence $(\forall x)x = x$ belongs to T. By the Extensionality Condition, then, $(\forall x)\phi(x)$ also belongs to T. Second, for any condition $\phi(x)$, the sentence $(\exists x)\phi(x)$ belongs to T only if $\phi(c/x)$ belongs to T for some $c \in \Gamma$. For, if for no $c \in \Gamma$ do we have $\phi(c/x) \in T$, then $\neg\phi(c/x) \in T$ for each $c \in \Gamma$, whence by the foregoing observation we have $(\forall x)\neg\phi(x) \in T$. By first-order logic, then, $\neg(\exists x)\phi(x) \in T$, whence by the consistency condition $(\exists x)\phi(x) \notin T$. This result may be interpreted as saying that each ontological commitment of the set T, represented by an existential generalization of the form $(\exists x)\phi(x)$, is realized therein by some individual constant in Γ.

Briefly, then, a frame for L is a collection of sentences in some extension of L that satisfies the completeness, consistency, diversity and extensionality conditions, and that is closed under first-order deducibility. A **modality** for L is a nonempty collection of frames for L; we view a modality for L as a

---

[18]Where if $\sigma = \langle \xi_1, ..., \xi_n \rangle$ is a finite sequence of expressions in the language of $\mathcal{F}$, the **type** of σ in $\mathcal{F}$ is the collection of all sequences $\langle \xi'_1, ..., \xi'_n \rangle$ such that ξ'_i is of the same syntactic category as ξ_i for each i, $1 \leq i \leq n$.

syntactic representation of a notion of possibility. We wish to characterize, for each modality M for L and each frame $\mathcal{F} \in M$, the extension in $\mathcal{F}$ of any expression in the language of $\mathcal{F}$, and we wish to say in terms of that characterization when an operator of L behaves invariantly over the field of possibilities described by M. If ϕ is a sentence and K a set of sentences in L, say that K **entails** ϕ in M if ϕ belongs to each member of M including K. It will turn out that, under quite general conditions, if each operator in a logic for L is invariant over all of the possible situations represented in M, then ϕ is a model-theoretic consequence of K in that logic only if K entails ϕ in M (see 4.4.3).

Let $\mathcal{F}$ be a frame $\langle T, \Gamma \rangle$ for L and $\mathcal{L}$ the language of $\mathcal{F}$. $\mathcal{L}$ is in general only *partially* interpreted, owing to the fact that we wish to take account of possible situations incorporating nonexistent objects. Clearly, if denotations for all of the individual constants in Γ are fixed, then an extensional interpretation for each operator in the situation described by $\mathcal{F}$ is fixed inductively in the obvious way. However, if $\mathcal{F}$ purports to describe a state of affairs in which there are more (or other) objects than there actually are, $\mathcal{L}$ will withhold reference from the corresponding individual constants. For our present purposes, I shall describe the nonexistent objects only in terms of properties specifiable in $\mathcal{L}$, and in terms of similarly specifiable relations that these objects bear to actual objects and to one another. The extension of a formula of $\mathcal{L}$ in the state of affairs described by $\mathcal{F}$ will then be represented metalinguistically, by sequences of individual constants in Γ. The remainder of the present subsection is devoted to implementing this idea.

In order to take account of the partially interpreted character of $\mathcal{L}$, identify Γ with a pair $\langle \Gamma_0, \Delta \rangle$, where Γ_0 is a set of individual constants and Δ is a partial denotation function on Γ_0, that is, a function defined on a subset of Γ_0. The constants for which Δ is defined are those assigned actual denotations in $\mathcal{L}$. If $\mathcal{F} = \langle T, \Gamma \rangle$ and $\mathcal{F}' = \langle T', \Gamma' \rangle$ are frames, $\mathcal{F}'$ is a **subframe** of $\mathcal{F}$ if $T' \subseteq T$ and, where $\Gamma = \langle \Gamma_0, \Delta \rangle$ and $\Gamma' = \langle \Gamma_0', \Delta' \rangle$, we have $\Gamma_0' \subseteq \Gamma_0$ and Δ' is the restriction of Δ to Γ_0'. If M is a modality, we say that a frame is **generated** by M if it is a subframe of some member of M.[19]

If $\mathcal{F} = \langle T, \Gamma \rangle$ is a frame, the **extension** of a formula $A(x_1, ..., x_n)$ in $\mathcal{F}$ is the set of sequences $\langle c_0, c_1, ... \rangle$ of constants from Γ such that $A(c_1/x_1, ..., c_n/x_n) \in T$. The extension of a term $t(x_1, ..., x_n)$ is the function

---

[19]The relation between the frames in M and the frames generated by M deserves brief comment. In the intended application, the members of M describe Karl's alternatives. In this case, then, M need not be closed under the subframe relation. The frames in M describe maximal possibilities; a frame is generated by M if it is a substructure of such a possibility.

f mapping each sequence $\mathbf{s} = \langle c_0, c_1, ... \rangle$ of constants from Γ to Γ such that $f(\mathbf{s}) = c$ if the formula

[i] $$c = t(c_1/x_1, ..., c_n/x_n)$$

appears in T.[20] If ξ is a finite sequence $\langle \xi_1, ..., \xi_n \rangle$ of formulas or terms in $\mathcal{L}$, by the extension of ξ in $\mathcal{F}$ we mean the structure $\langle A_1, ..., A_n \rangle$, where for each i, $1 \leq i \leq n$, A_i is the extension of ξ_i in $\mathcal{F}$. We write $\text{Ext}_{\mathcal{F}}(\xi)$ to denote the extension of ξ in $\mathcal{F}$. The extensions of operators are defined as follows. Suppose that α is an operator that applies to sequences of expressions from a product

$$\Pi = \sigma_1 \times ... \times \sigma_n$$

of categories in $\mathcal{L}$ to yield an expression of category τ, and set $\text{Ext}_{\mathcal{F}}(\Pi) = \{\text{Ext}_{\mathcal{F}}(\xi) | \xi \in \Pi\}$. The **extension** of α in $\mathcal{F}$ is then that function $J_{\alpha, \mathcal{F}}$ mapping $\text{Ext}_{\mathcal{F}}(\Pi)$ to $\text{Ext}_{\mathcal{F}}(\tau)$ that associates the extension of each sequence $\xi \in \Pi$ in $\mathcal{F}$ with the extension of the expression $\alpha(\xi)$ in $\mathcal{F}$.[21]

I am now in a position to say in somewhat more precise terms what it is for an operator of L to behave invariantly over the collection of possible situations described by a modality for L. Thus, let α be an operator applying to sequences of expressions from a product of syntactic types in L, and let $\mathbf{M}$ be a modality for L. Then α is said to be **invariant over M** if for each pair of frames $\mathcal{F}$ and $\mathcal{F}'$ generated by $\mathbf{M}$ and each sequence ξ an input for α, any function mapping the extension of ξ in $\mathcal{F}$ isomorphically onto the extension of a sequence ξ' in $\mathcal{F}'$ *also* maps the extension of $\alpha(\xi)$ in $\mathcal{F}$ onto the extension of $\alpha(\xi')$ in $\mathcal{F}'$. In an equivalent formulation, suppose

---

[20] Observe that f is well defined: first, since by the first-order closure condition the formula

$$(\exists x)x = t(c_1/x_1, ..., c_n/x_n)$$

appears in T, by the second consequence of the Extensionality Condition noted earlier there exists a constant $c \in \Gamma$ such that the sentence

[i] $$c = t(c_1/x_1, ..., c_n/x_n)$$

appears in T. Further, if c_1, c_2 are distinct constants in T such that the sentences

$$c_1 = t(c_1/x_1, ..., c_n/x_n),$$
$$c_2 = t(c_1/x_1, ..., c_n/x_n)$$

belong to T, by first-order closure the sentence $c_1 = c_2$ belongs to T. But since c_1, c_2 are distinct, the sentence $\neg c_1 = c_2$ also appears in T, which contradicts the consistency assumption for T. Thus the constant c in [i] is unique.

[21] Again, in view of the Extensionality Condition, it may be verified that the function $J_{\alpha, \mathcal{F}}$ is welldefined.

that $E = \mathrm{Ext}_{\mathcal{F}}(\xi)$, $E' = \mathrm{Ext}_{\mathcal{F}'}(\xi')$, and ϕ is a one-to-one correspondence mapping $|\mathcal{F}|$ onto $|\mathcal{F}'|$ such that $\phi(E) = E'$. The invariance condition requires in this case that

$$\phi(J_{\alpha,\mathcal{F}}(E)) = J_{\alpha,\mathcal{F}'}(E'),$$

the exact analogue of Mostowski's requirement enforced across all possible situations represented in **M**. My suggestion will be that α be counted a logical constant of Karl's language if and only if α is invariant over the entire collection of frames that describe his epistemic alternatives. It remains to be seen just what conditions a frame must meet in order to do this; I take up this question in section 4.5.

4.4   Completeness and Determinacy

4.4.1   Reflection

What is the evidence for such a characterization of the logical constants? If, as I suggested at the outset, a fundamental constraint on an interpretive definition of logical consequence for Karl's language is that its converse be a species of entailment therein, a fundamental fact that must be explained on any criterion for the logical constants is why this connection should obtain. Beyond that, we should want a reasonable fit with entrenched intuitions about the bounds of logic, in the sense that when the criterion is applied to our language, against the background of our indigenous concept of epistemic possibility, the resulting demarcation includes expressions which are clearly logical by our lights and excludes expressions which are clearly nonlogical. We should want it to imply the Mostowski constraint and related model-theoretic generalizations about logic. I believe that the identification of logical constanthood with the suggested invariance property accomplishes these aims, at least in the presence of a natural assumption about the modality **M** describing Karl's epistemic alternatives.

The required assumption, roughly put, is that *what is actual is possible.* I shall factor this informal requirement into two parts: first, that the actual interpretations of expressions of Karl's language can, in a suitable sense, be realized in **M**; second, that a complete description of any structure over an actual domain can be embedded in some frame of **M**. These two requirements together make up what I shall call the **Reflection Condition**; a modality fulfilling them will be called **reflective**.

In order to put these requirements more precisely, a couple of auxiliary notions will be useful. By a **structure** in the present context I mean a valuation for a possible extensional language. Secondly, if $\mathcal{F} = \langle T, \Gamma \rangle$ is a frame and $\alpha_1, ..., \alpha_n$ are operators in the language of $\mathcal{F}$, say that the pair

$$\langle \mathcal{F}, \langle \alpha_1, ..., \alpha_n \rangle \rangle$$

realizes a structure $\langle D, E_1, ..., E_n \rangle$ if the partial denotation function Δ_Γ associated with Γ correlates the constants of Γ with the domain D; for each i, $1 \leq i \leq n$, E_i is an extension of the sort appropriate for α_i over D, and Δ_Γ maps the extension of α_i in $\mathcal{F}$ isomorphically onto E_i. The Reflection Condition may now be put as follows.

(a) For each nonempty domain D and each sequence $\sigma = \langle \alpha_1, ..., \alpha_n \rangle$ of operators from L, there is a frame $\mathcal{F}$ such that $\mathcal{F}$ is generated by M and $\langle \mathcal{F}, \sigma \rangle$ realizes the structure

$$\langle D, J_{\alpha_1}(D), ..., J_{\alpha_n}(D) \rangle,$$

where for each i, $J_{\alpha_i}(D)$ is the extension of α_i over D.

(b) For each nonempty domain D and each structure $\mathfrak{A}$ over D, there exists a frame $\mathcal{F}$ and a sequence σ of the appropriate type in the language of $\mathcal{F}$ such that $\langle \mathcal{F}, \sigma \rangle$ realizes $\mathfrak{A}$ and $\mathcal{F}$ is generated by M.[22]

4.4.2 Invariance and Determinacy

One immediate consequence of the Reflection Condition is that any operator that behaves invariantly over a reflective modality must satisfy Mostowski's condition: if all actual structures are realizable in a certain modality M, any operator invariant under any isomorphism of the possibilities described in M is *ipso facto* invariant under isomorphisms of such structures. Another slightly less obvious consequence of the Reflection Condition is that a reflective modality uniquely determines the way in which an expression

---

[22]One aspect of the Reflection Condition that deserves comment is that it forces any reflective modality M to be set-theoretically large. It is clear that any modality satisfying the Reflection Condition must comprise a proper class of frames, for the assumption in this case is that every (actual) structure is represented, up to isomorphism, in M. It should also be clear that the frames themselves are not, in general, syntactic structures in the ordinary sense, for the same assumption requires them to incorporate sets of individual constants of arbitrarily large cardinality. It is convenient to identify the lexical primitives in a frame that outrun the devices of Karl's language L with ordinal numbers; the expressions of the language of the frame may then be embedded in a type structure defined over this set of primitives. Thus, for example, if α is an operator defined on a product of types $T_1, ..., T_n$ and $\sigma_1, ..., \sigma_n$ are members of these types, the expression $\alpha(\sigma_1, ..., \sigma_n)$ may be identified with the pair $\langle \alpha, \langle \sigma_1, ..., \sigma_n \rangle \rangle$.

invariant over that modality affects the extensions of the expressions on which it operates. The example of a quantifier symbol Q that applies to a one-variable condition $A(x)$ and the variable x to return a sentence is typical. Suppose we wish to determine the truth-value of the sentence $(Qx)A(x)$, where A has extension E over a domain D. Using (a), find a realization $\langle \mathcal{F}, A \rangle$ of the structure $\langle D, E \rangle$ in $\mathbf{M}$. $\mathcal{F}$ is thus a frame of $\mathbf{M}$, and the partial denotation function associated with $\mathcal{F}$ maps the extension of A in $\mathcal{F}$ isomorphically onto $\langle D, E \rangle$, and so maps the extension of $A(x)$ in $\mathcal{F}$ isomorphically onto the extension of $A(x)$ over D. We shall then count the sentence $(Qx)A(x)$ as true in D if it holds in $\mathcal{F}$. It is immediate from the invariance condition that this procedure yields the *same* truth-value for this sentence no matter which realization of $\langle D, E \rangle$ in $\mathbf{M}$ is considered. An analogous procedure is available for any operator that is rigidly invariant over $\mathbf{M}$. On the suggested demarcation of the logical constants, then, if a modality describing Karl's alternatives satisfies the Reflection Condition, the semantic interpretation of the logical expressions of Karl's language is fixed by the structure of that modality.

At this point, it might be objected that, although the foregoing procedure yields a *determinate* interpretation for each logical operator of L, we have been given no reason as yet to suppose that this procedure is not *arbitrary*. Thus, for example, why would it not have been equally appropriate to assign the truth-value to the sentence $(Qx)A(x)$ *opposite* to the one determined for it above? But the indicated procedure is not arbitrary. If $\mathbf{M}$ is reflective, no truth-value for $(Qx)A(x)$ *other than* the value determined above can be coherently assigned to it by the semantics for L being considered if in fact A has extension E over D. Suppose, for example, that in this case $(Qx)A(x)$ holds in the frame $\mathcal{F}$ as above, but that this sentence is false in L over D. Using (a), find a realization $\langle \mathcal{F}^{\#}, \langle Q, A \rangle \rangle$ of the structure $\langle D, J_Q(D), E \rangle$ in $\mathbf{M}$. Then since $(Qx)A(x)$ is false in L over D, this sentence must fail in $\mathcal{F}^{\#}$. However, since the denotation function associated with $\mathcal{F}^{\#}$ maps the extension of A in $\mathcal{F}^{\#}$ isomorphically onto $\langle D, E \rangle$, the extension of $A(x)$ in $\mathcal{F}^{\#}$ is isomorphic to that of $A(x)$ in the frame $\mathcal{F}$ above, whence, since Q is rigidly invariant over $\mathbf{M}$, the sentence $(Qx)A(x)$ holds in $\mathcal{F}$ if and only if it holds in $\mathcal{F}^{\#}$. It must therefore hold in $\mathcal{F}^{\#}$, a contradiction.

As applied to a modality $\mathbf{M}$ that purports to describe Karl's epistemic alternatives, the Reflection Condition may be thought of as an additional internal or structural constraint on a complete interpretation of Karl, and part (a) specifically as a condition of the coherence of the semantic description the interpretation gives of Karl's language with its demarcation of Karl's alternatives. Part (a) may be paraphrased by saying that the actual extensions of expressions of L must be realized in some alternative, so that the complete description of the world in L that is true according to the given interpretation must be among those that are *possible for Karl* according to that interpretation. The application of this constraint demands no prior semantic conception of Karl's language and attitudes: but it does prompt us to discard from the start those complete interpretations of Karl whose semantic description of L does not cohere in the indicated way with its description of what is possible for Karl. This means that the present account of the logical constants is not going to be able to handle one sort of pathological case. Suppose Karl's inductive method licenses the inference of a false sentence, say $(\exists x)Gx$, in *every* situation. There is then no frame describing an epistemically possible world for Karl in which this sentence is false. Consequently there is no frame $\mathcal{F}$ generated by the modality describing Karl's alternatives such that the pair $\langle \mathcal{F}, \langle G \rangle \rangle$ realizes the extension of G in the actual situation; and this contradicts part (a) of the Reflection Condition.

I do not wish to say that there *could not be* an agent whose attitudes and inductive method are properly described in this way. It is only that the interpretation problem for the agent's logic will have to be solved in something other than the present terms. But it seems worth observing that the inductive practices of such a being would have to be very unlike our own. In the imagined case, there is a false sentence that no possible life-history of evidence would prompt the agent to reject. The possible variations in life-history include deviations in the background of desires and values actually ascribed to the agent.[23] It may be that there are, for example, religious beliefs of the form $(\exists x)Gx$ the agent is so highly motivated to accept that no *further* accretion of evidence would dislodge them. In such a case, we need only consider counterfactual situations in which the agent has a different religious biography, perhaps a different upbringing, than the one he actually has. Obviously the attempt to produce an *example* of a sentence of the problematic sort in *our* language—a sentence which is false but to which we would assent in all epistemic circumstances—is necessarily self-defeating. Euclidean geometry, viewed as a theory about physical space, is perhaps a near case, but founders precisely because we have actually acquired evidence that undermines it.

I am uncertain how serious a limitation this sort of case represents for the present approach. They seem sufficiently far removed from any we are likely to encounter that I think we are justified in proceeding without producing a systematic response to them. However, such cases do underscore

---

[23] See sec. 1 of the postscript to chapter 2 for some observations about the sensitivity of belief-ascriptions to the desires and goals of the subject of interpretation.

a point that will appear elsewhere as well, that on the present account the semantic foundations of logic turn to a considerable extent on the fine-structure of the inductive method ascribed to the subject of interpretation.

4.4.3 Invariance and Completeness

The Reflection Condition is instrumental in fulfilling the main constraint I have placed on a model-theoretic characterization of the concept of logical consequence, namely that it lead to an explanation of why model-theoretic implications are instances of entailment. The connection is an easy consequence of the following result:

(C) Suppose that **M** is a reflective modality for L, let $\langle T, \Gamma \rangle$ belong to **M**, and let $\mathcal{L}$ be a logic for L. If each operator of $\mathcal{L}$ is invariant over **M**, then T is true in a valuation $\mathfrak{A}$ such that $\mathfrak{A}(\alpha) = J_\alpha(|\mathfrak{A}|)$ holds for each operator $\alpha \in \mathcal{L}$.[24]

How does this result yield the required connection between logical consequence and entailment? Consider in less technical terms what (C) asserts. If **M** is a reflective modality, (C) says something about what happens in case the expressions counted as logical in L behave invariantly over the entire collection of possibilities represented in **M**. The result in this case is that every description realized in **M** is in fact satisfied by a valuation that assigns to each logical term its intended interpretation over the domain of the valuation. If each operator in a logic $\mathcal{L}$ for L is invariant over **M**, then, a sentence ϕ is an $\mathcal{L}$-consequence of a set Σ only if Σ entails ϕ over **M**. Otherwise, for some T and Γ such that $\langle T, \Gamma \rangle \in \mathbf{M}$, we have $\Sigma \cup \{\neg \phi\} \subseteq T$ where ϕ is an $\mathcal{L}$-consequence of Σ. But in that case, by (C), there is a valuation $\mathfrak{A}$ for L in which Σ is true and ϕ is false, and which assigns to each expression of $\mathcal{L}$ its actual interpretation over $|\mathfrak{A}|$. But this contradicts the claim that ϕ is an $\mathcal{L}$-consequence of Σ. Thus ϕ is a logical consequence of Σ only if Σ entails ϕ in **M**.

To review: given a collection of frames representing Karl's epistemic alternatives, I described an entailment relation for Karl's language L: a set Σ entails a sentence ϕ in L if ϕ holds at any alternative realizing each member of Σ. I then characterized the logical constants of L as those expressions that satisfy a modal analogue of Mostowski's invariance condition defined with reference to the entire collection of Karl's alternatives. I showed in the last subsection that characterizing the logical constants in this way renders their semantic interpretation determinate relative to a complete specification of Karl's alternatives; and in this subsection we have seen why on that

---

[24]See my "Modality, Invariance, and Logical Truth," and postscript B to this chapter.

characterization the model-theoretic consequence relation for L is a species of the entailment relation for L. It remains to be seen how the relevant specification of Karl's alternatives is fixed by his inductive method. I take up this problem in the following section.

4.5   Characterizing Alternatives 1

In chapter 2 I described Karl's inductive method in terms of a function Φ that maps each of his possible epistemic situations onto a set of interpreted formal objects, the semantic representations of the sentences he holds true in that evidential situation. I shall first characterize an entailment relation in terms of the function Φ; Karl's epistemic alternatives will then be described by frames which are closed under this relation. Under quite natural conditions, this relation coincides with the entailment relation characterized earlier in terms of those alternatives.

Preliminarily, define a relation '$\Vdash_\Phi$', read 'Φ-forces' (or, when confusion is unlikely, simply 'forces') between sets of sentences of L by

[i] $\Gamma \Vdash_\Phi \Delta \ =: \ (\forall e)(\Gamma \subseteq \Phi(e) \rightarrow \Delta \subseteq \Phi(e)) \ \& \ (\exists e)\Gamma \subseteq \Phi(e).$

If ϕ is a sentence, we write $\Gamma \Vdash_\Phi \phi$ to mean that $\Gamma \Vdash_\Phi \{\phi\}$. $\Vdash_\Phi$ constitutes a strong entailment relation with respect to Karl's inductive method: to say that Γ forces Δ is to say that if Karl's inductive method generates each sentence of Γ at a given input e, it must also generate each sentence of Δ at e; and that Γ is in fact thus generated at some input.[25] However, there may be entailments that flow from Karl's inductive method that are not captured by the forcing-relation. To see this, first notice that Karl's inductive method may validate certain *infinitary* patterns of inference. Thus, for example,

---

[25]What is the role of the requirement that Γ is generated at some input, that is, that $\Gamma \subseteq \Phi(e)$ for some e? Suppose that the sentences of Γ are not simultaneously generated at any input. In that case, then, if we were simply to say that $\Gamma \Vdash_\Phi \Delta$ holds just in case

$$(\forall e)(\Gamma \subseteq \Phi(e) \rightarrow \Delta \subseteq \Phi(e)),$$

we would have that $\Gamma \Vdash_\Phi \Delta$ for every Δ, and thus that Γ is inconsistent with respect to $\Vdash_\Phi$. But Γ may nonetheless be fully coherent with respect to Karl's inductive method if, for example, Γ is simply too large or too complicated to be generated at any input. The indicated constraint restricts $\Vdash_\Phi$ to those sets which are *inductively realizable*, that is, to those sets that can be embedded in some state of information that arises by applying Karl's inductive method to some possible life-history of evidence. The idea is that an instance $\Gamma \Vdash \Delta$ of the forcing-relation should reflect a fundamental pattern of inference in Karl's inductive method: such a pattern must be instantiated in Karl's inductive practice, and for this it is required that Γ is sometimes generated by Karl's inductive method.

consider the ω-rule

$$\frac{A(0), A(1), \dots}{(\forall n) A(n)},$$

where '$(\forall n)$' represents the universal quantifier over the natural numbers. This rule is sound with respect to Karl's inductive method if Karl holds the universal statement $(\forall n) A(n)$ true when he bears the belief-relation to the set $\Gamma = \{A(0), A(1), \dots\}$ (an attitude that is manifested, for example, in his disposition to assent to each of the sentences $A(k)$). However, Γ need not in this case *force* $(\forall n) A(n)$. To say that Γ forces $(\forall n) A(n)$ is to say that if Karl's inductive method generates every sentence $A(k)$ in a given state of information, it must generate the sentence $(\forall n) A(n)$ therein.[26] But it need not do this if it fails to generate each sentence $A(k)$ *simultaneously*. Recall that the belief-describing function Φ is defined for any input e by setting $\Phi(e)$ equal to the limit of the sets $\Phi^{(n)}(e)$, where for any n, $\Phi^{(n)}(e)$ inscribes the propositions Karl projects to be true after n stages in the inductive evaluation of the evidence-base e. The set $\Phi(e)$ thus consists of those sentences that appear in $\Phi^{(n)}(e)$ for each sufficiently large n, that is, of those sentences which are stable at some stage; and $\Gamma \Vdash_\Phi \Delta$ holds when, for any input, if each sentence of Γ achieves stability, then so does each sentence of Δ. The difficulty in accommodating the ω-rule by the forcing-relation arises from the fact that

(α) At input e, there exists a stage n such that for each k, the sentence $A(k)$ is stable at stage n.

does not follow from the assertion

(β) At input e, for each k, there exists an n such that the sentence $A(k)$ is stable at stage n.

Claim (β) is the assertion that $A(k)$ belongs to $\Phi(e)$ for each k; but it is claim (α) that is required for the applicability of the ω-rule: for the ω-rule to be applied at a stage, Karl must have inferred *each* sentence $A(k)$ at that stage. The ω-rule, then, is not sound with respect to the forcing-relation.

The natural remedy for this descrepancy is to allow *sets* of sentences to appear in the sets $\Phi(e)$ describing Karl's epistemic states. The correctness of the ω-rule will then consist in the fact that the set $\{(\forall n) A(n)\}$ belongs to each $\Phi(e)$ of which the set $\{A(0), A(1), \dots\}$ is a member. For any input e, we thus (re)define $\Phi(e)$ to be the collection of all *sets* X of sentences such that X belongs to $\Phi^{(n)}(e)$ for each sufficiently large integer n; the sentences Karl holds true at e are then just the sentences belonging to some set in

---

[26]In what follows I use 'k' to range over numerals in Karl's language, that is, a natural set of natural number-specifying terms.

$\Phi(e)$, that is, the members of $\cup\Phi(e)$.[27] The forcing-relation may then be reconstrued correspondingly by replacing '$\subseteq$' with '$\in$' in [i]; that is, $\Gamma \Vdash_\Phi \Delta$ will mean that the set Δ belongs to any state of information $\Phi(e)$ generated by Karl's inductive method to which Γ belongs, and Γ is realized in some such state.

I shall now define a natural entailment relation corresponding to Karl's inductive method. A collection K of sentences will be said to be Φ-**closed** if for each Γ, Δ, if $\Gamma \subseteq K$ and $\Gamma \Vdash_\Phi \Delta$, then $\Delta \subseteq K$. It may be shown that, for any set K, there exists a *smallest* Φ-closed set including K, that is, a unique Φ-closed set including K and included in each Φ-closed set including K.[28] The sentences of L which are consequences of K within Karl's inductive method are precisely the members of this minimal Φ-closed set. We write '$K \vdash_\Phi \chi$' to indicate that χ stands in the present consequence relation to the set K.[29]

---

[27] Allowing infinite sets of sentences in the belief-sets $\Phi(e)$ is tantamount to equipping Karl's inductive logic with a limited form of infinitary truth-functional inference: the occurrence of the set $\{\phi_0, \phi_1, ...\}$ in $\Phi(e)$ reflects an ascription of belief in the conjunction

$$\phi_0 \ \& \ \phi_1 \ \& \ ...$$

to Karl. Such an infinitary expression is not, of course, available in Karl's language L. But an infinitary conjunction may be finitely representable, for example, in terms of an effective schema describing the set $\{\phi_0, \phi_1, ...\}$. Codes for such representations, not the sets themselves, would be the literal arguments and values for the rule of revision determining the function Φ.

[28] For later purposes, it will be convenient to have at hand a sketch of the proof. Define by transfinite induction sets Σ_α for each ordinal number α. $\Sigma_0 = K$. If α is a successor ordinal, say $\alpha = \beta + 1$, set

$$\Sigma_\alpha = \Sigma_\beta \cup \{\phi| \ (\exists X \subseteq \Sigma_\beta)(\exists Y)(\phi \in Y \ \& \ X \Vdash_\Phi Y)\}.$$

If, on the other hand, α is a limit ordinal, set $\Sigma_\alpha = \cup_{\lambda < \alpha} \Sigma_\lambda$. Clearly, the sequence $\{\Sigma_\alpha\}$ is increasing, that is, we have $(\forall\alpha)(\forall\beta)(\alpha < \beta \rightarrow \Sigma_\alpha \subseteq \Sigma_\beta)$. Since the collection of sentences $L(K)$ is of bounded cardinality, the sequence $\{\Sigma_\alpha\}$ must reach a fixed point; that is, for some α we have $\Sigma_{\alpha+1} = \Sigma_\alpha$. Let γ be the least ordinal with this property. Σ_γ is clearly Φ-closed. Moreover, $\Sigma_\gamma \subseteq X$ for each Φ-closed set X including K, so that Σ_γ is the smallest Φ-closed set including K.

[29] The relation $\vdash_\Phi$ has been defined explicitly only for Karl's language L. But we will want to apply it also to the language of alternatives for Karl that enrich L by expressions of an uninterpreted or partially interpreted character. From the standpoint of Karl's inductive method, the additional lexical items should not generate any additional entailment relations; they should behave essentially like schemata with respect to $\vdash_\Phi$. Thus if χ and K are respectively a sentence and a set of sentences in some extension of L, we put $K \vdash_\Phi \chi$ if $K^+ \vdash \chi^+$ holds for each set K^+ and sentence χ^+ that arise from K and χ by uniform substitution of expressions of the appropriate type in L for operators that do not appear in L. Observe that part (b) of the Reflection Condition is

The entailment relation $\vdash_\Phi$ generated by Karl's inductive method gives rise in the usual way to an associated notion of consistency: a set K of formulas in L is consistent in the relevant sense if for no formula ϕ do we have $K \vdash_\Phi \phi$ and $K \vdash_\Phi \neg\phi$. Karl's epistemic alternatives are to be thought of as configurations of the world that possess complete descriptions which are consistent with respect to his inductive method. My suggestion, then, is that Karl's alternatives be identified with those frames $\langle T, \Gamma \rangle$ such that T is closed under $\vdash_\Phi$, where T is a set of sentences in an extension of L arising from L by the addition of partially interpreted operators.

This demarcation of Karl's alternatives thus defines the entailment relation relevant to the completeness property described earlier: K entails ϕ if ϕ appears in each alternative including K. However, at this point we are faced with an embarrassing duplication of entailment relations for L; we should expect the present entailment relation, characterized in terms of Karl's alternatives, to coincide with the notion of entailment $\vdash_\Phi$ characterized directly in terms of Karl's inductive method. One half of the desired equivalence is immediate. Suppose that $\Sigma \vdash_\Phi \chi$ and $\langle T, \Gamma \rangle$ is an alternative realizing each member of Σ. Then $\Sigma \subseteq T$, and since T is closed under $\vdash_\Phi$, we have $\chi \in T$, which is to say that χ holds in $\langle T, \Gamma \rangle$. The other half of the equivalence requires an assumption of a rather special but, I shall argue, natural character. It is the supposition that every set of sentences in L that is consistent with respect to Karl's inductive method can be extended to an alternative for Karl.[30] I shall call the property expressed in this assertion the **Lindenbaum Condition**, for it is an analogue with respect to the notion of consistency generated by Karl's inductive method of the Lindenbaum property for first-order logic.[31] The Lindenbaum Condition immediately yields the other half of the desired equivalence. For, suppose that χ is a sentence and K a set of sentences in L such that not $K \vdash_\Phi \chi$. Then $K \cup \{\neg\phi\}$ is consistent with respect to $\vdash_\Phi$. By the Lindenbaum Condition, then, there is an alternative $\langle T, \Gamma \rangle$ for Karl such that $K \cup \{\neg\phi\} \subseteq T$. Thus ϕ fails in some alternative for Karl in which K holds.

What reason is there to suppose, or require, that the notion of consistency generated by Karl's inductive method should satisfy the Lindenbaum

---

then satisfied, since we may add to L operators of the appropriate sort designating the components of any chosen structure. Part (a) of the Reflection Condition is equivalent to the assumption that total descriptions which are true in L over a given actual domain are consistent with respect to the entailment relation generated by Karl's inductive method. For an airing of misgivings about this assumption, see the remarks at the conclusion of 4.4.2.

[30]To be precise, to a set T such that $\langle T, \Gamma \rangle$ is such an alternative for some collection Γ of constants in the language of T.

[31]That any consistent first-order theory has a consistent and complete extension.

Condition? As applied to Karl's language L, the Lindenbaum Condition requires that any story Σ in L that is epistemically possible for Karl be extendible to a complete description of the world that is epistemically possible for Karl. If Karl is an ideal hyper-rational cognizer, this condition will plausibly obtain. For the disjunction of all epistemically possible (that is, $\vdash_\Phi$-consistent) complete descriptions should in this case be a priori for Karl. If Σ cannot be embedded in any such description, then, Karl can infer a priori that Σ is false, whence Σ is not epistemically possible for Karl.

A less fanciful rationale for the Lindenbaum condition is suggested by a technical result based on the hypothesis that the notion of consistency generated by Karl's inductive method can be coherently combined with a certain infinitary logic. Suppose that any set of sentences in L that is consistent with respect to the entailment relation generated by Karl's inductive method remains so when it is closed under the consequence relation generated by the relevant infinitary logic. The result says in this case that any set that is consistent in the sense of that method can be extended to a frame that is closed under the corresponding entailment relation. A precise statement and proof of this result can be found in postscript B to this chapter. Thus the general requirement for the applicability of the Lindenbaum Condition is not that Karl's cognitive procedures actually *embody* an idealized infinitary analogue of the usual quantificational inferences, but only that they *admit* such an idealization.

To review: I have suggested a construction of the worlds, or of a set of representations thereof, which are epistemically possible for Karl. These are Karl's alternatives. Very roughly, I have said that a set of sentences in an extension of L specifies an alternative if it meets certain completeness and consistency conditions. The crux of the matter was to characterize notions of entailment and consistency generated by Karl's inductive method. This done, I defined an alternative as a frame $\langle T, K \rangle$ for L such that T is closed under the relevant entailment relation. Assuming the Lindenbaum Condition, I was then able to identify the possible worlds entailment relation for L characterized with reference to Karl's alternatives with the entailment relation generated by Karl's inductive method. Finally, I observed that the Lindenbaum Condition is met if any set of sentences in L that is consistent with respect to that entailment relation remains so under the introduction of certain infinitary inferences. On these conditions, then, specializing the considerations of 4.4.3 to the present context gives the result that the relation of logical consequence for Karl's language is a special case of the consequence relation generated by Karl's inductive method.

4.6   The Bounds of Logic 1

I have suggested that a logical constant of Karl's language L is an expression that behaves invariantly over the entire collection of Karl's alternatives, the collection of worlds which are epistemically possible for Karl. I will briefly consider some classes of expressions that count as logical by this criterion. Obviously the answer to the question of which expressions are logical turns on the strength of the relevant concept of epistemic possibility and thus, to some extent, on the fine structure of Karl's inductive method. Nevertheless, some general observations can be made.

4.6.1   Elementary Logic

Since Karl's alternatives are complete, consistent, and closed under first-order deducibility, the elementary connectives and quantifiers of L are logical constants. For example, let $\vee$ be the connective of L interpreted as disjunction.[32] Then for any sentences A and B and any alternative $\mathcal{F}$, $A \vee B$ holds at $\mathcal{F}$ if A holds at $\mathcal{F}$ or B holds at $\mathcal{F}$. Consider any function ϕ mapping the extensions of A and B at $\mathcal{F}$ isomorphically onto the extensions of a pair of formulas $A^{\#}$ and $B^{\#}$ in an alternative $\mathcal{F}^{\#}$. Then an instance of A or B holds at $\mathcal{F}$ if the corresponding instance of $A^{\#}$ or of $B^{\#}$ holds at $\mathcal{F}^{\#}$, whence the relevant instance of $A \vee B$ holds at $\mathcal{F}$ iff the corresponding instance of $A^{\#} \vee B^{\#}$ holds at $\mathcal{F}^{\#}$. Thus ϕ maps the extension of $A \vee B$ at $\mathcal{F}$ isomorphically onto the extension of $A^{\#} \vee B^{\#}$ at $\mathcal{F}^{\#}$, as required by the invariance condition. Similar arguments apply to the other connectives.

Next consider the quantifiers. Let $\exists$ be the device of L interpreted as existential quantification. For each one-variable condition $A(x)$ of L and each alternative $\mathcal{F} = \langle T, \Gamma \rangle$, we saw in 4.3.2. that $(\exists x)A(x)$ holds at $\mathcal{F}$ if $A(c/x)$ obtains therein for some constant $c \in \Gamma$. Let ϕ be a function mapping the extension of $A(x)$ at $\mathcal{F}$ isomorphically onto the extension of a formula $A^{\#}(x)$ at an alternative $\mathcal{F}^{\#} = \langle T^{\#}, \Gamma^{\#} \rangle$. If $(\exists x)A(x)$ holds at $\mathcal{F}$, then, ϕ must map some individual constant c in Γ onto a constant $c^{\#}$ in $\mathcal{F}^{\#}$ such that the sentence $A^{\#}(c^{\#})$ holds at $\mathcal{F}^{\#}$, and thus the sentence $(\exists x)A^{\#}(x)$ obtains at $\mathcal{F}^{\#}$. Similarly $(\exists x)A^{\#}(x)$ holds at $\mathcal{F}^{\#}$ only if $(\exists x)A(x)$ holds at $\mathcal{F}$. A symmetric argument applies to the universal quantifier.

4.6.2   Generalized Quantifiers

The operators of elementary logic, then, are logical on the suggested characterization of the logical constants. That much seems mandatory. Pressing

---

[32] In the sense of 4.3.2; see n. 17.

further, I now wish to ask which operators in various extensions of classical logic count as logical constants on the suggested criterion. In particular, which generalized quantifiers are logical constants? The literature of generalized model theory has emphasized the cardinality quantifiers, usually denoted Q_α, meaning "for at least $\aleph_\alpha$" for a fixed ordinal α. In capsule, I will show that Q_α is not a logical constant for any $\alpha > 0$, but that Q_0 may be. Thus 'for infinitely many' counts as logical (under some circumstances); 'for uncountably many' does not.

Consider first Q_0. For any positive integer k, let N_k be the (complex) elementary quantifier of L expressing "there are at least k". Again letting '$\vdash_\Phi$' signify entailment within Karl's inductive method, suppose that the following patterns of inference hold:

$(Q_0 I)$ $\qquad\qquad \{(N_1 x)A(x), (N_2 x)A(x), ...\} \vdash_\Phi (Q_0 x)A(x)$

$(Q_0 E)$ $\qquad\qquad (Q_0 x)A(x) \vdash_\Phi (N_k x)A(x) \ (k = 1, 2, ...).$

That is to say, the totality of sentences of the form "there are at least k As" entails that there are infinitely many; and "there are infinitely many As" entails "there are at least k As" for each k. Then the quantifier Q_0, "for infinitely many," is a logical constant of L. For example, consider a fixed alternative $\mathcal{F} = \langle T, \Gamma \rangle$ and a formula $A(x)$ in the language of $\mathcal{F}$, and suppose there is a function mapping the extension of $A(x)$ at $\mathcal{F}$ isomorphically onto that of a predicate $A^\#(x)$ at an alternative $\mathcal{F}^\# = \langle T^\#, \Gamma^\# \rangle$. Since, for each k, N_k is invariant over Karl's alternatives, for each k the same function must map the extension of the formula

(1) $\qquad\qquad\qquad\qquad (N_k x)A(x)$

at $\mathcal{F}$ isomorphically onto that of the formula

(2) $\qquad\qquad\qquad\qquad (N_k x)A^\#(x)$

at $\mathcal{F}^\#$. By the conditions $(Q_0 I)$ and $(Q_0 E)$, an instance of the formula

(3) $\qquad\qquad\qquad\qquad (Q_0 x)A(x)$

holds at $\mathcal{F}$ if and only if the corresponding instance of any formula of form (1) is true therein. Similarly, an instance of

(4) $(Q_0 x) A^{\#}(x)$

holds at $\mathcal{F}^{\#}$ if and only if the corresponding instance of any formula of form
(2) obtains therein. Thus an instance of (3) holds at $\mathcal{F}$ if and only if the
corresponding instance of (4) holds at $\mathcal{F}^{\#}$, as required for the invariance of
Q_0.

If Karl's inductive method sanctions the inferences $(Q_0 \text{I})$ and $(Q_0 \text{E})$,
then, Q_0 is counted as a logical constant by the suggested criterion. But
Q_1, "there are uncountably many," is not. In fact, for no $\alpha > 0$ is Q_α
counted as logical if the entailment relation $\vdash_\Phi$ preserves truth in L. The
argument showing this for Q_1 relies on a weak compactness property for
$\vdash_\Phi$:

($C\omega_1$) Let ϕ be a sentence and Σ a set of sentences in the language of some
  alternative. Then $\Sigma \vdash_\Phi \phi$ only if there is a countable subset Σ_0 of
  Σ such that $\Sigma_0 \vdash_\Phi \phi$.[33]

It is not difficult to see how ($C\omega_1$) leads to the noninvariance result for
Q_1. Suppose, for a contradiction, that $\vdash_\Phi$ preserves truth in L, and that Q_1
satisfies the invariance condition over the entire collection of Karl's alternatives. Let Γ be an uncountable collection of constants outside L included in
the language of some alternative. (Observe that such an alternative exists
by the Reflection Condition.) If Q_1 were a logical constant, then, for each
predicate $A(x)$, the sentence

(5) $(Q_1 x) A(x)$

would be a logical consequence of the set

$$\Sigma = \{A(c)| \ c \in \Gamma\} \cup \{\neg a = b| \ a, b \text{ distinct constants in } \Gamma\}.$$

Therefore, by the completeness property,

$$\Sigma \vdash_\Phi (Q_1 x) A(x),$$

---

[33] Here is a brief argument for ($C\omega_1$). Let $\{\Sigma_\alpha\}$ be the sequence of sets defined in
n. 28, and suppose that $\Sigma \vdash_\Phi \phi$ for some Σ and ϕ. Then we have $\Sigma \vdash_\Phi \phi$ if $\phi \in \Sigma_\alpha$
for some α. By the **rank** $\text{rk}_\Sigma(\phi)$ of ϕ over Σ we understand the least ordinal α such
that $\phi \in \Sigma_\alpha$. We show that Σ and ϕ satisfy the countable compactness condition by
induction on the rank of ϕ over Σ. If $\text{rk}_\Sigma(\phi) = 0$, $\phi \in \Sigma$ and the condition is trivially
satisfied. Assume, then, for a fixed α, that if $\text{rk}_\Sigma(\phi) = \beta$ for some $\beta < \alpha$, then $\Sigma_0 \vdash_\Phi \phi$
for some countable subset $\Sigma_0 \subset \Sigma$, and consider a sentence χ such that $\Sigma \vdash_\Phi \chi$ and
$\text{rk}_\Sigma(\chi) = \alpha$. Then for some sets X, Y we have $X \Vdash_\Phi Y$, $\chi \in Y$, $\text{rk}_\Sigma(\phi) < \alpha$ for each
$\phi \in X$. Clearly, X is countable (since X is included in some state of information for Karl,
or is derived by substitution from such a set.) Put $X = \{\phi_n| \ n \in \omega\}$. For each n, by the
induction hypothesis there is a countable subset Σ_n of Σ such that $\Sigma_n \vdash_\Phi \phi_n$. Hence
setting $\Sigma^* = \cup_n \Sigma_n$, Σ^* is countable and $\Sigma^* \vdash_\Phi \phi$, as required.

whence by $(C\omega_1)$, there is a countable subset Σ_0 of Σ such that

(6) $$\Sigma_0 \vdash_\Phi (Q_1 x)A(x).$$

Then we may put

$$\Sigma_0 = \{A(c_n)|\ n \in \omega\} \cup \{\neg c_n = c_m|\ n \neq m;\ n, m \in \omega\},$$

where $c_n \in \Gamma$ for each n. Since the constants of Γ do not occur in L, they behave like schemata with respect to the deducibility relation $\vdash_\Phi$ (see note 29). Thus, for each countable set $\{c_n\}$ of constants and each predicate $A(x)$ of L, the relation (6) must obtain. However, this contradicts the assumption that $\vdash_\Phi$ preserves truth in L: for example, for each n take c_n to designate n, and let $A(x)$ represent the predicate "x is a natural number". Then each sentence in the set Σ_0 is true in L but the sentence (5) is false. Similar considerations show that Q_α is noninvariant for any $\alpha > 0$.

4.6.3   How Many Alternatives?

It makes all the difference to the demarcation of the logical constants of Karl's language *which* frames are taken to describe possibilities for Karl. The wider the range of possibilities, the more stringent the corresponding invariance requirement; the stronger the invariance requirement, the narrower the logic. Suppose, for example, that Karl's alternatives are required to tell *metaphysically possible* stories. Then some of the frames that presently describe alternatives for Karl will no longer do so. Consider, for example, a frame that incorporates, for an uncountable set Γ of individual constants, each statement $\neg a = b$ for a, b distinct constants in Γ, assertions that the denotations of each of these fall under a predicate $A(x)$, and the assertion that there are only countably many As. The foregoing considerations show that this description is consistent with respect to the entailment relation generated by Karl's inductive method, but there is no counterfactual situation in which it is realized: the indicated frame does not describe a *metaphysically possible* world. If only properly possible frames were considered, the invariance requirement defining the logical constants of Karl's language would be weakened. If the cardinality quantifiers are understood rigidly—that is, if, for any α, $(Q_\alpha x)A(x)$ is understood to hold in any *possible* situation if and only if there are at least $\aleph_\alpha$ objects falling under $A(x)$ therein—then all such quantifiers would count as logical constants. The general point is that the bounds of logic vary inversely with the limits of the notion of possibility used to characterize the logical constants.

My claim is that the 'pathological' frame just described, including the assertion that there are at most countably many As and uncountably many denials of identity between objects asserted to fall under A, describes a 'world' that, though not metaphysically possible, is among those that are *possible for Karl*, and it is with reference to these that the invariance requirement for Karl's logic is to be specified. The root idea is that a frame should describe an epistemically possible situation for Karl if its claim to do so cannot be *defeated* by Karl's inductive method. Such a defeat would be at hand if there were a set of sentences holding in the frame that stands in the entailment relation generated by Karl's inductive method to the negation of some such sentence. This could not, however, be the case if the sentences in question are derived from the frame, precisely because of the consistency and closure properties of the frame.[34]

It might, however, be objected that this conclusion requires the assumption that the information in question be *internal* to the frame. Consider the following assertion, where α is the situation described above:

(P) There is an uncountable set Γ of individual constants such that for each $a, b \in \Gamma$, a distinct from b, the sentence $a = b$ is false in α, and for each $a \in \Gamma$, the sentence $A(a)$ is true in α.

Assertion (P) describes α correctly but *externally*, in terms of sentences in the language of the frame that hold in α; and (P) entails that there are uncountably many objects of which the predicate $A(x)$ is true at α. Since it is also true at α that there are at most countably many As, α would seem to realize inconsistent descriptions.

The difficulty with this argument is that unless α is assumed to be a metaphysically possible situation, the claim

[i]   It is true in α that there are uncountably many As[35]

does not follow from

[ii]   There are uncountably many things of which $A(x)$ is true in α.

[ii] does follow from (P); but it is [i] that is required to defeat the consistency of α. Indeed, if Q is a nonlogical quantifier, it is generally not the case that

[ii]$_Q$ $(Qa)\{A(x)$ is true of a in $\alpha\}$

entails

[i]$_Q$ $(Qx)A(x)$ is true in α.

---

[34]The distinction between possible worlds and epistemically possible situations originates, as far as I can tell, with Kripke's discussion of the relationship between necessity and a prioricity in *Naming and Necessity* (Cambridge, Mass.: Harvard University Press, 1980).

[35]That is, $(Q_1 x)A(x)$ holds at α.

Suppose, for example, that Qx means "for some red x", that is, that $(Qx)A(x)$ holds in any world w if and only if $A(x)$ is true at w of some thing that is red at w. Consider a world w_0 devoid of the color red but containing at least one object that is red in the actual world. Then setting α equal to w_0 and taking $A(x)$ to be the formula $x = x$, we find that $[ii]_Q$ is true but $[i]_Q$ is false.

The foregoing 'pathological' frame, then, involves a combinatorial anomaly, but is fully coherent with respect to Karl's inductive method. It is true that uncountably many objects exist in the frame, but it is false in the frame that there are uncountably many objects! This would not be too surprising if the 'external' identities of all but countably many of the objects were collapsed in the frame, but this is not so: there are uncountably many constants whose denotations pairwise diverge *according to the frame*. What is accurate to say in this situation is that there are two *pluralities*—the plurality of items falling under $A(x)$ and the plurality of natural numbers—which the frame cannot distinguish in terms of cardinality. Both pluralities are fully embedded in the situation described by the frame, but Karl's cognitive procedures do not size them up accurately in this situation.

4.6.4   Variations and the Second Design

I have been illustrating some consequences of the fact that the conception of possibility within Karl's language with which I have been working is very wide, demanding of a frame that describes a possibility for Karl only that it be closed under the entailment relation determined by his inductive method. But for a number of purposes it is appropriate to consider analogues of the logical constants that arise by requiring possibility-specifying frames to be subject to stronger conditions of closure. I have already mentioned that requiring these frames to be closed under relative metaphysical necessitation—in effect, allowing Karl omniscience concerning matters of metaphysical necessity—leads to a significantly wider class of rigidly invariant expressions, including each of the cardinality quantifiers Q_α. Under this interpretation, the abstract completeness result described in subsection 4.4.3 delivers the conclusion that $\Gamma \models \phi$ only if $\Gamma \cup \{\neg\phi\}$ is not metaphysically possible.

I now want to breifly revisit a question raised at the outset of this chapter. Following Tharp, I distinguished two broad designs for a theory of the nature of logic. The first aims for a relation of logical consequence that is coordinated with a notion of *demonstration* in Karl's language; the second for a set of logical *concepts* that enable characterizations of classes of structures of mathematical interest. The question is what, if anything, these two designs for logic have to do with one another.

One answer to this question emerges from an interpretation of the present framework that arises by allowing Karl access to facts about the mathematical realm. Suppose that, under the given semantic description, Karl's language L contains the language of set theory, which, for present purposes, we suppose to be formulated in the manner of von Neumann and Bernays.[36] The natural or standard interpretations of this language are relational structures of the form $\langle V_{\alpha+1}, E_\alpha \rangle$, where α is a strongly inaccessible cardinal and E_α the relation $\{\langle a, b \rangle \in V_\alpha \times V_{\alpha+1} | \ a \in b\}$.[37] A natural model of *mathematical possibility in L* arises by restricting the collection M of alternatives for Karl to the class M* of frames that describe standard interpretations of set theory; in effect, then, for the present purposes the closure condition on frames generated by Karl's inductive method is strengthened to require closure with respect to inferences correct with respect to all standard models. Observe that M* is in fact a modality. Applying the result of 4.4.3, we see that if the logical notions in L are invariant over M*, then a sentence ϕ is a consequence of a set Σ of sentences in L only if ϕ holds in each *mathematically possible* alternative for Karl that realizes Σ.[38] This suggests that the notions which are invariant over M*, the space of mathematical possibilities for Karl, would be natural candidates for characterizing mathematical structures, and that applying the result of 4.4.3 under the indicated restriction of alternatives may yield a link between the two conceptions of logic described by Tharp. I shall present some evidence relevant to this claim.

To get a sense of which expressions are invariant over M*, I shall introduce a notion of definability for quantifiers. For simplicity, I characterize it with reference to monadic generalized quantifiers Q. Say that Q is **set-theoretically definable in L** if there is a set-theoretic predicate Ω such that for each formula $A(y)$ of L the equivalence

(1) $(Qy)A(y) \leftrightarrow (\exists X)((\forall y)(A(y) \leftrightarrow y \in X) \ \& \ \Omega(X))$

is analytic over M.[39] To see how set-theoretic definability in L can bear on

---

[36]The theory is normally formulated with two styles of variable, lower-case (for sets) and upper-case (for classes), and a membership predicate $\in$; but quantifiers over sets may be regarded as restrictions of quantifiers over classes to the predicate $(\exists y) x \in y$, that is, to those classes which are members of other classes.

[37]The sets V_α are defined by transfinite induction on α by setting V_0 equal to a chosen collection of urelements, $V_\alpha = V_\beta \cup \mathcal{P}(V_\beta)$ if $\alpha = \beta + 1$ for some β, and $V_\alpha = \cup_{\lambda < \alpha} V_\lambda$ if α is a limit ordinal, where $\mathcal{P}(x) = \{y | y \subseteq x\}$. In structures of the indicated sort, the collections in V_α are values of set variables, and those of $V_{\alpha+1} - V_\alpha$ are values of class variables.

[38]It is clear that the modality M* satisfies the Reflection Condition if M does, which is required for the completeness result to apply.

[39]Recall that ϕ is analytic over M if $\neg\phi$ is not realized by any frame in M.

invariance over $\mathbf{M}^*$, consider the quantifier Q_1, "for uncountably many." I showed earlier that this device is not invariant over the full modality $\mathbf{M}$. But under a quite general and natural condition, it is so over $\mathbf{M}^*$. Suppose that for any $A(y)$ the equivalance

(2) $(Q_1y)A(y) \leftrightarrow (\exists X)((\forall y)(y \in X \leftrightarrow A(y))$ & $(\exists z)(z \simeq \omega_1$ & $z \subseteq X))$

is analytic over $\mathbf{M}$, where '$z \simeq \omega_1$' abbreviates the formula in L that says that z is a set of cardinality ω_1, the first uncountable cardinal. (This is roughly to say that Karl can know a priori that there are uncountably many As if and only if there is an uncountable set of things that fall under A.) Then Q_1 is invariant over $\mathbf{M}^*$. For, suppose that $\mathcal{F}$ and $\mathcal{F}^{\#}$ are frames generated by $\mathbf{M}^*$, that f is a function mapping the extension of $A(y)$ in $\mathcal{F}$ isomorphically onto that of a formula $B(y)$ in $\mathcal{F}^{\#}$, and that $(Q_1y)A(y)$ holds in $\mathcal{F}$. We must show that $(Q_1y)B(y)$ holds in $\mathcal{F}^{\#}$. By (2), sentential logic and the $\exists$-instantiation condition for frames, there is a constant $\mathbf{a}$ such that the sentences

$$(\forall y)(y \in \mathbf{a} \leftrightarrow A(y)), \; (\exists z)(z \simeq \omega_1 \; \& \; z \subseteq \mathbf{a})$$

obtain in $\mathcal{F}$, whence similarly there is a constant $\mathbf{b}$ such that the sentences

$$(\forall y)(y \in \mathbf{a} \leftrightarrow A(y)), \; \mathbf{b} \simeq \omega_1 \; \& \; \mathbf{b} \subseteq \mathbf{a}$$

hold in $\mathcal{F}$, so that

(3) $\mathcal{F} \models (\forall y)(y \in \mathbf{b} \rightarrow A(y))$ & $\mathbf{b} \simeq \omega_1$.

By (3) and the standardness assumption for $\mathcal{F}$, then, there are uncountably many constants $\{c_\lambda | \; \lambda < \omega_1\}$ such that $\mathcal{F} \models c_\lambda \in \mathbf{b}$ for each $\lambda < \omega_1$, whence

$$\mathcal{F} \models \{A(c_\lambda) | \; \lambda < \omega_1\} \cup \{\neg c_\gamma = c_\lambda | \; \gamma < \lambda < \omega_1\}.$$

For each λ we set $f(c_\lambda) = c_\lambda^{\#}$. By the hypothesis on f, then, we have

$$\mathcal{F}^{\#} \models \{B(c_\lambda^{\#}) | \; \lambda < \omega_1\} \cup \{\neg c_\gamma^{\#} = c_\lambda^{\#} | \; \gamma < \lambda < \omega_1\}.$$

Working the same line in the opposite direction, using the standardness assumption for $\mathcal{F}^{\#}$, we infer that the sentence

$$(\exists X)((\forall y)(y \in X \leftrightarrow B(y)) \; \& \; (\exists z)(z \simeq \omega_1 \; \& \; z \subseteq X)$$

obtains in $\mathcal{F}^{\#}$; whence by (2), with $B(y)$ for $A(y)$, the sentence $(Q_1y)B(y)$ holds in $\mathcal{F}^{\#}$, as required. Similarly, $(Q_1y)B(y)$ holds in $\mathcal{F}^{\#}$ only if

$(Q_1 y)A(y)$ holds in $\mathcal{F}$, so that Q_1 is in fact invariant over $\mathbf{M}^*$. By examining the foregoing argument, we see that the invariance property over $\mathbf{M}^*$ may be similarly established for any quantifier Q_α such that α is a definable ordinal.

Various generalized quantifiers have a similar status. An interesting example is provided by the branching quantifiers first introduced by Leon Henkin.[40] In the simplest and most typical case, one has a 2×2 branching structure

$$(H) \qquad\qquad \begin{pmatrix} \forall x & \exists \alpha \\ \forall y & \exists \beta \end{pmatrix} \phi.$$

Informally, (H) is read as saying that for each x, y there are α and β, where the choice of α depends only on x and the choice of β only on y, such that $\phi(x, \alpha, y, \beta)$; (H) may thus be interpreted by means of the Skolem form

$$(\exists f)(\exists g)(\forall x)(\forall y)\phi(x, f(x), y, g(y)).$$

The indicated Skolem form, of course, can easily be expressed in the von Neumann-Bernays notation; and if the equivalence of any branching sentence and its Skolem form is analytic with respect to $\mathbf{M}$, then via that very form the Henkin quantifier is set-theoretically definable in L. An argument rather similar to that just given for Q_1 will then show that the Henkin quantifier is invariant over the class $\mathbf{M}^*$ of mathematical possibilites. That is noteworthy, for it is known that branching or partially ordered quantification very greatly extends the expressive capacity of elementary logic. For example, Ehrenfeucht observed that the quantifier Q_0 is definable in terms of the Henkin quantifier. More generally, it is known that extensions of first-order logic by branching quantifiers enable categorical axiomatizations of many of the classical mathematical structures.[41]

To take stock: I have suggested that the modality $\mathbf{M}^*$ is a natural model of the states of affairs which are mathematically possible for Karl. These are roughly the world-stories which are epistemically possible for Karl

---

[40] See Leon Henkin, "Some Remarks on Infinitely Long Formulas," in *Infinitistic Methods* (Warsaw: Pergamon Press and Państwowe Wydawnictwo Navkowe, 1961), pp. 167–83.

[41] A basic result, from Walkoe, "Finite Partially Ordered Quantification," *Journal of Symbolic Logic* 35 (1970): 535-55, is that any Π_1^1 sentence is definable in terms of first-order forms allowing branching. Thus, for example, the second-order completeness axiom for the real numbers may be rendered in this form, as may the second-order replacement axiom for set theory. And this is enough to show that the standard model of analysis and the class of standard models of set theory can be completely described in terms of first-order notions plus branching quantifiers.

and closed under inferences correct for standard models of set theory. The expressions invariant over $\mathbf{M}^*$ constitute a powerful and flexible instrument for characterizing mathematical structures. Broadening the class of logical expressions of L by putting $\mathbf{M}^*$ in the role of $\mathbf{M}$ fits the second design for logic described by Tharp, which concerned precisely the model-theoretic capacity of a logic to describe structure. But it is also compatible with a form of Etchemendy's necessitation requirement and with a generalization of the first design.

Etchemendy argued that Tarski has not shown that the model-theoretic entailment relation is *necessarily truth-preserving*. Operating with the conception of necessity dual to the notion of epistemic possibility in Karl's language, by means of the result of 4.4.3 I was able to satisfy Etchemendy's requirement by identifying logical expressions with those which are invariant over the entire class of Karl's alternatives. The result is that model theoretic implication is a species of relative epistemic necessity, equivalent to an idealized sort of demonstrability in L. But for certain purposes it is appropriate to idealize even further: if our aim in deploying a logic for L is to enable Karl to characterize a class of structures—that is, to give a set of axioms that are satisfied by all and only the members of that class and that, more vaguely, *is an adequate description of that class for all mathematical purposes*—then it is not at all clear why we should require that the consequences of a successful characterization flow from it via the entailment relation generated by Karl's inductive method. In the case in which the isomorphism type of a single structure is thus characterized, that would be tantamount to requiring that if ϕ is any sentence true in the structure, then given knowledge of the characterization, Karl can know a priori that ϕ is true. It is, however, fully appropriate to require that any such sentence be *mathematically necessary* relative to the characterization; in general, that if θ is a characterization of a class of structures adequate for all mathematical purposes, and ϕ is any sentence that holds in each such structure, then $\theta \cup \{\neg\phi\}$ should not be mathematically possible. On the interpretation of mathematical possibility described earlier, that is precisely the conclusion delivered by the specification of the result of 4.4.3 to $\mathbf{M}^*$, the collection of properly mathematical possibilities for L, if the expressions of θ counted as 'logical' are invariant over $\mathbf{M}^*$. The result in this case provides that the consequence relation for a logic invariant over $\mathbf{M}^*$ goes along with a radically idealized sort of demonstrability, one that requires closure under inferences which are correct for all standard models of set theory.

4.7 Framework 2

4.7.1 Intensional Languages

Until now I have assumed that the languages under consideration have an extensional structure of a rather simple sort. This assumption is seriously limiting, and it is time to consider the fate of the foregoing observations in a more general setting. Suppose that Karl's language L is *intensional*. That is to say, there is a set IN of objects, called **indices** for L, relative to which the notions of reference and satisfaction for L are characterized within the given semantic description of L. The set IN will be called the **index space** for L. The description will assign to each primitive ξ of L a function mapping each index onto an extension of the appropriate type for ξ at that index; the extension of a compound expression at any index is determined by the assignment of extensions to its constituents *at that and other* indices, together with a function F mapping each index onto a nonempty domain (the objects *actual* relative to that index) and a binary relation R of *accessibility* between indices. The triple $\langle \text{IN}, F, R \rangle$ will be called an **indexical structure** for L. This framework is by now familiar, in large measure due to the work of Richard Montague.[42]

I now want to ask how logical relations are to be construed within the present framework. As in the extensional case, the crux of the matter will be to define an appropriate notion of invariance that characterizes the logical constants; and for this purpose we shall want to know what corresponds within the intensional setting to the notion of an *alternative* for Karl in the extensional case. The discussion will be structured as follows. Subsection 4.7.2 characterizes notions of logical truth and consequence for intensional languages relative to a variable base of expressions treated as logical constants. Section 4.8 introduces the concept of a modality in the intensional setting, and characterizes a corresponding concept of modal invariance. Finally, in section 4.9 the required specification of Karl's alternatives will be provided. As earlier, logical constanthood for Karl's language will consist in an invariance property of the constants specified with reference to the totality of his alternatives, but here we must contend with an ambiguity created by the role of the underlying indices with no counterpart in the extensional case. Since this is the only essential difference between the two cases, however, the treatment of the topics of invariance, completeness and determinacy can be abbreviated. In particular, I will omit detailed discussion of results and assumptions that are exact analogues of items in the

---

[42]See, for example, the articles reprinted in *Formal Philosophy: Selected Papers of Richard Montague*, edited by R. Thomason (New Haven: Yale University Press, 1975).

extensional case.

First consider a few examples of the semantical framework described above. Very typical is the arrangement required to interpret the temporal modifier A, 'it has always been the case that'. In this case, IN is the set of real numbers, representing times, and R is $\leq$. For any time t, $F(t)$ is the collection of objects existing at t. For any sentence ϕ (or any formula ϕ relative to parameters), $A\phi$ is true at an index $t \in$ IN if ϕ holds at t' for each t' such that $t'Rt$.

As a second illustration of the framework, consider a language L that arises from an extensional language L_0 by addition of a unary operator $\Box$, and suppose we are given a modality $\mathbf{M}$ for L_0. In this case the index space for L is the modality $\mathbf{M}$ itself, and if $\langle T, \Gamma \rangle$ is any frame in $\mathbf{M}$, $F(T, \Gamma) = \Gamma$. A sentence of L_0 holds at an index just in case it is true at that index considered as a frame. Let R be any binary relation on $\mathbf{M}$. If, for any formula ϕ, $\Box\phi$ holds at an index i iff ϕ holds at all indices j such that jRi, $\Box$ will be said to be the **necessity operator for $\mathbf{M}$ over R**. The relation R will differ according to the sort of necessity we wish to describe. In cases where an arbitrary index space IN is considered and R is a relation on IN, such a device will be called a **generalized necessity operator**. The modifier A above is the special case in which IN is the collection of real numbers and R is $\leq$.

As a third application of the framework, I shall give an interpretation of monadic second-order logic, and an alternative interpretation of the first-order quantifiers. Again, let L_0 be an extensional language. As earlier, by a valuation of L_0 we understand an assignment of interpretations of the appropriate type to each nonlogical primitive of L_0 over a nonempty domain. In the present application, the indices are valuations for L_0, and for a sentence of L_0 to hold at such an index is simply for the sentence to be true in that valuation. The function F maps each index onto the associated domain. The accessibility relation will vary with the context.

For the case of monadic second-order logic, we assume that L_0 contains countably many monadic predicate letters $P_0, P_1, P_2, \ldots$ and that L arises from L_0 by adding a corresponding collection of operators $\Box_0, \Box_1, \Box_2, \ldots$, each associated with an accessibility relation R_n. The index space IN being the class of all valuations for L_0, for any natural number n and any choice of indices $i, j \in$ IN, jR_ni if j differs from i at most in the extension it assigns to P_n. For any number n and index i, $\Box_n\phi$ will hold at i just in case A holds at all j such that jR_ni. For any n, then, the expression $\Box_n$ is the generalized necessity operator for IN over R_n; but it may equally be viewed as a universal second-order quantifier: $\Box_n\phi$ holds in a valuation $\mathfrak{A}$ just in case ϕ holds in each valuation differing from $\mathfrak{A}$ at most in the interpretation assigned to P_n. The predicate letter P_n, then, plays the role of a second-order variable and $\Box_n$ plays the role of $(\forall P_n)$. Essentially the same idea allows us to provide an intensional interpretation of ordinary *first-order* quantification. In this case, the language L_0 is assumed to contain a denumerable stock $c_0, c_1, \ldots$ of individual constants, and L arises from L_0 by adding corresponding operators $\Box_n$ as above. In this case, R_n comprises just the pairs $\langle j, i \rangle$ of valuations for L_0 such that j differs from i at most in the reference it assigns to c_n. The operator $\Box_n$ is a generalized necessity operator, but it may equally be viewed as a universal first-order quantifier.[43]

4.7.2   Intensional Logics

I now turn to the problem of characterizing logical relations in intensional languages. It will be useful first to have in hand a few definitions that are quite parallel to those in the extensional case. Let L be an intensional language associated with an indexical structure $\mathfrak{A} = \langle \text{IN}, F, R \rangle$. Where τ is a syntactic category of L, the **intensions of appropriate type for** τ are characterized as follows; an intension of appropriate type for an individual expression will be an intension of appropriate type for its category. If τ is the category of formulas or of terms, then the intensions apropriate for τ over $\mathfrak{A}$ are functions Φ defined on IN such that for each i, $\Phi(i)$ is a pair $\langle A_i, E_i \rangle$, A_i being a nonempty subset of $F(i)$ and E_i an extension of appropriate type for τ over A_i. If τ is a product $\tau_1 \times \ldots \times \tau_n$ of categories wherein each τ_i is either the category of all formulas, or the subcategory of variables, or the category of all terms, then the intensions appropriate for τ over $\mathfrak{A}$ are functions Φ defined on IN such that for each i, $\Phi(i)$ is an n-tuple $\langle \langle A_i, E_{i_1} \rangle, \ldots, \langle A_i, E_{i_n} \rangle \rangle$ wherein A_i is a nonempty subset of $F(i)$ and for each k, $1 \leq k \leq n$, E_{i_k} is an extension of appropriate type for τ_k over A_k (equivalently: for each k, the function on IN that sends each i onto $(\Phi(i))_k = \langle A_i, E_{i_k} \rangle$ is an intension of appropriate type for τ_k over $\mathfrak{A}$). If Q is an operator applying to such a product to yield formulas or terms, then the intensions of appropriate type for Q over $\mathfrak{A}$ are functions mapping intensions appropriate for that product to intensions appropriate for the target category. A **valuation** for L over $\mathfrak{A}$ is an assignment of intensions of appropriate type over $\mathfrak{A}$ to each primitive of L. Any valuation for L over $\mathfrak{A}$ then inductively determines an intension of the appropriate type over $\mathfrak{A}$ for each formula or term of L in the obvious way. Finally, if Q is an operator of L and θ a valuation of L over an indexical structure $\mathfrak{A}$, say that θ **respects** Q on a given interpretation of L if the intension that θ assigns to Q agrees

---

[43]This intensionalization of the elementary quantifiers was first described by Montague in his early paper "Logical Necessity, Physical Necessity, Ethics and Quantifiers," reprinted in *Formal Philosophy*.

with the intension determined for it over $\mathfrak{A}$ by the given interpretation.[44]

As in the extensional case, by a **logic** for L we understand a set of operators from L; we say that a valuation of L respects a logic when it respects each operator therein. If $\mathcal{L}$ is a logic for L, Σ is a set of sentences and ϕ a sentence of L, we say that ϕ is an $\mathcal{L}$-**consequence** of Σ if for any valuation θ for L respecting $\mathcal{L}$ and any index i of the relevant sort, if each member of Σ is true at i on θ, then φ is true at i on θ; a sentence is $\mathcal{L}$-valid if it holds at each index on every such valuation. We naturally want to say that the logical consequences of Σ in L are those sentences that are $\mathcal{L}$-consequences of Σ where $\mathcal{L}$ is the collection of all *logical* expressions of L. The question of how to characterize the logical expressions of L in the intensional case will be answered through a generalization of the account given in the extensional setting in terms of modalities and modal invariance. Its philosophical implications are substantially the same: we shall recover a relative type of interpretive determinacy for the logical constants, and an explanation of the interpretive significance of the relation of logical consequence.

4.8   Invariance 2

4.8.1   Modal Segments and Intensions

I shall discuss two notions of logical constancy for intensional languages. I first ask what it is for an expression of such a language to behave as a logical constant relative to the fixed indexical structure over which it is interpreted. Thus, for example, if IN is the set of real numbers, representing time, it will turn out that the modifier 'always' qualifies as logical relative to IN. In this case, I shall say that the operator in question is **relatively logical**. A logical constant will then be a relatively logical expression interpreted over an indexical structure that is itself characterizable in purely logical terms (in a sense to be made precise shortly). I begin by introducing analogues of the concepts of a modality and of modal invariance for the intensional case.

In the extensional setting, a modality was a collection of frames satisfying certain conditions of consistency and completeness; in the intended application, these objects describe Karl's epistemic alternatives. To obtain

---

[44]For this we require the assumption that the given interpretation *does* fix an intension for Q over any indexical structure for L, which is one way of framing the requirement that the semantic rule assigned to each operator of L fixes a reference for it in every intensional setting. Recall that there is a corresponding assumption for the extensional case: that the assigned interpretation fixes an extension for each operator over each nonempty domain.

THE GROUND OF LOGIC

an analogous construction for the intensional case, these notions must be suitably relativized to indexical features of Karl's language. Suppose, for example, that L is an extension of a first-order language by temporal modifiers and the relevant index space IN is the set of real numbers. Think of the frames in a modality for L in my previous sense as giving *momentary* descriptions of the world: complete descriptions which are possible (in some sense) *at a time*.[45] The temporal analogue of a frame would assign such a description to each time: it would represent a *possible world-history*. Such a history might then be identified with a function mapping the real numbers to the collection of all instantaneous state-descriptions. We might call such a function a *temporal segment*. The corresponding modality will be a collection of temporal segments, representing a collection of possible world-histories.

I shall now generalize this example, beginning with an arbitrary set IN of indices and a device $\mathcal{M}$ I call a **premodality**, the analogue in the general case of the collection of all instantaneous state-descriptions in the temporal case. Formally, $\mathcal{M}$ is a collection of syntactic structures satisfying each of the conditions in the definition of a frame except extensionality. A **modal segment for** IN **over** $\mathcal{M}$ is a function mapping IN to $\mathcal{M}$ satisfying a compositionality requirement to be described below. A modal segment **sg** for IN over $\mathcal{M}$ is thus an analogue with respect to IN of a temporal segment: $\mathcal{M}$ is a collection of descriptions that obtain or not relative to any index, and **sg** associates each index with such a description. If **sg** is a modal segment for IN over $\mathcal{M}$ and $i \in$ IN, a sentence ϕ of L will be said to be **true on sg at** i if ϕ holds in $\mathbf{sg}(i)$ (that is, if $\mathbf{sg}(i) = \langle T, \Gamma \rangle$, then $\phi \in T$); we write $\mathbf{sg} \models_i \phi$ to indicate this relation. If ϕ is a formula or term of L, the **extension** of ϕ on **sg** at i is its extension in $\mathbf{sg}(i)$; we write $\mathrm{Ext}_{\mathbf{sg},i}(\phi)$ to denote the extension of ϕ in **sg** at i. Finally, the **intension** $\mathrm{Int}_{\mathbf{sg}}(\phi)$ of ϕ in **sg** is the function defined for each $i \in$ IN by

$$\mathrm{Int}_{\mathbf{sg}}(\phi)(i) = \mathrm{Ext}_{\mathbf{sg},i}(\phi);$$

if $\sigma = \langle \phi_1, ..., \phi_n \rangle$ is a finite sequence of expressions, by $\mathrm{Int}_{\mathbf{sg}}(\sigma)$ we understand the corresponding sequence of intensions. The compositionality condition adverted to earlier requires intensions to behave compositionally *within a segment*: that is to say, the intension of an expression in a segment is preserved by substitution of expressions that are cointensional in that segment.

---

[45]Of course, such a description may constrain the world at other times: the description of the world at a time t may incorporate the sentence 'It is always the case that p', so that a compatible description at any other time must incorporate the sentence represented by 'p'. Thus the extensionality requirement previously imposed on frames will have to be weakened.

The analogue of a modality in the intensional case will be called a **diachronic modality**. A diachronic modality, then, is a collection **M** of modal segments for a fixed index space IN over a fixed premodality $\mathcal{M}$; in this case, we say that **M** is **for** IN and **over** $\mathcal{M}$. If Σ is a set of sentences and ϕ a sentence of L, Σ is said to **entail** ϕ over **M** if for each $i \in$ IN and each segment $\mathbf{sg} \in \mathbf{M}$, if every sentence of Σ is true in **sg** at i, ϕ is as well. We write $\vdash_{\mathbf{M}}$ to denote this relation. It is immediate that the entailment relation over **M** coincides with the entailment relation determined by the associated premodality $\mathcal{M}$ if any element of $\mathcal{M}$ is in the range of some segment in **M**. However, a more discriminating entailment relation is also available. Suppose that Σ and ϕ are as above and that $i, j \in$ IN. Define:

$$\langle \Sigma, i \rangle \vdash_{\mathbf{M}} \langle \phi, j \rangle =: (\forall \mathbf{sg} \in \mathbf{M})(\mathbf{sg} \models_i \Sigma \to \mathbf{sg} \models_j \phi).$$

This is to say that the story told by Σ at i entails the proposition expressed by ϕ at j if any segment of **M** that realizes each element of Σ at i also realizes ϕ at j. Thus, for example, if the language of **M** incorporates a generalized necessity operator $\Box$, the sentence $\Box\phi$ relative to a world w should entail the sentence ϕ over **M** relative to any world accessible, in the relevant sense, from w. Note that we have

$$\Sigma \vdash_{\mathbf{M}} \phi \;\leftrightarrow\; (\forall i)(\langle \Sigma, i \rangle \vdash_{\mathbf{M}} \langle \phi, i \rangle).$$

4.8.2   Invariance in Intensional Languages

Suppose that we have fixed a collection **M** of segments mapping IN to a premodality $\mathcal{M}$ that describe Karl's *diachronic alternatives*. These segments then constitute, with respect to a semantics that takes truth-conditions for sentences of L to be relative to members of IN, the collection of all complete descriptions of the world which are epistemically possible for Karl. Logical constanthood in Karl's language should be characterized by an appropriate notion of invariance defined with reference to this collection. I shall now implement the required definition of invariance, following as closely as possible its structure in the extensional case. In that context, an expression is invariant over a modality if the function it introduces preserves extensions across frames. In the case of a quantifier Q, that meant that if you consider any pair of frames $\mathcal{F}, \mathcal{F}'$ in the modality and any function mapping the extension of a formula ϕ in $\mathcal{F}$ isomorphically onto the extension of a formula ψ in $\mathcal{F}'$, that function also maps the extension of $(Qx)\phi$ in $\mathcal{F}$ isomorphically onto the extension of $(Qx)\psi$ in $\mathcal{F}'$. Roughly the same idea will apply in the intensional case, but with intensions replacing extensions and modal segments in the role of frames.

Suppose, then, that L is described by a diachronic modality $\mathbf{M}$, and as earlier let $\mathcal{M}$ be the premodality and IN the set of indices associated with $\mathbf{M}$. $\mathbf{M}$ is then a set of functions mapping IN to $\mathcal{M}$. For any $i \in$ IN and $\mathbf{sg} \in \mathbf{M}$, set

$$\mathbf{sg}(i) = \langle T_i, \Gamma_i \rangle,$$

and define

$$|\mathbf{sg}| = \bigcup_{i \in \mathrm{N}} \Gamma_i;$$

$|\mathbf{sg}|$ is called the **ontology** of $\mathbf{sg}$. Now let $\mathbf{sg}'$ be another modal segment belonging to $\mathbf{M}$ and suppose that ζ and ζ' are expressions of the same type in L. By an **isomorphism** of the intension of ζ in $\mathbf{sg}$ with the intension of ζ' in $\mathbf{sg}'$ we understand a one-to-one correspondence f of $|\mathbf{sg}|$ with $|\mathbf{sg}'|$ such that, for each i, the restriction $f \restriction \Gamma_i$ of f to Γ_i maps the extension of ζ in $\mathbf{sg}$ at i isomorphically onto the extension of ζ' in $\mathbf{sg}'$ at i. An isomorphism of intensions defined on two modal segments, then, is a one-to-one correspondence between the ontologies of the segments which is simultaneously an isomorphism of the extensions induced by the intensions at any index. If σ and σ' are two sequences of expressions which are componentwise of the same type, by an isomorphism of their intensions in $\mathbf{sg}$ and $\mathbf{sg}'$ we understand a function that is componentwise such an isomorphism.

The invariance requirement over the diachronic modality $\mathbf{M}$ is now quite parallel to the extensional case considered earlier. Suppose that α is an operator that applies to sequences of expressions from a product Π of syntactic categories. Then α is said to be **invariant over** the diachronic modality $\mathbf{M}$ if for each $\sigma, \sigma' \in \Pi$ and each $\mathbf{sg}, \mathbf{sg}' \in \mathcal{M}$, any isomorphism of the intension of σ in $\mathbf{sg}$ and the intension of σ' in $\mathbf{sg}'$ also maps the intension of $\alpha(\sigma)$ in $\mathbf{sg}$ isomorphically onto the intension of $\alpha(\sigma')$ in $\mathbf{sg}'$. My idea will be that α should count as logical relative to an indexical structure if α is invariant in the present sense over the class of segments describing Karl's diachronic alternatives with respect to that structure.

I can illustrate the present definition of invariance by considering an important special case, the generalized necessity operators. The necessity operators ordinarily so-called are subcases; but as noted earlier, so also are various devices not ordinarily construed as intensional operators. Thus, for example, I showed that the elementary quantifiers, and their second-order analogues, are interpretable as generalized necessity operators. The next observation shows that under a rather general condition on the operator and the relevant diachronic modality, an operator of this sort is invariant over the modality. Thus let $\square$ be a generalized necessity operator in L characterized with reference to an accessibility relation R over an index space IN, so that for any sentence ϕ and index $i \in$ IN we have that $\square\phi$

holds at i just in case ϕ holds at each index j such that jRi. Let $\mathbf{M}$ be a diachronic modality for IN over a premodality $\mathcal{M}$ for L. Say that $\Box$ is **normal** over $\mathbf{M}$ if for any segment $\mathbf{sg} \in \mathbf{M}$ and each index $i \in$ IN, the relation

$$\mathbf{sg} \models_i \Box\phi \;\leftrightarrow\; (\forall j \in \text{IN})(jRi \rightarrow \mathbf{sg} \models_j \phi)$$

holds for each sentence ϕ of L.[46] If $\Box$ is normal over $\mathbf{M}$, then $\Box$ is invariant over $\mathbf{M}$. For, consider any pair of segments $\mathbf{sg}$ and $\mathbf{sg}'$ from $\mathbf{M}$ and any pair of formulas ϕ, ψ. Let J be any isomorphism of $\text{Int}_{\mathbf{sg}}(\phi)$ and $\text{Int}_{\mathbf{sg}'}(\psi)$. Then for any $i \in$ IN and n-tuple of constants $c_1, ..., c_n$ from $|\mathbf{sg}|$, we have

$$
\begin{aligned}
\mathbf{sg} \models_i \Box\phi(c_1...c_n) \;&\leftrightarrow\; (\forall jRi)\, \mathbf{sg} \models_j \phi(c_1...c_n) && \text{(by normality)}\\
&\leftrightarrow\; (\forall jRi)\, \mathbf{sg}' \models_j \phi(Jc_1...Jc_n) && \text{(J is an isomorphism)}\\
&\leftrightarrow\; \mathbf{sg}' \models_i \Box\psi(Jc_1...Jc_n). && \text{(by normality)}
\end{aligned}
$$

Therefore, J maps $\text{Int}_{\mathbf{sg}}(\Box\phi)$ isomorphically onto $\text{Int}_{\mathbf{sg}'}(\Box\psi)$, as required.

On natural assumptions about the coherence and extent of $\mathbf{M}$, the present framework allows us to secure counterparts of the completeness and determinacy properties described for the extensional case in section 4.4. The assumptions are these: first, there are the completeness and consistency conditions fulfilled by the underlying premodality $\mathcal{M}$, exclusive of extensionality (as noted, in place of extensionality—the assumption that *extensions* behave compositionally within frames—we have the assumption that *intensions* of expressions behave compositionally within segments); second, there is an analogue of the Reflection Condition.[47] On these assumptions we are led to the following results: first, if the operators of a logic $\mathcal{L}$ for L are invariant over $\mathbf{M}$, then for each set Σ of sentences and each sentence ϕ of L, we have $\Sigma \models_{\mathcal{L}} \phi$ only if $\Sigma \vdash_{\mathbf{M}} \phi$ (completeness of $\mathbf{M}$ with respect to $\mathcal{L}$); second, the interpretation of any operator of L invariant over $\mathbf{M}$ is determined uniquely by $\mathbf{M}$ (determinacy of $\mathcal{L}$ with respect to $\mathbf{M}$). The arguments closely parallel those in the extensional case.

---

[46]This is roughly to say that the 'interior' semantics of $\mathbf{sg}$ respects the 'external' interpretation of $\Box$. The present condition is thus an analogue of the requirement that the interior semantics for segments respect the truth functional connectives, for example, that $\mathbf{sg} \models_i \phi \vee \psi$ holds iff $\mathbf{sg} \models_i \phi$ or $\mathbf{sg} \models_i \psi$, a condition assured by the assumption that $\mathbf{sg}(i)$ is closed under first-order deducibility.

[47]Let T be a syntactic type in L and let IN be the relevant index set. By a **structure for T over** IN we mean a pair $\langle D, E \rangle$ where E is an intension over IN mapping each index onto an extension of the appropriate type for expressions in T over the domain D. If $\mathbf{sg}$ is a segment and $\alpha \in T$, say that the pair $\langle \mathbf{sg}, \alpha \rangle$ **realizes** a structure $\langle D, E \rangle$ for T if for each $i \in$ IN, $\langle \mathbf{sg}(i), \alpha \rangle$ realizes $\langle D, E(i) \rangle$ in the sense of 4.4.1. The analogues of conditions (a) and (b) of 4.4.1 are now apparent.

In the intended application, M describes Karl's epistemic alternatives, so that the segments in M are functions mapping the relevant indices into the premodality $\mathcal{M}$ comprising state descriptions at-an-index that are epistemically possible for Karl. The question is now under what conditions such a function describes a *diachronic alternative*, that is, a configuration of the world at each index that is epistemically possible for Karl; such a configuration is the analogue in the general situation of an *epistemically possible history* in the temporal case. An expression of L will count as relatively logical—that is to say, as logical *relative to* the relevant indexical features—if it is invariant over the entire collection of such alternatives.

My strategy will again parallel that of the discussion in the extensional setting earlier. I said in that case that a frame constitutes an alternative for Karl if it is closed under an entailment relation generated by Karl's inductive method. I shall apply an analogous requirement here. As before, this will involve specifying a pertinent notion of entailment. The crux of the matter will be to make sense of 'diachronic' or cross-index entailments, typified by the relationship of a sentence $\Box\phi$ realized at a given index i to the realization of ϕ at all indices accessible from i. We begin by extending the account given earlier of the notion of 'inductive method' to the intensional setting.

In the extensional case, Karl's inductive method was represented by a function mapping Karl's evidence-bases onto collections of sets of sentences; the sentences expressed, under the relevant semantic description, belief-contents. But a *sentence* cannot express such a content in the intensional case, for what content it expresses depends on which index is considered. The obvious remedy was to take Karl's attitudes in general to be given not by sentences, but by couples consisting of a sentence and an index. In the context of a semantic description that relativizes truth-conditions to such indices, such a couple fixes a propositional content. I shall suppose, then, that Karl's inductive method is described by a function Φ that maps each of his possible evidential situations onto a collection of pairs $\langle S, i \rangle$ such that S is a set of sentences and i an index of the relevant sort. View such a pair as ascribing to Karl a belief that the members of S obtain at i.

I now turn to the required definition of entailment. If IN is the relevant index-space and Φ the function describing Karl's inductive method, we want to know not when one set of sentences from L entails another such sentence, but when such a set coupled with an index from IN entails another sentence coupled with that, or another, index. As in the extensional case, I shall first characterize an immediate consequence relation $\Vdash_\Phi$ holding between pairs $\langle S, i \rangle$ as above and a collection

$$X = \{\langle S_\alpha, i_\alpha \rangle \mid \alpha < \beta\}$$

of such pairs.[48] Fixing S, X and i, we define:

$$X \Vdash_\Phi \langle S, i \rangle \ =: \ (\exists e) X \subseteq \Phi(e) \ \& \ (\forall f)(X \subseteq \Phi(f) \rightarrow \langle S, i \rangle \in \Phi(f))).$$

The definiens says roughly that if each set S_α is assertible at an evidence-base relative to the index i_α, then S is assertible at that evidence-base relative to i; and that the S_α thus relativized are assertible at some evidence-base or other. We will then say that a set A is Φ-**closed** if

$$(\forall Y \subseteq A)(\forall K)(\forall j)(Y \Vdash_\Phi \langle K, j \rangle \rightarrow \langle K, j \rangle \in A);$$

$$(\forall j)\langle \bigcup \{K | \langle K, j \rangle \in A\}, j \rangle \in A.$$

Roughly, then, A is Φ-closed if A is closed under the immediate entailment relation $\Vdash_\Phi$ and under amalgamation of sets of sentences pegged to a single index. I shall finally say that the pair $\langle S, i \rangle$ is a Φ-**consequence** of X if it belongs to each Φ-closed collection including X; if ϕ is a sentence, $\langle \phi, i \rangle$ is a Φ-consequence of X if ϕ belongs to some set S such that $\langle S, i \rangle$ is a Φ-consequence of X. We write '$\vdash_\Phi$' to denote the corresponding entailment relation.[49]

I have thus defined an analogue for intensional languages of the notion of entailment within Karl's inductive method defined earlier for the extensional case.[50] The general requirement I wish to impose on the diachronic modality **M** generated by Karl's inductive method is that the segments comprising it exhibit closure with respect to the present entailment relation. A bit more explicitly, for any $\mathbf{sg} \in \mathbf{M}$, each χ and each set S of sentences, we have:

$$(\forall i, j \in \text{IN})((\mathbf{sg} \models_i S \ \& \ \langle S, i \rangle \vdash_\Phi \langle \chi, j \rangle) \rightarrow \mathbf{sg} \models_j \chi).$$

---

[48]Here β is an ordinal number, serving as an index set.

[49]As in the analogous construction for the extensional case, it may be shown that there exists such a minimal Φ-closed set including any set X.

[50]Note that the definition of $\vdash_\Phi$ allows for 'cross-index' entailments. Suppose, for example, that Karl's inductive method satisfies, with respect to an accessibility relation R defined on the index-space IN,

[i] $(\forall e)(\forall i \in \text{IN})(\langle \{\Box A\}, i \rangle \in \Phi(e) \leftrightarrow (\forall j \in \text{IN})(\langle j, i \rangle \in R \rightarrow \langle \{A\}, j \rangle \in \Phi(e));$

that is, the necessitation of a sentence is assigned to an evidence-base at an index if and only if that sentence is assigned to that evidence-base at each index accessible from that index. Clearly, then, for each i we have that

$$\langle \{\Box A\}, i \rangle \vdash_\Phi \langle A, j \rangle$$

for any index j accessible from i.

comprising it exhibit closure with respect to the corresponding entailment relation. A bit more explicitly, for any $\mathbf{sg} \in \mathbf{M}$, I wish to require for each sentence χ and each set S of sentences that

$$(\forall i, j \in \mathrm{IN})((\mathbf{sg} \models_i S \ \& \ \langle S, i \rangle \vdash_\Phi \langle \chi, j \rangle) \to \mathbf{sg} \models_j \chi).$$

Karl's **diachronic alternatives** are then just the segments satisfying the indicated closure condition, and the diachronic modality $\mathbf{M}$ consists exactly of Karl's diachronic alternatives.

As earlier, we may argue that the entailment relation $\vdash_\Phi$ generated by Karl's inductive method coincides with the entailment relation $\vdash_{\mathbf{M}}$ generated by the diachronic modality $\mathbf{M}$ if, as in the extensional case, we assume a maximality condition pertaining to the possibilities represented in $\mathbf{M}$, an analogue of the Lindenbaum condition. What was required before was that any set consistent with respect to Karl's inductive method can be embedded in some frame in the relevant modality. Here I shall make an analogous assumption involving the obvious diachronic analogue of the notion of consistency. Let S be a set of sentences and χ a sentence in the language of $\mathbf{M}$, and let i and j be indices. The pair $\langle \chi, j \rangle$ will be said to be **incompatible** with the pair $\langle S, i \rangle$ with respect to Φ if

$$\langle S, i \rangle \vdash_\Phi \langle \neg\chi, j \rangle;$$

pairs are **compatible** if they are not incompatible. The required condition is that if the pairs $\langle S, i \rangle$ and $\langle \chi, j \rangle$ are compatible then there exists a segment that unifies them, that is, a segment $\mathbf{sg} \in \mathcal{M}$ such that $\mathbf{sg} \models_i S$ and $\mathbf{sg} \models_j \chi$. It follows easily from the present condition that the entailment relations $\vdash_\Phi$ and $\vdash_{\mathbf{M}}$ extensionally coincide.[51]

4.10   The Bounds of Logic 2

I have now arrived at a characterization of Karl's diachronic alternatives: they may be thought of as the segments that specify indexed stories that are coherent with respect to Karl's inductive method. My suggestion is that

---

[51]To see this, we must show that for any S, χ, i, j that

$$\langle S, i \rangle \vdash_\Phi \langle \chi, j \rangle \leftrightarrow \langle S, i \rangle \vdash_{\mathbf{M}} \langle \chi, j \rangle.$$

The implication from left to right is clear from the condition that the range of any segment in $\mathbf{M}$ is closed under $\vdash_\Phi$. For the right-to-left direction, suppose that not $\langle S, i \rangle \vdash_\Phi \langle \chi, j \rangle$. Then $\langle \neg\chi, j \rangle$ is compatible with $\langle S, i \rangle$, whence by the maximality condition there is a segment $\mathbf{sg} \in \mathbf{M}$ such that $\mathbf{sg} \models_i S$ and $\mathbf{sg} \models_j \neg\chi$. Thus not $\langle S, i \rangle \vdash_{\mathbf{M}} \langle \chi, j \rangle$.

an expression of Karl's language counts as logical *relative to the indexical structure over which it is interpreted* if it behaves invariantly over the entire collection of his diachronic alternatives. In this case, I will say that the expression is **relatively logical**. I observed that there is then a rather close parallelism to the extensional setting: in particular, precisely parallel completeness and determinacy results apply. However, in the intensional case, we have to contend with a distinction with no counterpart in the extensional one. It might be suggested that an expression of Karl's language characterized with reference to a fixed indexical structure is a logical constant if and only if it is relatively logical. The difficulty for this suggestion is created in the case in which the structure itself is in some sense clearly *non*logical. The problem can be illustrated by temporal modifiers such as 'always', 'never', 'sometimes', and so on. These devices are relatively logical: nevertheless, they seem to be 'absolutely' nonlogical expressions. They are analogous, with respect to the usual semantics for them, to sortal quantifiers *relativized to times*. But a sortal quantifier is not a logical expression unless the underlying *sort* is logical. The corresponding requirement here would be that the relevant indexical structure be characterizable in purely logical terms.

How is this requirement to be understood? An indexical structure consists of an index set IN, an accessibility relation R, and a domain-specifying function F, and so the question is what it should mean to say that IN, R, and F are definable in logical terms. The question, posed in these terms, has an air of circularity, for we are attempting to use the relevant notion of definability to say what a logical constant is. But the apparent circularity is easily eliminable. We proceed inductively: assuming the logical expressions of a given level to be fixed, an expression of an intensional language is a logical constant of the next level if it is a relatively logical expression interpreted over an indexical structure definable in terms of logical expressions of the given level. The logical constants of level 0 are just the expressions covered by the criterion for this notion in the extensional case.

The question, then, is what it is for an indexical framework to be characterizable in terms of a given extensional logic. Recall that a model, in the usual sense, of a set X of sentences is a relational structure arising from a valuation of the nonlogical expressions in the language of X that satisfies each sentence in X. It is natural to say that a class K of such structures is **definable** in a logic $\mathcal{L}$ if K consists of all and only the models of some set of sentences in the logic; that is to say, there is a set Σ of sentences in $\mathcal{L}$ such that

$$K = \{\mathbf{A} : \mathbf{A} \models_{\mathcal{L}} \Sigma\}.^{52}$$

What about relations on structures? Let K be a class of structures, all of the same type. Say that a relation $R \subseteq K \times K$ is **homogeneous** if for each $\mathbf{A}, \mathbf{B} \in K$, $\langle \mathbf{A}, \mathbf{B} \rangle \in R$ only if $|\mathbf{A}| = |\mathbf{B}|$. It is quite easy to say, in analogy to the foregoing notion of definability for classes, when a homogenous relation on K is definable in $\mathcal{L}$. Let τ_0 and τ_1 be disjoint copies of a vocabulary for structures in K, and set $\tau = \tau_0 \cup \tau_1$.[53] Then R may be said to be definable in $\mathcal{L}$ if it is characterizable by some theory in $\mathcal{L}(\tau)$; a bit more explicitly, if T is the relevant theory, we have

$$R = \{ \langle \mathbf{A} | \tau_0, \mathbf{A} | \tau_1 \rangle : \ \mathbf{A} \models_{\mathcal{L}} T \},$$

where $\mathbf{A} | \tau_i$ indicates the restriction of $\mathbf{A}$ to τ_i. Homogeneous relations of arbitrary degree are handled similarly. It is thus natural to suggest that the *logical* index spaces are classes of structures definable in a proper logic; and that a notion of accessibility is logical if it is similarly characterizable. An indexical structure will be said to be **definable over** an extensional logic $\mathcal{L}$ if both the index space and the accessibility relation for it are definable over $\mathcal{L}$.[54]

To sum up: I have suggested that an intensional operator Q is a relatively logical expression if Q is invariant over the entire class of alternatives arising from the indexical framework over which it is interpreted; and that

---

[52]The classes definable in $\mathcal{L}$ are thus analogues for a general logic of generalized elementary classes.

[53]If $\mathbf{A}$ is a relational structure $\langle D, R_1, ..., R_n \rangle$, $|\mathbf{A}| = D$ (the domain of $\mathbf{A}$); a **vocabulary** τ for $\mathbf{A}$ is an n-tuple $\langle P_1, ..., P_n \rangle$ of predicates such that, for each i, $1 \leq i \leq n$, P_i and R_i are of the same arity. If τ is a vocabulary and $\mathcal{L}$ a logic, $\mathcal{L}(\tau)$ is the language whose primitives are just the operators in $\mathcal{L} \cup \tau$.

[54]There is no need for a separate requirement of definability for the domain-specifying function associated with the structure, since the domain of any index i in this case is simply the domain of i considered as a model. There is a technical problem created here for cases in which the index space for L is a cartesian product of a collection of index sets. Some of these may not be definable over a set of logical constants but this circumstance should not disqualify an intensional operator as logical if the indices and accessibility relation that are *relevant* to interpreting it are so definable. The question is then what it should mean to say that an indexical sort is 'relevant' to interpreting an intensional device in the case where the needed set of indices is a product of such sorts. The corresponding notion of *irrelevance* is perhaps somewhat more intuitive: a factor in such a product is semantically irrelevant for an operator Q if the valuation of Q at any index i coincides with its interpretation at an index j if i and j diverge in at most the component corresponding to that factor. And so to solve our problem we will say that a relatively logical expression Q interpreted with reference to a cartesian product Π of indexical sorts is a logical constant if the following conditions are satisfied: Let Π_R result from Π by omitting each factor irrelevant to Q. Then, first, Π_Q is definable over some set of antecedently given logical constants; and second, if R is the accessibility relation on Π, then the restriction, in the obvious sense, of R to Π_Q is similarly definable.

Q is a logical constant *tout court* if in addition that framework is itself definable in terms of logical notions. I shall illustrate these criteria by considering two examples.

The monadic second-order quantifiers comprise the first example. Let L be a monadic second-order language and L_0 the first-order fragment of L. L arises from L_0 by adding quantifiers on monadic predicate places. L_0 is assumed to contain a denumerable stock $P_0, P_1, \ldots$ of 1-place predicate letters, which play the role of the second-order variables of L; as above the combination $(\forall P_n)$ will be interpreted as a generalized necessity operator $\Box_n$. The relevant indices are structures for L_0, truth at an index consists in truth in that structure, and the accessibility relation associated with $\Box_n$ is the relation R_n on such structures such that for any $\mathbf{A}$, $\mathbf{B}$, $\mathbf{A} R_n \mathbf{B}$ holds if $\mathbf{B}$ differs from $\mathbf{A}$ at most in the set it assigns to P_n.[55] Thus $\Box_n \phi$ holds at an index $\mathbf{A}$ if ϕ holds under every variation of $\mathbf{A}$ assigning a new extension to P_n. If the $\Box_n$s satisfy the normality condition,[56] they are counted as relatively logical expressions; thus, to show that they are logical operators it suffices to show that each R_n is definable in first-order logic. For each n, I shall assemble a theory T_n to this end. The language of T_n consists of L_0 and a disjoint copy $L_0^{\#}$ of L_0. T_n contains, for each primitive ζ of L_0 other than P_n, a sentence that asserts the extensional coincidence of ζ and $\zeta^{\#}$. Then setting τ_0 equal to the vocabulary of L_0 and $\tau_1 = \{\zeta^{\#} \mid \zeta \in \tau_0\}$, we have for any n and any structure $\mathbf{A}$ for $\tau_0 \cup \tau_1$ that $\mathbf{A} \models T_n$ if $\langle \mathbf{A}|\tau_0, \mathbf{A}|\tau_1 \rangle \in R_n$, whence R_n is definable in elementary logic via T_n. Thus if the $\Box_n$s satisfy the normality condition, and so count as relatively logical, these expressions are counted as logical constants by the suggested criterion. In this case, then, monadic second-order logic is counted as logic.

The second example arises by associating a generalized necessity operator with each elementary theory. Let T be a theory in an elementary language L. L_T is a language resulting from L by adding a unary modality $\Box_T$. $\Box_T$ is a generalized necessity operator that is characterized with reference to an index space consisting of all structures for the language L and an accessibility relation R_T such that $\langle \mathbf{A}, \mathbf{B} \rangle \in R_T$ if $\mathbf{A}$ is a model of T. We then have for any sentence ϕ in L_T and structure $\mathbf{A}$ that $\Box_T \phi$ is true at $\mathbf{A}$ if ϕ is true in each model of T. In effect, then, the operator $\Box_T$ expresses conditional logical necessity relative to the theory T; $\Box$ (logical necessity) is the special case in which T is the empty theory. It is clear that the relation R_T is definable over elementary logic, in terms of the theory

---

[55] I here depart slightly from the treatment of this example in 4.7.1. There the indices for L were taken to be valuations of L_0; here they are relational structures for L_0 corresponding to such valuations.

[56] See 4.8.2.

T itself. Thus on the suggested criterion $\Box_T$ will be counted a logical constant if it is relatively logical; and it is relatively logical if, again, it satisfies the normality condition. Obviously for the purposes of this construction I could equally well have considered, in place of an elementary theory, a theory T in an extension of elementary logic by means of additional logical constants.

One case of this more general situation is of some interest. For this example, let L be the language that results from the language of elementary number theory by addition of the generalized quantifier Q_0, 'for infinitely many'. I argued earlier that under quite natural conditions this quantifier should count as properly logical. **Robinson's Arithmetic** is the elementary theory Q axiomatized by the following sentences

$$(\forall x)\neg 0 = x'$$
$$(\forall x)(\neg x = 0 \to (\exists y)x = y')$$
$$(\forall x)x + 0 = x$$
$$(\forall x)(\forall y)(x' = y' \to x = y)$$
$$(\forall x)x \cdot 1 = x$$
$$(\forall x)(\forall y)x + y' = (x + y)'$$
$$(\forall x)(\forall y)x \cdot y' = (x \cdot y) + x.$$

Define T to be the result of combining Q with the sentence:

$$(\forall x)\neg(Q_0 y)y \leq x.$$

Robinson's Arithmetic completely characterizes the structure of the *finite* (standard) integers; the added sentence says that there are no nonstandard integers, by saying that each natural number has only finitely many predecessors. These items together imply that the theory T characterizes the standard model of arithmetic uniquely, in the sense that any model of T is isomorphic to the intended or standard one. We have now arrived at the following equivalences: on the one hand, a sentence of L is true in the standard model of arithmetic if and only if it holds in each model of T. On the other hand, a sentence ϕ holds in each model of T if and only if $\Box_T \phi$ is true and, in fact, logically true. Thus the mapping that sends any arithmetic statement ϕ onto the modal sentence $\Box_T \phi$ is truth-preserving and, in fact, necessarily truth-preserving. Some philosophers, call them 'modal structuralists', have argued that such a modal correlate of an arithmetical statement can be taken to provide a representation of its meaning.[57] Using devices illustrated in this chapter, such modal-logical translations can be developed for other parts of mathematics, in particular for analysis (the theory of the real numbers) and Zermelo-Frankel set theory.[58] The root idea is that a mathematical assertion makes a claim about what *would* hold in any structure of a certain sort (an isomorphism type). The foregoing translation scheme for number theory reflects this idea: the modal translate of an arithmetical assertion says roughly that the sentence in question holds in all possible standard models, where these are regarded as indices for a generalized necessity concept. The issues surrounding this

---

[57]The view originates, as far as I can tell, with Hilary Putnam in "Mathematics without Foundations," reprinted in his *Philosophical Papers*, vol. 1 (Cambridge: Cambridge University Press, 1975). A detailed defense of it can be found in Geoffrey Hellman, *Mathematics without Numbers* (New York: Oxford University Press, 1989).

[58]See Hellman, *Mathematics without Numbers*, chs. 2, 3, for a detailed discussion; the key ideas may be noted briefly. Let OF represent the (finite) set of axioms for the theory of ordered fields. We adjoin monadic second-order quantifiers to the language of OF to obtain a language $\mathcal{L}$. Where X represents a monadic second-order variable of $\mathcal{L}$ and y a variable of the first-order fragment, we define

$$X \leq y := (\forall z)(Xz \to z \leq y).$$

OF^+ is then the theory in $\mathcal{L}$ that results from OF by adding the sentence

$$(\forall X)(((\exists y)Xy \ \& \ (\exists y)X \leq y) \to (\exists y)(X \leq y \ \& \ (\forall z)(X \leq z \to y \leq z)),$$

which asserts that every bounded nonempty set has a least upper bound. The models of OF^+ are isomorphic to the field of real numbers, and so OF^+ characterizes the structure of the real number system uniquely. Thus a sentence ϕ in the language of analysis is true if and only if the sentence $\Box_{OF^+}\phi$ is true. The other example of this situation mentioned trades on the fact that the standard models of Zermelo-Frankel set theory (ZF) are characterizable in terms of a second-order logical construction. In this case, $\mathcal{L}$ is the language of ZF, augmented with monadic second-order quantifiers. Define

$$fcn(X) :=$$
$$(\forall y)(Xy \to (\exists u)(\exists v)y = \langle u,v\rangle) \ \& \ (\forall y)(\forall u)(\forall v)((X(\langle y,u\rangle) \ \& \ X(\langle y,v\rangle)) \to u=v).$$

The sentence

(R) $(\forall X)(\forall y)(fcn(X) \to (\exists z)(\forall u)(u \in z \leftrightarrow (\exists v)(v \in y \ \& \ X(\langle v,u\rangle)))$

formulates the second-order replacement axiom. Zermelo showed that adjoining (R) to his 1908 axioms yields a theory (Z^2) that characterizes the standard models of ZF, namely the structures

$$\langle V_\alpha, \{\langle a,b\rangle \in V_\alpha \times V_\alpha \mid a \in b\}\rangle$$

where α is a strongly inaccessible cardinal. The sentence $\Box_{Z^2}A$ then says that A holds in all set-theoretically standard models.

proposal, in particular the opposition between modal-structuralist and Platonist interpretations of classical mathematics, are complex, and somewhat
tangential to the main concerns of this chapter.[59] But it is worth observing
that the ingredients of the modal-structuralist picture of classical mathematics are interpretable in terms of devices which, on the present account
of the nature of logic, qualify as properly logical.

4.11   Endpoint

At the outset, I distinguished constitutive principles from enabling proposals. A constitutive principle of radical interpretation sets out a fundamental
constraint on the enterprise of understanding a system that in the broadest
sense may be called a person, an agent who is a subject of intentional states
and who instantiates what I have called an 'inductive method'—roughly,
a rule-based conception of epistemic rationality. The constitutive principle
that guides the account of logic in this chapter is the *Completeness Principle*: that the model-theoretically characterized entailment relation for
Karl's language should be a species of entailment therein. My deployment
of the principle required that an account be given of how Karl's inductive
method fixes a notion of entailment in Karl's language. That accomplished,
the question then became how to characterize the logical constants in such
a way as to explicate the connection between the notions of logical consequence and entailment. Beyond this, however, there was the question of
the relevance of the present account of logic to the problem interpretational
determinacy.

The account I have given of what a logical constant is has the status
of an enabling proposal with respect to satisfaction of the Completeness
Principle. On that account, a logical constant of Karl's language is roughly
an operator whose semantic role is invariant under structure-preserving
transformations defined across situations which are epistemically possible
for Karl. These in turn have been identified with suitable representations
of worlds which are coherent with respect to Karl's inductive method; and
I argued that Karl's inductive method fixes a set of such representations
uniquely. In the extensional case, the relevant representations are sets of
sentences maximal, in an appropriate sense, among those that are closed
under the entailment relation generated by Karl's inductive method. In
the intensional case, they are functions mapping the relevent index space
into a collection of representations of this sort. The Completeness Principle
is a consequence of a technical observation that, in the context of a given

---

[59]For a discussion of these issues, see my critical notice of Hellman, *Mathematics
without Numbers*, in *Notre Dame Journal of Formal Logic* 38 (1997): 136–61.

interpretation of Karl, says roughly the following: if the logical constants of Karl's language are invariant over the totality of his epistemic alternatives, then each set of sentences that is epistemically possible for Karl has a realization that assigns to each logical term its proper or intended reference with respect to that interpretation.

What of the second question? The suggested characterization of the logical constants implies a relative determinacy result: the interpretations of the logical terms in Karl's language are fixed by the role they play in stories describing worlds that are epistemically possible for Karl; and that role is fixed, or so I argued, by Karl's inductive method. The result is that both the demarcation of the logical expressions of Karl's language and the interpretations of the devices counted as logical are fixed by a suitable representation of Karl's inductive method. Such a representation is a computational rendering of the structure of Karl's understanding.

POSTSCRIPT TO CHAPTER 4

These postscripts present two technical results that are used in this chapter.

A.   An Abstract Completeness Property

PROPOSITION. *Let* **M** *be a reflective modality for L and* $\mathcal{L}$ *a logic for* **M**. *Suppose that each expression in* $\mathcal{L}$ *is rigidly invariant over* **M**. *Then for any set T of sentences and sentence* ϕ *in L, $T \models_{\mathcal{L}} \phi$ only if $T \vdash_{\mathbf{M}} \phi$.*

1.   Definitions and Notation

Where ϕ is a sentence of $L(T)$, recall $T \vdash_{\mathbf{M}} \phi$ means that for no $\langle S, \Gamma \rangle \in \mathbf{M}$ do we have $T \cup \{\neg\phi\} \subseteq S$. For any domain D and expression ζ, $\mathrm{Ext}_D(\zeta)$ is the extension of ζ in L over D and if $\mathcal{F}$ is a frame we write $\{\zeta\}_{\mathcal{F}}$ for the extension of ζ over $\mathcal{F}$. If $\mathcal{F} = \langle S, \Gamma \rangle$, $\mathcal{F}' = \langle S', \Gamma' \rangle \in \mathbf{M}$ and ζ is in $L(S)$, a ζ-**morphism** of $\mathcal{F}$ and $\mathcal{F}'$ is a translation f mapping $L(S)$ to $L(S')$ such that $f|\Gamma$ is an isomorphism mapping the structure $\langle \Gamma, \{\zeta\}_{\mathcal{F}} \rangle$ onto $\langle \Gamma', \{f(\zeta)\}_{\mathcal{F}'} \rangle$. An **embedding** of $\mathcal{F}$ in $\mathcal{F}'$ is a translation mapping $L(S)$ to $L(S')$ which is a ζ-morphism for each formula or term ζ of $L(S)$. A frame $\mathcal{F} = \langle S, \Gamma \rangle$ will be called **proper** if the denotation function associated with Γ is total and S is true when interpreted over the domain consisting exactly of the denotations of the constants in Γ. A **realization** of a frame is an embedding of it in a proper frame.

2.   Proof of Proposition

Let **M** be a reflective modality and $\mathcal{L}$ a logic invariant over **M**. If ζ is any formula or term, the complexity of ζ is defined inductively as follows. If ζ is a variable $|\zeta| = 0$, and if ζ is a constant $|\zeta| = 1$. If α is an operator that applies to expressions $\zeta_1, ..., \zeta_n$ to form an expression ζ, then $|\zeta| = 1 + \max\{|\zeta_i| \mid 1 \le i \le n\}$. Since each realization of a frame $\langle T, S \rangle$ fixes a valuation of $L(T)$ satisfying T, it suffices to show the following.

(1)   For each frame $\mathcal{F} \in \mathbf{M}$, there is a realization of $\mathcal{F}$ that leaves $\mathcal{L}$ fixed.

Thus, fix a frame $\mathcal{F} = \langle T, \Gamma \rangle \in \mathbf{M}$. By the Reflection Condition, there exists a frame $\mathcal{F}' = \langle T', \Gamma' \rangle \in \mathbf{M}$ such that, where Δ is the denotation function associated with Γ', we have

[i] Δ maps Γ' one-to-one and onto Γ;

[ii]   for each operator α of $L(T)$, there is an operator $\alpha^{\#}$ in $L(T')$ whose extension in $L(T')$ over Γ coincides with the extension of α in $\mathcal{F}$;

[iii] T' is true over Γ.

The frame $\mathcal{F}'$ comprises a complete diagram of the extensions of each primitive of $L(T)$ in $\mathcal{F}$. We define a translation and mapping $L(T)$ to $L(T')$ as follows: if ζ is a primitive term, we take

[iv] $$\zeta^{+} = \begin{cases} \zeta & \text{if } \zeta \text{ is a variable.} \\ \Delta^{-1}(\zeta) & \text{if } \zeta \in \Gamma. \end{cases}$$

If α is a primitive operator of $L(T)$, we take α^{+} to be an operator $\alpha^{\#}$ satisfying [ii] if α is not invariant over $\mathbf{M}$; if α^{+} is invariant over $\mathbf{M}$, set $\alpha^{+} = \alpha$. To show that $+$ is a realization of $\mathcal{F}$ in $\mathcal{F}'$, we argue by induction on the complexity of ζ that $+$ is a ζ-morphism for each formula or term ζ of $L(T)$. The basis case is immediate from [iv]. Now assume that ζ is $\alpha(\zeta_1, ..., \zeta_n)$ for some operator α in $L(T)$ and for the induction hypothesis that $+$ is an ζ_i-morphism for each i, $1 \leq i \leq n$.

   Case 1. α is invariant over $\mathbf{M}$. Then α^{+} is α itself and ζ^{+} is the expression $\alpha(\zeta_1^{+}, ..., \zeta_n^{+})$. Thus by the induction hypothesis and the definition of invariance, $+$ is a ζ-morphism of $\mathcal{F}$ and $\mathcal{F}'$, as required.

   Case 2. α is not invariant over $\mathbf{M}$.

   LEMMA. *For each formula or term ζ of $L(T)$, $+$ is a ζ-morphism of $\mathcal{F}$ and $\mathcal{F}'$ iff* $\text{Ext}_{\Gamma}(\zeta^{+}) = \{\zeta\}_{\mathcal{F}}$.

   PROOF. We consider only the case in which ζ is a formula $\phi(x_1, ..., x_n)$. Suppose first that $+$ is a ζ-morphism of $\mathcal{F}$ and $\mathcal{F}'$. Then for any sequence $\mathbf{s} = \langle c_n \rangle \in \Gamma^{\omega}$, $\mathbf{s} \in \text{Ext}_{\Gamma}(\zeta^{+})$ if $\phi^{+}(\mathbf{c}_1^{+}, ..., \mathbf{c}_n^{+})$ holds in $L(T')$ over T, which by [iii] obtains precisely when

[v] $\mathcal{F}' \models \phi^{+}(\mathbf{c}_1^{+}, ..., \mathbf{c}_n^{+}).$

On the other hand, $\mathbf{s} \in \{\zeta\}_{\mathcal{F}}$ iff

[vi] $$\mathcal{F} \models \phi(\mathbf{c}_1, ..., \mathbf{c}_n).$$

Since $+$ is a ζ-morphism of $\mathcal{F}$ and $\mathcal{F}'$, [v] and [vi] are equivalent, whence, since $\mathbf{s} \in \Gamma^\omega$ was arbitrary, we have

[vii] $$\mathrm{Ext}_\Gamma(\zeta^+) = \{\zeta\}_{\mathcal{F}}.$$

A similar argument shows that [vii] implies that $+$ is a ζ-morphism of $\mathcal{F}$ and $\mathcal{F}'$.

Case 2 is now handled as follows. By the induction hypothesis and the Lemma, it follows that

$$\mathrm{Ext}_\Gamma(\zeta_i^+) = \{\zeta_i\}_{\mathcal{F}} \quad (1 \le i \le n).$$

We thus have

$$\begin{aligned}
\mathrm{Ext}_\Gamma(\zeta^+) &= \mathrm{Ext}_\Gamma(\alpha^+)(\mathrm{Ext}_\Gamma(\zeta_1^+), ..., \mathrm{Ext}_\Gamma(\zeta_n^+)) \\
&= \{\alpha\}_{\mathcal{F}}(\{\zeta_1\}_{\mathcal{F}}, ..., \{\zeta_n\}_{\mathcal{F}}) \\
&= \{\alpha(\zeta_1, ..., \zeta_n)\}_{\mathcal{F}} \\
&= \{\zeta\}_{\mathcal{F}},
\end{aligned}$$

whence again using the Lemma we obtain that $+$ is a ζ-morphism of $\mathcal{F}$ and $\mathcal{F}'$, as required. This completes the induction, and the proof of the theorem.

B.   The Lindenbaum Condition

In this postscript I describe a general setting for the applicability of the Lindenbaum Condition to the notion of consistency generated by Karl's inductive method.

Let κ and λ be infinite cardinals. $\mathcal{L}_{\kappa,\lambda}(L)$ is the smallest collection containing the sentences of L and closed under the finitary first-order operations, the operations $\vee S$, $\wedge S$, where S is a set of sentences of cardinality $< \kappa$, and the operator

$$(\forall v_1)(\forall v_2)...\phi,$$

where ϕ is a given formula and $\langle v_1, v_2, ... \rangle$ is a sequence of variables of length $< \lambda$.

The entailment relation $\vdash_{\Psi,\kappa,\lambda}$ for $\mathcal{L}_{\kappa,\lambda}(L)$ is the smallest relation on $\mathcal{L}_{\kappa,\lambda}(L)$ closed under both $\vdash_\Psi$ (the entailment relation generated by Karl's inductive method) and entailment in the infinitary logic $\mathcal{L}_{\kappa,\lambda}$. We say that $\mathcal{L}_{\kappa,\lambda}$ is **conservative over** L if for each Σ, ϕ in any extension by constants of L, $\Sigma \vdash_{\Psi,\kappa,\lambda} \phi$ only if $\Sigma \vdash_\Psi \phi$. Clearly, $\vdash_{\Psi,\kappa,\lambda}$ is conservative over L if and only if any set consistent in the sense of $\vdash_\Psi$ is consistent in the sense of $\vdash_{\Psi,\kappa,\lambda}$. I shall now show that, if $\lambda = \omega_1$, the first uncountable ordinal, and $\kappa = 2^\omega$, the cardinal of the powerset of the natural numbers, then $\vdash_{\Psi,\kappa,\lambda}$ is conservative over L only if any set consistent in the sense of $\vdash_\Psi$ can be embedded in an alternative.

PROOF. In what follows we write CON_Ψ to denote the consistency property generated by $\vdash_\Psi$, and for any κ, λ, $\mathrm{CON}_{\Psi,\kappa,\lambda}$ is the consistency property generated by $\vdash_{\Psi,\kappa,\lambda}$. Now suppose that Σ is given such that $\mathrm{CON}_{\Psi,\kappa,\lambda}(\Sigma)$. Let $\{\phi_n(x_{i_n})\}$ be an enumeration of the formulas of L in one free variable and $\{c_n\}$ a countable collection of constants not appearing in L. Define a sequence $\{\Sigma_n\}$ by induction on n:

$$\Sigma_0 = \Sigma;$$
$$\Sigma_{n+1} = \Sigma_n \cup \{(\exists x_{i_n})\phi_n(x_{i_n}) \to \phi(c_{k_n}))\}$$

for the least k_n such that c_{k_n} does not appear in Σ_n. Set $\Sigma^+ = \bigcup_{n \in \omega} \Sigma_n$. Then:

[i] $\mathrm{CON}_{\Psi,\kappa,\lambda}(\Sigma^+)$.

Otherwise, we have

$$\Sigma \vdash_{\Psi,\kappa,\lambda} \neg \bigwedge_n \{(\exists x_{i_n})\phi(x_{i_n}) \to \phi_n(c_{i_n})\}$$

whence by quantifier-introduction

$$\Sigma \vdash_{\Psi,\kappa,\lambda} (\forall x_{i_1})(\forall x_{i_2})...\neg \bigwedge_n \{(\exists x_{i_n})\phi_n(x_{i_n}) \to \phi_n(x_{k_n})\}.$$

A little manipulation yields

$$\Sigma \vdash_{\Psi,\kappa,\lambda} \bigvee_n \{(\exists x_{i_n})\phi_n(x_{i_n}) \land (\forall x_{i_n})\neg\phi_n(x_{i_n})\}.$$

But by the conservativeness assumption, this contradicts $\mathrm{CON}_\Psi(\Sigma)$.

Next, I show that there is a complete extension Σ^* of Σ^+ such that $\mathrm{CON}_\Psi(\Sigma^*)$. Let Ω be the collection of all complete extensions of Σ^+ in $L^+ = L + \{c_1, c_2, ...\}$. Then $\overline{\overline{\Omega}} = 2^\omega$. If

$$(\forall T \in \Omega)\neg\, \mathrm{CON}_\Psi(T),$$

we must have

[ii] $$\vdash_{\Psi,\kappa\lambda} \neg \bigvee \Omega.$$

However, we have

$$\vdash_{\Psi,\kappa,\lambda} \bigwedge \Sigma \to \bigvee \Omega,$$

which with [ii] yields

$$\vdash_{\Psi,\kappa,\lambda} \neg \bigwedge \Sigma,$$

whence $\neg \operatorname{CON}_{\Psi,\kappa,\lambda}(\Sigma)$ so that, again by the conservativeness assumption, $\neg \operatorname{CON}_{\Psi}(\Sigma)$, a contradiction.

Thus, let Σ^* be a complete extension of Σ^+ consistent in the sense of $\vdash_{\Psi}$. I claim that if

$$\mathcal{F} = \langle \Sigma^*, \{\mathbf{c}_n \mid n < \omega\}\rangle,$$

then $\mathcal{F}$ is a frame realizing Σ. Since Σ^* is $\vdash_{\Psi}$-consistent, complete, and includes Σ, we need verify only the extensionality condition. I consider the case of a unary quantifier symbol Q as typical. We must show that, for any formulas ϕ, χ, if

[iii] $$\operatorname{Ext}_{\mathcal{F}}(\phi) = \operatorname{Ext}_{\mathcal{F}}(\chi)$$

then

[iv] $$\operatorname{Ext}_{\mathcal{F}}((Qv)\phi) = \operatorname{Ext}_{\mathcal{F}}((Qv)\chi).$$

Thus, assume [iii]. Then if $A(\phi, \chi)$ is the sentence

$$(\forall x_1)...(\forall x_n)(\phi \leftrightarrow \chi),$$

where $x_1, ..., x_n$ exhaust the variables free in ϕ, χ, we have $\Sigma^* \vdash_{\Psi} A(\phi, \chi)$. Otherwise, by the completeness property of Σ^*, either

$$\{\phi(\mathbf{c}_1/x_1...\mathbf{c}_n/x_n), \neg\chi(\mathbf{c}_1/x_1...\mathbf{c}_n/x_n)\}$$

or

$$\{\neg\phi(\mathbf{c}_1/x_1...\mathbf{c}_n/x_n), \chi(\mathbf{c}_1/x_1...\mathbf{c}_n/x_n)\}$$

is included in Σ^*, which is in contradiction to [iii]. Thus if $B(\phi, \chi)$ is the formula

$$(Qv)\phi \leftrightarrow (Qv)\chi,$$

we have

$$\Sigma^* \vdash_{\Psi,\kappa,\lambda} (\forall x_1)...(\forall x_n)B(\phi, \chi),$$

whence by the conservativeness assumption this entailment must obtain also for the relation $\vdash_{\Psi}$. Thus for each choice of constants $\mathbf{c}_{i_1}, ..., \mathbf{c}_{i_n}$, we have

$$\Sigma^* \vdash_\Psi B(\phi, \chi)(c_{i_1}/x_{i_1}, ..., c_{i_n}/x_{i_n}),$$

which gives [iv]. The verification of other instances of the extensionality condition being similar, this completes the proof.

INDEX